STUDIES IN RELIGIOUS PHILOSOPHY AND MYSTICISM

STUDIES IN RELIGIOUS PHILOSOPHY AND MYSTICISM

by

ALEXANDER ALTMANN

CORNELL UNIVERSITY PRESS

Ithaca, New York

First published 1969

Library of Congress Catalog Card Number: 68–24050

PRINTED IN GREAT BRITAIN

To my dear brother Manfred

CONTENTS

INTRODUCTION

The papers presented here were originally published individually in a number of journals, *Festschriften*, and other collective works, some of which are not easily accessible. I felt that gathering them within the covers of a single volume would help to make them more readily available and might, at the same time, bring the various topics of research treated therein into some more cohesive pattern.

As a glance at the table of contents will show, the studies selected for inclusion in this Volume fall into three distinct groups which may be designated, respectively, as Arabic and Judaeo-Arabic philosophy, as Jewish mysticism, and as modern philosophy. They all come within the broad area of "Studies in Religious Philosophy and Mysticism" indicated by the title of this book. Published papers of mine dealing with Jewish theology in various phases of its development are purposely not included. I believe that a firm line is to be drawn between theology as such and the philosophical and mystical traditions of interpreting religious themes. The border line, on the other hand, between philosophy and mysticism is often blurred, and this is particularly true of the medieval period in which Neoplatonism serves as a focal point in both spheres. The studies comprising the first two sections of this book clearly indicate this situation. Even Maimonides' determined stand against mysticism, wavering as it does between Neoplatonism and Aristotelianism, belongs to the context of the two impinging domains. In a sense, then, there is a common patrimony to the philosophical and mystical traditions in medieval thought, which might well be traced back to Philo of Alexandria, as Professor Harry A. Wolfson has never tired of emphasizing. It is this fact which justifies, we submit, the joining together in a single volume of the papers here collected.

As far as the individual topics themselves are concerned, a few introductory remarks will suffice. When surveying them, I was struck by the observation that one particular theme appears in many of them in various guises and from different angles. I am referring to the theme of the images in which God and the Divine realm are portrayed: Primordial Man, the kabbalistic Tree, the Sanctuary, the Figure on the Throne, even the structure of the nut and its shells, all these and other symbols belong to the mystical way of thought, yet they are given a conceptual, philosophical meaning by Moses Narboni in his "Epistle"; not to speak of the *homo imago Dei* motif as understood in connection with the variegated interpretations of the Delphic maxim, "Know thyself." Self-knowledge and the knowledge of God enter into intimate relationship. One may say that a considerable portion of this Volume deals with the emergence of images of the Divine, and the manner in which philosophers tried to grapple with the problem of anthropomorphism thus posed. Saadya's theory of revelation, Maimonides' negative theology stressing the unity of essence and existence in God, and Narboni's bold exegesis of the *Shiᶜur Qomā* (Measure of the Divine "Body") in Averroistic terms are cases in point. Closely allied to this theme is that of man's ascent to the vision of God (the "Ladder of Ascension") and that of his ultimate felicity through achieving the angelic stage of mystical union with the Active Intellect as discussed by Ibn Bājja (Avempace), the first Muslim philosopher in Spain and one of the major influences on Maimonides.

In the third section of the book three thinkers take the floor. The English Deist William Wollaston (1659–1724), who was highly regarded in the eighteenth century, is shown to be steeped in the knowledge of medieval Jewish philosophy and mysticism. Next follows Moses Mendelssohn (1729–86), whose thesis of the indebtedness of Leibniz to Spinoza is critically examined. Finally, Franz Rosenzweig's understanding of History and of the place of Judaism in it comes up for discussion. While Wollaston and Mendelssohn represent, each in his own way, the intellectual climate of eighteenth-century Enlightenment—both being, at the same time, heirs to the tradition of medieval Enlightenment—Rosenzweig (1886–1929), the most brilliant religious philosopher produced by modern Jewry, offers an "existentialist" eschatology more in tune with the Biblical outlook, which takes Time and History seriously.

A few remarks of a technical nature. The references in the footnotes have been brought up to date and fresh material has been occasionally added. Minor modifications of style have been applied to the text, where it seemed advisable. Greek, Arabic, and Hebrew words and sentences, which appeared in Greek, Arabic, and Hebrew characters in the original papers, have been transliterated. Where transliterations were the rule in the papers as they first appeared, they were left unchanged, without attempting to adopt a uniform system of transliteration. The disparity is due to the fact that each paper follows the type of transcription customary in the journal in which it was published or preferred by me at the time of writing.

I wish to express my thanks to Mr. Bernhard Kendler, Editor of Cornell University Press, and to Mr. Colin Franklin, Publisher of Routledge & Kegan Paul, London, for the warm interest they took in the project of this Volume. I also acknowledge with appreciation the permission granted to me by the original Publishers to reprint the papers in this form. My thanks are due to the American Academy of Jewish Research, the East and West Library (Phaidon Press), London, the Hebrew University Press, Harvard University Press, the Jewish Historical Society of England, the John Rylands Library, Manchester, the Journal of Jewish Studies (Jewish Chronicle Publications), London, Manchester University Press, and Routledge & Kegan Paul.

Brandeis University,
Waltham, Massachusetts A. A.

THE DELPHIC MAXIM
IN MEDIEVAL ISLAM AND JUDAISM

The Islamic Ḥadīth attributes to Muḥammad (or ʿAlī) a saying which is obviously based on the famous Delphic exhortation, "Know thyself." It appears, as Ibn al-ʿArabī testifies,[1] in two formulae: "He who knows himself knows his Lord" and "He among you who knows himself best knows his Lord best."[2] The Ikhwān al-Ṣafāʾ quote both in the name of the Prophet.[3] The author who first introduced this sentence as a *ḥadīth* is the early mystic Yaḥya b. Muʿādh (d. 871).[4] Ibn Sīnā,[5] who quotes the first of the two formulae, describes it as a saying (*kalima*) on which the philosophers (*al-ḥukamāʾ*) and the Saints (*al-awliyāʾ*) are in agreement. As for the philosophers, he recalls a statement by the "Head" (*raʾīs*) of the philosophers: "He who is incapable of the knowledge of himself, will naturally be incapable of the knowledge of his Creator. How will he consider what is reliable in the science of any of the things, being ignorant of himself?" The "Head" of the philosophers to whom this saying is attributed is, no doubt, Aristotle. The quotation must be assumed to derive from some

[1] *Kitāb ʿuqlat al-mustawfiz*, ed. H. S. Nyberg (*Kleinere Schriften des Ibn Al-ʿArabī*) (Leiden, 1919), p. 52.

[2] (1) *Man ʿarafa nafsahu faqad ʿarafa rabbahu*: (2) *ʾaʿrafukum bi-nafsihi ʾaʿrafukum bi-rabbihi.*

[3] *Rasāʾil Ikhwān al-Ṣafāʾ* (Cairo, 1928), III, 351.

[4] Cf. L. Massignon, *Essai sur les origines du lexique technique de la mystique musulmane* (Paris, 1929), p. 107 (quoted by S. van den Bergh, *Die Epitome der Metaphysik des Averroes*, Leiden, 1924, p. 250). For the literary history of this *ḥadīth*, see Muḥammad Thābit al-Fandī, *Mashriq* (1934), p. 325, n. 7 (quoted by G. Vajda, *Archives d'histoire doctrinale et littéraire du moyen age*, XV (Paris, 1946), 193, n. 3). On Yaḥya b. Muʿādh, see L. Massignon, *Recueil des textes inédits* . . . (Paris, 1929), p. 27.

[5] In his early *opusculum* on the soul published by S. Landauer, "Die Psychologie des Ibn Sina", *Zeitschrift der deutschen Morgenländischen Gesellschaft* 29:340, 374 (1875).

apocryphal text similar to the one from which ʿAlī ibn Rabban Sahl al-Ṭabarī (d. after 855) cited Aristotle's alleged statement: "Whosoever possesses the knowledge about the intelligent soul recognizes his essence, and whosoever recognizes his essence is able to recognize God."[6] As for the Saints, Ibn Sīnā does not cite any religious authority but links the *ḥadīth* with the Qurʾān verse (59, 19): "Be not as those who forget God, and so He caused them to forget their souls." He points out that according to this verse the knowledge of God and the knowledge of the soul are interdependent.[7] Al-Ghazālī likewise quotes this verse and interprets it in the same way.[8] He may have borrowed this piece of exegesis from Ibn Sīnā or from a source common to both. It should be noted that "knowing oneself" is understood here as "knowing one's soul", the Arabic *nafsahu* having both meanings.[9]

A third formula expressing the same idea is still closer to the original Delphic inscription. It reads, "Know thyself [thy soul], O man, and thou wilt know thy Lord."[10] Ibn Sīnā introduces it in the same context as the first one in the following words: "I have read in the writings of the Ancients that they invited profundity in the knowledge of the soul on account of a revelation [*waḥy*] that came down to them in one of their sacred temples, saying . . ." He adds that according to his source this saying was found on the altar (*miḥrāb*) of the temple of Aesculapius, who was known to them as a prophet.[11] This third formula is thus not considered a *ḥadīth* but is recognised as of Greek origin. Ibn Sīnā's source confused the temple of the Pythian Apollo at Delphi with the temple of Aesculapius and shows other inaccuracies, but he at least preserves some semblance of historical record.[12] It should be noted that in his quotation the Delphic maxim appears with the addition, "and thou wilt know thy Lord". There existed then an Arabic version of some "ancient", most probably late-Hellenistic, text which

6 Quoted by F. Rosenthal, "On the Knowledge of Plato's Philosophy in the Islamic World," *Islamic Culture* 14:410 (1940).

7 *Ibid.*

8 See *Kitāb Mīzān al-ʿamal* (Cairo, 1946), p. 23.

9 Cf. Landauer's remark, "Die Psychologie des Ibn Sina", p. 375, n. 5, and M. Steinschneider, *Hebräische Bibliographie*, XV (1875), 43.

10 *Iʿrif nafsaka, yā insān, taʿrif rabbaka.*

11 Landauer, "Die Psychologie des Ibn Sina," 341, 374–375.

12 Alexander of Aphrodisias' *De anima* contains at the beginning a reference to the Delphic maxim by stating the necessity of obeying the injunction given and proclaimed by the Pythian (Apollo). See *De anima*, ed. I. Burns, p. 1, lines 4–6. But the Arabic version—as we may infer from the Hebrew one which was based on it—substituted "the Prophet" for "the Pythian" (*ibid.*, ed. Bruns, p. 1, lines 3–5).

stated the Delphic inscription in the full-fledged form "Know thyself and thou wilt know thy Lord" or simply: "God". Ibn Rushd quotes the same formula from "the Divine laws"[13] which seems to be a vague reference to the Ḥadīth and the Qurʾān exegesis mentioned above, but there is no reason to doubt the clear and detailed statement of Ibn Sīnā concerning his "ancient" source. It is possible to assume that the *ḥadīth* actually originated in some such source. If the Delphic maxim already existed in the two-stage form (self-God) in some Hellenistic text translated into Arabic, it was a simple matter to recast it from the imperative into the indicative form, "He who . . ." That the two-stage formula is found earlier in the Hellenistic tradition is attested also by Ḥunain ibn Isḥāq, whose Florilegium of Sayings of the Philosophers (*Kitāb al-ādāb al-falāsifa*) contains a paraphrase of it in the name of one of "Seven Greek Philosophers": "It is fitting that we should first know ourselves before attempting to know God."[14]

From Islam the concept of self-knowledge leading to the knowledge of God passed also into medieval Judaism. The earliest references to this notion appear in some Karaite authors of the ninth and tenth centuries (Daniel al-Qumisī, Qirqisānī, Joseph al-Baṣīr)[15] but use neither the *ḥadīth* formulae nor the enlarged Delphic maxim. They quote as *locus probans* a verse from Job (19:26), "From my flesh I behold God", which is understood to mean that God's existence can be inferred from His creation. This Scriptural proof continues to be employed throughout medieval Jewish literature. It occurs—still unconnected with the *ḥadīth* formulae or the Delphic maxim—in such twelfth- and thirteenth-century writers as Abraham bar Ḥiyya, Joseph ibn Ṣaddīq, Samuel ben Nissīm Masnūt, Baḥya ben Asher, and others.[16] Isaac Albalag, on

[13] In his *Epitome* of Aristotle's *Metaphysics*. Cf. S. van den Bergh, *Die Epitome*, p. 117.

[14] See A. Loewenthal's edition of Jehuda ben Solomon al-Ḥarīzī's Hebrew version, *Sēfer Musērē ha-Pilōsōfīm* (1896), p. 11.

[15] Cf. G. Vajda, *Archives*, XV, 193, n. 3, and *Revue de l'Histoire des Religions* (January–March 1959), p. 89, where he points out that the interpretation of Job 19:26 in the sense of self-knowledge leading to the knowledge of God is attested for the ninth century, if the Karaite text edited by J. Mann (*JQR*, N.S. 12:274 [1921–22]) has indeed Daniel al-Qumisī for its author.

[16] See Abraham bar Ḥiyya, *Sefer Hegyon ha-Nefesh* (Leipzig, 1860), p. 1b; Joseph ibn Ṣaddīq, *Sefer ʿOlam ha-Qatan*, ed. A. Jellinek (Leipzig, 1854), p. 20 and XIX; *idem*, ed. S. Horovitz (Breslau, 1903), p. 21; Samuel ben Nissīm Masnūt, *Maʿyan Ganīm*, ed. S. Buber (Berlin, 1889), p. 61; Baḥya ben Asher, *Beʾūr ʿal ha-Torah* (Amsterdam, 1726), fol. 9r, col. a; Joseph ben Jehuda, *Sefer Musar*, ed. W. Bacher (Berlin, 1910), p. 75.

the other hand, connects the Job verse with the saying, "Know thy soul and thou wilt know thy Lord", which he introduces as "the word of the Sage".[17] He points out that the Arabic word *nafs* is homonymous, meaning both "soul" and "essence", and that in this particular instance it denotes the latter. Likewise, the Hebrew word *basar*, he says, means either "flesh" or (as in Gen. 2:24) "essence". In the Job verse it stands for the latter.[18]

In Hebrew texts the Arabic *rabbaka* ("thy Lord") is usually rendered *elohekha* ("thy God") or *bōrʾekha*, also *yōṣerkha* ("thy Creator").[19] Thus, Shemtob ibn Falaqēra and Simon ben Ṣemaḥ Durān quote the formula, *daᶜ nafshekha wa-tedaᶜ bōrʾekha*.[20] Jehuda Hallevi's poem, *im nafshĕkha yeqarah be-ᶜēnēkha* contains a paraphrase of it: "If thy soul be precious in thine eyes, know thou her essence [*mā hīʾ*] and seek her Creator."[21] Abraham ibn Ḥasday's Hebrew version of al-Ghazālī's *Mīzān al-ᶜamal* translates it: *Ben adam, daᶜ nafshĕkha, tēdaᶜ elohēkha*.[22]

What was the meaning associated in the medieval Islamic and Jewish mind with this exhortation to know oneself in order to know God? The formula as such is rather vague and lends itself to a variety of interpretations.[23] Porphyry's treatise, *On "Know Thyself"*,[24] lists several distinct ways of understanding the Delphic sentence. We shall endeavour to answer our question by sifting the various strands of interpretation in the sources at our disposal.

I. THE MOTIF OF THE SOUL'S "LIKENESS" TO GOD

The inscription on Apollo's temple at Delphi originally meant: "Know that you are but man, not divine." It was a warning against

[17] Cf. G. Vajda, *Isaac Albalag* (Paris, 1960), p. 117.

[18] *Ibid.* and Steinschneider, *Hebräische Bibliographie*, XV, 43.

[19] Vajda, *Isaac Albalag*, p. 117.

[20] Shemtob ibn Falaqēra, *Iggeret ha-Wikuaḥ*, ed. A. Jellinek (Vienna, 1875), p. 13 (quoted by Steinschneider, *Hebräische Bibliographie*); Simon ben Ṣemaḥ Durān, *Magen Abōt* (Leghorn, 1785), fol. 49a (quoted by L. Dukes, *Philosophisches aus dem zehnten Jahrhundert*, Nakel, 1868, p. 59).

[21] Quoted by L. Dukes, *Shīrē Shĕlomoh* (Hannover, 1858), p. 82 from an Oxford MS.; see *Dīwān des Abū-l-Ḥassan Jehuda ha-Levi*, ed. H. Brody (Berlin, 1903), p. 242.

[22] *Sefer Moʾzĕnē Ṣēdeq*, ed. J. Goldenthal (Leipzig–Paris, 1839), p. 28.

[23] In the Confucianist School (*The Mencius*, VIIa, I) it was similarly stated; "He who knows his nature knows Heaven" (see *History of Philosophy Eastern and Western*, ed. S. Radhakrishnan, London, 1952, I, 564).

[24] In Stobaeus' *Florilegium*, ed. A. Meineke, I (Leipzig, 1855), 332ff. For the history of the Delphic maxim in the Classical and Hellenistic periods, see also Ulrich von Wilamowitz-Moellendorff, *Reden und Vorträge*, II (Berlin, 1926), 171–189.

hubris and taught the Apollinic virtue of temperance (σωφροσύνη). Thus it expressed the essence of Greek piety.[25] In Socrates, the Delphic oracle assumes a new significance. Turning away from the cosmological speculations of his predecessors, he poses the problem as to the nature of man. He wants to examine himself. Hence he chooses the maxim: "Know thyself." Plato goes beyond Socrates' use of the Delphic saying. In his *First Alcibiades*[26] he introduces Socrates as offering a fresh interpretation. "I will tell you what I suspect to be the real advice which the inscription gives us." Just as an eye viewing another eye will see itself as in a mirror, the soul too, if she is to see herself, must look at the Divine. For the best part of the soul resembles God, and it is only by looking at the Divine that she will gain the best knowledge of herself. The Divine, to be sure, is true prudence or temperance, and here the original meaning of the Delphic oracle again emerges. But the new thing is the idea of God being akin to the soul, and the implicit use of the Empedoclean motif of "like being known only by like". "Know thyself" now means: "Know thyself by knowing God"; in other words, "He who knows God knows himself." As W. Jaeger has shown, this theological trend is evident also in other literary documents of the later Academy. It appears in Plato's *Epinomis* and in Aristoxenus' *Life of Socrates*, in which an Indian (representing the later Plato) explains that man cannot know himself until he knows God.[27] The connection of self-knowledge and knowledge of God is reasserted in the Platonizing Stoa. Posidonius' *Commentary* on Plato's *Timaeus* says that "Just as light is apprehended by the luciform sense of sight, and sound by the aeriform sense of hearing, so also the nature of all things ought to be apprehended by its kindred reason."[28] This elaborates the Empedoclean principle of "like knowing like" which Plato had

[25] Cf. W. Jaeger, *Aristotle* (Oxford, 1934), p. 164; Karl Kerényi, *Apollon*, 2nd ed. (Amsterdam—Leipzig, 1941), p. 268; Martin P. Nilsson, *Greek Piety* (Oxford, 1948), pp. 47–52. Philo, *Spec. Leg.*, I, 10, 44, reflects this interpretation of the Delphic maxim.

[26] At 127e, 132b; see also *Philebus*, 48c; *Charmides*, 164d. On the influence of Proclus' *Commentary* on the *First Alcibiades* see my account in A. Altmann and S. M. Stern, *Isaac Israeli* (Oxford, 1958), pp. 184ff., 204ff.

[27] Cf. W. Jaeger, *Aristotle*, pp. 164–166. The Aristoxenus fragment referred to by Jaeger (from Eusebius, *Prep. Ev.*, XI, 3) reads: "*Nisi divina . . . prius perspecta et cognita habeam praevideri a nobis humana non possunt.*" Cf. *Fragmenta Historicorum Graecorum*, II, ed. C. Müller (Paris, 1878), 281.

[28] See Sextus Empiricus, *Adversus Dogmaticos*, I, 93 (ed. R. G. Bury, *Loeb Classical Library*, II, 49).

used in the *Timaeus* (45 C),[29] and Sextus Empiricus reports that "Empedocles called himself a god because he alone had kept his mind free from evil and unmuddied and by means of the god within him apprehended the god without."[30] Cicero's interpretation of the Delphic maxim, "*ut ipsa se mens agnoscat conjunctamque cum divina mente se sentiat*" (*Tusc.* V, 70) and similar statements have been traced to Posidonius.[31] The kinship between God and the ruling part (*ἡγεμονικόν*) of the soul is frequently stressed in Stoic doctrine.[32] Even as God sees and hears everything, so the soul perceives everything.[33] In the purity of the *pneuma* the soul is divine.[34]

Chalcidius (fourth century) in his *Commentary* on the *Timaeus*[35] combines the Empedoclean motif with the Biblical notion of the Divine "spirit" in man. Re-echoing Philo's statement that "in many passages the Law of Moses pronounces the blood to be the essence of the soul",[36] he explains, like Philo,[37] that this view applies only to the irrational part of the soul. The likeness between God and the soul is due to the fact that God breathed the Divine Spirit into man. "Knowledge [*cognatio*] is common to us with Divinity, and we are said to be children of God."[38] It is strange, however, that Chalcidius failed to connect the Empedoclean motif with the Biblical notion of man being created in the "image" of God.[39]

[29] See Sextus Empiricus, *Adversus Mathematicos*, I, 303 (ed R. G. Bury, *Loeb Classical Library*, IV, 174–177).

[30] *Ibid.* From Sextus Empiricus' testimony we gather that Posidonius said of "the nature of all things" that it ought to be apprehended by its kindred reason; and that Empedocles said of himself to be able to apprehend the god without because of the god within. Karl Gronau (*Poseidonius und die Jüdisch-Christliche Genesisexegese*, Leipzig, 1914, p. 170) counfounds these two distinct testimonies when declaring that, according to Sextus Empiricus, Posidonius used Plato's image of the luciform eye in order to prove the soul's ability to know God by virtue of its kinship with God. This statement goes beyond the evidence furnished by the above texts. Its veracity can, however, be confirmed by reference to the Cicero passages adduced by I. Heinemann, *Poseidonios' metaphysische Schriften*, I (Breslau, 1921), 69–70.

[31] See end of preceding note.

[32] Cf. Emile Bréhier, *Chrysippe et l'Ancien Stoïcisme* (Paris, 1951), p. 166.

[33] "Quem in hoc mundo locum deus obtinet, hunc in homine animus" (Seneca, *Ep.* 65, quoted by Gronau, *Poseidonius*, p. 165, where also further references are given). The Talmudic fivefold comparison of God and the soul in BT *Berakhot* 10a reflects this Stoic theme.

[34] Cf. Gronau, *Poseidonius*, p. 165.

[35] *Chalcidii Commentarius in Timaeum Platonis* in *Fragmenta Philosophorum Graecorum*, II, 226–227.

[36] See H. A. Wolfson, *Philo* (Cambridge, Mass., 1947), I, 387.

[37] *Ibid.*

[38] Chalcidius, ch. 207.

[39] He quotes the Empedoclean principle, "*similia non nisi a similibus suis comprehendi*", but connects it only with the Biblical concept of the inbreathing of the Spirit into man.

Similarly, Gregory of Nyssa (end of the fourth century) uses the Empedoclean motif when saying that by the Divine Spirit within him man knows God, and by the senses which are part of his earthly nature he knows things earthly.[40] The Biblical notion of the "Spirit" is woven into the discussion but, again, the *homo imago Dei* concept is not taken into account. There is, on the other hand, an earlier attempt to combine the Delphic maxim with the *homo imago Dei* motif, though without any reference to the Empedoclean principle. It occurs in Origen's homily on the verse, Cant. 1:8[41] (translated by him: "Unless thou know thyself, o fair one among women . . ."). The Greek maxim "Know thyself", Origen declares, had been anticipated by King Solomon, who addresses the soul: "Unless thou hast known thyself and hast recognized whence the ground of thy beauty proceeds—namely, that thou wast created in God's image, so that there is an abundance of natural beauty . . ."[42] The soul is exhorted to know "both what she is in herself, and how she is actuated".[43] The first of the two tasks is not immediately explained. All interest seems to concentrate on the second aspect: the soul should examine her dispositions, inclinations, and actions. "Know thyself" is an invitation to reflect on one's moral and spiritual condition. But the soul should also know the Trinity and God's creation. Knowing the creation implies "a certain self-perception"; that is, "how she [*scilicet*, the soul] is constituted in herself"—reverting to the first of the two tasks—"whether her being is corporeal or incorporeal, and whether it is simple, or consists of two or three or several elements", et cetera.[44] There follows a listing of practically the whole gamut of problems of the nature of the soul posed in Patristic and medieval psychology. Origen's exegesis of Cant. 1:8 in the sense of "Know thyself" has a solitary later parallel, obviously without any literary connection, in a passage in the *Zohar Ḥadash* on Canticles which will be discussed below.[45]

[40] Cf. Gronau, *Poseidonius*, p. 170, where the relevant passages are quoted.

[41] See Origen, *The Song of Songs, Commentary and Homilies*, trans. and annotated by R. P. Lawson (London, 1957), pp. 128–139 (in *Ancient Christian Writers*, no. 26). See also Walter Völker, *Das Vollkommenheitsideal des Origenes*, in *Beiträge zur Historischen Theologie* (Tübingen, 1931), p. 23; H. Crouzel, "L'image de Dieu dans la théologie d'Origène", *Studia Patristica*, ed. K. Aland-F. L. Cross (Berlin, 1957), II, 194ff.

[42] Origen, *The Song of Songs*, p. 128.

[43] *Ibid.*, p. 130.

[44] *Ibid.*, p. 134.

[45] See p. 18.

In Islam the Biblical *homo imago Dei* motif had found expression in the *ḥadīth*, "Allāh created Adam in his image", which seems to have given rise to some perplexity and conflict among the theologians.[46] Al-Ghazālī accepted it as authentic, and devoted a great deal of effort to its interpretation.[47] What interests us here is the way he combined this particular *ḥadīth* with the theme of self-knowledge. This he did in his esoteric works, especially in the *Mishkāt al-Anwār* ("The Niche of Lights"), which he wrote toward the end of his life. It is in this fusion of the two *ḥadīths*, the one stemming from the Biblical, the other from the Hellenic tradition, that his deepest thought on the subject is provoked. In his early *Mīzān al-ᶜAmal* ("The Balance of Action") he interprets the *ḥadīth* on self-knowledge without any reference to the image motif.[48] In the *Iḥyāᵓ ᶜUlūm al-Dīn*, his great compendium on theology, and in his *Kitāb al-Imlāᵓ*, which answers some doubts concerning a certain section in the *Iḥyāᵓ*, he elaborates two ways of interpreting the *ḥadīth* on Adam's creation in God's image without linking them with the theme of self-knowledge.[49] But once he is on esoteric ground, he connects the two. This happens in the *Al-Maḍnūn al-ṣaghīr*,[50] one of the books "to be guarded stingily against those unworthy of them", where the two *ḥadīths* are placed alongside each other, and Ghazālī records an actual question asked of him: What is the meaning of the sentence, "He who knows himself knows his Lord"? He answers that things are known by virtue of kinship, and that man could not know his Creator by knowing himself unless a certain kinship existed between man and his Creator. This, clearly, is an echo of the Empedoclean theory, and it is by no means an isolated utterance of al-Ghazālī's. In the *Iḥyāᵓ* (IV, 263) he speaks of the necessity of loving God as founded on a "hidden correspondence" between God and man,[51] and in his *Al-Maqṣad al-asna fī asmāᵓ Allāh al-ḥusna* he develops the notion of a

[46] Cf. Farid Jabre, *La Notion de la Maᶜrifa chez Ghazali* (Beirut, 1958), p. 86.

[47] Cf. Jabre, *La Notion de la Maᶜrifa*, pp. 86–108; W. H. T. Gairdner, *Al-Ghazzālī's Mishkāt Al-Anwār*, A Translation with Introduction (London, 1924), pp. 31ff.; A. J. Wensinck, *La Pensée de Ghazzālī* (Paris, 1940), pp. 39ff.

[48] Cf. *Mīzān al-ᶜAmal*, ed. Kurdi (Cairo, 1342 [1923]), p. 18; Hebrew version, *Mozěnē Ṣedeq*, ed. J. Goldenthal (Leipzig–Paris, 1839), p. 28.

[49] Cf. *Iḥyāᵓ ᶜUlūm al-Dīn*, ed. Ḥalabi, IV (Cairo, 1352/1933), pp. 215–216; *Kitāb al-Imlāᵓ*, printed in the margin of *Iḥyaᵓ*, I (Cairo, 1346/1927), pp. 138–141, 165–171. These passages are reproduced as Appendices 11 and 12 in Jabre, *La Notion de la Maᶜrifa*, pp. 186–193.

[50] Cf. Wensinck, *La Pensée de Ghazzālī*, pp. 40–42.

[51] *Iḥyāᵓ*, IV, 263; cf. Jabre, *La Notion de la Maᶜrifa*, p. 88.

"common term" existing between God and man.[52] But in the *Maḍnūn ṣaghīr* he adds that the kinship spoken of consists in man being a microcosm and, more specifically, in possessing a soul which resembles God.[53]

The microcosm motif is one which seems to have been very dear to al-Ghazālī. We find it in the *Mīzān al-ᶜAmal*: "It is an effect of the mercy of God that man is a copy *en miniature* of the form of the universe; by contemplating it he comes to know God."[54] The *Imlāᵓ* offers a detailed list of correspondences between man as a microcosm and the world at large.[55] But it is hard to see how the knowledge of the macrocosm achieved by introspection can yield a knowledge of God. Al-Ghazālī therefore adds that it is the soul which by virtue of her kinship with God leads us to the knowledge of the Creator. The soul, he says distinctly, and hereby reflects Plato's view, is the essence of man, and thus the *ḥadīth* describing man as created in the image of God must be understood to refer to the soul of man.[56] Hence, we conclude, only he who knows his soul knows his Lord.

The two *ḥadīths* are even more fully discussed in the *Mishkāt al-Anwār*[57] where the theme crops up again and again. In one of the major passages on this topic[58] al-Ghazālī starts out by explaining that Adam was created in the image not of Allāh himself but of "the Merciful One". A distinction is thus drawn between God in his transcendence and what al-Ghazālī also calls the "Divine Presence" (*ḥaḍra*). "For it was the Divine mercy that caused the image of the Divine Presence to be in that 'image'. And then Allāh, out of his grace and mercy, gave Adam a summary 'image' embracing every genus and species in the world, insomuch that it was as if Adam were all that was in the world, or were a summarized copy of the world." Adam created in the image of the Merciful One, therefore, means simply that his being a microcosm

[52] Cf. *Al-Maqṣad*, ed. Sharaf (Cairo, 1324/1905), pp. 17–27; cf. Jabre, *La Notion de la Maᶜrifa*, p. 93.

[53] Cf. Wensinck, *La Pensée de Ghazzālī*, p. 40.

[54] See n. 48.

[55] Cf. Jabre, *La Notion de la Maᶜrifa*, pp. 96–97.

[56] Cf. Wensinck, *La Pensée de Ghazzālī*, p. 42.

[57] Gairdner's translation is based on the text of the Cairo edition of 1322/1903; see *Al-Ghazzālī's Mishkāt*, p. 1, n. 1; Jabre's analysis on the text in *Al-Jawāhir ᵓl-ghawāli*, pp. 110–146; cf. his *La Notion de la Maᶜrifa*, p. 142. The work was rendered twice in Hebrew. The third section of Isaac ben Joseph al-Fazi's version has been published by L. Dukes, *Shīrē Shelōmō*, pp. ix–xiii, 90. M. Steinschneider quotes Joḥanan Alemano's comparison of al-Ghazālī's grading of lights with the kabbalistic doctrine (*Hebr. Übersetzungen*, no. 196, p. 136).

[58] Cf. Gairdner, *Al-Ghazzālī's Mishkāt*, pp. 75–76.

is due to God's mercy. We assume that the exegesis implied in this view is identical with the one offered in the *Imlāʾ*: "in *his* image" signifies the macrocosm which is "his", that is, belongs to God; as distinct from the other (second) exegesis which interprets "his" image as God's attributes.[59] Our passage in the *Mishkāt* would seem to adopt the (first) interpretation and to elaborate it in the sense that as Adam's creation in the image of the macrocosm was due to the Divine mercy, the *ḥadīth* may also be understood as saying that Adam was created in the image of the Merciful One. He actually quotes a version (according to Bukhari) which reads: "Allāh created Adam in the image of the Merciful One."[60] We may note that this exegesis or, for that matter, this text is already presupposed in the passage in the *Mīzān al-ᶜAmal* (quoted above) which attributes man's being a miniature copy of the world to the "effect of the mercy of God". "But for this mercy", al-Ghazālī says in the *Mishkāt* passage, "no son of Adam would be capable of knowing his Lord; for 'only he who knows himself knows his Lord'."[61] Thus the two *ḥadīths* are once more connected with each other. The microcosm motif, it would appear, holds the key to the understanding of the *ḥadīth* on self-knowledge.

But this is not the whole story in this highly esoteric treatise. In an earlier passage of the same work[62] al-Ghazālī discusses the "light" of the intellect (*al-ᶜaql*). "In the twinkling of an eye it [*scilicet*, intellect] ascends to the highest heavens above, in another instant to the confines of the earth beneath . . . For it is a pattern or sample of the attributes of Allāh. Now the sample must be commensurate with the original, even though it does not rise to the degree of equality with it. And this may move you to set your mind to work upon the true meaning of the tradition: 'Allāh created Adam after his own likeness.'" It is to be noted that here the *ḥadīth* is quoted differently from the usual text. Obviously, a new exegesis is worked into the quotation. Allāh created Adam after *his own* likeness. We may recognise in this exegesis the one offered as a second possibility in the *Imlāʾ*: "his" image meaning the image of God's own attributes. Moreover, it is the intellect which is here described as being in the image of God. This links up with the passage in the *Maḍnūn ṣaghīr* which speaks of the soul

59 Cf. Jabre, *La Notion de la Maᶜrifa*, pp. 89–90.
60 Cf. Gairdner, *Al-Ghazzālī's Mishkāt*, p. 76.
61 *Ibid.*
62 Gairdner, *Al-Ghazzālī's Mishkāt*, p. 48.

as the true essence of man. Man in the image of God here, therefore, means the intellect as "a pattern of the attributes of Allāh". And our mind that is to be set working on this new interpretation is directed toward the mystery of the intellect as a spiritual "light". Al-Ghazālī refuses, at this stage, to be drawn more deeply into the matter.[63]

There is, however, a third passage in the *Mishkāt*[64] which brings us to the acme of al-Ghazālī's mystical interpretation of the *ḥadīth* on self-knowledge. It relates to the experience of mystical union. In that experience man may, like the Prophet, become so fully immersed in the Divine Unity as to utter in rapture: "I have become His hearing whereby He heareth, His vision whereby He seeth, His tongue wherewith He speaketh"; or as to exclaim, like al-Ḥallāj, "I am the ONE REAL!"; or, like another, "Glory be to ME!" Al-Ghazālī sees in this assertion of identity with Allāh a self-delusion comparable to mistaking the form seen in a mirror for the mirror itself.[65] Yet, as W. H. T. Gairdner remarked,[66] the *Mishkāt* could have been written only after al-Ghazālī had been deep in the study of al-Ḥallāj, and "his inmost thought may have been, 'Perhaps al-Ḥallāj has penetrated here to something of what the Koran itself left obscure. I neither assert nor deny'." We have to bear this thought in mind when contemplating al-Ghazālī's final hint at what the *ḥadīth* on *homo imago Dei* may mean: "From that heaven of intellect he [*scilicet*, the mystic] fares upward to the limit of the ascension of created things . . . thereafter 'settleth he himself on the throne' of the Divine Unity, and therefrom 'taketh command' throughout his storied heavens. Well might one, in looking upon such an one, apply to him the saying, 'Allāh created Adam after the image of the Merciful One.'" There is the sobering afterthought that such an interpretation stands condemned just like the self-delusory "I am the ONE REAL" or "Glory be to ME."[67] But it is noteworthy that al-Ghazālī considered, albeit for a fleeting moment and with great hesitation, the possibility of understanding the *ḥadīth* about man being in the image of God and, obviously, also the *ḥadīth* about self-knowledge, in terms of an ultimate identity.

[63] *Ibid.*

[64] Gairdner, *Al-Ghazzālī's Mishkāt*, pp. 64–65; see also pp. 60–61.

[65]. *Ibid.*, p. 61.

[66] *Ibid.*, pp. 33–34.

[67] *Ibid.*, p. 65.

Although al-Ghazālī rejects the claim of the mystic to union with Allāh, he seems to suggest that in the experience described the human intellect merges with the supernal Intellect. In the third section of the *Mishkāt*, which deals with the degrees of ascent, the third grade is said to be reached when God ("the Lord") is conceived in terms of the Vicegerent, the first Mover of the Heavens, who is, however, but one of His creatures, an Angel who issues the command (*amr*), and is "the Obeyed One" (*al-Muṭāᶜ*).[68] Gairdner has argued that this Vicegerent is the Spirit of Allāh, the Divine Word of Command or *Logos* but does not include, as R. Nicholson had suggested, the archetypal spirit of Muḥammad, the Heavenly Man, nor, as L. Massignon had proposed, the figure of the *quṭb* ("axis") as embodied in an earthly mystic who, unknown to the world, administers the affairs of the heaven and the earth.[69]

We suggest that this figure of "the Obeyed One" is identical with Philo's *Logos* as "ruler" and "second God" in whose image man is created (man thus being an image of the image of God),[70] and that he is, therefore, the archetypal man. Moreover, he is identical also with the Plotinian Intellect, as has already been pointed out by Jabre.[71] In his *Kitāb al-Maᶜārif al-ᶜaqliyya*[72] al-Ghazālī quotes a *ḥadīth* of Neoplatonic origin in which the Intellect is described as the first of God's creations. He says of this Intellect (which obviously represents the Plotinian *Νοῦς*) that *it knows its Lord*, humbly *obeying* His command, and *exercising dominion* over the decrees of Providence and the mystery of predestination contained in the Word (*kalima*) of the Creator. The supernal Intellect, thus, possesses the features of the Vicegerent ("exercising dominion") and of the *Muṭāᶜ* who is obeyed because he obeys the Divine Command. What is of particular interest to us here is the characterization of this figure as "knowing its Lord". This phrase is clearly taken from the *ḥadīth*, "He who knows himself knows his Lord." Intellect, knowing itself, knows its Lord.

If we put all the threads together, the final interpretation of the

[68] *Ibid.*, p. 96.

[69] Cf. Gairdner, *Al-Ghazzālī's Mishkāt*, pp. 10–25.

[70] Cf. H. A. Wolfson, *Philo*, I, 339, 234.

[71] Cf. Jabre, *La Notion de la Maᶜrifa*, p. 107.

[72] Cf. M. Asín Palacios, *La Espiritualidad de Algazel*, III (Madrid, 1936), 254–255; Dario Cabanelas, "Un Opusculo inedito de Algazel," *Al-Andalus*, 21:28 (1956).

two *ḥadīths* as implied in al-Ghazālī's doctrine is as follows. Man is essentially intellect. He is created in the image of the Merciful One, which we take to signify the supernal intellect or Vicegerent. In the act of union the mystic becomes identical with this supernal intellect and, like it, by virtue of the intellect's self-knowledge knows his Lord. But as experience shows, the mystic rather tends to mistake this identity with the Intellect for one with Allāh Himself. Here the danger lurks which al-Ghazālī tries to warn against.

Ibn al-ᶜArabī follows in the footsteps of al-Ḥallāj and al-Ghazālī. The soul or self referred to in the *ḥadīth* formulae is the Intellect (*ᶜaql*); it is the "Pen", a symbol of the "handwriting of Allāh", by which, in a passage in the *Mishkāt*, al-Ghazālī had described Adam's form; it is the Spirit of Allāh, again as in al-Ghazālī. There is also the reference to the mystic's "settling oneself on the throne" as expressed by al-Ḥallāj.[73] But Ibn al-ᶜArabī goes beyond al-Ghazālī in identifying the perfect soul or self with the Vicegerent of God on earth. Here he resumes entirely al-Ḥallāj's tradition which saw in the perfect saint a semi-divine power put in charge of the governance of the world, and who taught that the saint becomes *al-Muṭāᶜ* (the Obeyed One) and *Quṭb* (Axis) of his time.[74] In a more specific sense Muḥammad is the "perfect man", the *Logos proforikos* of Christian theology.[75] But potentially every man is a claimant, as it were, to the throne. For man is created in the image of God.[76] "God formed a knowledge of Himself; thereby He knew the world, and for this reason, it emerged in a Form [*ṣūra*]. And God created man as an exalted design by summarizing the ideas [*maᶜānī*] of the macrocosm, and made him a manuscript containing in miniature everything in the macrocosm . . . With regard to him the Prophet has said, God created Adam after His own image."[77] Now, "he who has his existence in the form of something contains that something in his form so that by the very same act by which he perceives his own form he perceives also that in whose form he exists".[78] Hence, he

[73] See *Kitāb ᶜuqlat al-mustawfiz* (ed. Nyberg), p. 52.

[74] Cf. Gairdner, *Al-Ghazzālī's Mishkāt*, pp. 14ff.; R. A. Nicholson, *The Idea of Personality in Ṣūfism* (Cambridge, 1932), pp. 44ff.

[75] Cf. H. S. Nyberg's account in his Introduction to *Kleinere Schriften des Ibn Al-ᶜArabi*, pp. 100ff.

[76] *Kitāb ᶜuqlat . . .*, p. 45.

[77] Cf. Nyberg's translation and discussion of this text, *Kleinere Schriften*, pp. 98ff.

[78] Cf. *Kitāb ᵓinshaᵓ al-dawāᵓir*, p. 15 (quoted and discussed by Nyberg, *Kleinere Schriften*, pp. 99ff.).

who knows himself knows his Lord.[79] God, man, and world coincide. They are three aspects of the same entity, and man is the connecting link. Man who is created in the image of God is the throne upon which Allāh is seated, while the physical world is the throne on which the Merciful seats himself. The Merciful is the *Logos*, the Spirit of Allāh, the perfect man, Muḥammad, and ideally man as such.[80]

It is a long way from Plato's interpretation of the Delphic maxim to the complex pattern of al-Ghazālī's and Ibn al-ᶜArabī's mystical understanding of the *ḥadīth* formula. The Philonic *Logos*, the mythological *Adam Qadmon* motif, Neoplatonic elements, and Biblical notions as reflected in the Qurʾān and the Ḥadīth have a share in it. The position is somewhat similar in medieval Jewish mysticism. Here too a variety of motifs, developed from Neoplatonic, Gnostic, and other late-Hellenistic sources, overlay the original Platonic theme of the soul's kinship with God, and enter into combination with the Biblical idea of man's creation in the image of God. But there is little stress here on self-knowledge, although—as we shall see—this aspect is not entirely missing and, in fact, somehow continues to loom in the background even where it is not articulated.

The *Sēfer Bahīr* (no. 55) sees in the seven (or six) limbs of the body of man an image of the seven (six) lower *Sefirot* or six mystical Days of Creation, and applies to this analogy the verse, "For in the image of God made He man" (Gen. 9:6). This passage is reflected in *Tiqqūnē Ha-Zohar* (130 b), where it is said: "The limbs of man are all arranged in the order of the Beginning [*ᶜal sidrē bĕrēshīt*]"—that is, of the mystical days of creation which are identical with the six lower *Sefirot*—"and man is therefore called a microcosm [*ᶜolam qaṭan*]".[81] The mystical interpretation of the microcosm motif[82] becomes increasingly important and furnishes one of the decisive aspects for the kabbalistic exegesis of the Genesis passages speaking about man being made in the image of God. The most outspoken passage—which is significant also because of its clear reference to the theme of self-knowledge leading

[79] *Kitāb ʾinshāʾ al-dawāʾir*, p. 18; *Kitāb ᶜuqlat* . . ., p. 52; *Kitāb al-tadbīrāt*, p. 209. See Nyberg, *Kleinere Schriften*, p. 100. [80] Cf. Nyberg, *Kleinere Schriften*, p. 101.

[81] It is interesting to note that the term is preserved in its Hebrew form, although the context is in Aramaic.

[82] As distinct from its use in philosophical literature, which will be investigated below (Section 2).

to the knowledge of God—is found in the *Sēfer Tĕmūnah* (Lemberg, 1892, fol. 25a–b): "The *Sefirot* which are the image [*dĕmūt*] of man—for man is a microcosm [*ᶜolam qaṭan*] according to 'Let us make man in our image, in our likeness'—are seven Forms, and the soul [*ha-nĕshamah*] is in the body and is the hidden light which is in his head. For in it [*scilicet*, the body] is the mystery of the 'small image' [*tĕmūnah qĕṭanah*], for it is written, 'And from my flesh I behold God'; and the mystery of the 'supernal image' [*tĕmūnah ᶜelyōnah*]." The quotation of Job 19:26 (see above, pp. 3–4) immediately links the kabbalistic notion expounded here with the philosophical tradition in medieval Judaism which uses this verse as *locus probans* for the concept of self-knowledge leading to the knowledge of God. The *Sēfer Tĕmūnah* thus implies that from the mystical understanding of the human body one may arrive at an understanding of the "supernal Image" which is the world of the *Sefirot*. In making the contemplation of the body the point of departure for the knowledge of the Sefirotic realm the *Sēfer Tĕmūnah* obviously follows the precedent of the *Sēfer Bahīr*. Other kabbalistic passages describe the totality of man (body and soul) as comprising both the supernal and lower grades of existence. Thus Isaac the Blind says in his *Commentary on Sefer Yeṣirah*[83] that "Man is a great seal in which the beginning and the end, the totality of all created things, are contained." Man is "composed of the supernal and the lower [forces], and he belongs to the world, the year and the soul [*ᶜolam*, *shanah*, *nefesh*]. For all that is in the world is in the year, and all that is in the world and in the year is in the soul."[84] There are also several *Zohar* passages which speak of man as a totality "comprising everything": that is, both the supernal and lower grades.[85] Likewise in Menaḥem Recanati's *Sēfer Taᶜamē Ha-Miṣwōt* (Basle, 1581, fol. 2b): "All that exists of all created beings is in the image [*ᶜinyan dugmaᵓ*] of the Ten Ineffable [*bĕlīmah*][86]

[83] MS. Hebrew Union College, Cincinnati, fols. 35, 36.

[84] Quoted in part by J. Tishby, *Pērūsh Ha-Aggadōt Le-Rabbi ᶜAzriel* (Jerusalem, 1945), p. 5, n. 7, together with parallels from the writings of ᶜEzra ben Solomon, ᶜAzriel of Gerona, and Naḥmanides; and by G. Scholem, *Rēshīt Ha-Qabbalah* (Tel-Aviv, 1948), p. 114. The analogy between *mundus* (*ᶜolam*), *annus* (*shanah*), *homo* (*nefesh*), which is one of the themes of *Sēfer Yeṣirah* (chap. iii), is a variant of the microcosm-macrocosm motif which has a parallel in Isidor of Seville, as J. G. Weiss has suggested (in a lecture at the Institute of Jewish Studies, Manchester, in 1959).

[85] *Zohar*, II, 75b; III, 117a, 141b.

[86] On the term *bĕlīmah*, see G. Scholem, *Major Trends in Jewish Mysticism* (New York, 1946), p. 77.

Sefirot, and when man below came to be created, he was made in the image of the supernal Form [*ha-ṣūrah ha-ᶜelyōnah*], the Ten *Sefirot* being formed [*meṣuyyar*] in him."[87] Yet other passages are content to leave it open as to whether the reference is to man as a totality of body and soul or to him *qua* soul alone. Thus, we hear simply that "God created man in His image, in the manner [*ke-gawna*] of the Ten *Sefirot*" (*Tiqqūnē Ha-Zohar*, 90b). Still another passage says distinctly that only the soul resembles the supernal world, while the body is not worthy of being united to the supernal, although the image of the body too is fashioned in the mystery of the supernal (*Zohar*, I, 140a).

A decidedly Platonic view is taken by Moses de Leon in his Hebrew writings and taken over into the *Zohar* when man is said to be identical with the soul.[88] An exposition of this view occurs in the *Sēfer Sheqel Ha-Qōdesh* (ed. Greenup, pp. 33–34): "They said that He, blessed be His Name, created man in the 'image and likeness' and fashioned him in the supernal Form, as He says, 'And God created man in His image' . . . They said in [the exposition of] the mysteries of the Torah[89] that the intellectual Form [*ha-ṣūrah ha-sikhlīt*] which is in man is the one called 'man'; for skin, flesh and bones are but the garment of man. Therefore, they said, it is written (Job 10:11), 'Thou hast clothed me with skin and flesh, and knit me together with bones and sinews.' And if skin and flesh are the garment, consider who is the man." Similarly in the *Sēfer Ha-Mishqal* (Basle, 1608, fol. 1 Cd, 2 Cb): "One has to search and inquire as to who is the 'man', whether it is the body

[87] Similarly in Recanati's *Pērūsh Ha-Tefilōt* (quoted from MS. Munich, 112 in M. Steinschneider's *Die Hebräischen Handschriften . . . München*, 1895, pp. 96ff.): "In all created beings is something (*ᶜinyan*) corresponding to the Ten *Sefirot*, like the shadow following the form."

[88] Cf. *Zohar*, I, 20b, 22b; the main passage is *Zohar*, II, 75b–76a, which has striking parallels in the texts quoted above. The term "the inner man" goes back to Porphyry's *On "Know Thyself"* (see Note 24), ed. Meineke, i, 334: "Such is the precision of Plato who sought most eagerly to know himself above all other things . . . and again to know himself wholly in order that the immortal *inner man* might be known and the *outer man* which is an image might not be unknown, and that the things which make a difference to these might become well known. For an all-perfect mind makes a difference to the *inner part* of us, in which Man himself is, and of which each one of us is an image."

For Plotinus' discussion of Plato's view, see *Enn.*, I, 3, 3; VI, 7, 5; for his assertion that the soul is man, see *Enn.*, III, 5, 5; IV, 7, 1; for his use of the term "image" in this connection, see *Enn.*, VI, 4, 10, 16. Plotinus does not, however, use the term "inner man". It occurs in St. Augustine's *Confessiones*, X, 6, 9.

[89] Clearly a reference to the *Zohar* passages quoted in the preceding Note.

or the Form. To say that of the body that comes from a fetid drop and which is flesh [destined to become] full of worms and maggots, it is said, 'In the image of God created He him', is, Heaven forfend, something that will never occur to a wise man. And they said in [the exposition of] the mysteries of the Torah,[90] 'Thou hast clothed me with skin and flesh', etc.—If skin and flesh are the garment, consider who is the 'man'. He is what matters [*ha-ᶜiqqar*], and skin and flesh are but the garment and the covering accruing to man." The passage goes on to say that only the "inner man" is in the image of God. There is, however, a sequel to the former passage in which it is explained in terms of the most profound secrecy that the inner man is arranged in three distinct orders (*tiqqūnīm*)—that is, three souls: *nefesh* (appetitive soul), *rūaḥ* (vital spirit) and *neshamah* (intelligent soul)[91]—and that this threefold structure of the soul has its prototype in the Heavenly Man (*Adam Qadmon* or *Sefirot*) of whom it is said: "And upon the likeness of the throne was a likeness as the appearance of a man upon it above" (Ez. 1:26). This introduces the Ezekiel passage as an elaboration of the Genesis verses speaking of man as in the image of God. ᶜAzriel of Gerona too says in his *Pērūsh ᶜEser Sefirot* (ed. Goldberg, 4b) that the doctrine ascribing "a measure of limit and corporeality" to the *Sefirot* occurs in the Torah ("in our image, after our likeness"), in the Prophets ("and upon the likeness of the throne", et cetera) and in the words of the Sages, the latter being a reference to the *Shīᶜūr Qōmah*.[92] This aspect is, however, not touched upon in the *Sēfer Ha-Mishqal*, which is primarily concerned with the nature of the human soul and its fate after death. In posing the problems of the mystery of the soul (*sōd ha-neshamah*) it reveals a truly Platonic concern with self-knowledge, and in comparing the soul with God it stresses in rather homely fashion the kinship of God and the soul: "Even as God sees and is not seen, the soul sees and is not seen", et cetera.[93] It is with this Stoic-Talmudic aspect of the kinship between the two in view that it

[90] See preceding note.

[91] For the psychology of the *Zohar*, see Scholem, *Major Trends*, pp. 240ff.; R. J. Z. Werblowsky, "Philo and the Zohar", *JJS* 10:38–44, 112–114 (1959).

[92] The linking of the *Genesis* passage with the *Shīᶜūr Qōmah* mysticism shows the radical possibilities inherent in the *homo imago Dei* concept and throws into bold relief the reticence with which this notion is treated in classical Rabbinic sources. For the Rabbinic attitude, see A. Geiger's note on *ṣelem ʾelohīm* in *Oṣar Neḥmad*, ed. I. Blumenfeld, III (Vienna, 1860), 4–6, 119. On the *Shīᶜūr Qōmah* see below p. 180ff.

[93] *Sefer ha-Mishqal*, fol. 2 C 2.

finally interprets the Biblical notion of man being created in the image of God.[94]

We conclude this account by quoting the passage from the *Zohar Ḥadash* (Warsaw ed., 70b) on Canticles to which a fleeting reference has already been made (see above, p. 7) in connection with Origen's exegesis of Cant. 1:8. It presents a curious mixture of motifs and thereby shows the extent to which kabbalistic texts are prone to gather their material from a variety of sources: "The wisdom which man requires: Firstly to know and contemplate the mystery of his Lord [*rāza de-marē*], and, secondly, to know himself [*lĕ-mindaᶜ lē lĕ-gufē*]." This interprets the Biblical verse, Can. 1:8 (*ʾim lō tēdĕᶜī lakh ha-yafah ba-nashīm*, et cetera) in the same way in which Origen had understood *lakh* as an object in the reflexive sense, meaning the "self" or the "soul". The reference to God as "his Lord" recalls the *ḥadīth* use of *rabbahu*. Knowing oneself and knowing one's Lord are coupled together as in the *ḥadīth* formula. The text continues: "And to make himself aware who he is"—this is the question we met twice in Moses de Leon—"and how he was created; whence he comes and whither he goes"—quoting the well-known passage in *Abōt* 3, 1 which reflects Gnostic influence, as S. Lieberman has shown[95]—"and how his body has been arranged [*tiqqūna dĕ-gūfa hēʾakh ittaqen*]"—This reflects a philosophical motif which will be more fully discussed below (pp. 23, 25, 27): from the arrangement of his body man can infer the wisdom of his Maker. The term *tiqqūna* used in our passage has a precedent in, for example, Samuel ben Nissim Masnūt's *Maᶜyan Ganīm* (twelfth century), where the meaning of Job 19:26, "From my flesh I behold God", is explained: "From the formation of my limbs and from the arrangement of my body [*we-taqqanat gūfī*]—contemplating them—I behold God" (ed. Buber, 61). The text goes on: "And how he is destined to appear in judgment before the King of the universe"—reverting to the *Abōt* passage ("and before Whom thou wilt render account and reckoning"). That the theme from *Abōt* and the philosophical motif are merely interjected becomes apparent from the resumption of the original subject of self-knowledge in what follows: "And, secondly, to know and contemplate the mysteries of the soul; what this soul in him is, and whence it comes, and

[94] For this theme, see above, p. 6, and n. 33.

[95] Cf. his article "How much Greek in Jewish Palestine?", *Biblical and Other Studies*, ed. by Alexander Altmann, (Cambridge, Mass., 1963), pp. 135–137.

why it entered this body, a fetid drop, which is here today and in the grave tomorrow. Moreover, to contemplate this and know the world in which he finds himself, and why it has been established. And afterward to contemplate the supernal mysteries [*bĕ-rāzīn ʿilāʾīn*] of the supernal world to become aware of his Lord [*le-marē*]." One looks in vain in this entire passage for any development of the theme of self-knowledge as a road to the knowledge of God or the supernal world. The two kinds of knowledge are co-ordinated rather than causally related. But there is still vaguely discernible in this discussion the outline of the two-stage formula connecting man's self-knowledge with the knowledge of God.

2. THE MICROCOSM MOTIF

In the Platonic tradition, which has just been analyzed, knowing God proceeds from knowing one's soul (or vice versa), and the "self" which the Delphic oracle bids us know is not the body nor the totality of soul and body but the soul alone. It is in the spirit of this tradition that St. Augustine could say: "Deum et animam scire cupio: Nihilne plus? Nihil omnino."[96] In tracing this line of thought in medieval Islam and Judaism we noticed the intrusion upon it of the Neoplatonic concept of the Intellect as the archetype of the truly divine soul. This development will be more fully discussed in the next section (3). We also came across the microcosm motif, which extends the base of the desired knowledge of God to include the body beside the soul. Jewish mysticism, we saw, wavers uneasily between the purely Platonic approach and an attempt to see in the totality of man as body plus soul an image of the Divine realm of the *Sefirot*. The microcosm motif is used here in a profoundly mystical sense, which completely annihilates any Gnostic disparagement of the body. This line of approach shall not be pursued further. We propose, instead, to investigate the microcosm idea as reflected in the philosophical literature of medieval Islam and Judaism and to do so only insofar as this idea is linked with the theme of self-knowledge and the knowledge of God.

Speaking about the microcosm-macrocosm motif, A.-J Festugière says, "There is no more famous image in antiquity, amongst Christians and pagans, and it continued to be employed in the Middle Ages."[97] (He should have included "Jews" in the

[96] *Soliloquies*, 1, 7; *De ordine*, 2, 30, 44, 47; *De quantitate animae*, 24E, *et passim.*

[97] A.-J. Festugière, *La Révélation d'Hermès Trismégiste*, 2nd ed. (Paris, 1949) I, 92.

Hellenistic as well as medieval period, as will be shown below.) It is found in Democritus (fragment 34 Diels), Aristotle (*Physics*, VIII, 2, 252b, 26–27), and there is an allusion to it in Plato (*Timaeus*, 30 D; 44 D). According to the *Vita Anonymi* of Pythagoras,[98] "Man is called μικρὸς κόσμος not because he consists of the four elements—this applies also to each of the animals, even to the lowest—but because he possesses all potencies (δυνάμεις) of the cosmos. For in the cosmos are the gods and also the four elements, and [in it] are also the irrational animals and the plants. All these potencies man possesses. For he has the divine rational potency; he has the nature of the elements, the potency of nourishment, growth and reproduction." There existed, then, a tradition tracing this motif back to Pythagoras.[99] It is this tradition which underlies al-Shahrastānī's account of Pythagoras' doctrine: "He says that in his natural disposition man corresponds to the whole world, and is a microcosm, whereas the world is a Great Man."[100] Possibly Aristotle drew on that tradition when using the terms "small world" and "large world" as current concepts, and Philo distinctly re-echoes it when recording the opinion of "some" who "have ventured to affirm that the tiny animal man is equal to the whole world, because each consists of body and rational soul, and thus *they* declare that man is a small world and alternatively the world a great man".[101]

[98] In *Photii Bibliotheca*, cod. 249, quoted by M. Joel in "Ibn-Gebirol's (Avicebrons) Bedeutung für die Geschichte der Philosophie" (first published in *MGWJ*, 1857, 386ff., 420ff.; 1858, 59ff.), *Beiträge zur Geschichte der Philosophie* (Breslau, 1878), Supplement, p. 30, n. 2.

[99] According to H. Siebeck, *Geschichte der Psychologie* (1880–84), I, 43 (quoted by S. Horovitz, *Die Psychologie bei den jüdischen Religions-Philosophen des Mittelalters von Saadia bis Maimuni* [Breslau, 1898], p. 129, n. 110), the microcosm motif is first found in Heraclitus. Diels, *Vorsocratiker*, 4th ed., 55 B 34, traces it to Democritus, while G. P. Conger, *Theories of Macrocosms and Microcosms* (New York, 1922), p. 6, cites the passage in Aristotle's *Physics* as the first authentic occurrence of the term, though he admits that Aristotle draws on an earlier tradition. Cf. the note (b) in P. H. Wicksteed's and F. M. Cornford's edition of the *Physics* in the *Loeb Classical Library*, II, 286–287.

[100] See al-Shahrastānī, *Kitāb al-milal wa-l-niḥal*, ed. Cureton, p. 275 (in T. Haarbrücker's German translation, *Religionspartheien und Philosophen-Schulen*, II, 106), quoted by J[acob] Guttmann, *Die Philosophie des Salomon ibn Gabirol* (Göttingen, 1889). p. 117, n. 3.

[101] *Heres* 155; see also *Migr.* 39, 220; *Opif.* 82 (quoted by H. A. Wolfson, *Philo*, I, 424–425, n. 5). The notion that man is "equal" to the whole world may be indebted to Rabbinic sources (cf. *Abōt de-Rabbi Nathan*, ed. Schechter, Version A, chap. 31, p. 91). I. Heinemann, *Philons griechische und jüdische Bildung* (Breslau, 1932), is silent on this point.

In the Hellenistic period the microcosm motif is strongly allied to astrological ideas. It is now "no longer a matter of imagery but one literally speaks of limbs of the world and finds relations between each part of the heaven and each member of the body".[102] We meet this new doctrine of the microcosm in the astrological texts of Manilius, Firmicius, and of the *Corpus Hermeticum*. The principal work of "Egyptian" astrology by Nechepso and Petosiris bears testimony to it.[103] In Rabbinic literature too an echo of this doctrine is quite audible. Thus, *Abōt de-Rabbi Nathan* (ed. Schechter, Version A, chap. 31, pp. 91–92) contains a long description of analogies between man and the world, ending with the sentence: "Hence you learn that everything which the Holy One, blessed be He, created in His world He created in man."[104] The astrological concern plays some part in a late midrash published by A. Jellinek and entitled by him *Aggadat ᶜOlam Qaṭan*.[105] The *Sēfer Yeṣirah*, above all, employs the microcosm motif on the threefold level of *mundus-annus-homo* (see above, p. 15), and its commentators develop this scheme. In Shabbatai Donnolo's Commentary *Sefer Ḥakmōni* (in the Warsaw 1884 edition of *Sefer Yeṣirah*, pp. 121ff.) a large-scale account of the microcosm-macrocosm is offered in an exegesis of the Genesis verse, "Let us make man in our image" (edited and explained by Adolph Jellinek in *Pērūsh Naᶜaseh Adam* . . ., Leipzig, 1854).

The connection of the microcosm motif with the Delphic maxim is first attested in Porphyry's *On "Know Thyself"* (ed. Meineke, i. 332), as I have shown elsewhere.[106] The relevant passage reads: "Others who assert that man has been well described as a microcosm claim that the [Delphic] saying is an exhortation to know man, and that since man is a microcosm it commands him only to philosophize . . . proceeding from our own perception to the contemplation of the Whole." I suggested that this passage

[102] Cf. Festugière, *Hermès Trismégiste*, 2nd ed., I, 92; on the influence of this motif, especially in its Stoic form of a "universal sympathy", see the note in S. van den Bergh, *Averroes' Tahafut al-Tahafut* (London, 1954), II, 90.

[103] Cf. Albert Dieterich, *Eine Mithrasliturgie* (1923), pp. 55ff.

[104] See also *Kohelet Rabba*, XII, 2, 1. For further references see A. Jellinek, *Der Mikrokosmos von R. Josef Ibn Zadik* (Leipzig, 1854), p. x; B. Beer (in a review of Jellinek's edition of Ibn Ṣaddiq's work), *MGWJ* 3:159–161 [1854]).

[105] *Bet Ha-Midrash*, V, 57–59. In his Introduction (p. xxv) Jellinek makes it clear that the title *Aggadat ᶜOlam Qaṭan* was chosen by *him*. The term *ᶜolam qaṭan* for microcosm, he points out, does not occur in haggadic literature and was adopted into Hebrew literature only under the influence of Arabic philosophy.

[106] Cf. Altmann-Stern, *Isaac Israeli*, p. 204.

might be regarded as one of the sources for the definition of philosophy as self-knowledge which is found in al-Kindī and Isaac Israeli. It also underlies the combination of the theme of self-knowledge with the microcosm motif which we meet in the *Ikhwān al-Ṣafāʾ*.[107] The salient point common to the *Ikhwān*, al-Kindī, and Israeli is that by knowing himself as a microcosm man knows himself "in both his spirituality and corporeality" and therefore knows "everything": that is, "the spiritual and corporeal substance". This point is neatly expressed by al-Masʿūdī (d. 957/8), who attributes to Aristotle the saying: "Whosoever knows himself, knows thereby everything."[108] It should be noted that this interpretation of self-knowledge as leading to the knowledge of "everything" omits any reference to God as the ultimate goal of the quest for knowledge. Neither the *ḥadīth* formulae nor the Delphic exhortation in its two-stage form is quoted in this context, although the *Ikhwān* use the *ḥadīth* when interpreting self-knowledge as the knowledge of the soul.[109] Obviously, knowing the macrocosm is the be-all and end-all according to the tradition which is here followed. It is clear that the microcosm-macrocosm motif holds a great fascination for the *Ikhwān* in particular, as is evident from the ample treatment they accorded it in their writings.[110] When dealing with it, they are absorbed in the vistas it offers, and theology recedes into the background.

It is characteristic of medieval Jewish philosophy that it goes beyond the aspect of the macrocosm when employing the Delphic maxim in the sense of the microcosm-macrocosm motif. Isaac Israeli already moves in this direction. Explaining the definition of philosophy as meaning that one who knows himself knows

[107] *Ibid.*

[108] Quoted by F. Rosenthal, "On the Knowledge of Plato's Philosophy in the Islamic World" (see note 6), p. 410. Rosenthal surmises that the saying is taken from the *Theology of Aristotle*, ed. Dieterici, p. 19. But there is nothing in that or any other passage of the *Theology* which could be considered the source of al-Masʿūdī's quotation. Rosenthal (p. 409) also cites al-Masʿūdī as reporting: "On the gates of the temple of the Sabians in Harrān there was written in Syriac language the saying of Plato, the translation of which is: Whosoever recognizes his essence is divine (*taʾallaha*)."

[109] Cf. F. Dieterici, *Die Philosophie der Araber im* X. *Jahrhundert n. Chr.*, 2, *Mikrokosmus* (Leipzig, 1879), p. 185; *idem*, *Die Philosophie der Araber*, *Achtes Buch* (1872), pp. 167–168.

[110] Cf. the passages quoted by me in Altmann-Stern, *Isaac Israeli*, p. 203, n. 2, and the references given by G. Vajda, "La Philosophie et la théologie de Joseph ibn Çaddiq," *Archives*, 17:96–97 (1949).

"everything"—that is, "the spiritual and corporeal substance"—he adds: "and also knows the first substance which is created from the power of the Creator without mediator . . ."[111] This suggests that self-knowledge eventually leads to knowing the supernal wisdom, but not to the knowledge of God who, like Plotinus' "One", is unknowable.[112] Shorn of its Neoplatonic orientation which is implied in the notion of the supernal wisdom,[113] Israeli's reference to the ultimate goal of self-knowledge could be interpreted to mean that the contemplation of the macrocosm or totality of being (corporeal and spiritual) shows the wisdom of the Creator and proves His existence. This step is taken in Joseph ibn Ṣaddīq's *Sēfer ʿOlam Qaṭan.*[114] It quotes Israeli's definition of philosophy as self-knowledge by which man "knows everything" (that is, the corporeal world and the spiritual world), and adds: "And this is the science of philosophy, which is the science of sciences and their final purpose, because it is the preliminary step (*madregah*) and road (*shebhīl*) to the knowledge of the Creator and Initiator of everything, blessed and exalted be He."[115] In another passage, which once more quotes Israeli's definition of philosophy as self-knowledge, he adds: "and he will thence reach the knowledge of his Creator, as it is written in Job (19:26), 'And from my flesh I shall behold God.'"[116] This verse, we have already noted, represents the Jewish version, so to speak, of the *ḥadīth* formula, "He who knows himself, knows his Lord." Joseph ibn Ṣaddīq thus interprets this saying to mean that by knowing oneself as a microcosm one will eventually know God.[117] In portraying man as a microcosm he draws on such sources as Israeli's "Chapter on the Elements", which sees in man a balancing of the four elements[118]; and on "the Ancients"—probably a version of some Hellenistic text which compared the limbs of the human organism to the heavenly bodies (viz., the head to the [all-encompassing] sphere, the eyes to sun and moon, the ears to Saturn and Jupiter, the nostrils to Venus, the mouth to Mars, the tongue to Mercury,

[111] Cf. Altmann-Stern, *Isaac Israeli*, p. 27, lines 104–108; pp. 28, 202–203.

[112] *Ibid.*, pp. 207–208.

[113] *Ibid.*, pp. 159–164.

[114] The quotations which follow are from S. Horovitz' edition (Breslau, 1903).

[115] Page 2.

[116] Page 21.

[117] Cf. Altmann-Stern, *Isaac Israeli*, p. 208. See also G. Vajda, "La Philosophie et la théologie de Joseph Ibn Çaddiq", in *Archives*, pp. 113ff.

[118] The passage in *Microcosm*, p. 24, lines 14–19, is clearly based on Israeli's "Chapter on the Elements" (Altmann-Stern, p. 121, no. 3). For the sources of the passage in *Microcosm*, p. 24, lines 19–24, see Vajda, *Archives*, p. 114, n. 1.

and the vertebrae of the spinal cord to the signs of the Zodiac); the arteries to the seas and rivers; the bones to the mountains; the hair to the plants; and the four temperaments to the four elements.[119]

While Ibn Ṣaddīq is content to develop the microcosm motif along traditional lines and link it but loosely with the theme of knowing God, one of his predecessors, Baḥya ibn Paqūdah,[120] treats it with much greater seriousness and independence. (The Neo-platonic outlook which determines his approach will be discussed in the next section [3].) He too quotes "some philosophers" as saying that "philosophy is man's knowledge of himself", which he explains to mean that from the "traces of wisdom" exhibited in man as a microcosm we are able to recognize the Creator. Job 19:26 is cited as proof text.[121] The "philosophers" referred to are the *Ikhwān*[122] and, possibly, Israeli, but the context in which this passage occurs (*Hidāya*, II, 4–5) clearly shows the freshness of Baḥya's treatment of the theme. The dominant topic is a meditation on the "traces of wisdom" (*āthār al-ḥikma*) found in the "roots and elements" of the world, in man as a microcosm, in the construction of man and in the composition of his body as well as in the faculties of his soul and the light of intellect, in the entire animal world, in plants and metals, in the sciences, arts, and purposive actions of man, in the laying down of the Law (*al-sharāʾiʿ*) and the statutes (*al-suna*).[123] The microcosm idea is used here only as one among seven aspects serving the purpose of the discussion.

Abraham bar Ḥiyya[124] closely follows Baḥya in interpreting Job 19:26 to mean that "from the formation of your body [literally,

[119] This passage (p. 24, line 24, to p. 25, line 12) is introduced by a reference to "the Ancients" (*ha-rishonīm*). A pictorial presentation of the analogies mentioned by Joseph ibn Ṣaddīq is found in the microcosm drawing of Prüfening (1165) reproduced in F. Saxl, *Lectures*, II (London, 1957), Plate 37a.

[120] In his *Al-Hidāya ʾilā Farāʾid al-Qulūb*, ed. A. S. Yahuda (1912).

[121] *Ibid.*, 106.

[122] On Baḥya's indebtedness to the *Ikhwān*, see D. Kaufmann, "Die Theologie des Bachja Ibn Pakuda", *Gesammelte Schriften*, ed. M. Brann, II (Frankfort, 1910), 15–17; G. Vajda, *La Théologie ascétique de Baḥya Ibn Paquda* (Paris, 1947), p. 25, n. 3.

[123] The exposition of this theme is given in a lengthy discussion (pp. 103–124). The term "traces of wisdom" occurs also in Ibn Gabirol (cf. Arab. Fragment 12.3, ed. S. Pines, *Tarbiṣ*, vol. XXVII [Scholem Jubilee Number], January 1958, p. 230: *al-āthār al-ḥikmīya*; in Falaqēra's *Liqqūṭīm*, V, 65, ed. Munk: *rishūmē ha-ḥokmah*; *Fons Vitae*, ed. Baeumker, V. 41: *impressionibus Sapientiae*). It goes back to Plotinus' use of the term τύπος in *Enn.*, *passim* (see Bréhier, Index, *s.v.*). The Hebrew Empedocles Fragments, ed. Kaufmann, render it *rishūm* (as in Falaqēra's *Liqqūṭīm*), whereas Jehudah ibn Tibbon's version of Baḥya's *Hidāya* has *simanē ha-ḥokmah*.

[124] *Sēfer Hegyōn Ha-Nefesh* (Leipzig, 1865).

'flesh'] and the arrangement of your limbs you can see and understand the wisdom of your Creator".[125] This theme becomes a popular topic in the twelfth and thirteenth centuries. Samuel ben Nissīm Masnūt,[126] who lived in twelfth-century Aleppo, quotes Job 19:26 as meaning to say that "From the formation of my limbs and from the arrangement of my body—contemplating them—I behold God (that is, the wonders of the Creator); for by seeing the created, man knows the wonders of the Creator, in the way in which it is said, 'The heavens declare . . .' (Ps. 19:2), which the *Targum* renders, 'Those who contemplate the heaven tell the glory of the Lord.'" Likewise, Joseph ben Jehudah[127] cites Job 19:26 as *locus probans* for the meritoriousness of studying medicine, for this verse means to say, "From the wondrous formation of my body I recognise the wisdom of my Creator as manifold and wondrous." As G. Vajda has pointed out, the Job verse figures in ninth- and tenth-century Karaite literature as proof text of a similar character.[128] But the texts at our disposal use this verse merely in the sense of clinching the cosmological argument. Thus Joseph al-Baṣīr says: "Since God is not visible, He can be known by us only through His works, because they—for example, our body—cannot be created by us. Job also declares: 'Out of my flesh I know God.' Now our method is prescribed: First we have to recognise the createdness of the bodies; then we can prove therefrom that they require a wise Creator."[129] The Job verse is used here in support of the Kalam method (later attacked by Maimonides) which seeks to prove the existence of God from His creation. From Baḥya onward it is employed in the sense of the teleological rather than cosmological argument. We have seen above (p. 18) that its traces can be found even in a kabbalistic text such as the *Zohar Ḥadash*. In Abraham ibn Ezra the microcosm motif is linked with the mystical notion of the Sanctuary as the "intermediate world" (*ᶜolam ᵓemṣaᶜī*) which, like the heart in the human body receiving the power of the soul in larger degree than any other organs, is the place in which the Divine power is most concentrated. "And if God has given you wisdom, you will understand the mystery of the Ark and the curtain and the Cherubim which spread their wings . . . And these things are the 'glory' of God . . . And he who knows the mystery of his soul [*sōd nishmatō*] and the arrangement of his body [*matkōnet*

[125] Fol. 1b.

[126] Cf. above, n. 16, for references.

[127] Cf. above, n. 16, for references.

[128] See above, p. 3 and n. 15.

[129] Cf. P. F. Frankl, *Ein mutazilitischer Kalam aus dem* 10. *Jahrhundert* (Vienna, 1872), p. 185.

gūfō] is able to know the things of the supernal world. For man is in the image of a microcosm [*ki-dĕmūt ᶜolam qaṭan*]. He was the end of His creation on earth. This is alluded to in the verse (Gen. 44:12), 'beginning with the great and ending with the small.'"[130]

The sentence, "And *he who knows* . . . is able to know the things of the supernal world" re-echoes both the *ḥadīth* ("*He who knows* himself knows his Lord") and Israeli's definition of philosophy as self-knowledge: "the mystery of the soul" and "the arrangement of the body" reflect Israeli's "spiritual and corporeal substance", and the "supernal world" described by Ibn Ezra as the goal of knowledge corresponds to Israeli's "First Substance" or "supernal Wisdom".[131] The doctrine interposing the "intermediate world" of the Sanctuary is quoted in the name of "the Gaon": that is, Saadya Gaon, who in his *Commentary* on the *Sēfer Yeṣirah* (ed. Lambert, 67ff., 91) mentions eighteen analogies between the three worlds.[132] That the Sanctuary and its furniture mirror the cosmos is an old midrashic motif, particularly pronounced in *Midrash Tadsheh*.[133] The observation that creation began with the macrocosm and ended with the microcosm is already found in Philo (*Opif.* 82) and Abraham bar Ḥiyya (*Hegyōn Ha-Nefesh*, 1b).

There is further reference to self-knowledge in Ibn Ezra. He links this theme also to that of the love of God which plays a cherished part in his thinking.[134] "It is the root-principle of the commandments that one should love God with all his soul and cleave unto Him. A man will not be perfect unless he recognizes the work of God in the supernal and lower worlds and knows His ways . . . and he will not be able to know God, unless he knows his own soul [*nefesh*] and his body and his intelligent soul [*nishmatō*]; for one who does not know the essence of his soul, what wisdom does he possess?"[135]

[130] *Commentary ad* Ex. 25:40, end.

[131] It denotes, however, the entire world of Spiritual Substances or Angels.

[132] Cf. H. Malter, *Saadia Gaon, His Life and Works* (Philadelphia, 1942), pp. 186–187 and n. 436, where the references to the literature on the subject are given.

[133] S. Z. Netter in his supercommentary on Ibn Ezra *ad loc.* offers a wealth of detail concerning these analogies.

[134] Cf. G. Vajda, *L'Amour de Dieu dans la Théologie Juive du Moyen Age* (Paris 1957), pp. 109–115.

[135] Quoted from the recension of Ibn Ezra's *Commentary* in Cod. 53 of the Breslau Seminary, as reported in D. Rosin's valuable essay, "Die Religionsphilosophie Abraham ibn Esra's", *MGWJ* 43 (N.F. 7):231 (1899). This recension has a fuller text, but the last sentence is corrupt. It reads: *kī kol mī shelōᵓ lamad ḥokmah ḥokmah mā lō.* In our translation of the passage (see above) we have substituted the reading of the printed edition in the last sentence.

This reflects the saying of the *Ikhwān* that one who regards the soul as a mere accident or mixture of the body "knows neither his soul nor his true essence; how then should he know the true essence of things and their First Cause?"[136] But while the *Ikhwān* mention only the soul, Ibn Ezra—bearing in mind the microcosm motif—regards the knowledge of the body *and* soul as a precondition for the knowledge of God.

Similarly, Netanʾel Berab Fayūmī, a Yemenite scholar of the twelfth century, who was greatly influenced by the *Ikhwān al-Ṣafāʾ* and by Baḥya ibn Paqudah, describes in his *Bustān al-ᶜUqūl* ("Garden of the Intelligences", edited and translated into Hebrew by Joseph ben David Qafaḥ, Jerusalem, 1954) the body and soul of man as a microcosm mirroring the macrocosm. The three worlds of (1) the Universal Intellect (*al-ᶜaql al-kullī*), (2) the spheres (*al-aflāk*), and (3) the coarse (*scilicet*, material] world (*al-ᶜālam al-kathīf*) are reflected in man's spirit, body, and three-dimensionality respectively. Hence it is said, "And out of my flesh I behold God" and "Thou has made him but a little lower than the angels" (Ps. 8:6). "It thus befits us to consider and contemplate all his attributes of body and soul, the manifest and the hidden [*scilicet*, the corporeal and spiritual] in order to know the exaltedness of his Maker and Creator, blessed be He" (pp. 5, 13).

An interesting variation of our theme is offered in one of the interpretations of Gen. 1:26 recorded by Baḥya ben Asher in his *Commentary on the Torah* (9a, col. a–b): "Some explain 'in our image' as 'in the image which is ours but distinct from Us," i.e., the image of the world in its structure [*bi-tekhūnatō*], comprising the world of the angels, the world of the spheres, and the lower world. These three parts make up the totality of existence. Hence man is called a microcosm [*ᶜolam qaṭan*]; for he corresponds to the macrocosm [*ᶜolam gadōl*], and Job alluded to this when saying 'And out of my flesh I behold God.' He meant to say that from the three parts of his body one beholds the three parts of existence in creation, which is the work of God. For man's head, which receives the emanation of Intellect, corresponds to the supernal world in which the separate intelligences reside. The part from the neck to the loins is man's intermediate part . . . corresponding to the intermediate world which is the world of the spheres . . . From the loins downward is the third part . . . corresponding to this world

[136] Cf. the passages in Altmann-Stern, *Isaac Israeli*, pp. 205–206.

of generation and corruption." In this account the body as such is conceived as a microcosm reflecting all stages of existence, including the supernal realm. The closeness of this view to the kabbalistic interpretation mentioned in a previous context (pp. 14 ff.) is obvious.

The same is true of the interpretation of Gen. 1:26 offered by Joshuᶜa ibn Shuᶜeib (first half of the fourteenth century), who, like Baḥya ben Asher, was a disciple of Solomon ben Adret of Barcelona. In his *Sefer Dĕrashōt al Ha-Torah* (Constantinople, 1522, and Krakow, 1573, the latter edition being quoted here) he describes the body of a man as made in the image (*ṣelem*) and archetype (*dugmā*) of everything found in the Ten *Sefirot* and in the Ten Heavens (symbolised by his ten fingers and ten toes respectively). His 248 limbs correspond to the 248 positive commandments and his 365 veins and sinews to the 365 negative commandments of the Torah. This is referred to in Job 19:26 and in Ps. 35:10 ("All my bones shall say: 'Lord, who is like unto Thee'"). The limbs of man, though resembling those of the animals, contain "something supernal mixed with them" and must therefore be guarded in their purity (fol. 60*v*, col. a). Gen. 1:26 teaches us "the rank of the creation of his body and of the form of his limbs" which have their counterpart in the world of the *Merkabah*, as known to the Kabbalists (fol. 2*v*, col. 1). It is interesting to note that both Ibn Shuᶜeib and Baḥya ben Asher, though steeped in Neoplatonic concepts and philosophically inclined, interpret the *homo imago Dei* motif by reference to the body of man as a microcosm.

3. SOUL AND INTELLECT

The third line of approach in interpreting the Delphic maxim is the neoplatonic one. According to Plotinus (*Enn.*, V, 3, 3ff.), the soul has two modes of knowing intrinsic to her: sensation, which is turned toward the external things, and discursive reason which separates or combines the images presented by the senses, and judges them in the light of standards derived from intellect. In all these operations the soul is concerned with the external world, not with itself. In the act of judging the soul turns toward the intellect, but standing midway between sensation and intellect, it cannot wholly identify itself with intellect and know itself. Intellect is ours and is not ours. It is ours when we act by it. The sensitive principle is our "scout" (*angelos*); intellect is our king.

But we too are kings, when we take our fill of intellect. Man becomes intellect when, ignoring all other phases of his being, he knows himself in the dual sense of knowing the nature of the discursive thinking of the soul and knowing its own conformity to intellect. Thus, essentially, the soul knows itself by looking upward to Intellect, not by looking merely into itself. The difference between soul and intellect is this: while the soul knows itself within something else (that is, intellect), the latter knows itself as self-depending and achieves its self-knowledge by simple introversion upon itself. In the act of self-contemplation the intellect and the intelligible are one. The precept, "Know thyself" addresses itself, therefore, only to those beings which are multiple and have to learn which of their parts is the dominant one and causes them to be "themselves" (*Enn.*, VI, 7, 41).

The salient points of this doctrine may be said to be the following. (1) The soul knows itself only by looking upward, not by looking upon itself. This tallies with Plotinus' theory of emanation which describes the emanant as becoming fully substance and reality at the second phase when it looks back to its source. (2) The act of self-knowledge implies a withdrawal from the sensible world. (3) The final goal of self-knowledge must lie beyond Intellect and can be found only in "union" with the One. There is no ecstasy in self-knowledge. Plotinus describes ecstasy in *Enneads*, VI, 9, 10–11, and in the famous passage IV, 8, 1, as a state in which the soul stands above the intelligible world. In this state the soul is divested of the body and it "enters into itself", but it reaches the end of the journey only when the image of the One takes shape in the soul. The desire for "contact" (ἁφή) is the keynote of this ultimate stage (V, 3, 17; VI, 9, 11). Here our concern is no longer the soul or self-knowledge. The soul is no longer itself. It becomes what it is in the very source of its being.[137]

In *Enneads*, V, 3, 7, Plotinus answers the view of the mystics who hold that by turning away from the sensible world we turn not to ourselves but to God. The view referred to is, as E. Bréhier remarks,[138] the Philonic doctrine according to which the exodus of the soul from the realm of sense leads not to self-knowledge but to the realisation of the nothingness of the soul

[137] Cf. Louis Gardet, *La Pensée religieuse d'Avicenne* (Paris, 1951), pp. 148–149, where the Plotinian view is compared and contrasted with Ibn Sīnā's.

[138] Plotinus, *Ennéades*, ed. Bréhier, 2nd ed. V, 41–42.

and of God as the only true Being. Philo had indeed interpreted the Delphic maxim as an exhortation to remember "thine own nothingness in all things" so as to remember the transcendence of God in all things (*Sacrif. Ab.*, 54). Socrates' quest for self-knowledge—represented in the Hebrew Scriptures by the character of Teraḥ—is not the ultimate end. "Abraham who gained much progress and improvement towards the acquisition of the highest knowledge" supersedes Teraḥ: "For when most he knew himself, then most did he despair of himself, in order that he might attain to an exact knowledge of Him Who in reality IS . . . And the man who has despaired of himself is beginning to know Him that IS" (*De Somniis*, 57–60).[139] Plotinus rejects this view because it ignores the fact that in knowing God the soul, at the same time, knows itself as derived from God. The tranquility (ἡσυχία) achieved in the act of knowing God is not "ecstatic" in the sense that the soul goes out of itself but means, on the contrary, that the soul rests entirely in itself: that is, in the self-knowledge of the intellect. This anticipates the critique medieval philosophers applied to the *Ṣūfī* doctrine of ecstasy as disregarding the essential role of intellect for the attainment of the ultimate stage of union.[140] For Plotinus, "knowing God"—he uses this term on this rare occasion—cannot be divorced from the self-possession of the soul in the pure act of intellect.

The Plotinian interpretation of the Delphic maxim is taken up in Porphyry's treatment of the theme in his *Sententiae*, in the *De abstinentia*, and in his large work *On "Know thyself"*. "To them that are able to withdraw thinkingly into their own substance and to know their own substance by that very same knowledge, and to receive themselves back (αὑτοὺς ἀπολαμβάνειν) by the vision of this knowledge according to the unity of knower and known—to them, being present to themselves, Being too is present. But those who slip past their own being towards the other things are far from themselves and Being is far from them" (*Sententiae*, ed. Mombert, ch. 40, p. 38).[141] The characteristic phrase describing self-know-

[139] Cf. also *Migr Abr.* 8 (interpreting the Biblical *hishshamēr lekha* as "give heed to thyself": i.e., "know thyself"); *Migr. Abr.* 195 (moving from self-knowledge to the contemplation of Him who IS).

[140] E.g., in Ibn Bājja's *Risālat al-wadāʿ*, ed. M. Asín Palacios ("La Carta de Adiós de Avempace", *Al-Andalus*, vol. VIII, §8, pp. 21–22 [53–55]).

[141] Cf. W. Theiler, *Porphyrios und Augustin* in *Schriften der Königsberger Gelehrten Gesellschaft*, vol. X, fasc. 1 (Halle [Saale], 1933), pp. 43ff., where this passage is discussed.

ledge as a "receiving oneself back" corresponds to the phrase "returning to oneself" by which Proclus denotes the essential movement of intellect, and which also appears in the Arabic paraphrase of the Plotinus passage on ecstasy in the *Theology of Aristotle* (ed. Dieterici, p. 8). It is re-echoed in St. Augustine's *De ordine*, I, 3: "Ut se noscat magna opus habet consuetudine recedendi a sensibus et animum in se ipsum colligendi atque in se ipso retinendi . . . ita enim *animus sibi redditus* . . ." In turning inward, man finds not only himself but Being as such; he loses both when turning away from himself to the "other" which is non-being. He renounces his interior riches and becomes impoverished.[142] Porphyry is particularly emphatic about the need of practising the virtues appropriate to the contemplative life. Only at the stage of the "paradigmatic virtues" may we expect the distance between soul and Intellect to be eliminated.[143]

In Proclus' scheme of the soul's ascent[144] self-knowledge is tacitly assumed to be identical with the first stage: that of "purification". "For whence else does it befit our self-purification and perfection to start than from the point where the Delphian god has commanded us? For to those entering the Eleusinian temple a notice was shown, 'Let none of the uninitiated and unexpiated enter here.' Indeed, the inscription 'Know thyself' upon the entrance to the Delphian temple likewise, I believe, indicated the manner of the ascent to the Divine and of the readiest way of purification, evidently as if to say to those capable of understanding that he who knows himself, starting as he does from the right beginning, can achieve union with God, the interpreter of all truth and leader of the purgative life."[145] The passage quoted shows clearly that the notion of self-knowledge merges here imperceptively with that of purification. The soul is capable of a true introversion only if it turns away from the things of the sensible, external world and, thus purified, rests entirely in the intellect from which it has its true being. There is an interesting parallel to the identification of self-knowledge and purification in Philo (*Leg. Spec.*, I, 263–264): "For he [Moses] holds that the most profitable form of purification is just this, that a man should know himself..."

142 For the relevant passages in Porphyry and parallels in Hierocles, see Theiler, *Porphyrios und Augustin*, p. 44.

143 Cf. Theiler, *Porphyrios und Augustin*, p. 44, n. 1.

144 Cf. Altmann-Stern, *Isaac Israeli*, pp. 185ff.

145 Cf. Altmann-Stern, *Isaac Israeli*, p. 205.

The impact of this neoplatonic view of self-knowledge upon medieval thought is very considerable. It is mediated in large measure by the neoplatonic pseudepigrapha sailing under the flags of Aristotle, Empedocles and others.[146] We propose to trace some of the themes to which reference has been made in a number of medieval writings. In many instances these themes are explicitly connected neither with the Delphic maxim nor the *ḥadīth* or its Hebrew equivalent, but the pattern of the two-stage formula is always in the background.

The theme of the soul's withdrawal from the external world in order to find itself illumined by the Intellect occurs in the many medieval passages quoting the *Theology of Aristotle*'s paraphrase of Plotinus' portrayal of ecstasy. How closely the text of the *Theology* follows its prototype will be clear from a glance at the passages concerned in juxtaposition to each other:

Enneads, IV, 8, 1:	*Theology*, p. 8:
Many times it has happened:	Sometimes,
Lifted out of the body into myself becoming external to all other things and self-centered	I was, as it were, alone with my soul: I divested myself of the body, put it aside, and was as it were a simple substance without a body. Then I entered into my essence by returning into it free from all things. . .
beholding a marvellous beauty	I saw in my essence so much of beauty, loveliness and splendour. . .
then more than ever assured of community with the loftiest order, enacting the noblest life	I knew that I was a part of the exalted . . . divine upper world, and that I was endowed with an active life
acquiring identity with the divine	I rose in my essence . . . to the divine world and I was as it were
stationing within it by having attained that activity, poised above whatsoever within the intellectual is less than the Supreme	placed there and attached (*muta'alliq*) to it. I was above the whole intelligible world . . .

[146] Cf. Altmann-Stern, *Isaac Israeli*, pp. 149–150.

As I have shown elsewhere,[147] the passage from the *Theology* is quoted by al-Fārābī, Moses ibn Ezra (most probably from the *Epistles of the Ikhwān*), Shemtob ibn Falaqēra, and is reparaphrased by Solomon ibn Gabirol. The latter's chapter on ecstasy in his *Fons Vitae* (ed. Bäumker, III, 56–57)[148] is obviously based on the passage of the *Theology*, as already suggested by Jacob Guttmann.[149] To this list we should add Aaron ben Joseph's *Sēfer ha-Mibḥar* and al-Batalyawsī's "Imaginary Circles"[150]; also Moses de Leon's *Mishkan ha-ᶜEdūth* (ms. Berlin, fol. 32a), where it is ascribed to the "true Teacher" (*mōreh ṣedeq*): "Regarding suchlike matters the true Teacher said, 'When I was alone with my soul and divested myself of my body and put it off and was like a soul without a body and contemplated the supernal world, I enjoyed a spiritual bliss like the bliss of the world-to-come such as mouths are unable to describe, and the image of which hearts are unable to contain. Hence a man must prepare himself with all his being before God as if he were an altar of atonement prepared before Him.'"[151] A faint trace of the *Theology* passage is also found in ᶜObadyah's (grandson of Moses Maimonides) *Treatise of the Bowl.*

[147] Altmann-Stern, *Isaac Israeli*, pp. 191–192.

[148] Also extant in the *Arabic Fragments*, ed. Pines, fragm. 2, pp. 221–222; Falaqēra's *Liqqūṭīm*, ed. Munk, III, 37.

[149] *Die Philosophie des Salomon ibn Gabriol*, p. 165, n. 2.

[150] See the reference in Guttmann, cited in n. 149.

[151] G. Scholem was the first to notice Moses de Leon's use of the *Theology* passage in the *Mishkan ha-ᶜEdūt*. See *Major Trends in Jewish Mysticism*, p. 203 and p. 398, n. 155. The text of Moses de Leon's paraphrase does not, however, bear out Scholem's description of it as quoting Plotinus' account of the philosopher's "ecstatic ascent into the world of pure intelligence *and his vision of the One*" (p. 203). It is clear from the text that for Moses de Leon the highest stage is the contemplation of the supernal world, not the vision of the One. He says of this contemplation (*wa-etbōnēn ba-ᶜolam ha-ᶜelyōn*) that its bliss (*taᶜanūg rūḥanī*) is "like" (*dugmat*) the bliss of the world-to-come: i.e., like enjoying the splendour of the Shekhinah—if we interpret the phrase *taᶜanūg ᶜolam ha-bāᵓ* as a reference to the well-known passage in BT *Běrakhōt* 17a—but he does not indicate any ascent beyond the contemplation of the supernal world, i.e. beyond the spiritual substances. This interpretation is corroborated by another passage (fol. 2b) of the same work describing the highest stage (i.e. that of prophecy) again as the vision, not of the One, but of the supernal Form: "For when the prophet enters into union, at the stage of his wisdom, so as to be attached (*lě-hiddabēq*) in his form to the supernal Form, he divests himself of all corporeal things and of all elements of this world." A parallel to the description of the vision of the supernal world of pure intellect occurs also in Moses de Leon's *Or zarūᶜa* (MS. Pococke 296:11, fol. 196a) where it becomes clear that the supernal Form is conceived in terms of the Spiritual Matter known from the Pseudo-Empedoclean Fragments (on which see Altmann-Stern, *Isaac Israeli*, pp. 159–164). For he speaks there of the *maᶜalat zohar ha-yesōd*, the vision of which "tongues cannot describe".

"When thou remainest alone with thy soul after mastering thy moral qualities, a gate will open before thee through which thou wilt contemplate wonders. Indeed, with the suppression of thy five outward senses thy inner senses will awaken, and thou wilt be shown a dazzling light with the light of the Intellect."[152] The account given of the ecstatic experience is more in the Sūfī tradition but the neoplatonic background is sufficiently attested by the opening phrase and the reference to the light of the Intellect. "When thou remainest alone with thy soul" is obviously a literal borrowing from the *Theology* ("I was as it were alone with my soul").

The theme of "looking upward" to the Intellect is predominant in the Hebrew Pseudo-Empedocles Fragments published by D. Kaufmann.[153] According to the ontological scheme of this text the hypostasis of (intelligible) Matter is interposed between God and the Intellect.[154] Hence Intellect loses its prerogative of being the ultimate goal of the soul's self-knowledge, short of her union with the One. But otherwise the mode of interpretation which we traced in Plotinus is fully preserved. "Likewise, the soul looks to Intellect beyond herself, and is lit up by looking to Intellect, and is raised and becomes truly soul and one with Intellect. When she looks to the things below which are caused by her, she becomes diffused and darkened. But in looking at herself, she looks at the part of herself which is Intellect in the same way in which Intellect looks at the part in itself which comes from (intelligible) Matter. She continues looking at Intellect until lit up by its light."[155] The equation of self-knowledge and purification which we met in Proclus is also much in evidence in the Pseudo-Empedocles Fragments. "It is *necessary* for us *to investigate* the soul which is within us [that is, to obey the precept, 'Know thyself'] and to speculate as to her nature. Such investigation should not relate to the soul as existing in this body of ours, a soul full of passions and held in the grip of animal pleasures of an evil nature so that it is dominated by anger, injustice, violence, and similar vices. But we are *obliged* [that is, to obey the Delphic precept] to investigate the soul which has abandoned all this and which is

[152] Cf. G. Vajda, "The Mystical Doctrine of Rabbi ᶜObadyah, Grandson of Moses Maimonides", *The Journal of Jewish Studies* 6:218 (1955).

[153] In his *Studien über Salomon Ibn Gabirol* (Budapest, 1899), pp. 17–51.

[154] Cf. Altmann-Stern, *Isaac Israeli*, pp. 162–164.

[155] Cf. Kaufmann, *Studien*, p. 21.

cleansed of all filth. In her we shall know what she really is . . . For the soul which has abandoned those evils and is clean while still in the body is, as it were, no longer in it nor tied to it. Once we know what this soul is, what her essence and her attributes are, we shall not be mistaken in our statements nor in whatever we ascribe to her . . . When the soul receives the divine and exalted virtues . . . it becomes apparent without doubt that the soul is an exalted substance of the genus of the Upper World: spiritual, divine and simple . . . when she becomes one in us and we one in her, she puts us on the level of that exalted world."[156]

The influence of the Pseudo-Empedocles Fragments on Solomon ibn Gabirol cannot be gainsaid.[157] We propose to offer a detailed analysis of this influence elsewhere. It appears that amongst the Arab philosophers in Spain Ibn Bājja too succumbed to the spiritual temper of the Pseudo-Empedoclean tradition. His neoplatonic leanings are pronounced, and his description of the ultimate stage of man's union with the Agent Intellect is wholly neoplatonic. At that stage, he says, the unity of knower and known is complete and man truly knows himself.[158] It is highly significant that he explicitly links the theme of self-knowledge with that of union. From Proclus he borrows the notion of the intellect's "returning to itself", which was mediated to him by an Arabic version of some of Proclus' Propositions attributed to Alexander of Aphrodisias.[159] In following the trend of the neoplatonic emphasis on purification, he makes the attainment of self-knowledge and union dependent upon a conversion from the world of the senses to the pure intelligibles. When saying that at the ultimate stage man is "simple, divine"[160] he literally quotes the Pseudo-Empedocles passage cited above. It may be noted in passing that Ibn Rushd's summary of Ibn Bājja's *Treatise on the Union of Intellect with Man* in his *Epitome* of Aristotle's *De anima* finds occasion to quote

156 *Ibid.*, p. 36.

157 The problems clustering around Falaqēra's allegation (in the Preface to his *Liqqūṭīm*) that Ibn Gabirol followed (Pseudo-) Empedocles' *Book of the Five Substances* have been briefly touched upon in my article, "Problems in Jewish-Neoplatonic Research", in *Tarbiṣ* 27:505 (July, 1958).

158 Cf. *Risālat al-wadāʿ* (see n. 140), 30, p. 39 [85].

159 See below, p. 96ff.

160 Cf. *Tadbīr al-mutawaḥḥid*, ed. M. Asín Palacios (*El Régimen del Solitario por Avempace*, Madrid-Granada, 1946) p. 61 [100–101].

the two-stage formula in the form, "Know thyself, know thy Creator."[161]

In Baḥya ibn Paqūdah's *Hidāya* the neoplatonic pattern of the treatment of self-knowledge is preserved but given a meditative and moralistic turn by the motif of the "scrutiny" (*muḥāsaba*) of the soul which is said to result in "all virtues" and in the "excellence, i.e. purity (*ṣafā*ʾ)" of the substance of the soul from the "darkness" of ignorance.[162] This stage of the "scrutiny" of the soul corresponds to Proclus' stage (1) of self-knowledge, and as in Proclus it is identified with that of purification. This is followed up, again as in Proclus, by stage (2) of illumination: "For when you have done this . . . your intellect will be lit up . . . and you will be of the rank of the best friends of God, and there will arise within you a strange exalted power . . . then you will discern the glorious things and see the subtle mysteries by the purity of your soul and the cleanness of your heart."[163] To Proclus' stage (3) of union there corresponds in Baḥya the vision of the spiritual substances: "And the supernal and exalted Forms which you have no way of seeing with your eyes is the Wisdom of the Creator and His Power and totality of the supernal world."[164]

Baḥya's dialogue between the soul and Intellect, described as the "admonition" (*tanbīh*) of Intellect and as an "inspiration" (*ilhām*) which comes from God to man through the intermediacy of Intellect, is also cast in the neoplatonic mould and akin to the Delphic maxim. I. Heinemann suggested that the dialogue form and other features of this passage indicate Baḥya's dependence on a Hermetic source. This has been disputed by D. H. Baneth[165] and

[161] Cf. *Talkhīs Kitāb al-Nafs*, ed. Ahwānī, p. 93. He makes the point that metaphysics deals with intelligibles which exist by themselves—i.e. are simple substances. (On this interpretation of the nature of metaphysics, see S. Pines, "Studies in Abul-Barakāt al-Baghdādī's Poetics and Metaphysics" in *Studies in Philosophy*, Scripta Hierosolymitana, VI (Jerusalem, 1960), 156, and n. 115.) Yet metaphysics deals with these abstract intelligibles only in relation to the material intelligibles. The "science of the soul", however, need not begin in the way metaphysics begins. Hence, it has been said: "Know thyself, and thou wilt know thy Creator." In his *Epitome* of the *Metaphysics* Ibn Rushd goes beyond this in suggesting that metaphysics presupposes what has been demonstrated in psychology. In other words, it starts out from psychology. Hence: "Know thyself, and thou wilt know thy Creator". Cf. van den Berg, *Die Epitome . . .*, pp. 117, 250–251. For the notion that psychology is the beginning of the sciences, see Plotinus, *Enn.*, IV, 3, 1, and Alexander of Aphrodisias, *De anima*, ed. Bruns, p. 1.

[162] *Hidāya*, III, 4, p. 349.

[163] *Ibid.*, p. 350.

[164] *Ibid.*, p. 351.

[165] Cf. D. H. Baneth, *Kiryat Sēfer*, 3:136.

G. Vajda.[166] The form of dialogue, Vajda has shown, is not unknown in the ascetic literature of Islam, and the term *tanbīh* is no proof for direct Hermetic influence, as it is a current term in totally un-Gnostic writings. We are not concerned here with the literary *Vorlage* of Baḥya's dialogue but may point out in this connection that the dialogue between soul and Intellect has a close parallel in the medieval "Streitgedicht" and in the Hebrew literary genre of *tōkhēḥah*.[167] The discussion between body, soul, and intellect in Jehudah al-Ḥarīzī's *Taḥkemōnī*[168] is a case in point. What interests us in particular is the description of the soul and her relationship to intellect offered in his text. The soul depicts herself as having once upon a time been "dwelling on high and occupying the first rank in the Kingdom", "like a dove nesting in the bosom of God" (4, 1–2); she had "descended from the ranks of the higher beings and become separated from the Divine world" (4, 3); she is now "held in bondage" by the body, "bitten by the serpent of the [evil] inclination", and "alone, desolate", "caught in their prison" (7, 3–4). Having been "in the palace of God like a burning candle", her light is now "dimmed in the darkness of the body" (7, 31). Intellect reminds the soul of her origin, and does so with certain Gnostic overtones: "Wake up, O soul, who art pure, hewn from the glory of God, and held captive in the prison of the body" (6, 4). It exalts the soul to purify herself (6, 6; 11) and to provide herself with food for her "long journey" (6, 14). Let her not be asleep while *intellect* is drowned in the sea of passions (6, 15–16).

Intellect is here not the universal *Nous* of Neoplatonism but man's individual reason, "thy intellect" (6, 16). Intellect itself is "drowned in the sea of passions" owing to the forgetfulness of the soul. It depends on the soul's return to God for its own salvation (6, 28). Intellect is thus not entirely separate from the soul but involved in its spiritual fate. There is, nevertheless, an echo of the neoplatonic *Nous* in this dialogue. The soul is admonished by Intellect. Hence the two are not identical, and it is only by rising to the level of intellect that the soul achieves her true essence.

In Ibn Gabirol's and Jehudah Hallevi's poetry we possess many

[166] G. Vajda, *REJ* 102:98–103 (1937); *idem*, *La Théologie Ascétique* . . ., pp. 57ff.

[167] Cf. B. Sutorius, *Le Débat provençal de l'âme et du corps* (Freiburg, 1816); H. Walther, *Das Streitgedicht in der lateinischen Literatur des Mittelalters* (Munich, 1914) (quoted by José M. Millás Vallicrosa, *Šĕlomo Ibn Gabirol como Poeta y Filósofo*, Madrid-Barcelona,.1945, p. 101).

[168] Ed. Paul de Lagarde (Hannover, 1924), pp. 67–71.

examples of the Hebrew genre of *Zurechtweisungsgedicht* or admonitory poem ((*tōkhēḥah*). The poet—not the Intellect—addresses his soul, but the neoplatonic flavour is still discernible. In Ibn Gabirol, in particular, I. Heinemann was able to lay bare the neoplatonic orientation toward the world of Intellect.[169] The soul is compared to a "king in captivity"[170] and the poet praises wisdom and exhorts her to seek wisdom and its Lord.[171] Gnostic motifs such as the image of the "pearl" for the soul reinforce the neoplatonic trend.[172] A good example of this kind of poetry is the *tōkhēḥah* "Forget thy sorrow" (*shikhĕḥī yegōnēkh*), which Karl Dreyer has analyzed.[173] Jehudah Hallevi's poem, "If thy soul be precious in thine eyes, know thou her essence and seek her Creator", has already been mentioned above (p. 4). The allegorical interpretation of Canticles as a dialogue between the soul and Intellect belongs essentially to the same category of *tōkhēḥah*. As A. S. Halkin has shown, Maimonides was the first to introduce this type of allegorization.[174] It is followed by Moses ibn Tibbon, Joseph ibn Kaspi, Gersonides, and Joseph ben Jehudah ibn ᶜAḳnīn. The "lover" is the Agent Intellect and the rational soul is the "beloved".

We conclude this analytical survey with an account of the *homo imago Dei* motif as it appears at the very end of medieval Jewish history in Spain in Shemtob ben Joseph Shemtob's philosophical *Homilies* (*Dĕrashōt Ha-Torah*, Salonica, 1525, fol. 2a–b), where all the three variations of the theme we have traced—namely, the Platonic one of the soul's likeness to God, the microcosm idea, and the neoplatonic notion of the upward way—occur together. Discoursing on Gen. 1:26, the author first points out that it is in the nature of all beings to produce their like (*she-yaᶜasū dĕmūtam*). Thus the elements assimilate whatever comes into contact with them to their own essence, fire making things fiery, water making them watery, and so on. If this be true of the lower ranks of existence, it applies *a fortiori* to the supernal world. Hence God, who is the archetypal pattern (*dĕmūt u-dĕfūs*) of all existing things,

169 Cf. his *Die Lehre von der Zweckbestimmung des Menschen* . . . (Breslau, 1926), p. 56.

170 Cf. Dukes, *Shirē Shĕlōmo*, I, 4.

171 *Ibid.*, poems nos. 7, 8, 9, 10, 12.

172 *Ibid.*, pp. 16, 35.

173 Cf. Karl Dreyer, *Die religiöse Gedankenwelt des Salomo ibn Gabirol* (Leipzig, 1930), p. 120. For the literature on this poem, see Dreyer, p. 120, n. 99.

174 A. S. Halkin, "Ibn ᶜAḳnīn's Commentary on the Song of Songs", in *Alexander Marx Jubilee Volume* (New York, 1950), pp. 396ff.

willed that there be in this world an image of the Divine Form: moreover, that there be found in it an image of the macrocosm (*ha-ᶜōlam bi-kĕlalō*): that is, man, who is a microcosm (*ᶜōlam qaṭan*). Obviously, two different motifs are placed here alongside each other. The idea that God willed to create his own image is formulated in the bold sentence that "God formed his own self (*et ᶜaṣmō*) in this matter", it being "in the Divine nature" which knows no envy to be desirous to create its like, seeing that even lower beings show the same propensity. In truly Platonic fashion the self or essence (*ᶜaṣmūt*) of man is identified with his soul, compared with which the body is but a "stranger and alien" (*zar we-nokhrī*). No motivation is offered for God's further desire to make man an image of the macrocosm. The author quotes Job 19:26 but discards the traditional interpretation according to which the contemplation of man as a microcosm leads to the knowledge of God. Instead he explains this verse as meaning that by knowing his true self—that is, his own high rank—man will pursue the intellectual virtues, "for it befits him who resembles a divine being [*lĕ-bar elōhīn*] to conduct himself in action and speech in perfect order so as to preserve his form". But "it is impossible for man to know the macrocosm by knowing himself, for he is neither in heaven nor beyond the seas to be able to comprehend the 'measure' of the Creator and thereby gain the bliss of the world-to-come", a reference to the statement of the Tannaitic *Shiᶜūr Qōmah* Gnostics that "Whoever knows the measurements of our Creator and the Glory of the Holy One, praise be to Him, which are hidden from the creatures, is certain of his share in the world-to-come."[175] The contemplation of the microcosm is therefore abandoned as a way to the knowledge of God, except in the sense that on the analogy of soul and God as the hidden, incorporeal, guiding forces in the human body and in the cosmos respectively man becomes aware of God. Shemtob quotes the account of this analogy as offered by Maimonides (*Guide*, I, 71).

The neoplatonic theme of ascent and union is developed by stressing man's endowment with intellect: "Since in his intellectual form man resembles the Holy One, blessed be He, and the separate intelligencies, the prophets called the Holy One, blessed be He, by the name of 'man', as is said, 'And upon the likeness of the throne

[175] Cf. Gershom G. Scholem, *Jewish Gnosticism, Merkabah Mysticism, and Talmudic Tradition* (New York, 1960), p. 40.

was a likeness as the appearance of a man upon it above' (Ez. 1:26), and as they said in Gen. R. (24:1), 'How great is the power of the prophets who liken the form to its Former.'" By actualizing his material or potential intellect man is able to rise to the angelic stage and achieve union with the separate (agent) intellect during his lifetime, a possibility which, we may note, had been advocated already by the author's father, Joseph ben Shemtob, in his *Commentary* on Averroes' *Epistle on the Possibility of Conjunction.* The angelic stage is also described as one of self-knowledge, which reflects the neoplatonic notion of intellection as a return of the intellect upon itself as found in Proclus and Ibn Bājja (see above, p. 35). It cannot be said that Shemtob succeeded in making the three motifs completely consonant with one another, but his attempt highlights the significance which they had attained in the course of the development which we have traced.

2

THE LADDER OF ASCENSION

One of the most cherished features in the life story of Muḥammad is the traditional account of his nocturnal journey (*isrāʾ*) from the "holy mosque" (*al-masjid al-ḥarān*) of Mecca to the "further mosque" (*al-masjid al aqṣā*) which originally denoted the celestial sanctuary or the seventh heaven near the throne of Allāh. The scant allusion to this *Himmelsreise* in the Qurʾān passage 17:1 (supplemented by 53:4–18) came to be elaborated in a dazzling variety of ways.[1] The most decisive development took place when, probably at the time of ʿAbd al-Malik, the Umaiyad caliph, the "further mosque" was identified with the site of the Temple in Jerusalem, and the night journey was, therefore, split into two parts: the ride, on the celestial steed Burāq, from Mecca to Jerusalem, and the ascension, by means of a ladder of sublime beauty, to the seventh heaven and into the presence of God.[2] The term *isrāʾ* was henceforth used to denote the first part of the journey while the ascent to heaven came to be designated as *miʿrāj*, a word which originally simply meant "ladder" but eventually acquired the meaning of

[1] They are presented, according to the various recensions of the different cycles, by Miguel Asín Palacios, *La Escatología Musulmana en la Divina Comedia*, Segunda Edición, Madrid-Granada, 1943 (1st ed., 1919). For a critical evaluation of the origin and growth of the story see the excellent studies by B. Schrieke, "Die Himmelsreise Muhammeds", *Der Islam*, VI (1916), 1–30; Josef Horovitz, "Muhammeds Himmelfahrt", *Der Islam*, IX (1919), 159–183; Richard Hartmann, "Die Himmelsreise Muhammeds und ihre Bedeutung in der Religion des Islam", *Vorträge der Bibliothek Warburg, 1928–1929* (Leipzig-Berlin), 1930, 42–65; Martin Plessner, "Muḥammed's Clandestine ʿUmra . . .", *Rivista Degli Studi Orientali*, XXXII (Roma, 1957), 525–530.

[2] Schrieke, *op. cit.*, p. 13, and Horovitz, *op. cit.*, pp. 167ff.; *idem*, *Koranische Untersuchungen* (Berlin-Leipzig), 1926, p. 140. For a condensed account see *Shorter Encyclopaedia of Islam*, ed. H. A. R. Gibb and J. H. Kramers (Leiden, 1953), *s.v.* Burāḳ (p. 65), Isrāʾ (pp. 183–184), Miʿrādj̲ (pp. 381–384).

ᶜurūj, ascension.[3] The ladder motif is found already in Ibn Isḥāq (d. *c.* 767 C.E.) as attested in Ibn Hishām's *Kitāb sīrat Rasūl Allāh* and al-Ṭabarī's *Tafsīr.*[4] It was not difficult to introduce it since Sūra 70 of the Qurʾān bears the title "The Stairways" (*al-maᶜārij*) and Allāh is there called *Dhū ᶜl-maᶜārij* ("the Lord of the Stairways") to whom "the angels and the Spirit mount up in a day whereof the measure is fifty thousand years".[5] As has been pointed out by Josef Horovitz, it is most likely that the Qurʾānic term *maᶜārij* is a borrowing from Ethiopic maᶜāreg, and that the phrase "Lord of the Stairways" has its origin in the Ethiopic *Book of Jubilees* (27:21) which renders the word *sullam* of the Hebrew text by *maᶜāreg.* The ladder by which Muḥammad was said to have ascended to heaven thus goes back to the ladder which the patriarch Jacob saw in his dream.[6] The motif of the ladder as a means of reaching heaven is found also in other places in the Qurʾān, where, however, the term *sullam* is used (6:35, 52:38). Horovitz assumes that Muḥammad was familiar with the apocalyptic writings (Books of Enoch, *Ascensio Isaiae*, the Baruch apocalypses) and that he sought to imitate the ecstatic experiences related therein. He is inclined to assume even direct influence of Jewish mystics such as the visionaries of the Hekhalot, and he quotes the description of their ecstatic technique found in Hai ben Sherira's famous responsum.[7] He might have added that a passage in the *Greater Hekhalot* (ch. 15) describes the truly pious man as one "who has a ladder in his house". According to one of the variant readings the ladder is a reference to the visionary's "descent to the Merkabā".[8]

The question whether the night journey and the ascent took place in a literal or spiritual sense or in both senses together is already discussed by al-Ṭabarī (d. 923 C.E.), who opts in favour of

[3] Horovitz, *op. cit.*, pp. 174–175. The latter meaning is already found in Ibn Hishām (d. 834 C.E.).

[4] Horovitz, *ibid.*, n. 6.

[5] *Sūra* 70:3–4. For the relation of the traditional material to the *Qurʾānic* texts see L. Gardet, *Expériences mystiques en terres non-chrétiennes* (Paris, 1953), pp. 116–117. On the rabbinic background see Horovitz, *op. cit.*, pp. 176–177.

[6] Horovitz, *op. cit.*, pp. 175–176.

[7] Horovitz, *op. cit.*, p. 165. Cf. Gershom G. Scholem, *Major Trends in Jewish Mysticism*, Revised Edition, p. 49; and *idem*, *Jewish Gnosticism, Merkabah Mysticism, and Talmudic Tradition* (New York, 1960), 14–19 *et passim.*

[8] See Abraham Wertheimer, *Batē Midrashōt* (Jerusalem, 1954), Vol. I, p. 90. For an explanation of the term "descent" see Scholem, *Jewish Gnosticism . . .*, p. 20, n. 1. For Mandaean and other parallels to the ladder motif see *Shorter Encyclopaedia of Islam*, p. 382.

the literal meaning (Tafsīr XV:5; XV:12): Both *isrāʾ* and *miʾrāj* were performed by the Prophet with his body and while awake. The Muʿtazilites, on the other hand, did not feel obliged to accept the literal sense of the story as an article of faith.[9] The matter is discussed at some length by Saʿd al-Dīn al-Taftāzānī (14th century) in his commentary on the Creed (*al-ʿAqāʾid*) of Najm al-Dīn al-Nasafī (d. 1142), which had stated: "The ascension (*al-miʿrāj*) of the Prophet, while awake, in his person (*bi-shakhṣihi*) to heaven and thence to whatsoever exalted place Allāh willed is a reality." Al-Taftāzānī understands this to mean that the event happened not by spirit only but by spirit and body, and he infers that the ascension "in sleep or in spirit" is not to be ruled out absolutely. He quotes a tradition from Muḥammad's wife ʿĀʾisha who said, "The body of Muḥammad was not absent during the night of the ascension."[10] In Islamic mysticism, on the other hand, the story of the Prophet's night journey and of his ascension became the archetypal pattern of the soul's itinerary to God. Ḥasan Baṣrī (d. 772 C.E.) was probably the first to interpret the *miʿrāj* as a vision of the Divine essence.[11] Ḥallāj (*ca.* 858–922) makes the theme one of mystical contemplation in his *Kitāb al-ṭawāsīn* (chs. IV–V).[12] The Persian Sūfī Abū Yazīd (Bāyazīd) al-Bisṭāmī (d. 874 C.E.) was several times banned from his native city because he attributed a *miʿrāj* similar to the Prophet's to himself.[13] Al-Hujwīrī (d. between 1072 and 1076) speaks of Abū Yazīd's mystical voyage as "a long narrative" and adds: "The Sūfīs call it the *miʿrāj* of Bāyazīd; and the term *miʿrāj* denotes proximity to God." He distinguishes, however, between the ascension of prophets which takes place outwardly and in the body, and the ascension of saints which happens inwardly and in the spirit only.[14] The popularity of the theme

[9] Reported by Abū ʾl Muʿīn al Nasafī (d. 1114 C.E.) in his *Baḥr al-Kalām fī ʿIlm al-Tawḥīd* (English translation in *A Reader on Islam*, ed. Arthur Jeffery, 'S-Gravenhage, 1962, p. 423).

[10] See *A Commentary on the Creed of Islam* . . . Translated with Introduction and Notes by Earl Edgar Elder (New York, 1950), pp. 136–137.

[11] See G.-C. Anawati–Louis Gardet, *Mystique Musulmane* (Paris, 1961), p. 24.

[12] See *ibid.*, p. 78, n. 10; 269.

[13] See Louis Massignon, *Essai sur les Origines du Lexique Technique de la Mystique Musulmane* (Paris, 1954), p. 277; R. A. Nicholson, "An Early Arabic Version of the *Miʿrāj* of Abū Yazīd al-Bisṭamī", in *Islamica*, 1926, pp. 402–415; Margaret Smith; *Studies in Early Mysticism in the Near and Middle East* (London, 1931), pp. 240–241, Anawati–Gardet, *op. cit.*, pp. 110ff.

[14] See *The Kashf Al-Mahjūb The Oldest Persian Treatise on Sufism* by . . . Al-Hujwīrī, New Edition by Reynold A. Nicholson (London, 1959), pp. 238–239.

among the Ṣūfīs is attested by the collection of the entire material in al-Qushairī's (d. 1072) *Kitāb al-miʿrāj*.[15] Ibn al-ʿArabī, in his *Kitāb al-isrāʾ ilā maqām al-asrā*, calls the Ṣūfīs the "heirs of the Prophet" who imitate his life and doctrine.[16] In another work of his, the *Al-Futūḥāt al-Makkiyya*, he portrays a believer and a philosopher as fellow-travellers: The philosopher does not reach beyond the seventh heaven, whereas the pious Muslim enters into the Divine mystery.[17] And Ibn al-Fāriḍ (1189–1245) describes the nocturnal journey in his Odes as the third stage of Oneness in which the mystic returns from the "intoxication of union" to the "sobriety of union".[18]

It is obvious that to the mystic the "ladder" figuring in the story of the *miʿrāj* is but a symbol of an inward experience. In the words of al-Hujwīrī, "When a saint is enraptured and intoxicated he is withdrawn from himself by means of a spiritual ladder and brought near to God; and as soon as he returns to the state of sobriety all those evidences have taken shape in his mind and he has gained knowledge of them."[19] To the literalist on the other hand, the shining ladder studded with all kinds of jewels is as real as the fabulous Burāq on which the Prophet rode to Jerusalem. In between these two types of interpretation, the literal and the mystical, we may discover a third, which so far seems to have passed unnoticed, viz. the allegorical. It is this type of interpretation which concerns us in this paper. Its allegoricism is neoplatonic in character, and for this reason it made an impact on medieval Jewish philosophers and mystics. The term *sullam ha-ʿaliyyā* which is found in medieval Hebrew literature derives from this impact.

We find this kind of allegorism in the *Rasāʾil Ikhwān al-Safāʾ*. The eighth epistle of Part Two (which represents epistle 22 of the total work according to the Cairo edition, 1928) contains the following passage[20]:

> We have explained in one of our epistles that the forces of the Universal Soul (*al-nafs al-kulīya*) when coming-to-be, immediately penetrate to the bottom of the bodies from the highest level of the

[15] See A. J. Arberry, *Revelation and Reason in Islam* (London, 1957), pp. 94, 116, n. 34; *idem*, *Sufism* (London, 1950), pp. 28–29.

[16] See Asín Palacios, *La Escatología . . .*, pp. 77ff.

[17] *Ibid.*, pp. 79ff.

[18] See R. A. Nicholson, *Studies in Islamic Mysticism* (Cambridge, 1921), p. 239.

[19] *The Kashf Al-Mahjūb . . .*, p. 239.

[20] *Rasāʾil Ikhwān al-Safāʾ* (Cairo, 1928), Vol. II, pp. 156–157.

[all-] encompassing sphere down to the centre of the earth. Having penetrated the spheres, the stars, the elements (*al-arkān*) and places of birth, and having reached the centre of the earth as the utmost extension of their limit and as their farthest extreme, they then turn in reverse direction toward the [all-] encompassing [sphere], and this is the "Ascent" (*al-miʿrāj*) and the "Arousing" (*al-baʿth*) and the great "Resurrection" (*al-qiyāma*).

Consider now, my brother, how thy soul should depart from this world to that place, for it is one of those forces that were dispersed from the Universal Soul which penetrates the world. It had already reached the centre [of the earth] and had departed from, and escaped, existence in minerals, plants and animals. It had already passed the ill-directed path (*al-ṣirāṭ al-mankūs*) and the crooked path (*al-ṣirāṭ al-muqawwas*) but is now on the straight path (*ṣirāṭ mustaqīm*), the last of the grades of hell, that is in the form of humanity. Once it has safely passed this [road], it enters paradise by one of its portals, that is [it enters] the angelic form which thou acquirest by pious acts, beautiful qualities of character, sound opinions, and true gnosis. . .

The cosmological scheme presupposed in this passage is essentially Plotinian and familiar from many other epistles of the Ikhwān where it appears in greater detail. "The Universal Soul", we hear elsewhere,[21] "is but a spiritual force which emanated from Intellect with the permission of the Creator." Its rank, we are told, is beyond the all-encompassing sphere, yet its forces penetrate all parts of the heaven and all particular bodies below the lunar sphere. There is only one Universal Soul but its forces are dispersed in all that exists, from the all-encompassing sphere down to the centre of the earth.[22] We are, again, on familiar neoplatonic ground when man's individual soul is exhorted to retract the steps of the downward way and return to its home in the supernal world. What is new is the combination of this theme with an allegorical interpretation of Islamic eschatology. The upward way means the abandoning of the "grades of hell", viz. of bodily existence, and the entering into the angelic stage of pure spirituality. In terms of traditional eschatology it is, ultimately, the "Resurrection" from the grave after the "Arousing" or "Quickening" of the dead. In the epistle on "Definitions and Descriptions" (III: 10)

[21] *Rasāʾil* . . . 3:1 (31), Vol. III, p. 191.

[22] *Rasāʾil* . . . 3:1 (31), Vol. III, p. 192. See also 2:15 (28), Vol. II, pp. 54f. A description of the celestial spheres and their motions by virtue of the Universal Soul is found in 2:2 (15), Vol. II, pp. 20ff.

we read: "The paradise of the vegetative soul is the form of animality; the paradise of the animal soul is the form of humanity; and the paradise of the soul of the human form is the angelic form . . . And the 'Arousing' is the alerting (*intibāh*) of the souls from the sleep of indifference and the slumber of ignorance . . . And the 'Resurrection' is the rising of the soul from its grave which is the body . . ."[23] The Ikhwān equate the neoplatonic upward way with "the straight path" (*al-ṣirāṭ al-mustaqīm*) which the Qur'ān commends in numerous passages,[24] and they see in the downward way into bodily existence of various grades the "ill-directed" or "crooked" path. It is in keeping with this neoplatonic allegorism that they interpret the Prophet's "Ascension" (*al-miʿrāj*) as the taking of the upward way or "straight path" that leads to the angelic stage or man's paradise.[25] The *miʿrāj* thus becomes synonymous with the *anagōgē* or Ascension spoken of by Plotinus.[26] The ladder motif is not specifically mentioned but it is tacitly implied in the reference to the "grades of hell" which the soul has to traverse in its flight from bodily existence. The extension of the *miʿrāj* or upward way may be said to cover the entire corporeal universe from the centre of the earth to the all-encompassing sphere. Since the Universal Soul is said to penetrate all bodies from the outermost sphere down to the centre of the earth, it was not difficult to imagine the Universal Soul as the "ladder of ascent". This more specific elaboration of the theme was, however, left to the Spanish philosopher Ibn al-Sīd al-Baṭalyawsī (1052–1127). His *Kitāb al-Ḥadā'iq* ("Book of the Circles") contains the following passage on "The Properties of the Universal Soul"[27]:

> The rank (*martaba*) of this Soul, according to the philosophers who admit it, is below the horizon (*ufq*) of the Agent Intellect, and the Intellect encompasses it on all its sides, and it [the Universal Soul]

[23] *Rasā'il* . . . 3:10 (41), Vol. III, p. 370. For a discussion of Islamic eschatology in traditional terms see al-Taftazānī's *Commentary*, transl. by Elder (see n. 10), pp. 99ff.

[24] See *Al-Muʿjam al-Fihris*, ed. Muḥammad Fuwūd ʿAbd al-Bāqī, *s.v. al-ṣirāṭ al-mustaqīm*.

[25] Cf. Plotinus, *Enneads* I.6.8 where Odysseus' flight from Circe or Calypso is allegorized in a similar way.

[26] See Émile Bréhier, *Plotin, Ennéades*, Vol. VI, 2 (Paris, 1954), 'Index analytique des matières', p. 257.

[27] M. Asín Palacios published the Arabic text of the *Kitāb al-Ḥadā'iq* with a biographical and analytical introduction and with a Spanish translation in *Al-Andalus* 5 (1940), 45–154. For Hebrew versions see below. The English rendering of the passage quoted here follows the Arabic text, p. 71 (Spanish version, p. 110).

> encompasses the globe of the spheres. It has according to what they assume, two circles (*dāʾiratāni*) and a straight line (*khaṭṭ mustaqīm*), and the first circle is contiguous with the [all-] encompassing sphere, the latter being its [viz. the Universal Soul's] supernal limit. The second circle is the lowest limit, and its place is the centre of the earth. This is an approximate way of speaking (*taqrīb*), for intelligible substances cannot be described by the attributes of place and the six directions. They [sc. the philosophers who admit the existence of the Universal Soul] hold that between its supernal limit and its lowest limit there is a line (*khaṭṭ*) which connects [the two circles], which they call "the ladder of the ascensions" (*sullam al-maᶜārij*). It causes [Divine] inspiration to reach the pure individual souls, and on it descend [the angels] and ascend the purified spirits to the supernal world. They [sc. the philosophers] discourse on it [sc. the Universal Soul] at length. We have, however, limited ourselves to this résumé, since our purpose in this book is different from theirs.

The "philosophers" referred to by al-Baṭalyawsī are most probably the Ikhwān who do admit the hypostasis of a Universal Soul, discourse at length on it, and describe it as beyond the all-encompassing sphere and yet penetrating the whole corporeal world down to "the centre of the earth". In the "straight line" (*khaṭṭ mustaqīm*) connecting the uppermost and the lowest circle we recognise the Qurʾānic term "the straight path" (*al-ṣirāṭ al-mustaqīm*) which the Ikhwān apply to the upward way or *miᶜrāj*. Although al-Baṭalyawsī makes no direct reference to the Prophet's Ascension, he alludes to it by saying that the philosophers [viz. the Ikhwān] call the [straight] line "the ladder of ascensions". The phrase *sullam al-maᶜārij* which he uses combines the Qurʾānic term *al-maᶜārij* ("the stairways") found in Sūra 70 (where it is unrelated to the Prophet's Ascension) with the term *sullam* that had not merely Qurʾānic overtones but had come to be associated with the story of the Ascension. It definitely points to the ladder motif familiar from the accounts of the *miᶜrāj*, and *maᶜārij* denotes here not "stairways" (as in Sūra 70) but "ascensions" or simply "ascension". The eschatological perspective of the ascension which we met in the Ikhwān is also present here: On the ladder the purified spirits ascend to the supernal world. The ladder or "straight line" thus becomes a symbol of the souls' return to their home, and the story of the Prophet's Ascent to Heaven which the Ikhwān unhesitatingly allegorized may be said to bear a similar connotation for al-Baṭalyawsī, seeing that the "ladder of ascension" is identified with the upward way of the pure souls, and is, furthermore, described as the path on which the angels descend and [prophetic] inspiration comes to the pure individual souls, the angels being probably conceived here as the mediators of inspiration. A direct reference to the Prophet's Ascension occurs in a gloss at the end of our passage in the treatise *Mozenē Ha-ᶜIyyunim* where it is almost verbatim reproduced.[28] It reads:

> And this is where the Prophet was during the night of the Assumption [V, A: *leyl ha-leqiḥā*; P: *leyl ha-peridā*][29] and it is this which a man [V: *ha-adam*; P, A: *ha-met*] sees at the time when his soul departs [A: *be-ᶜet zeʾt nafshō*; V: *ᶜad zeʾt ha-nefesh*; P: *be-ᶜet gewiyᶜatō*] and there is still a body wherewith to see [V: *we-yesh guf yirʾehu bō*; A: *we-yesh lō guf yirʾehu*; P: *we-yesh ᶜezem ʾish yirʾē ʾōtō*],[30] as the Prophet, peace be upon him, said [P; A: *kakh ʾamar ha-ʾīsh*; V: *ʾamar ha-ʾīsh*].

The popularity which al-Baṭalyawsī's *Kitāb al-Ḥadāʾiq* achieved in medieval Jewish circles is attested in many ways, as David Kaufmann was able to show in his elaborate monograph on the subject.[31] No less than three Hebrew translations of the work are known to us. Kaufmann published a critical text of Moses ibn Tibbon's version entitled *Sefer Ha-ᶜAgullot Ha-Raᶜyoniyot* ("Book

[28] The *Mozenē Ha-ᶜIyyunīm* is a Hebrew translation by Jacob ben Makhir (d. *ca.* 1308) of an Arabic treatise attributed to al-Ghazālī. Steinschneider's tentative suggestion that it might be identical with al-Ghazālī's *Al-Qusṭās Al-Mustaqīm* (in *Hebr. Hss. Berlin* (1878), pp. 107–108) has been adopted in ᶜAbd al-Raḥmān Badawī's recent work *Muʾallafāt Al-Ghazālī*, to which Dr. Hava Lazarus-Yafeh has drawn my attention. She herself disputes this assumption and rejects al-Ghazālī's authorship of whatever Arabic original may underlie the *Mozenē Ha-ᶜIyyunīm*. In fact, Steinschneider already doubted the authenticity of the work as one by Ghazālī in his *Hebr. Übersetzungen* (p. 340) and so did M. Bouyges, *Essai de Chronologie des oeuvres de Al-Ghazali* (Beirut), pp. 116–117, after quoting Steinschneider.

The *Mozenē Ha-ᶜIyyunīm* is extant in a large number of mss. (see *HÜ*, *loc. cit.*). Chapters 10–12 were published by L. Dukes in *Ozar Neḥmad* (ed. Ignaz Blumenfeld), Vol. II (1857), pp. 196–199, on the basis of a Paris ms. I have established a critical text of ch. 12 ("On the Property of the Universal Soul") based on Dukes' text (P) and mss. Vaticana (V), Hebr. 209, fol. 55*r*, and Ambrosiana (A), Hebr. S 20 Inf., fol. 14*v*. The author obviously plagiarised al-Baṭalyawsī's *Kitāb al-Ḥadāʾiq*, and both he and the Hebrew translator inserted glosses of their own.

[29] This term, which does not seem to derive from an exact Arabic equivalent, probably seeks to express the notion of *isrāʾ* and *miᶜrāj* in a single word. The term *leqiḥā* reflects the phrase used in Gen. 5:24 to denote Enoch's Ascension.

[30] Cf. Horovitz, *op. cit.*, p. 175, where Ibn Hishām's statement in the name of Abū Saᶜīd al-Khudrī is quoted as saying that to the ladder of ascent the dying turn their eyes.

[31] David Kaufmann, *Die Spuren Al-Baṭlajûsis in der jüdischen Religions-Philosophie* . . . (Leipzig, 1880).

of Imaginary Circles") together with Samuel ibn Moṭoṭ's translation of the first four chapters which had been incorporated in ibn Moṭoṭ's commentary *Meshobeb Netibot* on the *Sefer Yeẓirā*.[32] A third less literal but more elegant translation was brought to the attention of Professor Georges Vajda by Professor Gershom Scholem. It is contained in Hebr. ms 853 of the Bibliothèque Nationale, Paris, and has been briefly described and specimens of it from chapters 1 and 5 have been published by Vajda.[33] Since the question of the terminology employed in the Hebrew versions is of considerable relevance to our inquiry, I shall quote here the anonymous (third) Hebrew translation of the chapter on "The Property of the Universal Soul" which has hitherto not been published[34]:

> *Sĕgūlat Ha-Nefesh Ha-Kĕlalīt. Maᶜalat ha-nefesh ha-kĕlalīt ha-ẓōt ᶜal daᶜat ha-pilosofim ha-omrim ki yeshnā hiᵓ taḥat ha-daᶜat ha-pōᶜel. Ve-ha-daᶜat ha-pōᶜel ha-sōḇeḇ ōtah mi-kol ẓedadehah ve-hīᵓ muqefet be-kīdōr ha-galgalim. U-lĕfī seḇaratam yesh lah shĕtē ᶜiggulōt ve-qav mīshōr. Ve-ha-ᶜiggulā ha-riᵓshonā nōgaᶜat ba-galgal ha-muqaf ve-hīᵓ qĕẓatah ha-ᶜelyōn. Ve-ha-ᶜiggulā ha-shēnīt hīᵓ qĕẓatah ha-taḥton u-mĕqōm ha-ᶜiggulā ha-ẓōt huᵓ ṭībūr ha-areẓ ve-ẓeh derek qarob ki ha-haruẓim [ha-ᶜaẓamim?] ha-yĕdūᶜīm be-seḵel ᵓēn mĕsappĕrīn ᶜalehem meqōmōt ve-lō ha-pinnōt ha-shēsh. Ve-amrū ki yesh bēn qĕẓatah [ha-ᶜelyōn] u-qĕẓatah ha-taḥton qav. Ve-hūᵓ meḥubbar [meḥabber?] bēn shĕtē ha-ᶜiggulōt. Ve-qōrīn ōtō sullam ha-ᶜaliyyā u-ḇō yagiᶜa ha-ḥiẓayōn ba-nefesh ha-pĕraṭit ha-ṭehōrā u-ḇō yardū ha-malᵓaḵim ve-yaᶜalū ha-nĕfashōt ha-ẓakōt el ha-ᶜōlam ha-ᶜelyōn. Ve-yesh lahem deḇarim ᵓaruḵīm ba-nefesh ha-ẓōt ẓaḵarnū mehem ha-kĕlalīm ha-eleh ha-reᵓuyīm le-ḥibbūr ẓeh.*

A Hebrew translation of the passage on the Universal Soul independent of the other versions was made by Shemtob ben Isaac ibn Shapruṭ (end of fourteenth century) and quoted by him in his *Zofĕnat Paᶜneaḥ* (Hebr. ms. 852 of the Bibliothèque Nationale, Paris, fol. 82r). The text reads as follows[35]:

32 *Ibid.*, Hebrew Section, pp. 2–55.

33 Georges Vajda, "Une version hébraïque inconnue des 'Cercles Imaginaires' de Baṭalyawsī" (Extrait du "Semitic Studies in Memory of Immanuel Löw"), (Budapest, 1947), pp. 3–5.

34 Hebr. ms. Bibliothèque Nationale, Paris, 853.2, fol. 26. The corresponding texts of the first two Hebrew versions are found on pp. 17–18 in Kaufmann's edition.

35 I wish to express my sincere thanks to Dr. Colette Sirat for her and her colleagues' helpfulness in letting me have, at short notice, hand-written copies of the two passages from the Paris mss. quoted here.

Ha-nefesh ha-kĕlalīt maᶜalatah taḥat maᶜalat ha-sekel ha-pōᶜel ve-hūᵓ maqīf ōtah mi-kol ẓedadehah ve-hīᵓ maqefet kol ha-galgal ha-ᶜelyōn ve-yesh lah shĕtē ᶜiggulōt aḥat le-maᶜalā ve-aḥat le-maṭā ve-qav yashar bēnēhem ve-ha-ᶜiggulā ha-riᵓshonā magaᶜat ᶜad ha-galgal ha-maqīf ve-hūᵓ qeẓatah ha-ᶜelyōn ve-ha-ᶜiggulā ha-shēnīt muẓab arẓah ve-hūᵓ qĕẓatah ha-taḥton ve-ha-qav ha-yashar matḥīl me-ha-ᶜiggulā ha-riᵓshonā shĕ-hīᵓ ha-roᵓsh ᶜad ha-qaẓē ha-taḥton shĕ-hūᵓ ha-merkaẓ ve-niqrāᵓ sullam ha-ᶜaliyyā ve-amrū ha-pilosofim she-bō ᶜōlōt ha-nefashōt ha-zakōt la-ᶜōlam haᶜelyōn u-bō yordim ha-malᵓakim. ᶜad kān leshōnō.

The two points of terminology that concern us here relate to the Hebrew rendering of the Arabic phrases *khaṭṭ mustaqīm* ("straight line") and *sullam al-maᶜārij* ("ladder of ascension"). As for the first term, most versions (Ibn Tibbon, Ibn Moṭoṭ, Ibn Shapruṭ; mss. P, V of Mozenē Ha-ᶜIyyunīm) have *qav yashar*; ms. Paris 853 has *qav mīshōr*; and ms. A of Mozenē Ha-ᶜIyyunīm has *qav ha-yōsher*. As for the second term, the expressions used are *sullam ha-ᶜaliyyā* (Ibn Tibbon O²L, Kaufmann, Ibn Moṭoṭ [adding: we-ha-yerīdā], ms. Paris 853, Ibn Shapruṭ); *sullam ᶜolim we-yordim* (in the margin of ms. A of *Mozenē Ha-ᶜIyyunīm*); and the strange form *sullam ha-ḥigerūt* ("ladder of lameness") which occurs in the Ibn Tibbon text adopted by Kaufmann and in ms. A of *Mozenē Ha-ᶜIyyunīm*. It appears in the corrupted form *sullam ha-ḥagōrōt* in one of the variant readings of Ibn Tibbon noted by Kaufmann and in ms. P of *Mozenē Ha-ᶜIyyunīm*. Ms. V omits the phrase altogether. The explanation for the form *sullam ha-ḥigerūt* as the Hebrew equivalent of Arabic *sullam al-maᶜārij* is simple enough, as has already been shown by Steinschneider.[36] Arabic *ᶜaraja* (from which *maᶜraj*, stairway; pl. *maᶜārij*; and *miᶜrāj* are derived) means "to ascend", while *ᶜarija* denotes "being lame", or "to limp", and *ᶜaraj* means "lameness". It is hard to believe that any of the translators misunderstood the phrase *sullam al-maᶜārij* as "ladder of lameness". Probably some of the copyists who were aware of the dual meaning of the root in Arabic half playfully, half maliciously called Muḥammad's "ladder of ascent" a "ladder of lameness", and later copyists who were ignorant of Arabic corrupted the form into *sullam ha-ḥagōrōt*, "ladder of girdles", which makes no sense whatsoever. The polemical intent comes to the fore in Moses Narboni's characterization of the lower forms of prophecy as aptly designated by the term *sullam ha-ḥigerūt*, ladder of lameness: "Hence the

[36] M. Steinschneider, "Aus Handschriften", in *Israelietische Letterbode*, ed. M. Roest, 8 (1882–1883), Amsterdam, 61–62.

ancients called it the 'divine illness' . . . and, likewise, the author of the *Imaginary Circle* called the event of the Vision (*ᶜinyan ha-maḥazē*) [viz. of Muḥammad] the 'ladder of lameness', and the sages of Israel, peace be upon them, said, 'Balaam was lame in one foot' [b. Sanhedrin 105a]. They indicated thereby that his prophecy was through the intermediacy of an angel, that is to say, through the faculty of imagination, which is a corporeal faculty . . . But our teacher Moses, peace be upon him, did not employ the imaginative faculty."[37] Narboni thus seizes upon the phrase *sullam ha-ḥigerūt* in order to contrast Muḥammad's Ascension with the superior prophecy of Moses. In a somewhat similar way the copyist of ms. A of *Mozenē Ha-ᶜIyyunīm* adds the following gloss to the text mentioning the *sullam ha-ḥigerūt*: "That means to say that the prophet comprehends at times, and does not comprehend at times."[38] The "lameness" of his vision consists in the irregularity of his prophetic faculty. In spite, however, of this rather "lame" excuse for using the term *sullam ha-ḥigerūt*, medieval Jewish writers quoting al-Baṭalyawsī must have been aware of the true meaning of the term *sullam al-maᶜārij*, particularly in view of the fact that many mss. rendered it correctly as *sullam ha-ᶜaliyyā*. Besides, the phrase *sullam ha-ᶜaliyyā* did pass into the medieval Hebrew vocabulary. It is found not merely in translations from the Arabic but in original Hebrew texts. Thus Pseudo-Maimonides' *Maʾamar Ha-Yiḥūd* speaks of the *sullam ha-ᶜaliyyā* "which our Father Jacob, peace be upon him, saw in his dream",[39] and Jehuda Alboṭini's work on prophetic Kabbala (written in Jerusalem after the expulsion of the Jews from Spain) bears the title *Sullam Ha-ᶜAliyyā*.[40] This term must not be confounded with the phrase *sullam ha-ḥokhmot* which enjoyed equal popularity but stemmed from a

[37] The passage quoted is found in Moses Narboni's Commentary on Averroes' *Epistle on the Possibility of Conjunction*, Bodleian ms. Michael 119, fol. 112*r* and mss. Munich 108 and 110 (the latter being quoted by Steinschneider, *Letterbode*, 8, p. 61). See also Narboni's Commentary on Maimonides' *Guide*, ed. Jacob Goldenthal, 43a.

[38] *Be-sullam ha-ḥigerūt kelomar she-hanabiʾ yasig paᶜam u-faᶜam lō yasig.*

[39] See Steinschneider's edition of the text of the *Maʾamar Ha-Yiḥūd* in his *Shenē Ha-Meʾorot* (Berlin, 1847), p. 12, and his note on "Lesarten zu Maimonides, *Maʾamar Ha-Yiḥūd*" in *Magazin für die Wissenschaft des Judenthums*, ed. A. Berliner–D. Hoffmann, 19 (1892), pp. 86–88. The authenticity of the *Maʾamar Ha-Yiḥūd* as a work of Maimonides, which was firmly upheld by Steinschneider, is no longer assumed. Cf. G. Vajda, *L'Amour de Dieu dans la Théologie Juive du Moyen Age* (Paris, 1957), p. 126, 3; Gershom Scholem, *Ursprung und Anfänge der Kabbala* (Berlin, 1962), p. 287. n. 235.

[40] See Scholem, *Kiryat Sefer*, 2 (1925), 107, 138–141; 22 (1945), 161–171; *idem*, *Kitebē Yad Be-Qabbalā* (Jerusalem, 1930), pp. 32–33.

totally different background, viz. from the philosophical view of the classification and hierarchical order of the sciences. Thus, Isaac ibn Laṭīf speaks in his *Ginzē Ha-Melekh*[41] of seven rungs of the ladder of human knowledge. Naḥmanides sees the value (*toᶜelet*) of all sciences in their function as a "ladder" to the knowledge of God.[42] Abraham ibn Ḥasday's Hebrew version of al-Ghazālī's *Mīzān al-ᶜAmal* supplies the simile of Jacob's ladder *à propos* the discussion of the various grades and connections of the sciences.[43] Isaac ibn Abū Sahūla speaks of poetry (*melᵓekhet ha-shīr*) as *sullam ha-ḥokhmōt*.[44] A responsum by Yiẓhaq ben Yaᶜaqob Ha-Kohen uses the phrase already as a *façon de parler* synonymous with "ways of thoughts" (*darkhē meẓīmōt*) in solemn literary style,[45] and Moses de Leon mentions in a similar sense the "rising on the grades of the ladder".[46] Reverting to the scientific connotation of the phrase, Yoḥanan Allemano calls geometry and astronomy a "ladder by which to ascend to heaven",[47] an obvious allusion to the Ikhwān's saying: "Ptolemy loved astronomy; he made mathematics into a ladder by which he ascended to heaven."[48]

The allegorical interpretation of Muḥammad's Ascension which we found in the Ikhwān and in al-Baṭalyawsī is reflected in the way in which medieval Jewish philosophers and mystics treated the motif of the ladder in Jacob's dream. Both the Ikhwān concept of the *miᶜrāj* as the soul's upward way and al-Baṭalyawsī's notion of the "straight line" as well as the concept of the Universal Soul common to them re-appear in some form or another in the Jewish writers. We shall turn our attention to the philosophers first and then deal with the Kabbalists. The remarkable thing is that the

41 See *Kokhebē Yiẓhaq*, ed. Menaḥem Mendel Stern, Vol. 29, pp. 8ff.

42 See Ḥayyim D. Chavel, *Kitebē Rabbenu Moshē Ben Naḥman* (Jerusalem, 1963), Vol. I, p. 155.

43 *Mozenē Ẓedeq*, ed. J. Goldenthal (Leipzig-Paris, 1839), ch. 27, p. 166. The Arabic original does not contain the simile of the ladder.

44 See his Introduction to his Commentary on Shīr Ha-Shīrīm published by Ḥayyim Brody in *Maṭmonē Mistarim* (Cracow, 1894), p. 31.

45 See the text published by Scholem in *Madaᶜē Ha-Yahadut*, Vol. II (Jerusalem, 1927), p. 244.

46 See Moses de Leon, *Or Zaruᶜa*, Bodleian ms. Pococke 296.11, fol. 193*r*, col. b, line 17.

47 See his *Sefer Shaᶜar Ha-Ḥesheq* (Livorno, 1790), 3b. For further examples of the use of this term see Steinschneider, *Shenē Ha-Meᵓorot*, p. 12, n. 12.

48 Quoted by F. Dieterici, *Die Philosophie der Araber . . . Erster Theil Einleitung und Makrokosmos* (Leipzig, 1876), pp. 178–179.

latter showed themselves more amenable to neoplatonic allegorism than to the Sūfī view of the "ladder" as a symbol of an interior experience.[49]

Solomon ibn Gabirol is reported by Abraham ibn Ezra[50] to have seen in Jacob's ladder "an allegory of the supernal soul" (*remez la-neshamā ha-ᶜelyonā*) and in the "angels of God" ascending and descending on it "the thoughts of wisdom" (*maḥashabōt ha-ḥokhmā*). Wilhelm Bacher suggested the possibility of interpreting the term *neshamā ᶜelyonā* as denoting the Universal (World) Soul since Ibn Gabirol, again according to Ibn Ezra's report, considered the phrase *kol ha-neshamā* (Ps. 156:6) as an "allegory" (*remez*) of the "supernal soul which is in heaven" (*la-neshamā ha-ᶜelyonā she-hīʾ ba-shamayim*).[51] The "thoughts of wisdom" Bacher was inclined to identify with Ibn Gabirol's "intelligible substances" by means of which the intellect ascends to the supreme knowledge.[52] This interpretation is, however, a forced one, notwithstanding the fact that Ibn Gabirol's neoplatonic system contains the hypostasis of a universal soul and assumes the existence of simple or intelligible substances. The term *neshamā ᶜelyonā* can, nevertheless, not mean "Universal Soul" (for which he uses the phrase *anima universalis*,[53] which Ibn Falaqera renders *ha-nefesh ha-kelalīt*,[54] and which obviously goes back to Arabic *al-nafs al-kulīya*) but signifies man's rational soul. The "supernal soul which is in heaven" may, on the other hand, well represent the Universal Soul since it is said to be expressed by the term *kol ha-neshamā* which is understood as *neshamā kelalīt*. Yet on no account can Jacob's ladder have been understood by Ibn Gabirol as an allegory of the Universal Soul since it makes no sense to say that the "thoughts of wisdom" ascend on it. What does ascend on it is the soul and not "thoughts", let alone the intelligible substances. Ibn Gabirol's

[49] Abraham Maimonides, on the other hand, clearly adopts a Sūfī stance when interpreting Jacob's dream about the ladder as an achievement of union with God through the practice of "solitude" (*khalwa*). See *The High Ways To Perfection of Abraham Maimonides Volume II*, by Samuel Rosenblatt (Baltimore, 1938), p. 393.

[50] See Abraham ibn Ezra's Standard *Commentary on Genesis*, 28:12.

[51] Wilhelm Bacher, *Die Bibelexegese der jüdischen Religionsphilosophen des Mittelalters vor Maimûni* (Budapest, 1892), pp. 49–50.

[52] Bacher, *op. cit.*, p. 49, n. 6.

[53] *Fons Vitae*, ed. Clemens Baeumker, III, 15, p. 111, 19; III, 51, p. 194, 8; III, 56, p. 204, 22.

[54] See S. Munk, *Mélanges de Philosophie Juive et Arabe* (Paris, 1927), Hebrew Section, 11b (3:14).

interpretation makes perfect sense if we take the *neshamā ᶜelyonā* to refer to the rational soul (as was already assumed by Munk[55] and Kaufmann[56]) which proceeds from stage to stage on the ladder of the sciences. For in the *Fons Vitae* he uses distinctly the terms "ascent" and "ladder" in this sense. He speaks of *sapientia* as the equivalent of *scientia* which has three parts, viz. *de materia et forma*, *de voluntate* and *de scientia prima* (V. 1; V. 36). He says that "*scientia materiae et formae est prima pars sapientiae et scala* (!) *ad ceteras*" (I. 8); "*scientia materiae et formae est scala ad secundam et tertiam partem sapientiae*" (V. 1). He lets the disciple ask: "*Est ergo uia ascendendi ad scientiam eius quod est supra materiam et formam?*" and lets the master give the answer: "*Ascensio ad essentiam primam altissimam impossibilis est; sed ascensio ad it quod sequitur* [viz. *voluntas*] *difficilis est valde*" (V. 35).[57] Since the three sciences or wisdom form a graded system, it is natural to speak of Jacob's ladder as an allegory of the rational soul and its ascent from one stage to another. The "thoughts of wisdom" are, then, the three sciences.[58] There is, therefore, no trace in Ibn Gabirol's allegorization of Jacob's ladder of any of the specific features met with in the Ikhwān beyond his use of the neoplatonic system, the broad outline of which he shared with them.[59] His well-attested tendency to allegorize Scripture[60] was in tune with the neoplatonic spiritual temper and in this sense akin to the Ikhwān's. It did not have to be inspired by Yequtiᵓel's allegorization of Jacob's ladder, as Jellinek assumed.[61] Nor can in Ibn Gabirol's case any influence of al-Baṭalyawsī have played a part, seeing that chronology defeats any such assump-

[55] Munk, *Mélanges*, p. 166.

[56] David Kaufmann, *Studien über Salomon Ibn Gabirol* (Budapest, 1899), pp. 73–74.

[57] The Arabic text retrieved by S. Pines (*Tarbiẓ*, XXVII, Numbers 2–3, Presented to Gershom G. Scholem in Honour of his Sixtieth Birthday (Jerusalem, 1958), pp. 218–233) from the excerpts preserved in Moses ibn Ezra's *ᶜArugat Ha-Bosem* contains the immediately preceding passage *Fons Vitae* V, 35, p. 321, 21–p. 322, 3 (Text 9:3, pp. 227–228 in Pines' article), but stops short precisely at the point where the question about the possibility of an *ascensio* to the *essentia prima* (God) is raised. The Arabic term used here by Ibn Gabirol for *ascensio* is thus not preserved.

[58] Ibn Gabirol says of *cogitatio*, *maḥashabā* that it is peculiar to man (III, 46; see also V, 13).

[59] See my article in *Tarbiẓ*, XXVII, Number 4, 1958, pp. 501–507.

[60] See Bacher, *op. cit.*, pp. 46ff.

[61] See Adolph Jellinek, *Beiträge zur Geschichte der Kabbala*, II (Leipzig, 1852), p. 31. Yequtiᵓel's allegorization of Jacob's ladder which has been preserved in Shemtob's *Sefer Emunot* VIII, 15 (see Jellinek, *op. cit.*, pp. 24, 26) follows the *Sefer Yeẓirā* and is entirely mystical.

tion.[62] There remains, however, the fact that by putting together Ibn Gabirol's short sentence on Jacob's ladder and the passages from *Fons Vitae* which we have quoted we have before us the clear concept of *sullam ha-ᶜaliyyā*. Ibn Gabirol obviously understood Jacob's ladder as an allegory of the type denoted by the term *sullam ha-ᶜaliyyā*, which expresses the ascent of the soul, and not as one which merely indicates the order of the sciences. Although the phrase "thoughts of wisdom" might seem to point in the latter direction—in which case the ladder would be a *sullam ha-ḥokhmōt* —such an assumption is refuted by the fact that the passages in the *Fons Vitae* referred to do not speak of the usual classification of the sciences leading up to metaphysics but confine the notion of *ascensio* and *scala* to the spiritual progress from the metaphysical knowledge of matter and form to the higher one of the Will and to the still higher one of the First Essence.

Abraham ibn Ezra rejects Ibn Gabirol's interpretation of Jacob's ladder and suggests instead, on the analogy of certain passages from Zecharia, Amos and Jeremiah, that Jacob's vision showed him an allegory (*mashal*) of a different kind. It taught him "that nothing is hidden from God, and that the things below depend on the supernal beings; there is, as it were, a ladder between them, on which the angels ascend after having gone to and fro in the earth [Zech. 1:11]; it is also written that other angels descend [Zech. 6:5–7] in order to carry out God's behest, as is the way of a king with his servants".[63] Shemtob ben Isaac ibn Shapruṭ explains this passage in his *Ẓofenat Paᶜneaḥ*[64] first by identifying the references to Zecharia, Amos and Jeremiah[65] and then adding the remark: "Note that he refers here to what is written in [al-Baṭalyawsī's] *Imaginary Circle*." There follows the text reproduced above, p. 50, and Ibn Shapruṭ's concluding observation: "Consider thou, reader, this wonderful allegory, and how they [viz. the Muslims] conceded to us the path which connects the supernal

[62] In his *Die Spuren*, etc., p. 10, Kaufmann assumed al-Baṭalyawsī to have died in the year 1030/31 (421 H.). Hence he felt justified in suggesting that Ibn Gabirol (b. 1022) might have known the *Kitāb al-Ḥadāʾiq*. In his review of the book in *Revue des Études Juives*, 7 (1883), 274–279, Hartwig Derenbourg corrected Kaufmann's mistake and showed that al-Baṭalyawsī died in 1127. In Vol. 8 (1884) of the *Revue*, pp. 131–134, Kaufmann accepted this date which is since then no longer in dispute.

[63] Ibn Ezra, Standard *Commentary on Genesis*, 18:12.

[64] See above, p. 10. The full text of Ibn Shapruṭ's comment on the Ibn Ezra passage is found on fol. 82*r*–82*v* of the Paris ms.

[65] According to him they are: Zech. 1:8, 10, 11; Amos 7:7; Jer. 1:11.

beings with those below and those below with the supernal ones; namely that this is done by the intermediacy of the Universal Soul, which is like a form to the rational soul ⟨and like matter⟩ to the Agent Intellect, and this whole world is connected, one part with another, like a flame connected with the coal; and do thou understand this."[66] The salient point of this interpretation of the Ibn Ezra passage in the light of al-Baṭalyawsī lies in the stress on the function of the Universal Soul as the bond or "ladder" between the upper and the lower worlds. In his *Pardes Rimonim*[67] Ibn Shapruṭ reverts to the same text from al-Baṭalyawsī's chapter on the Universal Soul, albeit in an abridged form, in order to explain the passage in Talmud Ḥullin 91b where it is said that the angels compared the image of the sleeping Jacob below with his image above.[68] The emphasis is again on the mediating function of the ladder = Universal Soul, but the purpose of this function is said here to facilitate the ascent of the pure souls to conjoin with the Agent Intellect, and the downward emanation [of forms] from the Agent Intellect. It is obvious that Ibn Shapruṭ was much enamoured with al-Baṭalyawsī's interpretation of the ladder motif as an allegory of the Universal Soul. Whether he was right in reading this concept into Ibn Ezra's allegorization of the ladder is a matter still to be investigated. As a Neoplatonist, Ibn Ezra did, of course, adopt the notion of a Universal Soul. In his *Commentary on Psalms* (49:16) he calls it *neshamā ha-ᶜelyonā she-hūᵓ nishmat ha-shamayim* ("the superal soul, viz. the soul of the Heaven"), a term which comes close to Ibn Gabirol's *neshamā ha-ᶜelyonā she-hīᵓ ba-shamayim*.[69] It seems, however, that he considered not only the Universal Soul but the intelligible substances too as forming, allegorically speaking, the "ladder" by which the soul might reach God. In his *Short Commentary on Exodus* (33:23) he speaks of the intelligible substances as "the ladder to ascend to the Exalted [viz.

[66] *Histakkel ᵓattā ha-meᶜayyēn ha-dimyōn ha-muflaᵓ ha-z̭eh we-ēkh hōdū lanū derekh deḇequt ha-ᶜelyōnīm ba-taḥtōnīm we-ha-taḥtōnīm ba-ᶜelyōnīm we-hūᵓ | she-z̭eh yēᶜaseh be-ᵓemz̭aᶜūt ha-nefesh ha-kelalīt ᵓasher hīᵓ ke-z̭urā la-nefesh ha-medabberet* [ ] *la-sekhel ha-poᶜel we-z̭eh ha-ᶜōlam kulō niqshar qez̭atō bi-qez̭atō ke-shalheḇet qeshurā be-gaḥelet we-haḇēn z̭eh*.

[67] *Sefer Pardes Rimonim ᶜal Haggadot Ha-Talmud*, ed. Eliezer Zebi Zweifel, Sitomir, 1866, 59a (p. 117). This passage is quoted by Kaufmann in his *Die Spuren*, etc., p. 51, n. 7.

[68] The Talmudic passage represents a condensed form of Gen. R. 68:12. For its Gnostic background see my article in *JQR*, N.S. XXXV (1945), p. 390.

[69] See above, p. 53.

God], an ascent which was vouchsafed to Moses.[70] Moreover, in his Standard *Commentary on Exodus* (33 : 12) he says: "Length is [the extension] between two points, and the point nearest to the Agent [viz. God] is the Prince of the Presence [viz. the Intellect (Nous) of the neoplatonic system], and the other point [viz. the centre of the earth] marks the end of the power." I have ventured to suggest elsewhere[71] that Ibn Ezra's concept of the "Length" between the two extreme points in the cosmos reflects the notion of the *khaṭṭ mustaqīm* ("the straight line") between the all-encompassing sphere and the centre of the earth found in al-Baṭalyawsī's *Kitāb al-Ḥadāʾiq*. Moses Narboni identifies it with the Body (*Qomā*) or Height of the Body (*gobah ha-qomā*) representing the totality of created beings, and sees in Jacob's ladder an allegorical presentation of it.[72] At all events, Ibn Shapruṭ was not misguided in linking Ibn Ezra with al-Baṭalyawsī. He did, however, fail to perceive that Ibn Ezra extended, so to speak, the "straight line" or "ladder" to cover the entire expanse of the universe from the centre of the earth to the Agent Intellect and made it the road of the soul's ascension to God.

Maimonides' view of the ladder departs from the neoplatonic pattern, since his cosmology no longer assumes a single Universal Soul but assigns a separate soul to each of the spheres only.[73] Nor does he offer a coherent treatment of the theme. In his Introduction to the *Guide* (7a Munk) he throws out the general remark that Jacob's ladder represents a type of prophetic parable in which every single feature carries a specific meaning. In his brief references to the subject in *Guide* I, 15, the angels ascending the ladder are said to denote the prophets, since they achieve a knowledge of God by moving up toward God who is "stably and permanently at the top of the ladder". They first ascend and having attained

[70] See Ibn Ezra's *Short Commentary on Exodus*, ed. S. J. Rapoport (Prague, 1840), p. 104; David Rosin, "Die Religionsphilosophie Abraham Ibn Esra's", *Monatsschrift für Geschichte und Wissenschaft des Judenthums*, 42, N.F. 6 (1898), p. 503. On Ibn Ezra's concept of the Universal Soul see *ibid.*, p. 209.

[71] In my article "Moses Narboni's 'Epistle on *Shiʿur Qomā*'" in *Jewish Medieval and Renaissance Studies*, Philip W. Lown Institute of Advanced Judaic Studies, Brandeis University, Studies and Texts: Volume IV, ed. Alexander Altmann (Cambridge, Mass., 1967), p. 267, n. 22.

[72] *Ibid.*, p. 261, lines 186–189 (English translation, p. 281); p. 263, lines 251–252 (286).

[73] See Harry A. Wolfson, *The Problem of the Souls of the Spheres from the Byzantine Commentaries on Aristotle through the Arabs and St. Thomas to Kepler*, The Dumbarton Oaks Centre for Byzantine Studies (A Paper delivered in May, 1961), p. 87.

whatever degree of prophecy is granted to them ("certain rungs of the ladder"), they descend in order to govern and teach the people in the light of their prophetic inspiration. This interpretation of the "parable" (*mathal*) of Jacob's dream re-echoes al-Baṭalyawsī's view of the "ladder of ascent" as an allegory of prophetic inspiration (as well as of the pure souls' ascent to heaven) and it reflects, in particular, the Sūfī concept of the "spiritual ladder" by which the saints rise toward their ecstatic visions. Yet these apparent analogies are not more than faint echoes. The way in which Maimonides describes here the prophets' ascent differs from both al-Baṭalyawsī's and the Sūfīs' concepts of the ladder, and reflects the notion of *sullam ha-ḥokhmōt* rather than that of *sullam ha-ᶜaliyyā*. For he portrays the ascent not as one by inspiration or ecstasy but as one by logical operations leading step by step from the observation of things on earth to the "top of the ladder", viz. to God as the Prime Mover. This is how the commentators (Efodi, Shemtob ben Joseph ben Shemtob, Asher ben Abraham Crescas, Isaac Abrabanel) understood his statement that "Everyone who ascends does so climbing up this ladder [one end of which is in heaven, while the other end is upon the earth] so that he necessarily [!] apprehends Him who is upon it."[74] It is, therefore, understandable that Shemtob in his *Commentary* (*ad locum*) ignores Maimonides' reference to the prophets and speaks instead of the ascent performed by the philosophers (*ha-maskilim we-ha-ḥakhamim ha-nebonim*) or by the "prophets and the philosophers". Moreoever, Maimonides' interpretation implies that Jacob saw in a dream what can only be comprehended by a speculative process. Abrabanel considers this a difficult assumption.[75] One can only conclude that the Maimonides passage under review represents a curious conflation of two divergent traditions, that is of the one expressed in the term *sullam ha-ᶜaliyyā* and of the one denoted by the phrase *sullam ha-ḥokhmōt*. How uncertain Maimonides was in his view of the ladder motif may be gauged from the fact that in *Guide* II, 10, he describes the angels figuring in Jacob's dream as an allegory of the four elements, air and fire having the natural

[74] S. Pines mentions an alternative possibility of translating the latter part of this sentence: "so that he apprehends Him who is upon it necessarily". He regards, however, the translation quoted by us as "probably the correct one". See *The Guide of the Perplexed Moses Maimonides Translated*... by Shlomo Pines, 1963, p. 41 and n. 7 *ibid.*

[75] See his *Commentary on Genesis*, 28:12, where various interpretations of Jacob's ladder found in midrashic and philosophical sources are reviewed.

motion of rising, and water and earth tending to descend. On the other hand, Maimonides established one firm point. He made it clear that in his view Jacob's dream was a prophetic experience and not merely an ordinary dream. This evaluation was, of course, not entirely novel. The symbolic interpretations of this particular dream in some of the *midrashim*[76] also presuppose that God showed the sleeping patriarch certain future events in a prophetic vision. Yet these *midrashim* relate Jacob's prophecy to the historical plane. Maimonides, on the other hand, saw in Jacob's dream a prophecy which expressed, by way of a parable, the ascent to metaphysical truths. He did not say that Jacob had a vision of the *Merkabā* in the way he said in *Guide* III, 6 (following a statement made in *Talmud Ḥagigā* 13b) that the description of the *Merkabā* by Ezekiel had its parallel, in a summary way, in Isa. 6. As we shall see, Maimonides' successors added Jacob's dream to the list of Biblical accounts of the *Merkabā*. The fact that Maimonides insisted on treating Jacob's dream as a prophetic one may not be unrelated to the Islamic legend about Muḥammad's *miʿrāj* by way of a ladder (which was originally Jacob's property). If this ladder figured in Muḥammad's prophetic experience, Jacob too must have been a prophet.[77]

It was Samuel ibn Tibbon who, in his *Maʾamar Yiqawwu Ha-Mayim*,[78] initiated the interpretation of Jacob's dream as a prophetic vision on a par with the celestial visions of Ezekiel and Isaiah. In his view, all three "allegorized the way by which man's intellect attained to its ultimate perfection" (ch. 11, p. 54). Jacob's story[79] is a brief account of the long road to be taken to this end:

[76] Gen. R. 68:12; Tanḥuma, Gen. 28:12; Tanḥuma Buber, Wilna, 1885, pp. 74b–75b; *Midrash Ha-Gadol*, ed. M. Margaliot, Sefer Bereʾshit (Jerusalem, 1947), pp. 500–504.

[77] Cf. Baḥya ben Asher's phrase commenting on Gen. 28:12 in his *Beʿūr ʿal Ha-Torā* (Amsterdam, 1726), 43a, col. 1: "And Jacob awoke from his sleep and, behold, it was a dream, but a dream of perfect prophecy (*ḥalōm shel nebuʾā gemūrā*)". This statement would seem to reflect Maimonides' influence.

[78] Edited by M. L. Bisliches (Pressburg, 1837). An analysis of this work is found in Georges Vajda, *Recherches sur la Philosophie et la Kabbale* . . . (Paris – La Haye, 1962), pp. 11–31.

[79] *Sippūrō shel Yaʿaqob Abīnū*. This term is rejected as an implicit denial of the Divine origin of the chapter in the Torā relating the event by Jacob ben Sheshet in his *Meshīb Debarīm Nekhoḥīm*, a polemical treatise directed against Samuel ibn Tibbon's work. See Bodleian ms. Oppenheimer 239 (1585 Neubauer), fol. 70*v*–71*r* (ch. 27). The passage is not found in Bodleian ms. Michael (1586 Neubauer) which contains only chapters 1–13, as the table in Vajda's *Recherches*, p. 34, shows. I am grateful to Professor Vajda for having put at my disposal the critical text of the *Meshīb Debarīm Nekhohīm* prepared by him.

It is not a road paved[80] upon the earth but one of ascent by a ladder (*derekh* ᶜ*aliyyā be-sullam*) reaching from the earth to heaven, as it is said, "The path of life is upward for him who is wise" (Prov. 15:24). We are here, it would seem, within the tradition of the *sullam ha-*ᶜ*aliyyā* concept, an impression that is reinforced by Ibn Tibbon's remark that Jacob's ladder was made of the trunk of the Tree of Life, the size of which, according to the rabbis,[81] corresponds to a walk of 500 years [as Maimonides, *Guide* II, 30, recalled] which is also the distance said by the rabbis[82] to separate the earth from the lunar sphere (ch. 11, p. 54). Ibn Tibbon may have wanted to allude here to the *Qur*ʾ*ān* passage (Sura 70:3–4), "To Him the angels and the Spirit mount up in a day whereof the measure is fifty thousand years",[83] since it refers to the "stairways" (*al-ma*ᶜ*ārij*) to Heaven and is directly related to the legend of the *mi*ᶜ*rāj*. His suggestion that Jacob's ladder was made of the trunk of the Tree of Life also points to an Islamic motif connected with the *mi*ᶜ*rāj*. According to one particular version of the legend, Muḥammad's Ascent took place by means of a tree which grew taller and taller until it reached into Heaven.[84] This legendary material is, however, used by Ibn Tibbon merely as grist to the mill of rationalistic allegorization. The upward road to be traversed by the soul in search of perfection is the *sullam ha-hokhmōt*. It starts with physics, extends to astronomy (which is part of the mathematical sciences) and culminates in metaphysics. God standing "on top of the ladder" means the existence of God and the supreme ranks of the separate intelligencies or angels. As for the ascending and descending angels in Jacob's dream, they are the philosophers (*maskīlīm*), who ascend to the knowledge of God,[85] and the lower orders of angels commissioned for certain purposes (like the seraph in Isa. 6:6–7) respectively.[86] Ibn Tibbon interprets the

[80] *Derekh selulā*, according to the quotation in Jacob ben Sheshet's text (fol. 69*v*), which is to be preferred to the reading *derekh ẓelulā* in Bisliches' edition, p. 54.

[81] Gen. R. 15:6. For parallels see the references in Theodor's edition of *Bereshit Rabba*, p. 138.

[82] b. Pesaḥīm 94b; Ḥagigā 13a.

[83] See above, p. 42, and the reference to Horovitz' article in n. 5. Horovitz assumes that Muḥammad was influenced by the rabbinic speculations on the subject.

[84] See Asín Palacios, *La Escatología* . . ., p. 19; Horovitz, *op. cit.*, 160, 165.

[85] Ibn Tibbon attributes this interpretation to Maimonides, notwithstanding the fact that the latter identified the angels with the prophets. He obviously felt the same misgivings about Maimonides' interpretation as were expressed subsequently by the commentators (see above, p. 58).

[86] Chapter 11, pp. 54–56.

difference between the visions of Isaiah and Jacob as one of method. Isaiah described the ultimate and perfect knowledge, viz. that of God and the angelic hierarchies, first, and then went down to the lower levels. Jacob, on the other hand, started from the bottom and worked his way upward (p. 56). In more technical language, Isaiah chose as it were the "analytical method" (*derekh ha-hatakhā we-ha-hataqā*), while Jacob employed the "synthetical method" (*derekh ha-harkabā*). The "ascending" and "descending" angels are, therefore, also equated with the philosopher's use of the synthetical and analytical methods (ch. 8, p. 38ff.). This ingenuous, yet far-fetched exegesis has no doubt for its source a passage in al-Fārābī's *The Harmony between Plato and Aristotle* which reads as follows:

> The same [viz. the possibility of reconciling Plato's and Aristotle's respective views] applies to the opinion held by people in regard to analysis (*qisma*) and synthesis (*tarkīb*) for the purpose of obtaining a complete definition. Plato thinks that a complete definition is obtainable only by the method of analysis, while Aristotle holds that a complete definition can be formed solely by the method of demonstration and synthesis. One should, however, know that questions like these may be compared to *a ladder on which one ascends and descends.* The distance is the same; the only difference is between the two who use the ladder in going up or down.[87]

Al-Fārābī's simile proved too tempting to Ibn Tibbon to be ignored, and thus it happened that Isaiah came to be depicted as a Platonist and Jacob as an Aristotelian.[88] Ibn Tibbon's interpretation was adopted by two Karaite writers, viz. by Aaron ben Joseph Ha-Rofēʾ (1250 [or possibly 1260]–*ca.* 1320) and Aaron ben Elijah (*c.* 1300–1369). The former says in his *Sefer Ha-Mibḥar* (written in 1294), Eupatoria, 1835, fol. 52b:

[87] See F. Dieterici, *Alfarabi's Philosophische Abhandlungen* (Leiden, 1892, pp. 13–14), and the notes on pp. 200–201 (3.17) and 204–205 (14.1).

[88] In his terminology Ibn Tibbon somewhat deviates from al-Fārābī's. While he renders *tarkib* by the exact Hebrew equivalent *harkabā*, he translates *qisma* (lit.: division) by the two cognate terms *hatakhā* (analysis, *resolutio*) and *hataqā* (division, which represents Aristotle's term *diairesis*). In the discussion of Aristotle's *Posterior Analytics* by the Ikhwān (*Rasāʾil* 1:14, Vol. I, pp. 343ff.) the terms used for "division" and "analysis" are *taqsīm* and *taḥlīl*, respectively. The distinction between the two methods is noted in Ibn Gabirol's *Fons Vitae* (see the analytical index in Baeumker's edition *s.v. resolutio* and *compositio*). The same holds true of Dominicus Gundissalinus. See Georg Bülow, *Des Dominicus Gundissalinus Schrift "Von dem Hervorgange der Welt" (De Processione Mundi)*, Beiträge zur Geschichte der Philosophie des Mittelalters. Texte und Untersuchungen (Münster, W., 1925), pp. 2–3, 24. For the discussion of the two methods by Jewish Aristotelians see Joseph ibn Kaspi's *Ẓerōr*

> And some say that Jacob's dream resembles the vision seen by Ezekiel and Isaiah who beheld God sitting upon a high and exalted throne and the angels standing before Him like servants, there being no difference between them [i.e. the three accounts] except that Jacob began his story (*sippūrō*) from below upward, and there being, likewise, but little divergence between the apprehension of Isaiah and the apprehension of Ezekiel. It need not be mentioned here.[89] Yet the three are identical.

Aaron ben Elijah writes in his Commentary on the Torā, *Keter Torā* (composed in 1362), Eupatoria, 1860, fol. 65a:

> Some explain . . . that each part of the allegory points to some specific subject matter . . . and they put together Jacob's dream with the visions of Isaiah and Ezekiel in the sense that the three mean the same thing. They call, however, Jacob's apprehension one by the method of synthesis (*derekh ha-harkabā*), because he gained understanding (*she-tafas*) from below and ascended upward; and [they called] Isaiah's apprehension the method of analysis (*derekh ha-hatakhā*) [because he gained understanding] from above downward.[90]

Joseph ibn Kaspi (*c.* 1280–*c.* 1340) devotes his treatise *Menorat Kesef*[91] to an interpretation of the theme of the *Merkabā* as presented in the Torā and in Isaiah, Ezekiel and Zechariah. He too, then, follows the pattern introduced by Samuel ibn Tibbon in trying to show that a vision of the *Merkabā* is alluded to already in the Torā, particularly in Jacob's dream. The *Merkabā* he identifies with the supernal world of God and the separate intelligencies, of which, he assumes there are ten, the lowest being the Agent Intellect which presides over the sublunar world of the elements (as had been suggested by al-Fārābī and Ptolemy [=al-Baṭalyawsī

[89] It is spelled out in the author's *Commentary on Isaiah* (ch. 6), as noted in the commentary *Ṭirat Kesef* (printed alongside the *Sefer Ha-Mibḥar*), *ad locum*.

[90] The method used by Ezekiel is said to have been "from the place of the cause of his apprehension", which is not a very clear statement. Ibn Tibbon (*op. cit.*, p. 56) said of Ezekiel that he used neither the method of synthesis nor the one of analysis but "began [to relate immediately] the cause of the perfection of [his] apprehension" (?).

In his philosophical work *ᶜEẓ Ḥayyīm* (completed in 1346), ed. Franz Delitzsch (Leipzig, 1841), Aaron ben Elijah differentiates between grades of prophecy and assigns to Isaiah the fourth and to Jacob the sixth grade.

[91] Edited by Yiẓḥaq Last in *ᶜAsarā Kelē Kesef*, Vol. II, 1903, pp. 75–142.

Ha-Mōr, Vatican ms. 283.8 (no numbering of folios), Section entitled *Ha-Maʾamar bi-gedarīm*; and Abraham Bibago's *Commentary on the Posterior Analytics*, Vatican ms. 350, fol. 2*v*.

whom he constantly confuses with the astronomer] as well as by Maimonides) and is not identical with the mover of the lunar sphere (as had been taught by Averroes). The nine intelligencies above the Agent Intellect Ibn Kaspi calls, with al-Fārābī, the "secondary ones" (*sheniyīm*), that is "secondary" in relation to God, the "First". They are also termed "sons of God", the "spiritual ones" (*rūḥaniyīm*), "angels", and "cherubim", which names may also be applied to the Agent Intellect which bears the specific name "holy spirit" (*rūaḥ ha-qodesh*). Ibn Kaspi rejects Averroes' thesis which equates the mover of the highest sphere with God. The nine spheres moved by the nine intelligencies are those of the moon, the sun, Mercury, Venus, Mars, Jupiter, Saturn, the sphere of the fixed stars and the starless sphere, and they are all endowed with souls (pp. 79–83, 102–103). Ibn Kaspi thus subscribes to the cosmology of the pre-Averroean Aristotelians which had also been adopted by Maimonides (*Guide* II, 9). It is all the more remarkable that he re-introduces, on the other hand, the concept of the Universal Soul as propounded by al-Baṭalyawsī in his allegorical interpretation of the "Ladder of Ascension".[92] The relevant passage in *Menorat Kesef* (p. 91)—to which he refers the reader in his *Maskiyot Kesef*, p. 31—reads as follows:

> Likewise, there is transmitted (*nimsar*) in the Torā with the utmost brevity and [by way of] allegory (*u-be-remez*) a parable-like story (*sippūr eḥad ha-mishlī*) from our Father Jacob, peace be upon him, namely the vision of the ladder. Ptolemy [=al-Baṭalyawsī] also mentions in the first [chapter] of the *Book of the Circles* the "Ladder of Ascension" (*sullam ha-ḥagōrōt*)[93] which is stolen from the Book of the *Torā*. He said there: "Through it prophecy attaches to the pure particular soul, and on it the purified spirits ascend to the supernal world, and on it the angels descend." Hence it seems to me highly probable that this [ladder] was the thing which Jacob conceived (*ᶜinyan ẓiyyūr Yaᶜaqob*)[94] in that he conceived the perfect Soul (*ha-nefesh ha-tammā*) [viz. the Universal Soul] mentioned by Ptolemy [=al-Baṭalyawsī]. When saying: "And behold, the Lord stood upon it", he referred to the First Cause or to the totality of the separate

92 It seems that Ibn Kaspi's principal guides in philosophy were, in addition to Maimonides, al-Fārābī and al-Baṭalyawsī ("Ptolemy"). See *Menorat Kesef*, pp. 78, 80, 91; *Maskiyot Kesef*, ed. S. Werblumer [*ᶜAmudē Kesef U-Maskiyōt Kesef*] (Frankfurt a.M., 1848), pp. 90, 91, 97 *et passim*.

93 See above, p. 50.

94 For Ibn Kaspi's use of the term *ẓiyyūr* in the sense of "concept" see *Menorat Kesef*, p. 84.

> Intelligencies which comprise God, the Secondary ones, and the Agent Intellect. The meaning of ["and the top of it reached] to heaven" is: to the convexity of the diurnal [all-encompassing] sphere, for there the Universal Soul is located [viz. beyond the last sphere, yet penetrating the entire universe of spheres and earth], as Ptolemy [=al-Baṭalyawsī] mentioned; *comp. op. cit.* For in my view this is exactly the meaning of this vision, and this Universal Soul is identical with the "sapphire stone" (*ʾeben sapīr*) mentioned by Ezekiel [1:26].

Writing in the fourteenth century, the Aristotelian Ibn Kaspi thus resumes the neoplatonic concept of the Universal Soul and, moreover, suggests the complete identity of al-Baṭalyawsī's notion of the "Ladder of Ascent" with the meaning of the ladder in Jacob's prophetic dream. He does not mention the symbol of the "straight line" as the equivalent of the ladder motif but must be presumed to have accepted it too since he speaks of the exact identity of the meaning of Jacob's vision and al-Baṭalyawsī's view of the Ladder of Ascent. The Universal Soul is, of course, not identical with the ladder passing from the centre of the earth to the all-encompassing sphere. It is beyond the "upper circle", beneath the horizon of the Agent Intellect, but its force is diffused throughout what is below it. Ibn Kaspi enlarges on the exact meaning of the Universal Soul (which, we saw, he equates with the "sapphire stone" in Ezekiel's vision) in a subsequent context (pp. 123–124) when explaining Ezekiel's description of the *Merkabā*:

> There appeared to Ezekiel on the plane of the chariot (*ʿal sheṭaḥ ha-ʿagalā*) which is the convexity of the celestial body,[95] "the likeness of a throne" [Ez 1:26] which is "the appearance of a sapphire stone". In reality, there is no body (*geshem*) above the convexity of the diurnal sphere nor is there any Intelligence close by except the Agent Intellect. Hence we have no choice but to assume Ezekiel's view to be to the effect that there is found there a Universal Soul, as posited by Ptolemy [al-Baṭalyawsī], which is under the horizon of the Agent Intellect, and that the [Agent] Intellect encompasses it from all its sides, and it [i.e. the Universal Soul] encompasses the globe of the sphere, and that he called this Soul "sapphire stone". I, for my part do not reject this [view], for this opinion was held by many ancient philosophers.

Ḥanokh ben Solomon al-Qosṭanṭini, who lived in the second half of the fourteenth century, continues the tradition of treating

[95] The terms *ʿagalā* and *ʿagullā* are obviously used here as synonyms.

Jacob's dream as a vision of the *Merkabā* parallel to Isaiah's and Ezekiel's. His *Marʾōt Elōhīm*[96] offers a detailed comparison of the three texts, and makes the point that Isaiah saw first the spiritual world, viz. God and the angels, and afterwards the throne, viz. the world of the spheres. Ezekiel, on the other hand, saw first the world of the spheres, then the sublunar world, and then, finally, the world of the separate intellects. Jacob, however, started from the world below and worked his way up. This account follows the by now familiar pattern that had been introduced by Ibn Tibbon. Ḥanokh does, however, draw a line between the prophetic visions of Isaiah and Ezekiel and the dream-vision of Jacob (p. 282). Of particular interest is his discussion of the phrase "the likeness of a throne, as the appearance of a sapphire stone" (Ez. 1:26). He says: "Certain philosophers admit that there exists a tenth sphere devoid of stars, immobile, crystalline; this one is no doubt denoted by [the term] 'the likeness of a throne, as the appearance of a sapphire stone', for a throne is immovable . . ." (p. 301). The tenth sphere mentioned here is obviously not Maimonides' highest heaven called *ʿarabōt* (*Guide* I, 70) which is said by him to be empty and without stars (*Guide* II, 9), since this heaven is distinctly identified with the ninth, all-encompassing diurnal sphere which far from being immobile is moved by the Power and will of God and communicates its motion to the entire system of the spheres. Nor is it the all-encompassing sphere of the Ikhwān since it too is clearly stated to be the ninth sphere and said to be moved by the Universal Soul.[97] Ibn Gabirol[98] and Ibn Ezra[99] do speak of ten spheres but the tenth sphere is equated with the hypostasis of Intellect (Gabirol) or the world of the throne and the intelligible substances (Ibn Ezra). Ḥanokh's reference to "certain philosophers" who assume a tenth sphere probably re-echoes Moses Narboni's statement in his *Commentary on the Guide of the Perplexed*[100] which

[96] Translated into French on the basis of a critical edition of the text (about to be published), with an introduction and notes, by Colette Sirat in *Revue des Études Juives*, Quatrième série, I (CXXI), 3–4, 1962, pp. 247–354.

[97] See the systematic account given of the Ikhwān's doctrine by Dieterici, *Einleitung und Makrokosmos*, pp. 178–184.

[98] In his *Keter Malkhūt*.

[99] See the references in Rosin's article cited above (n. 70), pp. 30, 243–245. In his *Ḥayy Ben Mēqīẓ* (see David Rosin, *Reime und Gedichte des Abraham Ibn Ezra* (Breslau, 1891), pp. 167–201) no mention is made of a tenth sphere. The ninth sphere is followed by the world of the angels and of human souls (pp. 195–196).

[100] Ed. J. Goldenthal, 48b. Narboni's *Commentary* was completed in the year 1362. Hence, it could have been used by Ḥanokh.

after quoting Maimonides' reference to "the likeness of a throne, as the appearance of a sapphire stone" adds the remark: "It [merely] appeared to them [all these objects of vision being somewhat uncertain], and this is the sphere which many assume [to exist] above the sphere of *ᶜarabōt* [which is the ninth sphere] and which they call 'the heaven of beatitude' (*shemē ha-haẓlaḥā*)."[101] Colette Sirat quotes Narboni's comment and suggests that the notion of a tenth sphere may have been derived from a certain misreading of al-Baṭalyawsī's description of the Universal Soul. She attributes this misreading to Ibn Kaspi rather than to Narboni. By interpreting the "sapphire stone" as an allegory of the Universal Soul, Ibn Kaspi, she asserts, "introduisait dans cette doctrine une équivoque certaine et Ḥanokh franchit allègrement le pas qui lui permet d'expliquer allégoriquement la *pierre de saphir qui se trouve au-dessus du firmament* de la vision d'Ezéchiel par une dixième sphère immobile et cristalline" (pp. 265–266). Ibn Kaspi's step of identifying the Universal Soul with the "sapphire stone" could indeed have led to the assumption of a tenth sphere, seeing that the image concerned related to the throne which Maimonides had equated with the ninth sphere and for which Ibn Ezra had postulated a tenth sphere. The Universal Soul = sapphire stone could thus easily have been transformed into a tenth sphere. This line of reasoning seems, however, to break down in the case of Narboni who would hardly have made the same illegitimate use of Ibn Kaspi. Moreover, Narboni's clear statement that "many" assumed the existence of a tenth sphere remains unexplained. It should also be noted that Maimonides' commentator Shemtob says à propos the passage in *Guide* III, 7, mentioning the "sapphire stone": "This sphere is one without stars above [the sphere of] *ᶜarabōt*, and this is the 'terrible ice' [Ez. 1:22] which the latter-day philosophers (*aḥaronē ha-ḥakhamim*) call 'heaven of beatitude'."[102] I have not yet been able to identify the philosophers referred to but it appears that the tenth sphere "admitted" by them goes ultimately back to Ibn Ezra's concept of the world of the throne as a tenth sphere.[103] There is, then, hardly any connection of this notion with al-Baṭalyawsī's Universal Soul.

We do, however, find traces of al-Baṭalyawsī's allegorization of

[101] See my article cited in n. 71, pp. 271–272, n. 50.

[102] See also Efodi's *Commentary ad locum*.

[103] Narboni's quotation of Ibn Ezra in this context (48b) tends to confirm this hypothesis.

the *miʿrāj* in some of the Kabbalists. In Moses de Leon's *Sheʾelot u-Teshubot* the following passage occurs[104]:

> This is the mystical meaning thereof (*sōdō*) [viz. of the midrashic *dictum*: "All that happened to Jacob also happened to Joseph"]: Even as Jacob broke down the fence of those oppressive confines (*mēẓarim*) [which in the preceding passage, p. 26, lines 47–51 are identified with the "shells" (*qelipōt*) or demonic forces] and *ascended by way of the ladder in a straight line* (*we-ʿalā derekh ha-sullam be-qav ha-mīshōr*) . . . so did his son, Joseph the Righteous (Yosef ha-Ẓaddīq) . . . Thus the Father and his Son [whose kabbalistic symbols are the linear letter] *waw* (ו) and the outdrawing (*meshekh*) of the *waw* [the *waw* itself being the symbol of the Sefirā Tifʾeret (Jacob) and its "outdrawing" or direct emanation in a straight line being the symbol of the Sefirā Yesod (Joseph)] *ascended* (*ʿalū*) and attached themselves *by way of the straight line* (*ʿal derekh qav ha-yashar*), the "middle bar" (*ha-beriaḥ ha-tīkhōn*) [Ex. 26:28, used as another symbol of the straight line], to the [highest Sefirā called] Supernal Crown (*Keter ʿElyōn*), after their souls had departed and when they betook themselves to the eternal life (*le-ḥayyē ʿad*) . . .

All the essential elements of the specific configuration of the motif found in al-Baṭalyawsī and in the Ikhwān, with the exception of the Universal Soul, are found here re-assembled. The notion of the *miʿrāj* as an allegory of the upward way and of the soul's escape from the prison of the corporeal world is expressed here by the simile of the breaking down of the fence of the oppressive confines of the *qelipōt*.[105] The "straight line"—al-Baṭalyawsī's term for the Qurʾānic *al-ṣirāṭ al-mustaqīm* used by the Ikhwān—is literally taken over. It appears both in the form *qav ha-yashar* which we found in ms. A of *Mozenē Ha-ʿIyyunīm* and in the more poetic form *qav ha-mīshōr* which Moses de Leon may have borrowed from the third Hebrew version of the *Kitāb al-Ḥadāʾiq* which translates *khaṭṭ al-mustaqīm* by *qav mīshōr*. Since the Sefirotic diagram employs the symbol of a middle line leading straight from Keter down to Tifʾeret, Yesod and Malkhut, and since the characteristic symbol of Tifʾeret is the linear letter *waw*, it was not difficult to connect this line with the concept of the *khaṭṭ al-mustaqīm*.[106] The

[104] Ed. J. Tishby, Qobeẓ ʿal Yad, V (XV) (Jerusalem, 1950), p. 26.

[105] On the neoplatonic origin of this term see my article in *The Journal of Jewish Studies*, Vol. IX, 1–2, 1958, pp. 73–80 [reprinted below, pp. 172–179].

[106] This straight middle line is usually called *ha-qav ha-ʾemẓaʿī*. See, e.g., Moses de Leon, *Sefer Sheqel Ha-Qodesh*, ed. A. W. Greenup (London, 1911), p. 114.

decisive proof that Moses de Leon took this term from al-Baṭalyawsī lies in the fact that he links it with the ladder motif and the concept of the ascent of the souls of the departed to the supernal world. This is exactly what we find in al-Baṭalyawsī and can be traced back to the Ikhwān and their allegorization of the *miᶜrāj*. The combination of these various features is too striking to be explicable on internal kabbalistic grounds alone. What, however, is entirely novel is the transference of this configuration of motifs from the level of the human soul to that of the Sefirotic realm.

A somewhat fainter echo of the same Islamic source material may be noticed in a passage of the anonymous commentary on *Sefer Ha-Temunā* which reads[107]:

> And the supernal angels ascend to that Image, and this Image symbolises (*romeẓet*) the order of emanation which contains the supernal Sanctuary (*miqdash ᶜelyōn*). Our Father Jacob, who saw the ladder [lit. "the subject-matter of the ladder", *ᶜinyan ha-sullam*] in his dream, knew that even as there is a Sanctuary in the [world of] emanation above, so there is a Sanctuary below, for it is written, "and this is the gate of heaven" [Gen. 28:17]. And from the Upper Sanctuary to the one below there is a kind of ladder (*ke-mīn sullam*), that is to say, *a well-known path* (*derekh eḥad yaduᶜa*) which leads from Sanctuary to Sanctuary, and *on this path the angels ascend and descend, and so do the souls likewise.*

There is, of course, nothing new in the basic concepts of this passage (upper and lower sanctuary, world of emanation), yet it would seem that the equation of the ladder with "a well-known path" on which not only the angels but the souls also ascend to heaven is a reference to the *ṣirāṭ al-mustaqīm* or *khaṭṭ al-mustaqīm*.[108] We venture to suggest that the phrase *qav ha-mīshōr* used in the sense of "flow of emanation" by members of the Gerona school of Kabbalā has the same origin, notwithstanding the fact that all traces pointing to the ladder motif are obliterated in the contexts in which the term appears. The choice of this particular term would, however, be inexplicable without the assumption of some literary precedent, and seeing that in the case of Moses de Leon's use of the term the connection with al-Baṭalyawsī is fairly obvious, there would seem no justification whatever to conjecture

[107] *Sefer Ha-Temunā* (Lemberg, 1892), 9b.

[108] Cf. Horovitz, *op. cit.*, p. 175: "Von einer solchen Leiter der Toten wissen die jüdischen und christlichen Quellen nichts."

a different source for the employment of the same term by the Kabbalists of Gerona. The texts concerned are Jacob ben Sheshet's *Meshib Debarim Nekhoḥim* and Azriel's *Perūsh Ha-Aggadōt*. The beginning of chapter 9 of the first-named work describes the first emanation (*ha-ne'ezal ha-ri'shōn*) from the hidden source[109] as a "very subtle essence" from which "there begins the straight line (*qav ha-mīshōr*) to emanate and to spread (*le-himashekh u-le-hitpashet*). This subtle essence is pure potentiality and contains seminally all forms. It is the *Sefirā Ḥokhmā*, the term *Ḥokhmā* being understood by the Gerona school in the sense of potentiality (*koaḥ mā*).[110] The *re'shit* or beginning of the account of creation is, in accordance with an old tradition, the *Sefirā Ḥokhmā* because this *Sefirā* is the ultimate reality which can be grasped by human understanding.[111] Azriel says similarly that all essences arise in matter (*gōlem*) or potentiality through limitation and form, and "before limitation was effected, He [God] extended upon it "the straight line" (*qav ha-yōsher*).[112] The *khaṭṭ al-mustaqīm* which denoted the ladder connecting the centre of the earth with the all-encompassing sphere and bore all the symbolic meanings of the *mi'rāj* had now become the path of the emanation flowing down from the Sefirā Hokhmā and extending into infinity in the upward direction.

By way of postscript another aspect of the *mi'rāj* legend and its repercussion in Jewish sources may be touched upon. Brief mention has already been made of the fabulous steed Burāq, which according to some accounts, conveyed Muḥammad to Jerusalem and, according to others, even carried him on his ascent through the heavens into the very presence of Allāh.[113] The versions which limit the function of Burāq to the *isrā'* relate that after his

[109] Viz. from *Keter*. Cf. Scholem, *Ursprung und Anfänge der Kabbala*, p. 239.

[110] See J. Tishby, *Perūsh Ha-Aggadōt Le-Rabbi 'Azri'el* (Jerusalem, 1945), p. 84, n. 4.

[111] Our résumé of the passage is based on the critical text prepared by Vajda (see above, n. 79). The text is found in ms. Opp. 239, fol. 28*r*–*v*, and in ms. Michael 294, fol. 61*r*.

[112] *Perūsh Ha-Aggadōt*, ed. Tishby, p. 89, line 14. Tishby *ad locum* (n. 6) refers to the parallel passage in *Meshīb Debarīm Nekhoḥīm*, and he identifies the term *kōaḥ ha-yōsher* used by Azriel (p. 25, line 13, and p. 116, line 17, as well as in other works of his as quoted on p. 25, n. 19) with the *qav ha-yōsher*.

[113] Horovitz, *op. cit.*, pp. 180–181, and before him Steinschneider, *Shenē Ha-Me'orot*, pp. 13–14 (following Gustav Weil, *Biblische Legenden der Muselmänner* (Frankfurt, 1845), p. 196), associate Burāq with the *susyā' barqā'* which figures in the conversation between Samuel of Nehardea and king Shapur I related in b. Sanhedrin 98b. On the etymology of Burāq see Horovitz, *op. cit.*, pp. 182–183.

arrival in Jerusalem the Prophet descended from Burāq and that either he or the angel Gabriel fastened it to the gate of the Shrine or to the great rock under the Dome of the Rock, whereupon, after the recital of prayers, the glittering ladder was brought for the Ascent.[114] The accounts which describe Muḥammad as riding to heaven either equip the fabulous beast with wings[115] or failing to do so, assume that Burāq carried the Prophet along the ladder which, properly speaking, was a stairway leading up to heaven. The beautiful painting "Muḥammad on Burāq" reproduced as plate LIII in Arnold's work shows the Prophet on a wingless Burāq trotting along among the angels in heaven on what looks like an ascending path or ramp, which would seem the nearest approach to what is called *sullam al-maᶜārij*. The shape of Burāq went through many metamorphoses. Originally, the animal was considered an ass. It was held to be the same beast as Abraham (according to Gen. 12:3) and Jesus (according to John 12:14) had ridden upon. Later it was felt that an ass was not a sufficiently dignified animal, and Burāq came to be described as larger than an ass but smaller than a mule. It was equipped with wings, a human face either masculine or feminine, and portrayed even like a sphinx.[116]

It may be safely assumed that the Islamic legends about Burāq were widely known also in Jewish circles within the orbit of the Islamic world. The Arabic original of the Latin version of the legend published by Enrico Cerulli had been rendered in Castilian by the Jew Don Abraham al-Faquīn at about the middle of the thirteenth century.[117] It may also be taken for granted that the Jews disbelieved the legend of Muḥammad's ascension to heaven and that they discounted, in particular, the story of Burāq carrying the Prophet to heaven on a stairway which amounted to Jacob's ladder. Being familiar with the midrashic tradition concerning the ass which served Abraham (Gen. 22:3), Moses' wife Zippora and

[114] See Najm al-Dīn al-Ghaiṭī's account, translated into English in *A Reader on Islam*, ed. Arthur Jeffery, pp. 625–627, and the text of the Latin version of the *Kitāb al-Miᶜrāj* in Enrico Cerulli, *Il "Libro della Scala" e la questione delle Fonti Arabo-Spagnole della Divina Commedia*, Città del Vaticano, MCMXLIX (Studi e Testi 150), pp. 43ff.

[115] See F. W. Arnold, *Painting in Islam* (Oxford, 1928), p. 118, and plates LV and LVI.

[116] See Arnold, *op. cit.*, pp. 118ff.; Horovitz, *op. cit.*, pp. 179–180.

[117] See Cerulli, *op. cit.*, p. 17; Steinschneider, *Cat. Libr. Bodl.*, 2747, and *HÜ*, p. 591. The French and Latin translations were made from the Castilian version.

his sons (Ex. 4:10), and which was destined (Zech. 9:9) to carry the Messiah[118] they correctly assumed that the Islamic legend had imitated the midrashic source and therefore took Burāq to be an ass and nothing more. In their view, then, the story of this particular ass called Burāq climbing up on Jacob's ladder was utterly fantastic and an assertion of the impossible. I suggest that it is this assertion which was made the target of good-humoured ridicule in the so-called *Pirqē Rabbenu Ha-Qadōsh* which is extant under various titles in different recensions and has been recognised as containing a great deal of late—post-Islamic—material.[119] Under the rubric "The Sages said four things" certain obvious impossibilities are listed and linked together in the form: If A were possible, B could be admitted as equally possible, the implication being that since A is ostensibly absurd, B is likewise unthinkable. The formulation of the four pairs of absurdities varies slightly in the several readings but one might suggest as a kind of critical text the following:

Arbaʿā deḅarim amrū ḥaḵamim
Im yitlabben ha-saq yitḥakem ha-kĕsil
Im yaʿalē ḥamōr be-sullam timẓaʾ daʿat ba-koḅesim
Ve-im yagōẓ gĕdī mēlat ba-talē tadūr kallā ʿim hamōtah
Ve-im yimaẓēʾ ʿōreḇ kulō laḇan timaẓēʾ kesherā ba-nashim

Four things the Sages said:
If a sack can be cleaned, a fool can become wise;
If an ass can ascend a ladder, knowledge can be found among launderers;
If a kid can shear a lamb's wool, a daughter-in-law can live with her mother-in-law;
And if a completely white raven can be found, a decent woman can be found.

[118] *Pirqē de-Rabbi Eliezer*, ch. 31, quoted by Horovitz, *op. cit.*, pp. 180–181.

[119] The version called *Midrash Maʿasē Torā* (contained in *Sefer Kolbō*, ch. 118) was edited by A. Jellinek in *Beth-Hamidrash*, II, pp. 92–101 (see Introduction, p. XXVII). Leopold Zunz, *Die gottesdienstlichen Vorträge der Juden*[2] (1892), p. 297, n. *e* lists some of the later material. The recension named *Ḥuppat Eliyahu Rabbāʾ* is found in Israel ben Joseph Alnaqāwā's *Menorat Ha-Maʾōr*, ed. H. G. Enelow, IV, and, according to Jellinek (*loc. cit.*) as an appendix to the Amsterdam edition (which of the three is not stated) of Elijah de Vidas' *Reʾshīt Ḥokhmā*. The recension called *Pirqē Rabbenu Ha-Qadōsh* was published by Samuel Schönblum in *Sheloshā Sefarīm Niftaḥīm* (Lemberg, 1877), and by Eliezer Grünhut in *Sefer Ha-Liqqutīm*, III (Jerusalem, 1900), pp. 33–90. A ms. of this version is extant among the Geniza fragments, Cambridge, Schechter C 1/3—D. The short text published by Abraham Wertheimer in *Batē Midrashōt*, II, pp. 47–73, under the title *Midrash Sheloshā We-Arbaʾā* may represent the original version, as is asserted in the Introduction, p. 45.

This delightful apophthegm has variant readings only in lines 1, 3 and 4 (not counting the introductory sentence), whereas line 2 remains the same in all texts. If our assumption is correct, we have here a piece of subtle polemic against the Islamic story about Muḥammad's ride to heaven on the ass Burāq using Jacob's ladder. We have, at the same time, an explanation of the origin of the well-known formula found in the colophons of many a Hebrew manuscript:

Ḥazaq ha-sōfer lō yūzaq
lō hayōm ve-lō le-ᶜolam
ᶜad she-yaᶜalē ḥamōr ba-sullam
shē-yaᶜakob abīnū ḥalam

Be strong! May the copyist suffer no harm
Either today or at any time
Until the ass ascends the ladder
About which our Father Jacob dreamt.

In his *Vorlesungen über die Kunde hebräischer Handscriften* (1897; 2nd ed., Jerusalem, 1937, p. 48), Moritz Steinschneider deals with the many variations in detail of this humoristic type of prayer, "dessen wahrscheinlich fremder Ursprung noch nicht genügend nachgewiesen ist, nämlich das Besteigen der Leiter durch einen Esel (jene und dieser auch abgebildet) als Bild der Unmöglichkeit". Steinschneider was obviously unaware of the midrashic quadruple in which this "Bild der Unmöglichkeit" appears, and which we believe to have shown to owe its origin most probably to the reaction provoked among Jews to the story of Burāq. A kabbalistic meaning was no doubt read into the copyists' formula in Nathan of Gaza's pseudepigraphical letter published by Scholem.[120] The authentic meaning is, however, a great deal simpler, as we have endeavoured to show.

120 Gershom Scholem, *Shabbatai Zebi* (Tel-Aviv, I, 1957), p. 183, n. 1.

3

IBN BĀJJA ON MAN'S ULTIMATE FELICITY

There is a remarkable unanimity amongst the medieval philosophers of Islam and Judaism as to what constitutes man's ultimate felicity: "For you see all philosophers agree that the ultimate felicity of man is in his apprehension of the separate intellects", Ibn Rushd was able to write in his *De animae beatitudine*.[1] This notion derives from the neoplatonic tradition in which the utmost happiness was said to consist in the contemplation of the supernal world of Forms. Thus, Plotinus had described the vision of the Good as yielding a delight surpassing all other delights, including those of beauty and knowledge (*Enn.* VI, vii, 34–36; see also the treatise "On Happiness", *Enn.* I, iv). The *Theology of Aristotle*, in its Arabic vulgate version (ed. Dieterici, p. 163 [161]), uses already the term "the felicitous" to denote those privileged to enjoy the beholding of the supernal world of Forms: "The heavenly and the earthly things are but images (*aṣnām*) and impressions (*rusūm*) of the things in the supernal world (*al-ᶜālam al-aᶜlā*); hence what is there is a wondrous sight which only the felicitous (*ahl al-saᶜāda*) and those reaching the limits (*ahl al-ḥudūd*) will behold." But whereas in the more strictly neoplatonic medieval writings (e.g. *Epistles* of the Ikhwān al-Ṣafāᵓ; Ibn Gabirol; Baḥya ibn Paqūdā) the object of the desired vision is the Platonic realm of the Forms

[1] Venice, 1572, p. 150 (quoted by Ludwig Hannes, *Des Averroes Abhandlung "Über die Möglichkeit der Conjunktion"*, Halle a. S., 1892, p. 10, n. 3). Ibn Rushd makes the same remark in another treatise; cf. J. Hercz, *Drei Abhandlungen über die Conjunction*, etc. (Berlin, 1869), pp. 28f. The Arabic, Hebrew and Latin terms denoting "the ultimate felicity" are *al-saᶜāda al-quṣwā* (*al-ākhira*); *ha-haṣlaḥā ha-aḥarōnā*; *ultima beatitudo*.

or Ideas (localised in the Supernal Intellect or Wisdom),[2] the position is different in the writings of the Aristotelian school (al-Fārābī, Ibn Bājja, Ibn Rushd). Here the denial of self-subsistent Forms (even though assumed to reside in some supernal hypostasis) enforces a shift of the object of ultimate knowledge to a different plane. Instead of the supernal Forms it is now the separate intellects to which the quest for ultimate felicity is directed. These separate intellects or intelligences are not the essences of the sensible things, as the Platonists maintained, but conceived as simple, i.e. immaterial substances of an ontological order. The hierarchy of these intellects, the last of which is the Agent Intellect, represents a series of emanations from God and is correlated with the celestial spheres. It is also identified with the angelic order so that knowing the separate intellects has the overtones of knowing the angelic hierarchy. Already in the neoplatonic tradition the Jewish-Christian-Islamic notion of paradise was linked with the felicity of contemplating the supernal Forms. This association persists in the Aristotelian orientation. It does not necessarily imply the purely eschatological character of man's ultimate felicity. It poses, however, the question whether man is capable of achieving this felicity already in this life. The problem is also formulated in the sense of inquiring into the possibility of reaching the knowledge of the separate substances in a natural way, i.e. by the innate possibilities of the human intellect, without requiring the prophetic intellect to come into operation by the help of a Divine agency. The question is also formulated in terms of the possibility of the conjunction (*ittiṣāl*) of the Agent Intellect with man.

The difficulties inherent in the admission of such a possibility within the framework of an Aristotelian epistemology have been reviewed in a grand manner by Ibn Rushd in his *Long Commentary* on Aristotle's *De anima* (III, comm. 36). Ibn Rushd, although historically reflecting the neoplatonic concept of man's ultimate felicity and using as a matter of course the neoplatonic concept of "conjunction", nevertheless takes for his starting-point a passage in Aristotle (*De anima* III, 7,431b, 16) which he interprets to mean that Aristotle himself had promised to investigate the possibility of knowing something of the "abstract things", i.e. of the separate

[2] On the history of the location of the Platonic Ideas see H. A. Wolfson's masterful article, "Extradeical and Intradeical Interpretations of Platonic Ideas", *Journal of the History of Ideas*, XXII, 1 (January-March, 1961), pp. 3–52 [reprinted in his *Religious Philosophy: A Group of Essays* (1961)].

intellects. This promise not having been redeemed, Ibn Rushd takes it upon himself to step into the breach, and he does so not only here but in other works of his as well. He wrote, in fact, no less than five treatises in order to demonstrate the possibility of conjunction,[3] which al-Fārābī had distinctly denied in his *Commentary* on the *Nichomachean Ethics*, after having admitted it previously in some form or another.[4] In the *Long Commentary* (*ibid.*), Ibn Rushd examines the doctrines of his predecessors (Alexander of Aphrodisias, Themistius, al-Fārābī, and Ibn Bājja), and it is this review of the earlier positions which Thomas Aquinas used in his own presentation and critique of the methods by which Ibn Bājja (Avempace), Alexander and Ibn Rushd (Averroes) himself had defended the possibility of knowing the separate substances. Thomas Aquinas' own view is that (a) man's ultimate happiness does not consist in the knowledge of separate substances and (b) that it is impossible in this life to understand the separate substances (*Summa contra Gentiles* III, 41–45; see also *Summa Theologica* I, qu. 88, a. 1–2).

Our present analysis seeks to clarify Ibn Bājja's view in this matter. Although the arguments reported by Ibn Rushd and reproduced by St. Thomas in his name have been sufficiently highlighted by these two eminent authors, they do not represent Ibn Bājja's

[3] Cf. M. Steinschneider, *Al-Farabi* (1869), p. 107.

[4] Al-Fārābī maintains the possibility of conjunction with the Agent Intellect at the prophetic stage in *Al-Madīna al-Fāḍila*, ed. F. Dieterici (1896), p. 58, lines 15ff.; also in *Siyāsat al-Madīna* (Hydarābād, 1346 A.H.), p. 49, lines 11ff.; Hebrew version: *Sēfer Ha-Hateḥalōt*, ed. Filipowski, in *Sēfer Ha-Asīf* (1849), p. 40, lines 25ff.; German version: *Die Staatsleitung von Alfarabi*, ed. P. Brönnle (1904), pp. 61–62. He alludes to it also in *Risāla fī'l-ʿAql*, ed. M. Bouyges (1938), p. 22, lines 1–2. Otherwise, the "ultimate felicity" (*al-saʿāda al-quṣwā*) attainable by man is the "acquired intellect" which is a stage below the Agent Intellect and closest to it, with no intermediate stage in between. Cf. *Madīna*, p. 46, line 10; p. 57; *Siyāsat*, p. 7, lines 10–11 (Hebrew: p. 5, line 15); p. 15, line 1 (Hebrew: p. 20, line 18); *Risāla fī'l-ʿAql*, p. 31, line 5. Man will, however, be able to reach the stage of the Agent Intellect in the after-life. Cf. *Siyāsat*, p. 3, lines 14–15 (Hebrew: p. 2, lines 4–6); *Fuṣūl al-madanī*, ed. D. M. Dunlop (Cambridge, 1961), 25. Al-Fārābī's denial, towards the end of his life, of the possibility of conjunction in his *Commentary on the Nicomachean Ethics* is attested by Ibn Rushd in several places. Cf. his *Commentarium Magnum in . . . De Anima Libros*, ed. F. Stuart Crawford (1953), pp. 433, 481, 485–486; S. Munk, *Mélanges de philosophie juive et arabe*, pp. 348–349 (n. 3); J. Hercz, *Drei Abhandlungen über die Conjunction*, pp. 45–47, 54; M. Steinschneider, *Al-Farabi*, pp. 99, 102.

R. Walzer's brief account of al-Fārābī's doctrine in *Journal of Hellenic Studies*, Fasc. 1 (1957), p. 144, fails to distinguish between al-Fārābī's earlier and later view. F. Rahmann in his analysis of al-Fārābī's doctrine of intellect (in *Prophecy in Islam*, 1958, pp 11–14, 21–25) does not seem to realise that in terms of temporal sequence the rejection of the possibility of conjunction in the *Comm. on Eth. Nic.* is later than the admission of that possibility.

treatment of the subject in its totality. What, then, was Ibn Bājja's doctrine concerning the possibility of conjunction? A perusal of Ibn Bājja's writings amply confirms Ibn Rushd's observation that "Ibn Bājja devoted a great deal of scrutiny to this question and elaborated the assertion that this conjunction is possible in his Epistle called [*Epistle on*] *the Conjunction of the Intellect with Man*; and in the *Book on the Soul* and in many other books it appears that this question did not recede from his thought for a single moment".[5] The *Book on the Soul*[6] has, unfortunately, come down to us only in a severely truncated text,[7] and the passages dealing with man's conjunction with the Intellect quoted by Ibn Rushd[8] do not appear in the text at our disposal. We know that Ibn Bājja left the book unfinished but judging from Ibn Rushd's and Ibn Bājja's own references to it,[9] the chapter entitled "Discourse on the Rational Faculty" must have contained considerably more than what is found in the only extant manuscript at our disposal. We have, therefore, to rely on Ibn Rushd's testimony concerning its treatment of our topic. Our text does, however, contain some relevant material in some of the earlier chapters. The *Letter of Farewell*[10]

[5] *Comm. Magnum*, ed. Crawford, p. 487.

[6] *Kitāb al-Nafs*, ed. Muḥammad Saghīr Ḥasan al-Maᶜṣūmī in *Majjalat al-Majmaᶜ al-ᶜIlmī al-ᶜArabī*, Vols. XXXIII-XXXV (Damascus, 1958–60).

[7] Bodleian ms. Pococke 206, which is now the only extant ms. containing Ibn Bājja's works, the Berlin ms. (see W. Ahlwardt, *Die Handschriften-Verzeichnisse der königlichen Bibliothek zu Berlin*, IV (1892), No. 5060, We 87) being untraceable. Cf. the Editor's remarks in *Majjalat*, XXXIII, 1, pp. 108–109. The text contains only a few passages of the "Discourse on the Rational Faculty" (*al-qawl fīʾl-quwwa al-nāṭiqa*), which represents chapter XI of the book, and the final chapter on the appetitive faculty (*al-quwwa al-nuzūᶜiya*) is altogether missing. Since the *Kitāb al-Nafs* follows the pattern of Aristotle's *De anima*, the discussion of the rational faculty should have been succeeded by a final chapter on the appetitive function, as is the case in Ibn Rushd's *Epitome* of the *De anima* (ed. Aḥmad Fuʾad al-Ahwani (Cairo, 1950), pp. 96–101 [under the erroneous title *Talkhīṣ Kitāb al-Nafs*]), which is based on Ibn Bājja's *Kitāb al-Nafs*.

[8] *Comm. Magnum*, ed. Crawford, pp. 487, 491. The "Discourse on the Rational Faculty" (*sermo de virtute rationali*) is quoted on p. 457. The references to Ibn Bājjas views on pp. 397, 400, 406, 469, 489 and probably also on p. 433 go likewise back to the *Kitāb al-Nafs*.

[9] Cf. *Letter of Farewell*, § 13, p. 26 [63]; *Regimen of the Solitary*, p. 21 [52]; *Treatise on Union*, § 5, p. 13 [30]; § 8, p. 14 [32]. For bibliographical references to these works see notes 10, 13, 16 below.

[10] *Risālat al-Wadāᶜ*, edited by M. Asín Palacios with a Spanish translation, summary and notes under the title "La *Carta de Adiós* de Avempace" in *Al-Andalus*, Madrid-Granada, VIII (1943), pp. 1–87; Hebrew version by Ḥayyīm ibn Vivas under the title *Iggeret Ha-Peṭirā* in a Leipzig ms. (cf. M. Steinschneider, Hebr. *Übersetzungen*, § 206, pp. 357–361), a copy of which was in the possession of Steinschneider (see *ibid.*, n. 739) and is now at the Jewish Theological Seminary of America; and in a ms. of the Bibliothèque Nationale, Paris (cf. S. Munk, *Mélanges*, p. 386, n. 2; the shelf-mark is now Hébr. 959).

offers a great deal more information. Its whole purport is, according to the introduction, to enable the friend to whom it is addressed[11] to join the ranks of the felicitous (*al-suʿadāʾ*), i.e. to reach the final goal (*al-ghāya*) of union with the Intellect.[12] The *Regimen of the Solitary*[13] is, regrettably, yet another of Ibn Bājja's unfinished works, and the text breaks off precisely at the point at which the discussion of our topic commences.[14] But it, nevertheless, contains a considerable amount of material bearing on our subject. Ibn Rushd found its style rather obscure but recognised the novelty of its approach.[15] The most extensive treatment of the theme is offered in Ibn Bājja's *Treatise on the Conjunction of the Intellect with*

[11] Ibn al-Imām, who was responsible for the preservation of Ibn Bājja's writings. Cf. M. Asín Palacios' remarks in his edition, pp. 3–4; 41, n. 1; D. M. Dunlop, "Philosophical Predecessors and Contemporaries of Ibn Bājja", *The Islamic Quarterly*, II (1955), pp. 100, 108–111; Muḥammad Sahgīr Ḥasan al-Maʿsūmī, "Ibn al-Imām, The Disciple of Ibn Bājja", *The Islamic Quarterly*, V (1959–60), pp. 102ff.

[12] *Op. cit.*, § 1, p. 15 [42].

[13] *Tadbīr al-Mutawaḥḥid*, ed. by M. Asín Palacios with a Spanish translation, summary and notes under the title *El Régimen del Solitario*, 1946. Moses of Narbonne's Hebrew paraphrase (*Bēʾūr . . . Hanhagat Ha-Mitbōdēd*), which S. Munk had rendered in French (*Mélanges*, pp. 388–409), was edited by D. Herzog in *Qōbeṣ ʿal-Yad*, XI (1895). Cf. also D. M. Dunlop, "Ibn Bājjah's Tadbīru ʾl-Mutawaḥḥid (Rule of the Solitary)", *Journal of the Royal Asiatic Society* (1945), pp. 71–72 [80–81]. For an analysis of the political aspects of the *Tadbīr* see E. I. J. Rosenthal, *Political Thought in Medieval Islam* (Cambridge, 1958), pp. 158–174.

[14] The unfinished character of the work is attested by Ibn Ṭufail (cf. *Ḥayy ben Yaqdhān*, ed. L. Gauthier, Beyrouth, 1936, p. 12 [10]) and Ibn Rushd (see next note). M. Asín Palacios observed that Moses of Narbonne's Hebrew paraphrase sought to supply the missing final section on man's union with the Agent Intellect by borrowing some passages from al-Fārābī's *Risāla fiʾl-ʿAql*. But his statement, "el opúsculo de Avempace se trunca en el ms. original justamente al llegar éste al punto de sutura en que Moises añadio el pasaje de al-Farabi" (*El Régimen del Solitario*, p. 11, cf. *Al-Andalus*, VII (1942), 391–394) is incorrect. Between the end of the Arabic text and the al-Fārābī passage there is an intervening passage (ed. Herzog, p. 19, line 28—p. 20, line 17) which must be considered as belonging to Ibn Bājja. The Arabic text breaks off in the middle of a sentence, and the Hebrew paraphrase completes the sentence as well as the discussion of the subject in a manner which entirely agrees with Ibn Bājja's terminology and doctrine as known from elsewhere.

[15] Towards the end of his *Letter on the Possibility of Conjunction* (Bodleian ms. Michael 119, fol. 139, viii; quoted by Munk, *Mélanges*, p. 388, and—correcting Munk's translation—by M. Steinschneider, *op. cit.*, p. 193; see also p. 361) Ibn Rushd says: "Abū Bakr ibn al-Ṣāʾigh [Ibn Bājja] attempted to lay down an order of the regimen of the solitary in these countries. But the book is incomplete and hard to understand. We indicate its tendency in another place. For this is his speciality, and it has not been anticipated by any one of his predecessors." E. Renan concluded from this passage that Ibn Rushd intended to write a commentary on Ibn Bājja's *Regimen*, but no such work has been preserved. Cf. Steinschneider, *op. cit.*, p. 190, n. 601; Munk, *op. cit.*, p. 388. See below, n. 19.

Man,[16] as Ibn Rushd already observed.[17] A summary of this treatise written by Ibn Rushd[18] underlines its focal points.

As our analysis hopes to show, Ibn Bājja's doctrine of conjunction, though starting from Aristotelian premises and decisively influenced by Alexander of Aphrodisias, the most outspoken anti-Platonist among the commentators, is steeped in the neoplatonic climate of thought, and does in fact represent a remarkable synthesis of the two trends in medieval philosophy. Its concern with man's liberation from matter; its imagery of darkness, shadow and light; its simile of the soul as a mirror to be polished; its use of Plato's cave image; its description of the intellectual process as an ascension (*irtiqāʾ*); and the concept of conjunction (*ittiṣāl*) as such testify to a profoundly neoplatonic orientation. Moreover, there is a clear reversion to the Platonic doctrine of Ideas, albeit in a modified form. In a manner reminiscent of Boethius' admission of Platonic Ideas ("intellectibles") over and above the Aristotelian species and genera ("intelligibles"),[19] Ibn Bājja differentiates between the material intelligibles (species and genera) which have a "universal relation" to individual sense data, and the pure

[16] *Kalām fī Ittiṣāl al-ʿAql biʾl-Insān*, ed. by M. Asín Palacios with a Spanish translation, summary and notes under the title "Tratado de Avempace sobre la Union del Intelecto con el Hombre" in *Al-Andalus*, VII (1942), pp. 1–47. This treatise is chronologically the last of the four mentioned, as is evident from its references to the preceding three. The *Book of the Soul*, on the other hand, is the first of the four. It is quoted in the other three works. Cf. above, n. 9.

[17] *Comm. Magnum*, ed. Crawford, p. 490.

[18] It appears at the end of the "Discourse on the Rational Faculty" in Ibn Rushd's *Epitome* of the *De anima* (ed. Ahwani, pp. 90–95), but is missing in the Hebrew version of the *Epitome* (Hebr. ms. 956 of the Bibliothèque Nationale, Paris). Possibly Ibn Rushd refers to this text when saying in *Comm. Magnum*, ed. Crawford, p. 487; "Et nos iam exposuimus illam epistolam secundum nostrum posse." This summary may also have been considered by Ibn Rushd to indicate the tendency of the *Regimen*, and the reference to "another place" in the passage quoted in note 15 may be to the Summary of the *Treatise on Union*. Steinschneider (cf. *Al-Farabi*, pp. 106–7; *Catalogus Codicum Hebraeorum Bibliothecae Academiae Lugduno-Batavae* [1858], pp. 19–20) already suggested that the reference was to the Commentary on Ibn Bājja's *Treatise on Union* listed among the titles in Ibn Abī Uṣaybiʿa. But he was at a loss to locate this Commentary. His original surmise (*Al-Farabi*, p. 107) identifying it with the *excursus* on the theme of union in *Comm. Magnum* III, 36 (ed. Crawford, pp. 479–502) is abandoned in *Hebr. Übers.*, p. 190, n. 601, and in a marginal gloss in his own hand in his author's copy (in the possession of the Jewish Theological Seminary of America) of the Leyden Catalogue, p. 20, by reason of the fact that the *excursus* itself refers to Ibn Rushd's exposition of the theme elsewhere.

[19] Cf. Boethius, *The Theological Tractates . . . The Consolation of Philosophy*, ed. H. F. Stewart (1946), pp. 381–391; Etienne Gilson, *History of Christian Philosophy in the Middle Ages* (1954), pp. 100–101.

intelligibles from which even the universal relation to the objects of sense perception and imagination has been erased. As we shall see, the pure intelligibles become in his doctrine the *locus* for the intelligible par excellence. They absorb into themselves all the characteristics of the intellect proper (identity of knower and known; possibility of self-knowledge; unity of intellect). They represent the "acquired intellect", and they, being no longer mere abstracts without ontological status, are raised to the level of reality ("one of the existents of the world"). The stage of the pure intelligibles, which is the stage of the acquired intellect, is the goal of the upward way. For at this stage, the Agent Intellect "from without" is no longer "without" but has taken full possession of the human intellect. The Agent Intellect does indeed conjoin with the human intellect at every stage—here Ibn Bājja, as we shall see, follows Alexander of Aphrodisias' doctrine in the *De intellectu*—but as long as the concern with the material world still colours the act of intellection, the conjunction is incomplete. The final goal can be reached only by a true Platonic conversion towards the pure intelligible, and is therefore dependent not on a merely logical operation (as Ibn Rushd and Thomas Aquinas seem to have assumed) but involves an "existential" break with the world of matter. Only in this way can the erasion of even the "universal relation" to individual sense data be accomplished. The neoplatonic character of this doctrine is obvious.

Ibn Bājja himself was conscious of the fact that his view of the possibility of conjunction, although indebted to his predecessors (notably Alexander of Aphrodisias and al-Fārābī), represented a novel doctrine.[20] It will be our task to show in what respects Ibn Bājja drew on some of the earlier theories, and in what way he differed from them.

I. THE STAGES OF THE ASCENT

In all his writings dealing with our topic Ibn Bājja emphasizes the hierarchical structure involved in the process of intellection. In fact, he observes this structure of graded levels even at the pre-intellectual stage. The forms (*ṣuwar*) or "intentions" (*maᶜānī*) residing in the internal senses (common sense, imagination, and memory) represent so many different levels of individual spiritual

[20] *LFarewell*, I, p. 15 [42–43].

forms according to the degree of their remoteness from matter.[21] At the intellectual level, the grading is determined by the difference between the material forms abstracted from matter and the pure intelligibles. This distinction amounts to the differentiation between the speculative sciences on the one hand and "the ultimate science" on the other. Ibn Bājja associates the speculative sciences with the physicist (*ṣāḥib al-ᶜilm al-ṭibāᶜī*), and it stands to reason to assume that the adept of the ultimate science is the metaphysician.

In the *Book on the Soul* only the barest reference to the hierarchical scheme has been preserved but it suffices to show the trend of Ibn Bājja's thought. After pointing out that form never exists in reality without matter and that, consequently, the study of nature must be concerned with forms-with-matter, he declares that when form is "found to be different", it is evident "that it is connected (*ittaṣala*) with a mover in proportion to its difference which depends on the degree of abstraction".[22] This abstraction, he says, is of various grades, and he mentions sense perception, imagination, and reasoning (*al-nuṭq*) as so many different levels of abstraction.[23] There is no reference here to the ultimate level of pure forms. The picture is different in the *Letter of Farewell* where a distinction is drawn between the sciences and the ultimate science which he

[21] *RegSol*, pp. 31–32 [64]; *TrUnion*, 4, p. 12 [28–29]. Ibn Sīnā, too, stresses the varying degrees of abstraction in the internal senses. Cf. *Avicenna's Psychology* by F. Rahman (1952), pp. 38–40; Avicenna's *De Anima*, ed. F. Rahman, p. 58.

The term "spiritual form" (*ṣūra rūḥānīya*) is used by Ibn Bājja both in a wider sense denoting the intelligibles as well as the forms residing in the internal senses, and more narrowly speaking, signifying only the latter. The "Treatise on the Spiritual Forms" in *RegSol*, pp. 18–21 [49–52] offers a classification of spiritual forms under four heads, viz. (1) the forms of the celestial bodies, i.e. the separate substances or intelligencies; (2) the Agent Intellect and acquired intellect; (3) the material intelligibles or universal spiritual forms, and (4) the "intentions" (*maᶜānī*) residing in the internal senses, also called "individual spiritual forms". The last group is, as a rule, designated as "spiritual forms" par excellence, corresponding to the term "spiritual internal senses". For the interchangeability of the terms "internal" and "spiritual" (as opposed to "external" and "corporeal") senses, cf. H. A. Wolfson, "The Internal Senses in Latin, Arabic and Hebrew Philosophic Texts", *Harvard Theological Review*, 28 (1935), pp. 69–70.

The Arabic text (*RegSol*, p. 19, lines 11–12; followed in the translation, p. 50) describes the fourth class as "intermediate between the material intelligibles and the spiritual forms", which makes no sense. The correct reading has been preserved in Moses of Narbonne's Hebrew paraphrase (ms. Bodleian Or. 116, fol. 122*v*, col. 2, lines 16–18): "intermediate between the material intelligibles and the material [viz. corporeal] forms". Cf. also Munk, *op. cit.*, p. 395.

[22] *Kitāb al-Nafs*, fol. 149*v* (*Majallat*, XXXIII, 625–626).

[23] *Op. cit.*, fol. 150*r* (*Majallat*, XXXIII, 626).

identifies with the acquired intellect.[24] This stage is one in which knower and known are identical, and in which there is no forgetting.[25] In the *Regimen of the Solitary* the same distinction occurs. The ultimate grade is said to be higher than mere "intellectuality" which belongs to the rational soul and is expressed in speculative science. At the ultimate level man thinks the simple substantial intelligencies, and thereby achieves union with the supernal world. Ibn Bājja describes the gradation of forms succinctly by reference to the types of existence of man corresponding to them. "By corporeality man is an existing being; by spirituality[26] he is a more noble being; and by intellectuality he is a divine and virtuous being. He who possesses wisdom is necessarily a virtuous, divine man . . . And when he reaches the ultimate end, i.e. when he has an intellection of the simple substantial intellects . . . he thereby becomes one of those intellects, and it is true to say of him that he is only divine (*ilāhī faqaṭ*), and there fits him the attribute of the simple, divine (*ilāhī basīṭ*)."[27] The distinction between intellectuality, even at the stage of "wisdom", on the one hand and the intellection of the simple substances on the other corresponds broadly to the one between the speculative sciences and the ultimate science.

The more elaborate treatment of the topic of gradation is found in the *Treatise on the Union of the Intellect with Man*. At the lowest level, we are told, the intelligible or universal is known only in its relation to the individual matter from which it is abstracted. This is the stage of the *vulgus* (*jumhūr*) which perceives the intelligible only from the individual form from which it is derived.[28] At a higher level, the relation to the material, i.e. corporeal form is still maintained but there is an added awareness of the spiritual forms, particularly those residing in imagination, as mediating between the corporeal forms and the intelligibles. This is the stage of the

[24] *LFarewell*, 15, p. 30 [69]. The reading *al-ʿilm al-aqṣar* (rendered by M. Asín Palacios "conocimiento más elemental") makes little sense. The Hebrew version in the Paris Ms. 959, fol. 90*v*, reads: *ha-ḥokhmā ha-aḥarōnā*, corresponding to Arabic *al-ʿilm al-aqṣā*.

[25] *Ibid.* Cf. Maimonides, *Guide of the Perplexed*, I, 62 (Munk, I, p. 277, n. 3).

[26] I.e. by possessing the spiritual forms residing in the internal senses.

[27] *RegSol*, p. 61 [100–101]. Cf. Pseudo-Empedocles, *Book of the Five Substances*, §239, in the Fragments published by D. Kaufmann (*Studien über Salomon Ibn Gabirol*, Budapest, 1899), p. 36, line 32, where the supernal world is described as "spiritual, divine, simple".

[28] *TrUnion*, 10, p. 16 [35–36].

speculative intellect (lit. "those given to speculation"). Whilst the *vulgus* connects the intelligibles directly with the objects of sense perception, the speculative scientist knows that his concepts are related to sensible objects *via* spiritual forms. Yet fundamentally, Ibn Bājja insists, there is no difference between the level of the *vulgus* and that of the speculative scientist.[29] At both levels, the "conjunction" (*ittiṣāl*) with the intelligibles, i.e. the pure intelligibles in the Agent Intellect, is not a direct one but operates through the mediacy of material and spiritual forms. "Their [sc. the speculative scientists'] conjunction with the intelligibles of the spiritual forms resembles that of the *vulgus* with the intelligibles of the material forms; for the relation of the intelligibles of the speculative thinkers to the spiritual form is the same as the relation of the intelligibles of the *vulgus* to the material forms."[30] The conjunction with the intelligibles at both levels is "of the same manner and rule"; the difference lies only "in the measure of excellence" achieved in the "formation of the concept" (*al-taṣawwur*).[31]

The third and highest level is said to be reached when the pure intelligible becomes an object of intellection. "Then the physicist performs yet another ascension in that he contemplates the intelligibles not *qua* intelligibles denoted as material or spiritual but *qua* intelligibles which are one of the existents of the world.[32] Let us suppose that one of them comes to exist in him. Its relation to the intelligible serving as its substratum will be the same as the

[29] Ibn Rushd reflects this basic dichotomy when, paraphrasing Ibn Bājja in his Summary of *TrUnion* (in the *Epitome*, ed. Ahwani, p. 91), he says that "Men are of two classes, the felicitous (*al-suʿadāʾ*) and the *vulgus*."

[30] *Op. cit.*, 11, pp. 16–17 [36].

[31] *Op. cit.*, 10, p. 16 [35]. The term *taṣawwur* renders the Greek terms νόησις and νοῦς. Cf. H. A. Wolfson, "The Terms *Taṣawwur* and *Taṣdīq* in Arabic Philosophy and Their Greek, Latin and Hebrew Equivalents", *The Moslem World*, XXXIII, 2 (1943), p. 121. According to Aristotle (*De anima*, III, 6, 430a, 26ff.), thinking is either the thinking of indivisible (simple) concepts or a compounding of concepts. Ibn Rushd (*Comm. Magnum*, ed. Crawford, pp. 454ff.) interprets this passage in terms of the distinction between *formatio* (*taṣawwur*) and *fides* (*taṣdīq*). As Wolfson (*loc. cit.*) points out, the coupling of intellect with *formatio* (*taṣawwur*) has no precedent in Aristotle. Ibn Bājja emphasizes the intellect's function of *taṣawwur* without referring to *taṣdīq*. He seems to follow Alexander of Aphrodisias' *De anima*, where the activity of the intellect is invariably spoken of as νόησις or νοεῖν, both of which terms are rendered in the Hebrew version by *ṣiyyūr sikhlī*, reflecting the Arabic *taṣawwur* in the original text. Cf. A. Günsz' edition of Alexander's *De anima*, p. 6, line 6 = ed. Bruns, p. 83, line 12; p. 7, line 18 = p. 84, line 22; p. 13, line 24 = p. 89, line 22. On the Latin terms *intellectus*, *imaginatio*, and *significatio* for *taṣawwur* cf. M. Alonso, *Al-Andalus*, XX (1955), pp. 142, 368–369.

[32] For the meaning of this term see below p. 106 and notes 124–125.

relation of that intelligible which serves as its substratum to the individual [sc. material form] thereof with the result that the intelligible of that kind [sc. the universal form] will be an intermediate term in the relation. Hence man conjoins with that intelligible of the third [sc. the ultimate] grade only through the first intelligible and will see it through it [sc. the first intelligible]."[33] Elaborating further, Ibn Bājja says: "Thus man has first the spiritual form in its various degrees [i.e. in the various degrees of abstraction in common sense, imagination and memory]; then, through it, he conjoins with the intelligible; then, through this intelligible [which is still tied to the individual spiritual form] he conjoins with that ultimate intelligible. Hence the rise (*irtiqāʾ*) from the spiritual form resembles an ascension (*ṣuʿūd*)."[34]

If we discard the first of these three levels as belonging to the pre-intellectual stage, we are left with two grades; but we have noted before that Ibn Bājja subdivides the first of the two, and we thus arrive at a tripartite gradation at the intellectual level. This tripartite division is summed up in the following passage: "It is already clear from what I have said that there are three degrees (*manāzil*). The first of them is the stage (*martaba*) of the *vulgus* which is the natural stage, i.e. possessing the intelligible only *qua* tied to the material forms, and knowing it only through them, with them, from them, and for them. Into this category enter all practical arts. The second is speculative knowledge (*al-maʿrifa al naẓarīya*), which represents the climax of the natural stage, except

[33] *Op cit.*, 13, p. 17 [36–37].

[34] *Op. cit.*, 13, p. 17 [37]. Alexander of Aphrodisias describes the transition from the perception of individuals to the vision of universals as a *μετάβασις* (*De anima*, ed. Bruns, p. 85, line 21). The Hebrew version (ed. Günsz, p. 8, line 20) renders this term by *ʿalīyyā*, which suggests *ṣuʿūd* or *irtiqāʾ* in the Arabic text. In the *De intellectu* (ed. Bruns, p. 108, lines 19–21) Alexander himself describes the process of intellection as an ascent: "This intelligible in its own nature and intellect *in actu*, having become the cause of the material intellect's abstracting and imitating [sc. the Agent Intellect] and thinking also each one of the material forms and making them too intelligibles by raising them (*κατὰ . . . ἀναφορὰν*) towards a suchlike form, is called the Agent Intellect from without." The extant Arabic version of this passage (ed. J. Finnegan in *Mélanges de L'Université Saint Joseph*, XXXIII, 2 [Beyrouth, 1956], p. 186, lines 2–5) is corrupt, and the rendition of the phrase "by raising them" is missing (see Finnegan, n. 10). But its equivalent did occur in the text, as is attested by Ibn Rushd's quotation of it in *Comm. Magnum* (ed. Crawford, p. 484): "*Illud igitur intellectum per suam naturam . . . ascendendo apud illam formam . . .*" Ibn Bājja could, therefore, understand Alexander of Aphrodisias' description of the intellectual processes as an "ascent". The passage quoted above from *TrUnion* is reproduced by Ibn Rushd (*op. cit.*, p. 494) in a shortened form: "Et cum Philosophus ascenderit alia ascensione, considerando in intellecto inquantum intellectum, tunc intelliget substantiam abstractam."

that the *vulgus* contemplates the substrata [i.e. the material forms] in the first place and the intelligibles in the second place and for the sake of the substrata, whereas the speculative scientists contemplate the intelligibles in the first place and the substrata in the second place and for the sake of the intelligibles by way of analogy. For this reason they contemplate the intelligible in the first place, yet together with the intelligible [they contemplate also] the material forms . . . The third is the stage of the felicitous (*al-suʿadā*), i.e. of those who see the thing itself."[35]

2. THE SIMILES OF LIGHT AND SUN

Aristotle had used the simile of light in order to describe the function of the Agent Intellect in producing the universals.[36] As Themistius noted, his use of imagery is different from that of Plato. Whilst Plato employs the image of the sun which denotes a unitary being—it is identical with the Good—Aristotle is content to speak of "light" which in a sense is one and in another sense is diffused into many.[37] Al-Fārābī slightly modifies the imagery of both Plato and Aristotle by introducing the concept of light in terms of "rays" emanating from the sun. "For this intellect [sc. the Agent Intellect] imparts to the material intellect—which is but potential intellect—something which is like the ray imparted to vision by the sun . . . The sun imparts to vision a ray by which it becomes illumined, and also imparts to colours a ray by which they become illumined . . . Likewise that intellect which is actual [sc. the Agent Intellect] imparts to the material intellect something which it impresses upon the latter."[38] Ibn Bājja reverts to the simile of "light" in order to explain the function of the Agent Intellect as the cause for the abstraction of universals from matter but takes up the image of the sun when portraying the stages of intellection in their entirety. In comparing the activity of the Agent Intellect at the penultimate stage to the light, he uses, like al-Fārābī, the notion of an "impression" produced in the eye. "It [sc. the Agent Intellect] is something that resembles more the light [sc. than the sun] . . . The faculty in which the intelligible is impressed resembles the eye. The [act of] intellect resembles vision,

[35] *Op. cit.*, 15, pp. 18–19 [38–39].
[36] *De anima*, III, 5, 430a, 16.
[37] *Themistii . . . De Anima Paraphrasis*, ed. R. Heinze (1899), p. 103, lines 34–36.
[38] *Madīna*, p. 44 [70]; *Risāla fi'l-ʿAql*, pp. 25-7; *Siyāsat* p. 7 (Hebrew, p. 5).

which is the form impressed in the visual sense. And just as that form exists through the light, since it is the light which causes it to exist *in actu*, and, through it, it impresses itself in the [visual] sense, so likewise the intellect *in actu* becomes something and impresses itself in the faculty by virtue of that Intellect which has no individual substratum related to it . . . What the physical light is in regard to the sensible form, it [sc. the Agent Intellect] is in regard to the intelligibles: it is in some respect light by way of analogy."[39] In another place: "It is it [sc. the Agent Intellect] that produces the universals, and when it illumines something natural, the universality thereof becomes visible."[40]

Though Ibn Bājja does make use of the Aristotelian simile of the Agent Intellect as "light", the Platonic image of the "sun" is much more prominently in evidence. The *Letter of Farewell* describes the three stages of the ascent from the pre-intellectual to the ultimate level in terms of varying degrees of beholding the sun. "For we do not see it [sc. the Agent Intellect] in itself (*bi-dhātihi*) but see it together with something else [sc. related to matter], just as we see the sun, e.g. while we are [submerged] in the water, and see it afterwards while we are in the air; and the air is sometimes dense and dark, and sometimes pure. For we cannot see that Intellect in itself but we see its trace (*athar*) in something else. And therefore we see it in some intelligibles with a vision which is near to its essence, and in others with a vision more remote, and those who see it do so with a vision varying in degree. As for the vision (*ru'yā*) of its essence—if it be possible—it is, therefore, like the vision of the sun without an intermediary—if that were possible— or through an intermediary which leaves no trace in the vision thereof—if this exists."[41] The three levels are also described as those of darkness, shadow, and clear daylight. There is an unmistakable tinge of neoplatonic thought in a sentence like the following: "And he goes out from the absolute darkness—the state of the irrational animal—and from the state of the shadow which is darkness in some degree—the state of the rational animal— . . . and comes-to-be in a state at which one sees in a clear atmosphere without the humidity with which it is sometimes mixed."[42] Seeing the Intellect in itself (*bi-dhātihi*) is like seeing the sun and constitutes the final goal of the ascent.[43] The description of that ultimate

[39] *TrUnion*, 16, p. 19 [39–40].
[40] *LFarewell*, 25, p. 35 [79].
[41] *Op. cit.*, 27, p. 37 [81].
[42] *Op. cit.*, 27, pp. 36–37 [81].
[43] *Op. cit.*, 27, p. 37 [81–82].

stage is, again, entirely neoplatonic. "Know also that one to whom this degree (*rataba*) is vouchsafed comes-to-be in a state in which neither nature will assail him nor the bestial soul will combat him. In that state in which there is release (*khalāṣ*) from these two combatants—i.e. nature and bestiality—he knows a state which cannot be described by reference to anything greater than it. This state is such that its grandeur, nobility, pleasure and delight defy language."[44]

In the *Treatise on Union* the simile is slightly changed by the introduction of the concept of reflected light. "Those who belong to the speculative stage see the intelligible [only] through a medium, even as the sun appears [reflected] in the water; for what is seen in the water is the image thereof, not he [= the sun] himself. And the *vulgus* see [only] the image of his image, just as when the sun, e.g. casts his image upon the water and this is [then] reflected in a mirror . . . The third is the stage of the felicitous, i.e. of those who see the thing itself." The same image occurs somewhat modified in a subsequent passage: "One whose body's leader is the spiritual form of whatever class, as explained in the *Book of the Solitary*, will perish and decay; he resembles an unpolished surface in which the light is mixed in a diffused manner. One in whom the second, intermediate stage arises resembles thereby a polished surface like the surface of a mirror which can itself be seen and in which others can be seen. He is nearer to liberation than those of the first grade but is still in a corruptible condition. One who has reached the third grade resembles thereby the sun itself. For this stage there is no comparison possible with material bodies . . . He is no longer in any manner material." This third and highest stage, "and only it", "is one from every aspect, imperishable and incorruptible".[45]

A novel feature introduced in the simile just quoted is the

[44] *Op. cit.*, 29, p. 38 [82–83].

[45] *Op. cit.*, 15, pp. 18–19 [39]; 19, p. 21 [44]. The image of the polished . . . mirror is widespread in neoplatonic literature. It is reflected in Ibn Sīnā's doctrine of the polishing of the soul's mirror to enable it to receive the emanation of the intelligible forms from the Agent Intellect. Cf. F. Rahman, *Avicenna's Psychology*, pp. 116–117; *Prophecy in Islam*, p. 32; *Ibn Sīnā, Livre des Directives et Remarques*, Traduction . . . par A.-M.Goichon (1951), p. 331 and n. 4. The simile is quoted by Ibn Rushd in *Epitome*, ed. Ahwani, p. 73 (see also pp. 66, 84). The simile of the soul as a mirror which reflects the Divine Truth only when adequately polished is a favourite theme also with al-Ghazālī (cf. *Iḥyāʾ ʿulūm al-din* (Cairo, A. H. 1356–1357), III, i, *et passim*). Ibn Bājja's simile of the spiritual forms as the body's "leader" (*raʾis*) reflects Plotinus' statement, "The sensitive principle is our scout (ἄγγελος), intellect is our king" (*Enneads*, V, iii, 3).

identification, at the ultimate stage, of the beholder with the sun. Translated into the doctrine of intellect, this means that at this level the conjunction of man's intellect with the Agent Intellect becomes complete. This motif is accentuated in Ibn Bājja's use of Plato's cave image. The first stage, i.e. that of the *vulgus*, Ibn Bājja says, resembles the condition of those who employ their faculty of vision inside the cave. "They do not see the sun but see all the colours in the shade. One who is in the interior of the cave sees in a manner resembling [seeing in] darkness; and one [placed] at the entrance of the cave sees the colours in the shade." We interpret this to mean that at the pre-intellectual level, i.e. that of "spiritual forms", vision varies from darkness to shade in accordance with the various degrees of abstraction possible at that stage. Those at the second stage, i.e. that of the speculative scientist, "occupy the position of such as are outside the cave in the open air: the light which is free from colours shines for them, and so they see all colours in their true being". As for those at the third stage, i.e. the "felicitous ones", "there is nothing in vision resembling them, since they become the thing itself [i.e. the light by which they see]. If it were possible to compare their condition with the condition of those who see [sc. the physical light] so as to become light [themselves], the analogy would be perfect [lit. 'such would be the condition of those felicitous ones']. The allegory (*al-alghāz*) of the condition of the felicitous in terms of the condition of one who sees the sun itself [which would be congruous with the use of Plato's cave image] is not analogous to the allegory of the condition of the *vulgus*. But the allegory of the condition of the *vulgus* is much more analogous and closer [to the image of physical vision] than the [other] one. For Plato, on the other hand, supposing as he does the [real existence of the] Forms, the allegory of the condition of the felicitous in terms of the condition of those seeing the sun is analogous to the allegory of the condition of the *vulgus*, and thus his allegory is analogous in all its parts."[46] In other words, Plato's cave image is, according to Ibn Bājja, not applicable in all its parts. The felicitous do not, as in Plato, see the sun itself because for Ibn Bājja the Forms or Ideas are not "things" which can be made objects of an intellection. The Forms or Ideas, Ibn Bājja explains, are the *intentiones* or "meanings" (*maʿānī*) of the forms abstracted from matter. They are the ultimate quiddities and

[46] *Op. cit.*, 17, pp. 19–20 [41–42].

as such of an ontological order, yet they are not self-subsisting things, as Plato assumed them to be, but are one with the Agent Intellect. Plato made the quiddity of the thing into a thing, whereas the intelligible is not a thing. Otherwise the idea of fire would burn just as fire burns.[47] Since, however, these pure forms are not "things" but have their reality in the Agent Intellect, they cannot be contemplated by the felicitous in a manner analogous to visualising the sun but can be comprehended only when the human intellect becomes one with the Agent Intellect. The ultimate stage is therefore one of conjunction or union.

3. IS THE ULTIMATE STAGE A NATURAL PERFECTION OR DIVINE GIFT?

In the *Treatise on Union* Ibn Bājja pictures the ascent from the intellection of material forms to that of pure forms as a natural development. This is clearly suggested by the phrase, "Then the physicist performs yet another ascension in that he contemplates the intelligibles not *qua* intelligibles denoted as material or spiritual but *qua* intelligibles which are one of the existents of the world."[48] The final stage, Ibn Bājja insists, can be reached only *via* the preceding ones, i.e. through the forms obtained in sense perception, imagination and intellection.[49] Ibn Rushd quotes this passage in his *Long Commentary* and infers from it that Ibn Bājja regarded the ultimate stage as a "natural possibility" and as "a part of the speculative sciences [sc. natural science]".[50] What he means by "a part of the speculative sciences" is obviously to be taken *cum grano salis*, since Ibn Bājja is emphatic in elevating the ultimate stage above that of the speculative scientist. Ibn Rushd, no doubt, means to say that according to Ibn Bājja's view in the passage quoted the final stage arises naturally from the penultimate one. This is also the way in which Ibn Ṭufail interprets Ibn Bājja. Paraphrasing the description of the ultimate stage in the *Treatise on Union*, Ibn Ṭufail characterises this stage as one "arrived at by the road of speculative science (*al-ʿilm al-naẓarī*) and by rational

[47] *Op. cit.*, 18, p. 20 [42]. [48] *Op. cit.*, 12, p. 17 [36].

[49] "Thus man has first the spiritual form in its various degrees; then, through it, he conjoins with the intelligible; then, through that intelligible he conjoins with that ultimate intelligible . . . Hence the conjunction with the intelligibles by the natural method is like the intermediate term of the ascent" (*TrUnion*, 13, p. 17 [37]).

[50] *Comm. Magnum*, ed. Crawford, p. 494.

investigation (*al-baḥth al-fikrī*)".[51] His paraphrase of Ibn Bājja's account reads: "When one has understood the desired object [sc. the Agent Intellect], it is manifest thereby that it is impossible for any one of the ordinary objects of knowledge to be of its level. What is conceived of it comes-to-be through the understanding of that object on a level at which one sees himself different from all that went before; with other beliefs which are not material, too sublime to be related to the natural life; cleansed of the composition of the natural life; worthy to be called 'divine states' (*aḥwāl ilāhīya*); granted by God to him who pleases Him amongst His servants. And this rank, which Abu Bakr [Ibn Bājja] points out, is arrived at by the method of speculative science and rational investigation, and there is no doubt that he reached it and did not miss it."[52]

One will note that Ibn Ṭufail, although describing the ultimate stage as resulting from the previous ones, introduces the concept of a special Divine favour by which the ultimate perfection is "granted". This raises the question as to whether Ibn Bājja did in fact consider the ultimate perfection to depend on a Divine favour. According to Ibn Rushd's observation in the passage quoted,[53] Ibn Bājja's view in the matter is not consistent. Whereas in the *Treatise on Union* he upholds the entirely natural character of the ultimate stage, he expresses a different view in the *Letter of Farewell*. "And Ibn Bājja seems to be ambiguous concerning this topic. For in the *Letter* which he called that *of Farewell* he said that possibility is twofold: natural and divine, i.e. that the intellection of that Intellect belongs to the divine possibility, not to the natural one."[54] The passage in the *Letter of Farewell* referred to reads as follows:

> Our Saints who preceded us said that possibility is of two kinds: of a natural kind and a divine one. The natural kind is one which perceives through science, and man can obtain information about it by his spontaneous effort. As for the divine kind, it perceives only through Divine help. Therefore God has sent the messengers and appointed the prophets in order that they may inform us, the society of men, of the divine possibilities, since He, His name be exalted, desired the perfection of that of His gifts which is the most valued for men, i.e. science. The revealed laws (*al-sharāʾiʿ*) invite, in effect, the exercise of science, and in our Divine Revelation there are sayings which point to this such as the passage where He, His name be exalted, says in the

51 *Ḥayy ben Yaqdhan*, ed. Gauthier, p. 5 [4].
52 *Ibid.*
53 See note 50.
54 *Ibid.*

revealed Book[55]: "And those firmly rooted in knowledge say: We believe in it; all is from our Lord", i.e. the divine possibilities. And His saying, be He exalted and praised[56]: "Even so only those of His servants who have knowledge fear God." For one who knows God with a true knowledge knows that the greatest misery is His anger and the distance from Him, and the greatest felicity (*saᶜd*) is His benevolence . . . and being near to Him. And man will not be near to Him except through the knowledge of the essence thereof [sc. of the Intellect].

Ibn Bājja quotes in support of his exegesis *a ḥadīth*:

God created Intellect and said to it: Advance! and it advanced. Then He said to it: Return! and it returned. And He said: By My power and majesty, I have created no creature more amiable to Me than you.[57] Hence Intellect is the most amiable of existing things to God, be He exalted and praised, and when man comes-to-be that Intellect itself (*bi-ᶜainihi*), without any difference between the two in any way or from any aspect, he will be the most amiable of creatures to Him . . . And his most exalted grade is that at which a man forms a concept of his own essence so as to form a concept of that Intellect about which we spoke before.[58]

It is clear from the above passage that in the *Letter of Farewell* Ibn Bājja regards the ultimate stage as a result not of man's "spontaneous effort" but as a gift from God. The same view is expressed in one of his minor treatises: "And when the Divine gift (*mawhiba*) emanates (*faḍat*) upon him, he sees by his rational faculty that gift, just as through the faculty of the eye the light of the sun is seen by the light of the sun, and the proximate cause for the perception (*idrāk*) of the intelligibles and of the rational faculty coming-to-be *in actu* is the Divine gift, like the light of the sun; and by it he has vision and sees the creatures of God, be He exalted, so that he becomes one who believes in God and His angels and His book."[59] In fact, the *Treatise on Union* too contains a passage in which the ultimate stage, notwithstanding its being the result of the preceding stage, is described in similar terms. It reads:

It is evident that this Intellect which is numerically one is a gift (*thawāb*) of God and His benefaction to those of His servants that

[55] *Al-Qurʾān*, 3:5. Ibn Bājja seems to interpret this verse in a way different from Ibn Rushd's in *Faṣl al-Maqāl*, ed. L. Gauthier (1948), pp. 10, 12, 42 (n. 25), 43 (n. 31).

[56] *Al-Qurʾān*, 35:25.

[57] See below, pp. 98–99.

[58] *LFarewell*, 30, pp. 38–39 [84–85].

[59] Quoted from the Bodleian ms. (fol. 136*v*) by M. S. Hasan in *Majallat*, XXXIII, p. 105, n. 1.

> please Him well, and therefore it is not "reward" or "punishment" (?) but the gift and benefaction for the totality (*majmū*ᶜ) of the faculties of the soul, whereas reward and punishment are only for the appetitive soul which is the one that sins or does the right thing. One who obeys God and does what pleases Him He will reward by this Intellect and for him He will make a light in front of him by which to be guided. And one who disobeys Him, and does what does not please Him He will deprive of it [sc. the Intellect] so that he will remain in the darkness of his ignorance that encompasses him until he is separated from the body, deprived of it [sc. the Intellect], and becomes a perpetual object of His anger. There are degrees of this which reason (*fikra*) does not perceive. Hence God has completed the knowledge thereof in the revealed law (*sharī*ᶜ*a*). And to one to whom He has granted that Intellect some light will remain which praises God and sanctifies Him, when he is separated from the body, in the company of the prophets, the righteous, the martyrs and the saints. What a beautiful company![60]

It may be due to this passage that in his Summary of the *Treatise on Union* (ed. Ahwani, p. 95) Ibn Rushd, contrary to his interpretation of it in the *Long Commentary*, describes Ibn Bājja's view of the ultimate stage as being entirely a Divine gift and not a natural perfection.[61] He insists, however, that the state of union (*ittiḥād*) achieved at this level is inconceivable without the preceding stages. He is at pains to make it clear that Ibn Bājja's view of the "Divine gift" (*mawhiba ilāhīya*) is radically different from the Sūfī concept of union. "This state of union is what the Sūfīs desire. And it is clear that they never arrived at it, since for arriving at it the knowledge of the speculative sciences is necessary. They perceived of these things only something resembling those perceptions, such as the union (*ijtimā*ᶜ) of the three faculties [sc. the three internal senses], and some other things besides."[62] This re-echoes Ibn Bājja's severe criticism of al-Ghazālī's alleged doctrine of union in the *Letter of Farewell*.[63] Ibn Ṭufail,[64] on the other hand, takes Ibn Bājja to task for his rebuke of al-Ghazālī. He distinguishes Ibn Bājja's ultimate stage from the truly mystical one as

[60] *TrUnion*, 7, p. 14 [32].

[61] The passage quoted in note 49 may have likewise suggested to him that the ultimate stage is a "Divine gift", seeing that it describes only the "intermediate term of the ascent" as a conjunction "by the natural method".

[62] *Epitome*, ed. Ahwani, p. 95.

[63] 8, pp. 21–22 [53–55]. See also *RegSol*, p. 27 [59–60] and M. Asín Palacios' notes 52 and 54.

[64] *Ḥayy ben Yaqdhan*, ed. Gauthier, pp. 5–8 [4–6].

described by al-Ḥallāj, al-Ghazālī and Ibn Sīnā. But he points out that even in the mystical experience nothing is revealed which differs from the natural, speculative, i.e. discursive thinking, except that things are seen with greater clarity. He illustrates this by the simile of the blind-born who, thanks to the other senses, knows everything appertaining to his environment except colours. Supposing his eyes were suddenly opened, he would still find himself in the same world he knows, except that he would know the things he knew before with a greater clarity. Those who engage in the speculative sciences are in the position of the blind. The colours which, in this state, he knows only by name are the things of which Ibn Bājja says that they are too sublime to be related to the material life, and which God grants to him with whom He is pleased. It is not clear whether Ibn Ṭufail equates the highest stage described by Ibn Bājja with the mystical-ecstatic stage described by the Sūfīs. On the one hand, he clearly sets off one against the other: Ibn Bājja's "perception" (*idrāk*) is the speculative one, whereas the Sūfī method is the method of familiarity with God (*wilāya*), which is the way of ecstasy.[65] On the other hand, it is difficult to understand how Ibn Ṭufail accounts for Ibn Bājja's description of the ultimate stage which hardly differs from the usual accounts of the mystical experience of union. When he says that Ibn Bājja reached the stage described by him as the ultimate one,[66] he must have had in mind a stage other than the ecstatic one. For later he reproaches Ibn Bājja for having censured al-Ghazālī, having himself never experienced the ecstatic state. "Do not call sweet the taste of something you have not tasted."[67] The mystical colour of Ibn Bājja's description of the ultimate stage will be apparent from the following passage: "At this highest grade, the faculties of the soul are affected in a powerful way. In imagination there arises something analogous to that Intellect, i.e. a light which, when diffused into a thing, shows everything else in a manner which cannot be expressed or which it is difficult to express. In the appetitive soul there arises at this stage a condition similar to fear, and resembling a certain state when something tremendous and beautiful is perceived by the senses. This condition is called stupefaction. The Sūfīs have given exaggerated descriptions of this state."[68] It is clear that to Ibn Bājja the ultimate stage,

[65] On the term *wilāya* see Gauthier's note 2, p. 6. [66] *Op. cit.*, p. 5 [4].
[67] *Op. cit.*, p. 10 [8]. [68] *TrUnion*, 21, pp. 21–22 [45–46].

although based on the preceding one, represents a mystical experience not far in its effects upon the soul from what the Ṣūfīs claim to experience in the state of union.

4. THE ACQUIRED INTELLECT

The ultimate stage described by Ibn Bājja is identical with the "acquired intellect" (*al-ᶜaql al-mustafād*). This identity is expressed in such terms as "the ultimate science which is the forming of a concept (*taṣawwur*) of Intellect, i.e. the existence (*wujūd*) of the acquired intellect"[69] which has an exact parallel in the Hebrew paraphrase of the missing Arabic section at the end of the *Regimen of the Solitary*: "The formation of an intellectual concept, i.e. the existing intellect which is intellect *in actu*, i.e. the existence of the intellect that has emanated [=acquired intellect], which most of all things resembles the Agent Intellect, and this form that has emanated has no relation to matter except in another sense, viz. that it perfects the material intelligibles."[70] In another passage: "This acquired intellect is *one* from every aspect, and it is at the extreme of remoteness from matter."[71] When Ibn Bājja describes the ultimate end as the intellection of the "simple substantial intellects",[72] he thinks of the stage of the acquired intellect when man becomes a simple substantial intellect himself and is "divine, simple".[73]

In the ultimate science, i.e. at the stage of the acquired intellect, intellect and intelligible are one. At this stage, "the first substratum [the subject of intellection] is the form, and it is a substratum from one aspect and the thing [object of intellection] from another; therefore it is intellect and intelligible in a certain sense, apart from the things said about it in the books on the intellect. But in the [speculative] sciences the object of intellection (*al-maᶜqūl*) is different from the intellect (*al-ᶜaql*), and the knower (*al-ᶜālim*) is other than the known (*al-maᶜlūm*)[74] In the *Treatise on Union*,[75] Ibn Bājja refers, in addition to "the writings of others on this [subject]" to what he himself had explained in his *Book on the Soul*[76] concerning the identity of the intellect *in actu* and the

[69] *LFarewell*, 15, p. 30 [69]. See n. 24.

[70] Ms. Bodl. Or 116, fol. 127*r*, col. b; ed. Herzog, p. 20, lines 13–17. Cf. *RegSol*, p. 19 [50].

[71] *LFarewell*, 29, p. 38 [84].

[72] *RegSol*, pp. 61–62 [100–101].

[73] *Ibid.*

[74] *LFarewell*, 15, p. 30 [69].

[75] 5, p. 13 [20].

[76] Not preserved in the extant text.

intelligible *in actu*. The fact that identity is here ascribed to intellect *in actu* and intelligible *in actu*, without distinguishing between the intellection of material and pure forms, need not disturb us. Alexander of Aphrodisias too states that in every act of intellection, i.e. even in the intellection of material forms, the intellect is but the intelligible form[77]—which is good Aristotelian doctrine—and yet differentiates between the partial identity in the case of the intellection of material forms and the total identity in the case of intellection of non-material forms. Only in the latter case does the whole object of intellection enter into identity with the intellect.[78] Ibn Bājja would seem to follow Alexander of Aphrodisias' treatment of the subject. But he introduces, in addition, a number of fresh aspects into the discussion of the nature and attributes of intellection at the ultimate stage.

Describing the highest stage of intellection, i.e. that of the acquired intellect, in the *Treatise on Union*[79] he interprets the identity of intellect and intelligible to be due to the fact that the "intention" or "meaning" (*maᶜnā*) which is made an object of intellection *is* a meaning but does not *have* meaning. "As the contemplation (*naẓar*) of a thing and its being an object of intellection consist only in the contemplation as coming-to-be the meaning of the thing and its abstraction from its matter; and as the meaning which one wishes to make an object of intellection *is* a meaning but does not *have* a meaning, [it follows that] the act (*fiᶜl*) of that intellect is identical with its substance (*jawhar*), and it will not be possible for it to decay or corrupt." This somewhat obscure statement receives light from a passage in Ibn Rushd from which it appears that Ibn Bājja had explained the point more fully in the *Book on the Soul*.[80] Ibn Rushd reports that "In the *Book on the Soul* . . . he [sc. Ibn Bājja] assumed first that if it were not conceded by us that the quiddity of the object of intellection *qua* object of intellection has no quiddity . . . and if it were said that the quiddity of that object of intellection *qua* object of intellection also has a quiddity . . . and if it were not conceded by us that quiddity is simple and that the being which comes from it is identical with the intellect, . . . this would necessarily go on *in infinitum* or, alternatively, intellect will have to make a stop (lit. 'be cut off', *secetur*) here. But as it is impossible for this to go on *in infinitum*, . . . it is necessary for the in-

[77] Ed. Bruns, p. 86, lines 14ff.
[78] Ed. Bruns, p. 87, lines 24ff.
[79] 14, pp. 17–18 [38].
[80] Again, the passage is not preserved in our text.

tellect to make a stop. Now, when stopped, it will either arrive at a quiddity which has no quiddity or else at something having a quiddity which, however, intellect is not naturally equipped to extract . . . But it is impossible to find a quiddity which intellect is not naturally equipped to extract from a quiddity . . . It therefore remains . . . that intellect arrives at a quiddity which has no [further] quiddity; and what is suchlike is an abstract form."[81] Ibn Rushd adds that Ibn Bājja followed Aristotle's rule which prescribes that "whenever it is necessary to preclude (*abscindere*) the infinite, it is better to do so in the beginning".[82] It is obvious that the term "intention" or "meaning" (*maᶜnā*) as used in the *Treatise on Union* corresponds to the term "quiddity" in the text just quoted.[83]

Ibn Bājja's point is that if an infinite regress is to be avoided, we might as well consider the quiddity of universals as the ultimate quiddity and as identical with the abstract, i.e. immaterial forms which appertain to the Agent Intellect, and which are apprehended at the stage of the acquired intellect. According to Ibn Rushd's report, which is reproduced in Thomas Aquinas (see above, p. 75), this represents one of Ibn Bājja's proofs for the possibility of knowing the separate intellects. (For the other proof see below, p. 102.) We quote the relevant passage from Thomas Aquinas (*Summa contra Gentiles*, III, 41; see also *Summa Theol.*, qu. 88, a. 2):

> Avempace maintained that by the study of the speculative sciences it is possible to arrive at a knowledge of separate substances from understanding those things which we know through phantasms. For we are able by the action of the intellect to extract the quiddity of a thing which has quiddity without being its own quiddity. For the intellect is naturally adapted to know any quiddity as such, since the proper object of the intellect is what a thing is. Now if that which is first understood by the possible intellect is something that has a quiddity, we can, by the possible intellect, abstract the quiddity of the thing first understood; and if this quiddity has again a quiddity, it will be again possible to abstract the quiddity of this quiddity. And since we cannot go on indefinitely, we must stop somewhere. Therefore by way of analysis our intellect can arrive at knowing a quiddity that has no quiddity; and such is the quiddity of a separate substance. Consequently, through its knowledge of these sensible things, acquired

[81] *Comm. Magnum*, ed. Crawford, pp. 491–492.
[82] *Ibid.*
[83] Similarly in *LFarewell*, 26, p. 36 [80].

from phantasms, our intellect can arrive at understanding separate substances (translation by Anton C. Pegis, *Basic Writings of Saint Thomas Aquinas*, II, 66–67).

Saint Thomas objects to this proof (1) that the quiddity of a universal (genus or species) includes both matter and form; consequently it is unlike the quiddity of a separate substance, which is simple and immaterial; (2) that the quiddity of a genus or species in the case of sensible things cannot be separated, in its very being, from a particular individual matter; unless, as the Platonists think, we suppose the essences of things to exist separately; consequently, the aforesaid quiddity is altogether different from separate substances, which are in no way matter; (3) even granting that the quiddity of a separate substance is of the same kind as the quiddity of a universal, it cannot be said to be of the same specific kind, unless we say that the essences of the sensible things are identical with the separate substances. These objections reflect Ibn Rushd's remark that Ibn Bājja's reasoning could be maintained only on the assumption of the univocity of the term "quiddity" as applied to material things and abstract intellects (*Comm. Magnum*, ed. Crawford, p. 493). From our previous analysis of Ibn Bājja's doctrine it is clear that the criticism offered fails to take into account Ibn Bājja's insistence that at the ultimate stage the intelligible is no longer a universal but achieves the status of a separate intellect. How this transformation is possible can be fully understood only when Ibn Bājja's theory of "conjunction" is taken into account (see below, section 5). It will then become clear that the achievement of knowing the pure intelligibles or separate intellects is due to the Agent Intellect's taking full possession of man, and that this happens only when as a result of an existential break with the world of matter even the universal relation of the intelligibles is discarded.

The passage in the *Treatise on Union* (§14) introduces, in its concluding sentence, a further aspect; "in it [sc. the act of intellection] the mover will be the very same as the moved, and will, according to what Alexander of Aphrodisias said in his book *On the Spiritual Forms*, return upon itself".[84] The reference is to the treatise "On the Proof [of the Existence] of the Spiritual Forms which have no Matter", the eighth of ten treatises ascribed to Alexander of Aphrodisias.[85] S. Pines and B. Lewin have shown that the treatise

[84] Pages 17–18 [38].

[85] Published by A. Badawi in his *Aristū ͑inda ͗l-͑Arab* (Cairo, 1947), pp. 257–308.

concerned represents an Arabic version of propositions 15, 16 and 17 of Proclus' *The Elements of Theology* (ed. by E. R. Dodds, Oxford, 1933, pp. 16ff.).[86] Ibn Bājja's quotation is taken from propositions 15 and 16 which affirm that all that is capable of reverting upon itself is incorporeal (*ἀσώματος*; *rūḥānī*), and has an existence separable from the body. His formula of the identity of mover and moved occurs in proposition 17. A juxtaposition of the parallels in the texts concerned will show Ibn Bājja's close dependence on his source:

Proclus	Ps.-Alexander of Aphr. (ed. Badawi, pp. 291–292)	Ibn Bājja, *Tr. Union* §14
15. *Πᾶν τὸ πρὸς ἑαυτὸ ἐπιστρεπτικὸν ἀσώματόν ἐστιν* 17. *Πᾶν τὸ ἑαυτὸ κινοῦν πρώτως πρὸς ἑαυτό ἐστιν ἐπιστρεπτικόν. εἰ γὰρ κινεῖ ἑαυτό, καὶ ἡ κινητικὴ ἐνέργεια αὐτοῦ πρὸς ἑαυτό ἐστι καὶ ἓν ἅμα τὸ κινοῦν καὶ τὸ κινούμενον*	*inna kulla mā rajaᶜa ilā dhātihi fa-huwa rūḥānīyyun ghairu jirmīyyin* *qāla: kullu mā kāna muḥarrikan li-dhātihi innahu awallan huwa rājiᶜun ilā dhātihi lā maḥālata. wa-dhalika annahu in kāna yuḥarriku dhātahu wa-kāna fiᶜluhu muḥarrikan li-dhātihi kāna lā maḥālata al-muḥarriku waʾlʾmutaḥarriku wāḥidan*	*wa-kāna . . . rājiᶜan ᶜalā nafsihi bi-an wa-yujarridahu ᶜan hayūlāhu* *wa-kāna al-muḥarriku fī-hi huwa al-muḥarraku biᶜaynihi*

As E. R. Dodds has pointed out,[87] "these three propositions logically prepare the way for the proof that the soul is incorporeal and independent of the body, and therefore imperishable". Ibn Bājja, too, connects the notion of the self-reverting nature of the intellect and of the identity of mover and moved with the concept of the intellect as a substance that "neither decays, or corrupts".[88]

[86] S. Pines, "Une Version Arabe de Trois Propositions de la *Στοιχείωσις θεολογική* de Proclus" in *Oriens*, VIII, 2 (1955), pp. 195–203; B. Lewin, "Notes sur un text de Proclus en traduction arabe" in *Orientalia Suecana* (1955), pp. 101–107. On further Proclus texts in Arabic versions, cf. R. Walzer's review of Badawi's *Al-Aflāṭuniyya al-muḥdatha ᶜinda ʾl-ᶜArab* (Cairo, 1955) in *Oriens*, X, 2 (1957), pp. 393–395.

[87] *The Elements of Theology*, pp. 202ff.

[88] *TrUnion*, 14, p. 18 [38]

Of particular interest is the idea of the self-reverting, i.e. self-knowing, intellect. Dodds finds the connection between self-knowledge and separability already in Aristotle's *De anima* (430 b, 24): "But if there is anything which has no contrary, it is self-cognizant, actual, and separately existent." It is obvious, however, that Ibn Bājja derives this notion from the Proclus text ascribed to Alexander of Aphrodisias. He links it with Alexander of Aphrodisias' notion of the total self-knowledge found in the intellection of pure intelligibles,[89] i.e. at the ultimate level which is that of the acquired intellect. In the *Letter of Farewell*[90] the same motif is quoted from the *ḥadīth* (cited above, p. 90) which depicts God as having commanded intellect [sc. the Agent Intellect or, better still, the Plotinian *Νοῦς*]: "Advance!" and "Return!" Obviously, the "advance" and "return" of the intellect reflect the idea of the outgoing and self-reverting intellect. I. Goldziher already recognized the neoplatonic background of this *ḥadīth*[91] which is quoted as authoritative by al-Ghazālī in the *Iḥyāʾ ʿulūm al-dīn* (Cairo, 1312/1894–5, I, 69, 9) and by the commentator of the *Iḥyāʾ*, Sayyid Murtaḍā (Itḥāf I, 453–5).[92] Al-Ghazālī also incorporates it in a lengthy passage in his esoteric work *Kitāb al-maʿarif al-ʿaqlīyya* ("Book of the Intellectual Intuitions"),[93] where Intellect is described as the first of God's creations, followed by the Soul and Matter. The notion of Intellect is here linked with that of the Logos or Word (*kalima*), and H. S. Nyberg[94] was right in pointing out this particular background. But he failed to see the clearly neoplatonic flavour of the concept of the Intellect as such. According to Plotinus, the first movement of emanation at all stages, including that of the Intellect emanating from the One, is an outgoing process of pure, uninformed potentiality, while the second is a turning back to the source in contemplation, resulting in the substantiality and full reality of the emanant (cf. *Enneads*, III, viii, 4–5). The first phase is called by al-Ghazālī one of "acquiring"

[89] Cf. above, p. 94.

[90] 30, p. 39 [85].

[91] In his article, "Neuplatonische und gnostische Elemente im Hadit", *Zeitschrift für Assyriologie*, XXII (1908), pp. 318–321 (quoted by M. Asín Palacios in his edition of *LFarewell*, p. 85, n. 1).

[92] Cf. M. Asín Palacios, *La Espiritualidad de Algazel* (Madrid, 1936), III, p. 255, n. 1; Darió Cabanelas, "Un Opúsculo inedito de Algazel, El Libro de las Intuiciones Intelectuales," *Al-Andalus*, XXI (1956), p. 28.

[93] Cf. M. Asín Palacios, *op. cit.*, pp. 254–255, where the Arabic text is quoted and translated. Darió Cabanelas, *op. cit.*, p. 28, reproduces the translation.

[94] H. S. Nyberg, *Kleinere Schriften des Ibn Al-ʿArabī* (Leiden, 1919), pp. 107–108.

(*istifād*), sc. form and substance; the second is called one of acquisition (*fāda*), sc. full information:

> It [sc. the Intellect which is a "spiritual, simple, perceptive, perfect and perfecting substance"] advances towards Him [sc. God] in the [act of] acquiring, and retires (*adbara*) from Him with the acquisition, as is said in the tradition of the Prophet, may God bless him, "The first which God created was the Intellect (*al-ᶜaql*). He said to it: Advance! and it advanced. Then He said to it: Retire! and it retired. It advanced towards the Word (*kalima*) by the acquiring, and became solitary (*fa-tawaḥḥada*). Then it retired, and the Soul appeared with the acquisition, and it became paired. Matter was then produced by the direct action of Intellect and Soul, thus completing the number, according to the saying of tradition: The minimum sum is three.[95]

Behind this somewhat blurred account of the neoplatonic doctrine (plus the shadow of the Logos concept) lies the unmistakable notion of the Plotinian Intellect. It may be suggested that al-Ghazālī also wished to evoke the association of this concept with that of the "acquired intellect" (*al-ᶜaql al-mustafād*), seeing that he uses the terms *istifāda* and *fāda*. It is this text which Ibn Bājja probably had in mind when quoting the ḥadīth. But he connects the ḥadīth not so much with the Plotinian notion of the outgoing and returning Intellect as with the Proclus passage which we quoted. The "return" of the Intellect is identical, in his interpretation, with the act of self-reverting or self-knowledge. Similarly, one of Ibn Bājja's as yet unpublished minor treatises[96] describes the intellect as self-perceiving: "The intellect, however, perceives (*yudriku*), and perceives its perception through the same faculty." This is said to be in contrast to sense perception in which the perceiver is a body and in which the perception is distinct from the body that perceives: "The body is perceiving, but it is not perception at all . . . whereas it [sc. the intellect] is a perceiver which is identical with its perception. It is clear that this applies to a form which is not in matter." Although the intellect thus described is referred to as intellect *in actu*, the statement will apply in an unqualified sense only to the intellection of pure forms, i.e. to the acquired intellect, as we noted above (p. 93).

Another fresh aspect introduced by Ibn Bājja is that of the unity

[95] Our translation differs in some respects from the Spanish version offered by Asín and Cabanelas.

[96] "About the things through which one can know the Agent Intellect", ms. Pococke 206, fols. 128*v*–129*v* (made available to me with English translation and notes by Dr. S. M. Stern, Oxford).

of intellect. Intellect, at the ultimate stage, is numerically one in all men. Ibn Bājja first developed this doctrine in the *Book on the Soul* (unfortunately, the passage concerned is not preserved), as he himself testifies in the *Treatise on Union*.[97] At the time when he wrote the *Treatise* he was still preoccupied with the problem. "Considering the intelligibles *in actu*, whether everyone of them is numerically one or not; [and] if this be not the case, whether one or more of them are numerically one, we have already more than once discussed, and this has been explained in the *Book on the Soul*. When all I have said on this subject will be complete, I shall send it to you [sc. Ibn Bājja's correspondent]. I believe, however, that I ought to speak on this [subject] here to the extent which, I know, will remind you of what has been said previously." Ibn Bājja then goes on discussing some of the problems involved in the assumption of the unity of intellect. "I say, then, that when we assume every intelligible to be numerically one, there necessarily follows a view similar to the one held by the adherents of [the doctrine of] metempsychosis (*ahl al-tanāsukh*)." He explains this analogy by pointing out that if every intelligible were one in number, all men, irrespective of their intellectual efforts, would share the same intelligibles of the same quality, once they possessed the intelligible. There would, therefore, nothing be gained from study except the acquisition of a greater quantity of intelligibles. On the other hand, he argues, the contrary assumption denying the numerical unity of the intelligible involves no less absurd consequences. For on this assumption the intelligible possessed by me and you will have to have another intelligible in common; as this is again shared by me and you, there will be yet another intelligible held in common, and so *in infinitum*.[98] The answer to this antinomy is furnished by the realization that numerical unity obtains only at the ultimate stage when the intelligible is free from all relation to individual sense-data and to matter. "This [ultimate stage of the intellect], and it alone, is *one* in every respect, imperishable and incorruptible. At it alone all those who went before and those who will come after are numerically one."[99] In other words, only in the

[97] 8, pp. 14–15 [32–33]. Cf. also Ibn Rushd, *Comm. Magnum*, ed. Crawford, p. 491.
[98] *Ibid.*
[99] *TrUnion*, 20, p. 21 [45]. For a discussion of the prior stages to which the unity of intellect does not apply, see *op. cit.*, 9, pp. 15–16 [33–35]. The unity of the intellect is already assumed by Themistius, as O. Hamelin, *La Théorie de l'Intellect d'après Aristote et ses Commentateurs* (Paris, 1953), pp. 42–43 has shown.

acquired intellect—which is, as we shall see, but the Agent Intellect operating in man without any let or hindrance from matter—is the intelligible numerically one; a solution of the problem which Ibn Rushd criticized for failing to account for both the multiplicity and unity in the intellection of material intelligibles abstracted from matter (called by him the "speculative intellect" as distinct from the Agent Intellect in which there are only pure forms): "For the intellect which he [sc. Ibn Bājja] demonstrates in that Epistle called *The Union of the Intellect with Man* to be one, when he laboured to solve that question, is other than the Intellect which he demonstrated there to be also many, since the intellect which he demonstrated to be one is the Agent Intellect inasmuch as it is necessarily the form of the speculative intellect; the intellect, however, which he demonstrated to be many is the speculative intellect itself. But this name, viz. "intellect" is used equivocally of the speculative and Agent Intellect."[100] Ibn Rushd's own solution of the alleged antinomy is that an intelligible shared by a number of people is many in the substratum by which it is true, i.e. in the spiritual form residing in the imaginative faculty, and is one in the substratum by which it is an existing intelligible, i.e. in the material intellect.[101] For Ibn Bājja, who identifies the material intellect with the disposition (*istiᶜdād*) for the reception (*qubūl*) of the intelligibles which resides in the imaginative forms, this solution is impossible.[102] Nor does he use the term "intellect" equivocally, since the Agent Intellect is for him the only intellect *par excellence*, and the intelligible is numerically one as and when it is received as a pure intelligible shared with the Agent Intellect. This happens at the stage of the acquired intellect.

[100] *Comm. Magnum*, ed. Crawford, p. 412.

[101] *Op. cit.*, pp. 411–412.

[102] Ibn Bājja's doctrine of the material intellect requires a monograph of its own. Only scanty references to it are found in his extant writings but Ibn Rushd's *Epitome* of the *De anima* follows, on his own admission (ed. Ahwani, p. 90), Ibn Bājja's view in the matter and thus enables us to reconstruct in some measure his Master's doctrine as developed in the (lost) section of the *Kitāb al-Nafs* dealing with the rational faculty. In his *Comm. Magnum* on the *De anima* Ibn Rushd offers a critical account of Ibn Bājja's view of the material intellect (ed. Crawford, pp. 397–398, 400–401, 406). According to his account, Ibn Bājja's view differs from both Alexander's and Themistius' in that it identifies the material intellect with the imaginative forms in as much as they possess the "disposition" for the reception of the intelligibles. This doctrine goes back to Aristotle's statement that "the soul never thinks without an imaginative form" (*De anima*, III, 7, 431a, 16) and, possibly, to Simplicius who seems to have identified the potential intellect with imagination (see F. Rahman, *Prophecy in Islam*, p. 24). John Philoponus (*De anima*, ed. M. Hayduck, 523, line 27) says of imagination that it is also called "passive intellect".

Hence Ibn Bājja is able to employ the concept of the unity of the intellect as proof for the possibility of conjunction or—what amounts to the same—for the possibility of knowing separate intellects. This is how Thomas Aquinas understood him to have argued in his second proof (which, again, is not found in any of the extant texts and which Thomas, in this case, merely inferred from Ibn Rushd's critique):

> He [sc. Ibn Bājja] goes on to prove the same conclusion by another and similar way. Thus, he lays down that which we understand of a thing, for instance of a horse, is multiplied in me and in you only through the multiplication of the spiritual species, which are diverse in you and me. It follows, then, that an understood thing which is not clothed with any such form is the same in you and me. Now, as we have proved, the quiddity of the understood thing, which our intellect can abstract, has no spiritual and individual species... Therefore our intellect has a natural aptitude to understand a quiddity of which the thing understood is one for all: Such is the quiddity of a separate substance: Therefore our intellect has a natural aptitude to know separate substances" (*Summa contra Gentiles*, III, 41; translation by Pegis, *op. cit.*, p. 67).

The numerical unity of the intelligible implies the unity of all souls at the stage of the acquired intellect. The passage from the *Treatise on Union* (§20) quoted above draws this conclusion, and the same concept is introduced at the very outset of the discussion: "If present, past and future men were not numerically one, that intellect would not be one. In short, if there exists an intellect which is one in number, the individual persons possessing a suchlike intellect will all be numerically one."[103] Ibn Bājja illustrates this idea by the simile of the magnet. "It is like taking a magnet and covering it with [a layer of] wax. It will move one piece of iron and another piece. Then you might cover it with [a layer of] tar, and it will move the iron with the same [kind of] movement. Then you might cover it with other bodies, and all these bodies which are movers [of the iron] will be numerically one, as is the case with the pilot of a ship. The same is the case with this [intellect]; except that in respect of bodies it is impossible for each one of them to exist in all bodies simultaneously, whilst it is possible in respect of the intelligibles. This is what the adherents of the doctrine of metempsychosis believe, except that they fail to hit the target."[104]

[103] *TrUnion*, 6, p. 14 [31–32].

[104] *Ibid.*

The simile compares the Intellect to a magnet which remains identical and moves the iron irrespective of the material with which it is covered. Similarly, the pilot remains the same in relation to all parts of the ship. But these two movers, being bodies, cannot be in different bodies at the same time, whereas the intellect can. The adherents of the doctrine of metempsychosis failed to "hit the target", because they assumed only a migration of souls successively into different bodies, whereas even Bājja's doctrine teaches the simultaneous presence of Intellect in all souls.[105]

5. THE NATURE OF "CONJUNCTION" (*ittiṣāl*)

In the Aristotelian doctrine of the intellect, the concept of "con junction" does not appear.[106] The intellect "becomes" the intelligible, and since all becoming is a transition from potentiality to actuality, i.e. from matter to form, the intelligibles are, in a sense, the "form" of the potential intellect. This relationship of matter-form must, in the case of intellect, not be understood on the analogy of things composed of matter and form, as Alexander of Aphrodisias reminds us when introducing the term "material intellect" as an alternative term for "potential intellect".[107]

The notion of "conjunction" (*ittiṣāl*) derives from Plotinus. It reflects the term συνάπτειν (to conjoin)[108] which occurs in such passages as the following: "But since the souls are themselves

[105] The doctrine of the unity of all souls is referred to by Maimonides in connection with the Kalām argument from immortal souls (cf. H. A. Wolfson, "The Kalām Arguments for Creation in Saadia, Averroes, Maimonides and St. Thomas", *Saadia Anniversary Volume*, American Academy for Jewish Research, 1943, pp. 229–230): "Hence all souls are numerically one, as has been shown by Abu Bakr ibn al-Ṣāʾigh [Ibn Bājja] and by others who applied themselves with courage to speaking about these profound matters" (*Guide*, I, 74, 7; Munk, 434–435; see also I, 70; Munk, 328, n. 4, and additional note, p. 462). Maimonides obviously adopts this doctrine, as did Ibn Rushd, who thereby gave rise to the famous controversy in Latin scholasticism.

[106] Occasionally, Aristotle uses the term θιγγάνειν (to touch) in order to describe the act of thinking. Cf. *Met.* IX, 10, 1051b, p. 24 (see S. van den Bergh, *Die Epitome der Metaphysik des Averroes* (1924), p. 188). A.-M. Goichon (*Vocabulaires Comparés d'Aristote et d'Ibn Sīnā* (1939), p. 39) suggested that Ibn Sīnā's use of the term *ittiṣāl* in the sense of contact between the Agent Intellect and the soul reflects the Aristotelian term mentioned. But there is hardly any notion of "conjunction" implied in the Aristotelian term itself.

[107] Cf. *De intellectu*, ed. Bruns, p. 106, lines 20–23; Arabic text, ed. Finnegan, p. 181, lines 1–5.

[108] See E. Bréhier, *Plotin, Ennéades*, VI, 2, Index s.v.

intelligible . . . one has to think that the conjoining (*συνάπτειν*) of the intelligent (*τὸ νοοῦν*) with the intelligible (*τὸ κατανοούμενον*) is achieved by different potencies (*δυνάμεσιν*), and, moreover, that the intelligent approaches [its object] by virtue of its similarity and identity, and conjoins (*συνάπτειν*) with it by virtue of its common nature, when there is no obstacle."[109] The term, therefore originally denotes the process of intellection viewed under the aspect of the Empedoclean motif of "like knowing like".[110] The notion of "union" (*ittiḥād*), on the other hand, goes back to the Neoplatonic concept of *ἕνωσις* in Plotinus and his successors, and designates the ultimate stage of mystical union.[111] In his *De anima Liber*,[112] Alexander of Aphrodisias follows Aristotle's terminology and line of thought, when describing the ultimate stage of intellection as one at which we "become" the pure intelligibles represented by the Divine "Intellect from without" (*ὁ νοῦς ὁ θύραθεν*), and at which this Intellect comes-to-be (*γινόμενος*) in us. In his *De intellectu*,[113] however, he speaks of a "co-operation" between the material intellect and the Intellect from without, i.e. the Agent Intellect: "The intellect which is suchlike by nature and is from without co-operates (*συνεργός*)[114] with the one in us. This suggests a notion approximating to Plotinus's "conjoining" of the rational soul and the Intellect. There is this further difference between the two texts: In the *De anima*, Alexander describes the Intellect from without as "coming-to-be" only at the ultimate stage,[115] whereas in the *De intellectu* he speaks of it as being active and present in all our thinking, including in the thinking of the material intelligibles. Indeed, the thinking of the material intelligibles is described here as necessary for the perfection of that very Intellect from without. "Perfected, it thinks both the intelligibles which are such by nature [sc. the pure forms] as well as

[109] *Enneads*, VI, ix, 8, ed. Bréhier, Vol. VI, 2, p. 183, lines 24–29. Plotinus speaks also of the ecstatic experience of union as a "contact" (*ἁφή*). Cf. *Enneads*, V, iii, 1; VI, ix, pp. 10–11. The correspondence of Ibn Sīnā's *ittiṣāl* and Plotinus' *ἁφή* has been pointed out by L. Gardet, *La Pensée religieuse d'Avicenne* (1951), pp. 148–149.

[110] Plotinus quotes Empedocles in his chapter on the descent of the soul into the body (*Enneads*, IV, viii, 1), but does not explicitly refer to his doctrine of "like knowing like".

[111] Cf. A. Altmann and S. M. Stern, *Isaac Israeli*, pp. 185–192.

[112] Ed. Bruns, p. 89.21–22 = ed. Günsz, p. 13.23–25; ed. Bruns, p. 90.19–20 = ed. Günsz, p. 14.18–19; ed. Bruns, p. 91.2 = ed. Günsz, p. 14–26.

[113] Ed. Bruns, p. 111.27 = ed. Finnegan, p. 194.2.

[114] Ed. Finnegan: "becomes a helper (*muʿīn*) to the intellect in us".

[115] Cf. the references in note 112.

those which are such according to its proper action and art."[116] By thinking also the material intelligibles, i.e. by abstracting them from matter, the Intellect from without is "increased and perfected".[117]

Ibn Bājja clearly follows Alexander's view as expressed in the *De intellectu.*[118] In his description of the three stages of intellection (see above, section 1, pp. 81–83), he says that at each of them we "conjoin" with the Intelligible [= Agent Intellect] in a certain way, viz. "as related to material [sc. corporeal] forms" or "as related to spiritual form" in its various degrees, and, finally, we conjoin with it without any material or spiritual form serving as a substratum. Only at the last stage is the conjunction complete. The whole discussion of the stages of the "ascent" in the *Treatise on Union* is dominated by the concept of "conjunction". The *Book on the Soul,* too, stresses the same idea. Here the Agent Intellect is called the "Mover" or "Mover from without (*min khārij*)."[119] In order to become intelligibles, i.e. material forms, the forms inherent in matter "always require this conjunction (*ittiṣāl*) which perfects them in existence".

The Arabic versions of both the *De anima*[120] and the *De intellectu*[121] substitute for Alexander of Aphrodisias' term "the

[116] Ed. Bruns, p. 112.3–4=ed. Finnegan, p. 195.1–2.

[117] Ed. Bruns. p. 112.2–3. Cf. E. Gilson, "Les Sources Gréco-Arabes de l'Augustinisme Avicennisant", *Archives d'Histoire Doctrinale et Littéraire du Moyen Age* (1930), p. 17, where—interpreting the passage we have quoted—the Agent Intellect is said to "enrich itself" and to be led "to its own perfection" by knowing the material intelligibles. The Arabic version (ed. Finnegan, pp. 194.9–195.3) obliterates this aspect and speaks only of the material intelligibles as "perfected" by the action of the Agent Intellect, the latter being in any case "perfect". Ibn Bājja reflects the Arabic version when describing the acquired intellect as "perfecting" the material intelligibles. Cf. *RegSol*, p. 19 [50].

[118] Al-Fārābī, on the other hand, is influenced by Alexander's *De anima.* This tends to confirm J. Finnegan's thesis in his article "Al-Fārābī et le *Περὶ Νοῦ* d'Alexandre d'Aphrodise", *Mélanges Louis Massignon*, II (1957), pp. 133ff. and in the Introduction to his edition of Alexander's *De intellectu* denying any influence of this work on al-Fārābī. Finnegan suggests that only the occidental philosophers, viz. Ibn Bājja and Ibn Rushd were influenced by it, but he hesitates to affirm that Ibn Bājja knew it first hand (Introduction, p. 169). As our analysis has shown, the traces of the *De intellectu* in Ibn Bājja, far from being "feeble", are pronounced and of decisive importance.

[119] *Kitāb al-Nafs*, fol. 148*v*, *Majallat*, XXXIII, p. 621.

[120] Ed. Günsz, p. 14.26: *ha-sekhel ha-niqnē*, corresponding to the Arabic *al-ᶜaql al-mustafād*. In two other passages the term is slightly paraphrased by *ha-sekhel asher niqnēhū* and *zeh . . . ānū niqnēhū* (pp. 14.19, 21–22). It may be assumed that the Hebrew version faithfully reflects the Arabic text.

[121] Ed. Finnegan, pp. 186.5; 189.11; 191.4.5; 194.2,5,8.

Intellect from without" (ὁ θύραθεν νοῦς) the term "acquired intellect" (*al-ᶜaql al-mustafād*). Obviously, this term denotes the Agent Intellect *qua* operating in man.[122] In the *De anima*, the Agent Intellect appears as "acquired intellect" in man only at the ultimate stage—acting as he does merely as "cause" for the coming-into-being of forms abstracted from matter at the lower level—whilst in the *De intellectu* the acquired intellect "co-operates" with the human intellect from the very start. Ibn Bājja seems to steer a middle course, as far as the terminology goes. Although he considers the Agent Intellect to be operative in man throughout the intellectual process, he reserves the term "acquired intellect" for the ultimate stage (see above section, 4, p. 93), and uses the term "Mover from without" in order to denote the activity of the Agent Intellect at all levels.

Ibn Bājja's doctrine differs from al-Fārābī's in that he assumes the acquired intellect to come into being as a result of the purification of forms from all relation to matter, whereas al-Fārābī sees the acquired intellect constituted as soon as the intellect, having abstracted all or most forms from matter, reflects upon itself.[123] Nothing is said about the degree of abstraction as conditional upon the coming-into-being of the acquired intellect. Al-Fārābī does not differentiate between degrees of abstraction at the level of intellect, as Ibn Bājja does. He says that when the Intellect possesses forms abstracted from matter and has thus "become" those forms, it can now think itself, thereby resembling the Agent Intellect which possesses forms which were never in matter. The forms in the acquired intellect, too, may be considered as having never been in matter, since through the process of abstraction they have achieved a new "ontological status".[124] They have become "one of the existents of the world (*aḥad mawjudāt al-ᶜālam*)".[125] Ibn Bājja quotes this phrase in the name of al-Fārābī,[126] but he gives

[122] E. Gilson, *op. cit.*, p. 21 rightly characterizes the substitution of the term "acquired intellect" for "Intellect from without" as a "duplication" of the Agent Intellect into *intellectus acquisitus* and *intelligentia agens*. This interpretation does not hold good for al-Fārābī's concept of the ᶜ*aql mustafād*, as F. Rahman (*Avicenna's Psychology*, pp. 90–93) has rightly pointed out against Gilson. But it exactly fits the position in Alexander as well as Ibn Bājja.

[123] Cf. Rahman's excellent analysis in *Avicenna's Psychology*, pp. 90–93, and *Prophecy in Islam*, pp. 11–14.

[124] See Rahman, *Prophecy in Islam*, p. 12, where this phrase is applied to al-Fārābī's notion of the material intelligibles after their abstraction from matter.

[125] *Kitāb al-Nafs*, fol. 149r, *Majallat*, XXXIII, pp. 622–623; *TrUnion*, 12, p. 17 [36].

[126] *Ibid.*

it a new connotation. It is only by an "ascent" to the contemplation of pure intelligibles, freed from all relation to matter, including the universal relation, that the Intellect proper is envisioned. Al-Fārābī's intelligibles remain, even in the acquired intellect, at the same qualitative level which they possessed when abstracted from matter. They are still abstracts from sense data and represent genera and species related to the sensible world. Ibn Bājja's acquired intellect is above the level of genera and species. It moves in the world of separate substances, and is attainable only through a Platonic conversion from the sensible to the Divine. As such it constitutes man's ultimate felicity.

4

ESSENCE AND EXISTENCE IN MAIMONIDES[1]

Maimonides defines existence (*wudjūd*) as "an accident (*ʿaraḍ*) affecting (lit. happening to) that which exists (*mawdjūd*), and therefore something (*maʿna*) superadded to the essence (*māhīya*) of that which exists". He immediately qualifies this definition by restricting it to "all beings the existence of which is due to a cause". The existence of such beings, and of such beings only, will be something superadded to their essence. But a being whose existence is not due to any cause will contain being in its very essence. The only such Being is God, the necessary Existent. In Him, therefore, essence and existence are perfectly identical. "The existence of such a Being is its essence and truth, and its essence is its existence" (*Guide*, I, 57).

It can hardly be doubted that the above statement reflects Avicenna's famous theory concerning essence and existence, and the commentators of the *Guide* have not been slow in pointing out this fact. Moses of Narbonne and Shemtob ben Joseph take the opportunity of assailing Maimonides from the point of view of Averroes' critique of Avicenna's doctrine, while others (Shemtob Ibn Falaquera and Asher Crescas) are content to reproduce some of the arguments used by Avicenna and Averroes respectively.[2] Maimonides himself introduces his statement by referring to the theory he is about to explain as one "well-known" and, to all in-

[1] The present article was one of a series presented to Dr. S. van den Bergh, the distinguished scholar, philosopher, and teacher, on the occasion of his seventieth birthday.

[2] We learn incidentally that Shemtob ben Joseph composed a treatise on this particular subject which, unfortunately, appears to be lost. Two other treatises of his, one on Matter and its Relation to Form, and one on Final Causes, are extant in manuscripts. Cf. *JE.*, *s.v.* Ibn Shemtob.

tents and purposes, commonly accepted. He has obviously not had an opportunity of becoming acquainted with Averroes' attack on Avicenna's doctrine.[3] He must also have had in mind the fact that Avicenna's theory of essence and existence had gained some currency in Jewish philosophical writings. Thus, among the Jewish Neoplatonists, Gabirol and Jehudah Hallevi clearly state that in the case of all beings except God existence is different from essence.[4] But the question arises in what sense Maimonides understood existence to be an "accident" to essence. Did he attribute to Avicenna the view which was made the target of Averroes' subsequent attack, or did he interpret him in a different manner? This question is of added interest in view of the fact that only recently an attempt has been made to re-interpret Avicenna's doctrine and to clear it of the criticisms levelled against it by Averroes.[5]

We shall best open our enquiry by examining Maimonides' notion of essence. Here Maimonides stands solidly on Aristotelian

[3] This corroborates the prevalent assumption that, at the time of his writing the *Guide*, Maimonides was as yet unacquainted with the work of Averroes. Cf. H. A. Wolfson, *Crescas' Critique of Aristotle* (1929), p. 323. The famous Letter to Samuel Ibn Tibbon in which Maimonides reviews the contemporary philosophical literature and mentions Averroes twice was written after the completion of the *Guide*. Cf. J. Sonne, *Tarbiẓ*, ed. J. N. Epstein (Jerusalem, 1939), X, p. 147. The Verona ms. of the Letter published by Sonne does not contain the relevant paragraph but merely alludes to it. Another version of the Letter published by Alexander Marx from Codex Adler 2031 proves again inconclusive by virtue of the fact that the ms. is mutilated just where the reference to Averroes occurs in the Constantinople edition. Cf. *JQR*, N.S., XXV (1934–35), p. 375. A critical edition of the Letter has been announced by D. H. Baneth in *Tarbiẓ*, XXIII (1952), p. 171. From a Letter written by Maimonides to his favourite disciple, Joseph ben Jehudah ibn Aḳnīn and dated 1190, more definite conclusions can be drawn. There he mentions the fact that he had just received all the writings of Averroes except one and praises Averroes as "hitting the mark". He expresses regret at not having as yet had an opportunity of going over all his books. Cf. D. H. Baneth, *ʾIggĕrot Ha-Rambam*, ed. Meḳiẓe Nirdamīm (Jerusalem, 1946), pp. 33, 70. Seeing that the *Guide* had been completed by 1190, it is obvious that he had not been able to draw on Averroes' writings at the time of its composition. Shemtob Ibn Falaquera's assertion to the contrary cannot be substantiated. Cf. *Moreh Ha-Moreh* (1837), p. 8.

[4] Cf. *Fons Vitae*, ed. C. Bäumker, V, 24; *Kuzari*, IV, 25 (Cassel, p. 354).

[5] As Dr. F. Rahman has shown, Averroes' reading of Avicenna is not borne out by the relevant texts of the Kitāb al-Shifāʾ. Unfortunately, it has misled all subsequent interpretations of Avicenna's doctrine. Dr. Rahman's thesis has been presented in a paper on "Essence and Existence in Avicenna" read before the Scottish Society for Ancient Philosophy, and kindly made available to the present writer. [Published in *Mediaeval and Renaissance Studies*, ed. Richard Hunt, Raymond Klibansky, Lotte Labowsky, IV (London, 1958), pp. 1–16.]

ground. Aristotle had defined essence as that which a thing is said to be *per se* and which has its formula in the definition (*Met.* VII, 4, 4–5). "Essence belongs to all things the account of which is a definition" (*Met.* VII, 4, 9). Maimonides says likewise that among the Five Praedicabilia "species" constitutes the "essence" of the individuals to which it is common. Seeing that species itself contains genus and specific difference, essence coincides with the definition which is composed of the same elements (*Treatise on Logic*, X, 1). Thus the terms "rational animal" which express the definition of man constitute the essence (*ḍāt*) and truth (*ḥaḳīḳ*) of man (*Guide*, I, 51, 52). It may be noted that Maimonides is fond of calling the essence the "truth" of a thing (*Guide*, I, 33, 51). He no doubt means thereby the true being of a thing in the same way in which Aristotle regards the essence as the very being of a thing. He does not seem to have noticed the difficulty of attributing essence to God which arises from his own concept of essence. Seeing that a definition consisting of the *genus* and the *differentia* is inapplicable to God, the term "essence" should be likewise inapplicable to God. Maimonides, like his Jewish predecessors, emphatically states that no definition can be given of God (*Guide*, I, 52).[6] Yet he does not hesitate to speak of God's essence.[7] We are therefore compelled to assume that Maimonides uses the term "essence" in two *toto coelo* different senses when speaking of God and all other beings respectively. From his statement that the *Tetragrammaton* "includes nothing but His essence" one might infer that "essence" in the case of God is identical with "necessary existence"; for this, he says, is the meaning of that proper name (*Guide*, I, 61). The *Tetragrammaton*, he says in another place, implies nothing except God's existence (I, 53, end). It expresses the notion of God as the necessary Existent, and is identical with the name "I AM THAT I AM" (Ex. 3:14) which God revealed to Moses (I, 63).[8] In God, essence and existence are one (I, 57). Maimonides prefers this formula rather than the more radical one of the Jewish

[6] Cf. Jehudah Hallevi, *Kuzari*, IV, 25 (Cassel, p. 354); Abraham Ibn Daud, *Emunah Ramah*, ed. Weil, pp. 46, 52.

[7] God is "a simple essence" (I, 53); Will and Wisdom are one with His essence (I, 69; III, 13); His essence is unknowable (I, 54, 58); and *passim*.

[8] The Latin schoolmen, too, interpreted the name "I AM THAT I AM" as denoting the very essence of God. Cf. Etienne Gilson, *The Spirit of Medieval Philosophy* (1950), pp. 51ff. This interpretation goes back to Philo of Alexandria. Cf. H. A. Wolfson, *Philo*, I, pp. 19, 210; II, pp. 120–121.

Neoplatonists and of Ghazālī who had described God as existence without essence.[9]

What kind of existence does Maimonides attribute to essence? Here again he is a strict Aristotelian. Form or essence, Aristotle had said, does not exist independently. It is not a self-subsistent substance, for otherwise it could not be contained in an actually existing substance (*Met.* VII, 8, 6). On the other hand, neither form nor essence are generated. The concrete whole is generated, for generation means inducing form or essence into particular matter (*Met.* VII, 8, 3–5). Maimonides likewise holds that, as a universal, essence has no independent existence. "It is an established fact that species have no existence outside our minds, and that species and other universals are concepts appertaining to the intellect, while everything that exists outside our minds is an individual or an aggregate of individuals" (*Guide*, III, 18). At the same time, forms, unlike the combinations of the elements, do not change. They remain in their self-same natures, and appear and disappear instantaneously according to the ability of matter to receive them (II, 12). Maimonides does not further analyze the peculiar mode of being that attaches to essence or form as something existing only in concrete individuals and yet transcending them. He might have assigned to essence the character of something mid-way between being and non-being which certain schools of Kalām had attributed to the universals. Maimonides does indeed make reference to this particular theory, but only to reject it. Speaking about the attributes of God, he mentions the Kalām doctrine according to which the attributes of God are neither His essence nor anything extraneous to His essence. "This", he adds, "is like the assertion of others that the 'states' (*aḥwāl*), i.e. universal concepts, are neither existing nor non-existent." This view he strongly repudiates. There is, he says, no mean between existence and non-existence (*Guide*, I, 51). Both the theological doctrine referred to and the *ḥāl* theory belong to the same school of

[9] Cf. Gabirol, *Fons Vitae*, V, 24; Shemtob Ibn Falaquera, *Moreh Ha-Moreh*, pp. 28f.; Joseph Ibn Ẓaddiḳ, *Microcosm*, ed. Horovitz, p. 48; Asher Crecas' Commentary on the *Guide*, I, 57. As to Ghazālī, see T. de Boer, *Die Widersprüche der Philosophie nach Al-Gaẓāli und ihr Ausgleich durch Ibn Rošd* (1894), pp. 53f.; H. A. Wolfson, *Crescas on Divine Attributes*, in *JQR*, N.S., VII (1916–1917), pp. 189–191. Avicenna's view has met with a twofold interpretation. Ghazālī understood him to suggest that God is existence without essence; Averroes attributed to him the view that in God essence and existence are one. Cf. Wolfson, *ibid.*

thought. Abū Hāshim introduced the *ḥāl* theory as a means of reconciling the concept of the unity of God, which implies simplicity of essence, with the affirmation of distinct attributes. Do the latter not constitute accidental qualities in God? The answer put forward is to the effect that there is a *tertium quid* between essence and accidental attributes, i.e. the "states" such as wisdom, power, life which are one with the essence and yet conceptually different.[10] This doctrine was accepted also by members of the Ashʿarite school. Al-Djuwainī, the teacher of Ghazālī, defined a "state" (*ḥāl*) as an attribute of an existing thing, being itself neither existent nor non-existent.[11] It would appear that Maimonides referred to this formula when rejecting the theory of *aḥwāl*.[12] It is obvious that it could not solve for him the problem of the mode of being attached to essence seeing that the *ḥāl*, according to this theory, stands in between the essence and the accident. It is a notion specifically designed to fit a theological requirement. But it should be borne in mind that the concept of *ḥāl* has also a wider significance in the thinking of Kalām, and re-echoes, as Dr. van den Bergh has shown, the Stoical concept of "states" (*pōs échon*) under which the Stoics, to the displeasure of Plotinus, had subsumed most of the accidental categories.[13] The facts designated under this term constitute a something "neither corporeal nor non-corporeal", i.e. a "meaning" (*ennóēma*) in an objective sense and akin to the Platonic Forms.[14] This realm of "meaning" includes not only universals and essences but also illusions and errors. Maimonides, however, does not avail himself of this notion. He says of fictitious beings such as the griffin, the centaur and similar figments of the imagination, simply that they are non-existent. On the other hand, a true essence exists only in the concrete individual. Its universality arises from the intellectual pro-

[10] Al-Shahrastānī, *Milal*, translated by Haarbrücker, I, pp. 83ff.; David Kaufmann, *Geschichte der Attributenlehre in der jüdischen Religionsphilosophie*, 1877, p. 35, n. 65; S. Horovitz, *Ueber den Einfluss der griechischen Philosophie auf die Entwicklung des Kalam*, (Breslau, 1909), pp. 54–69. [See now Harry A. Wolfson, *Religious Philosophy*: *A Group of Essays*, 1961, p. 52, and his forthcoming book *The Philosophy of the Kalam* in which the concept of the "modes" (*aḥwāl*) is to be fully discussed (*loc. cit.*, n. 86).]

[11] Cf. *Kitāb al-Irshād*, ed. Luciani, p. 48 (81).

[12] Neither Munk (*Guide*, I, 185, n. 2) nor Friedländer (*Guide*, I, 176, n. 1) seem to have understood this reference.

[13] Cf. H. von Arnim, *Stoicorum Veterum Fragmenta*, II, 131, 124.

[14] *Op. cit.* I, 19, 117.

cess of abstraction. Maimonides is thus a true Aristotelian.[15] It follows that essences do not exist in an ideal realm of their own but "appear" in individual substances in which alone they have their being.

This brings us to the important question of the relationship between essence and substance. A clarification of this issue will help us to appreciate Maimonides' view-point concerning essence and existence.

What emerges from Aristotle's discussion of substance is the fact that substance has two fundamentally different meanings. In one sense substance is identical with the "what" of a thing, i.e. its essence. In another sense, it is the concrete particular thing. Aristotle does not always clearly distinguish between these two distinct senses of substance. But that he was fully aware of their difference cannot be doubted. Substance, he says, has two senses: "the ultimate subject, which cannot be further predicated of something else; and whatever has an individual and separate existence", i.e. the essence of a thing (V, 3, 4). "Substance", he says in another context, "is of two kinds, the concrete thing and the formula" (VII, 15, 1). This broadly corresponds with the distinction between primary and secondary substance laid down in the *Categories* (ch. 5). Aristotle designates as "primary substances" the things "which are neither predicated of a substrate nor found in a substrate, e.g. this man or this horse". He describes as "secondary substances" the genera and species. The designation of the concrete thing as "primary substance" makes it clear that being attaches primarily to the particular thing, not to essence. In the *Metaphysics* too, Aristotle speaks of the concrete individual as "substance in the highest degree" (VII, 6, 2). On the other hand, he regards the concrete thing as inferior in being to the essence. It admits of generation and destruction while essence does not. "The essence of house is not generated, but only the essence of *this* house" (VII, 15, 1). He adds that for this reason there is no definition or demonstration of particular sensible substances, because they contain matter "whose nature is such that it can both exist and not exist" (VII, 15, 2). One has therefore to realize the

[15] Cf. Shemtob Ibn Falaquera, *Moreh Ha-Moreh*, pp. 129–130, where this point is made in the clearest possible terms. S. B. Scheyer, in his *Das Psychologische System des Maimonides* (1845), pp. 41ff., suggests that Maimonides' rejection of the objective existence of the universals (*Guide*, III, 18) refers only to logical and mathematical concepts. This interpretation cannot be upheld.

paradoxical fact that the primary substance, i.e. the concrete thing, exists and has its being by virtue of its endowment with secondary substance, i.e. essence. Concrete individuals are perishable (VII, 15, 2). "Once they have passed from the sphere of actuality it is uncertain whether they exist or not, but they are always spoken of and apprehended by the universal formula" (VII, 10, 18). We may, therefore say of essence that while it exists only in concrete things and never by itself, it has nevertheless being and unity in a higher degree than the concrete thing. On the other hand, the concrete thing is substance in the truest sense, and existence belongs to it absolutely and primarily. Yet its existence is but the result of a particular matter achieving its form, and therefore dependent upon a specific set of causes. It is due to a process of generation which means "inducing form or essence into particular matter" (VII, 8, 4).

If one bears in mind Aristotle's dual approach to the problem of substance, one will not be surprised by Maimonides' definition of the relationship between essence and existence as stated in the opening paragraph of this paper. It has to be noted that Maimonides describes existence as an accident not to essence—no statement is made as to the being or non-being of essence *qua* essence—but to "that which exists", i.e. the concrete thing. This we interpret to mean that the existence of a concrete thing composed of matter and form is due to the fact that, as a result of a causal process, a certain form has been induced into a certain matter. The term "accident" merely expresses the fact that the thing "happens" to exist. In a certain sense it also means that the essence "happens" to appear in this particular matter. It does not indicate that a non-existent or ideal essence has become "existent" by the grace of the accidental attribute of existence. Nor does it obliterate the recognition of concrete substances as having existence in a primary and absolute sense. It merely defines existence as being due to factors outside the essence, and for this reason uses the term "accident". As Dr. Rahman has suggested, Avicenna employed the same term in a similar sense, and it is not unlikely that this is the way in which Maimonides understood Avicenna.

A closer analysis of Maimonides' definition of existence will bear out the correctness of our interpretation. From the statement quoted it is obvious that to exist is, in Maimonides' view, tantamount to being caused. Only in the case of God is existence uncaused. But precisely for this reason the term "existence" is used homonymously of God and all other beings (*Guide*, I, 56). The efficient cause, Maimonides states in his *Treatise on Logic* (IX, 3), is He who causes form to exist in matter, that is to say God. The philosophers, he adds, are in agreement with this, except that they regard God as a remote agent and seek for every existing being that is created its proximate agent. Seeing that the efficient cause is invariably outside the essence,[16] it is understandable that existence is described as an "accident superadded to the essence of that which exists." The proximity of this view to Alfārābī's and Avicenna's is too obvious to need much emphasis. The "that", says Alfārābī, does not derive from the "what" but from something external to the "what".[17] In other words, existence is due to an external agent. It does not derive from the essence as such. Both Alfārābī and Avicenna use the phrase that "considered in themselves and apart from their relation to the necessary Being, essences deserve privation of being".[18] Maimonides does not go as far as that. He does not designate essence as a mere possible in itself, but he agrees that existence in the sense of an "instantiation" of essence is a happening due to an agent outside the essence.

There is another aspect to the accidentality which Maimonides attributes to existence. To exist means to be actual. But everything that passes from a state of potentiality to that of actuality is caused to do so by some external agent (*Guide*, II, Introduction, Prop. XVIII). It follows that existence is due to some external agent, and therefore accidental to the thing itself. We may also say that existence is merely potential being as long as certain conditions are as yet unfulfilled. Maimonides calls this element of uncertainty surrounding the actualization of the potential a "possibility". "Everything that exists", he says, "and whose essence includes a certain state of possibility (*ʾimkān*) may at some time be without actual existence" (Prop. XXIII). In his Letter to Samuel Ibn Tibbon, he explains that there is a difference between

[16] Cf. *Met.* VII, 8; Gabirol, *Fons Vitae*, V, 24.

[17] Cf. Alfārābī, *Ringstones of Wisdom*, ed. Dieterici, p. 67 (110). As for the Aristotelian origin of the distinction between essence and existence, see I. Madkour, *L'Organon d'Aristote dans le monde arabe*, Paris, 1934, and H. A. Wolfson, *The Philosophy of Spinoza*, I, 124.

[18] Cf. Alfārābī, *loc. cit.*; Avicenna, *Metaphysics*, VIII, 6, quoted by E. Gilson, *Being and Some Philosophers* (1949), p. 78.

potentiality and possibility which to grasp requires great subtlety and is a matter of utmost difficulty even to trained philosophers.[19] It appears that the possibility of which he speaks refers to the as yet unrealized presence of the conditions necessary for the actualization of a potential being. What Avicenna and the Latin schoolmen called *potentiae remotae* as distinct from *potentiae proximae* lies in the same direction.[20] But neither Aristotle nor Avicenna differentiates between potentiality and possibility.[21] According to Maimonides —if we understand him correctly—the element of possibility is bound up with external causation, whereas potentiality is the as yet unrealised being of the thing as such. Maimonides says distinctly, "A thing which owes its existence to certain causes has in itself (lit. in consideration of its essence) merely the possibility of existence" (Prop. XIX). Again, existence is seen to be purely accidental from the aspect of essence. In the case of God, existence is not merely actual but necessary. This is brought out in Maimonides' Fourth Argument for the existence of God, which from the impossibility of an infinite regress postulates the existence of a cause which is pure actuality and admits of no potentiality whatever (*Guide*, II, 1). "In the essence of this Cause nothing exists potentially, for if its essence included any possibility of existence it would not exist at all." It should be noted that Maimonides is not content to exclude from God potentiality but that he excludes possibility as well. A being devoid of potentiality is actual—such is the God of Aristotle—but a Being free from possibility as well must be necessarily existent. Maimonides defines it as Being "that includes no possibility whatever but exists actually by its own essence". In God, therefore, essence and existence are one.

There is yet a third aspect to Maimonides' view concerning the nature of existence. To exist is to be willed by God. It is not enough to say that existence is caused by God. For that might imply an existence which necessarily derives from Him in the same manner

[19] Cf. *Ḳobeẓ Tĕshubot ha-Rambam wĕ-ʾIggĕrotaw*, II, 27b.

[20] For the Aristotelian source of this distinction, cf. H. A. Wolfson, *Crescas' Critique of Aristotle*, pp. 691–692. Hillel of Verona, in his Commentary on the Twenty-Five Propositions of Maimonides (*Tagmulē Ha-Nefesh* (Lyck, 1874), pp. 38a–39a) offers a different interpretation. He explains that the potentiality of a substratum to become X implies (a) a natural disposition, (b) a general possibility, whilst (c) the potentiality of X (e.g. the man being potentially in the seed) is pure potentiality: being as yet non-existent, the X has neither disposition nor possibility.

[21] The term *dunamis* in Aristotle denotes both potentiality and possibility. As to Avicenna, cf. M. Horten, *Metaphysik des Avicenna*, p. 25.

"as the shadow is caused by a body, or heat by fire, or light by the sun" (*Guide*, II, 2).[22] But Maimonides holds the world to be created by design (*ḳaṣd*) and determination (*taḥṣīṣ*) (*ibid.*). The best proof for design in the universe he finds in the different motions of the spheres which cannot be explained as the necessary results of differences in their substance. One substance is common to all spheres, and yet each one has its own particular form, i.e. kind of movement and velocity. Who then, he asks, determined and pre-disposed these spheres to receive different forms? The answer he puts forward is: The Will of God (*Guide*, II, 19). If one assumed "Nature" as such to operate without any voluntary determination, the "Wisdom" of God would be equivalent to Nature, and the essences of things would achieve existence in accordance with causal necessity. But the fact is that existence does not follow a plain and intelligible pattern. It contains an opaque, irrational element, as we might say. It points to "Will" as a determining factor besides "Wisdom". It appears that on the whole Maimonides related essence to the Wisdom, and existence to the Will of God, although he is rather vague in his utterances on the subject. He sometimes speaks of God's Wisdom as responsible for determinations which are rationally inexplicable (II, 19), sometimes of "the Will of God or his Wisdom" (III, 13), but it is clear that what he really means is Will, voluntary determination (cf. II, 19). In God there is, of course, no duality of Will and Wisdom. They are both identical with His essence (I, 69; III, 13). But the distinction is a valid one from the aspect of existing things. Their analysis reveals two distinct elements, i.e. essence which represents the realm of nature in the timelessness and constancy of being, and existence by which essence is thrown into combination with matter beyond the strict confines of causal necessity. Existence is thus from yet another angle accidental to essence. But its accidental nature is now seen to derive from the Will of God. The final causes which Aristotle found in nature, Maimonides declares to terminate in the Will of God (I, 69; III, 13). But God's Will is not arbitrary; it is guided by His Wisdom. "The object of His Will is only that which is possible, and of the things possible only such as His Wisdom decrees upon" (III, 25). The duality of essence and existence in all created beings therefore corresponds in a way to the Wisdom and Will of God.

[22] Two of these examples occur also in Maimonides' *Aphorisms* (*Fuṣul Mūsā*). Cf. M. Steinschneider, *Al-Farabi* (1869), p. 236.

Maimonides' concept of God's essence as the Unity of Wisdom and Will marks his standpoint in the great controversy between Ashᶜariya and Muᶜtazila as to whether Will or Wisdom operates in the workings of Divine Providence (cf. *Guide*, III, 17). It seems to imply a compromise solution combining both features. But its real purport must be seen in the stand Maimonides takes in the larger controversy between Kalām and the philosophers. There the issue is that of creation. As Isaac Abrabanel has pointed out, the issue is not between creation and non-creation but between creation by will and design or creation by necessity.[23] Creation by will and design as conceived by Kalām left no room for a realm of essence, and, vice versa, creation by necessity as conceived by the philosophers seemed to ignore the nature of existence. The theologians of Kalām refused to call God the First Cause and designated Him either as Agent (*fāᶜil*) or Determinant (*muḫaṣṣiṣ*).[24] Maimonides assumes an intermediate position. He does not share the rejection of the term "Cause" for God (I, 69), and, at the same time, adopts the Kalām notion of *taḫṣīṣ* which expresses the concept of will and design. He recognizes most clearly that the denial by Kalām of the "true nature", i.e. the essences, of things stems from a desire to prove the determination (*taḫṣīṣ*) of things (II, 19). He, on his part, accepts the theory of *taḫṣīṣ* but wishes to demonstrate the operation of this principle in the natural universe. He does not wish to disregard the "nature of things", i.e. their essences. In the view of Kalām, the principle of *taḫṣīṣ* determines the composition, size, place, accident, and time of the spheres and the sublunar beings (cf. *Guide*, I, 74, Fifth Argument). Maimonides restricts the operation of *taḫṣīṣ* to the spheres and admits it only indirectly to the sublunar world.[25] But once the principle of voluntary determination is established, the universe as a whole is proved to be created.

Moses of Narbonne, in his *Commentary* on the *Guide*, passes the remark that Maimonides' arguments for creation by will and design were taken over from Ghazālī; moreover, that they did not represent Maimonides' esoteric view but were meant merely to please the religionists. In his own generation one could safely agree with Averroes that all causality was determined by the

[23] Cf. *Shamayim Ḥadashīm*, ed. Heidenheimer (1828), p. 1b.
[24] Cf. *Guide*, I, 69; S. Pines, *Beiträge zur Islamischen Atomenlehre* (1936), p. 38.
[25] Abrabanel, *loc. cit.*, pp. 2b–3.

nature of existing things, i.e. by the pure causality of form in the case of simple bodies, and by a combination of formal and efficient causes in the case of composite bodies.[26] Averroes does indeed eliminate the voluntaristic concept of final causes. He defines the Will of God as "the process of necessary action accompanied by knowledge".[27] Spinoza went even beyond that by denying both the Will and Intellect of God. He thus eliminated the final causes, and reduced the formal cause to the efficient cause.[28] Maimonides, on the other hand, upholds efficient, formal and final causes. There is no justification for the view expressed by Moses of Narbonne that Maimonides' arguments for creation by design were not meant seriously. As we have seen, there is a close correspondence between Maimonides' ontology of essence and existence on the one hand, and his theology of Wisdom and Will on the other.

How far Maimonides succeeded in establishing the voluntaristic principle is another matter. The question is: To what extent is the Will of God free to operate in a world already determined by essences, i.e. formal causes? Moses of Narbonne had said that Maimonides' arguments for the principle of *taḫṣīṣ* were borrowed from Ghazālī. Abrabanel strongly repudiates this contention. Ghazālī, he asserts, furnished only the first of Maimonides' arguments.[29] But this is beside the point. The question is: Does Maimonides follow the whole trend of Ghazālī's argumentation? The answer to this is in the negative. Ghazālī wished to disprove causality altogether, and to replace it by the causality of Will alone. In full accord with Ashʿarite Kalām, he denies the concept of essence and all it implies, i.e. formal causality and the reality of the potential. There is no such thing as a natural process of change, of becoming, and of matter receiving successive forms as a result of a predisposition to receive them. Existence is not the result of a series of formal and material determinations but arises from discrete acts of Will on the part of God. This position is a renewal of the Megaric doctrine which Aristotle had taken

[26] Cf. Moses of Narbonne, *Biʾūr lĕ-Sefer Moreh Nĕḇuḵim*, ed. J. Goldenthal (1852), pp. 34a–b.

[27] Cf. S van den Bergh, *Die Epitome der Metaphysik des Averroes* (Leiden, 1924), p. 270.

[28] Cf. H. A. Wolfson, *Spinoza*, pp. 316ff.

[29] Cf. Abrabanel, *loc. cit.*, p. 3a. The argument referred to is based on the fact that certain spheres move from east to west, others in the opposite direction. Cf. *Tahāfut*, I, 12.

pains to repudiate (*Met.* IX, 3). Maimonides' Aristotelianism has no use for such a radical application of the voluntaristic principle. He firmly upholds the concept of essence and formal causality but admits for the translunar sphere, and thus indirectly also for the sublunar world, the principle of *taḫṣīṣ*. Existence thus becomes something both caused and willed. It is caught in a nexus of causality which has its First Cause in God. Existence is therefore, metaphysicallly speaking, an "accident", something that "happens" to occur, and not something determined by essence as such.

In the light of the afore-going interpretation of Maimonides' concept of essence and existence, the criticisms levelled against it by the commentators will be seen to fall to the ground.

(1) Shemtob Ibn Falaquera (*Moreh Ha-Moreh*, p. 28) does not expressly criticize Maimonides but adduces by way of comment Averroes' critique of Avicenna and obviously wishes to apply it to Maimonides. He quotes Averroes as saying that "Our statement that a thing exists does not indicate something superadded to its essence *extra mentem* as would be the case in our stating that the thing is white. We found, however, that Avicenna mistakenly believed that unity is something superadded to the essence, and likewise existence, whenever we say that a thing exists; and that, moreover, an existing thing has no existence by virtue of its essence. This statement is most misleading, for it implies that the term 'existent' signifies an accident common to all categories *extra mentem*, which is the opinion of Avicenna. Concerning this 'accident' the question is asked whether in saying that it (*sc.* this accident) exists, we refer to the truth of the matter or to another accident existing in that (first) accident, in which case there would be an infinite series of accidents, which is absurd."

It is obvious that the target of Averroes' attack is the view supposedly held by Avicenna that existence is an accident like whiteness. The fallacy of this assumption has been demonstrated by Dr. Rahman. The concrete individual thing "happens" to exist, but its existence is not an "accident" like quality or quantity. Averroes' argument that such an "accident" would be common to all categories does not therefore apply.[30] The other argument from the impossibility of an infinite series of accidents is a favourite one, and occurs in a number of medieval Jewish

[30] For a more elaborate account of this particular argument cf. *Die Epitome der Metaphysik des Averroes*, ed. S. van den Bergh, pp. 8–9.

authors such as Joseph ben Jehudah ibn Aḳnīn, Isaac Albalag, Gersonides and Ḥasdai Crescas.[31] Aristotle employs a similar argument to prove the absurdity of separating a thing from its essence (*Met.* VII, 6, 11–12). Again, the argument has no *locus standi* if the "accidental" nature of existence is interpreted as a "happening" due to a causal process.

(2) Moses of Narbonne (*Biʾūr Narbonī*, p. 9a) reproaches Maimonides for having failed to distinguish between two fundamentally different senses of "being" to which Aristotle had already drawn attention, and which had been stressed anew by Averroes. Unfortunately, he says, Avicenna had ignored this distinction, and Maimonides had blindly followed him. "To be" and "is" may, according to Aristotle, sometimes mean that a thing is true, and "not to be" that it is false (*Met.* V, 7; VI, 2). In another sense, being attaches to the "what" of a thing, that is to say, primarily to substance and in a secondary sense to the other categories as well. For in asking what quality "is", we are using the term "is" in a different sense. We may even say that not-being *is* not-being (*Met.* IV, 2, 3; VII, 4, 12–13). "The senses of essential being are those which are indicated by the figures of predication (i.e. the categories): for being has as many senses as there are ways of predication" (*Met.* V, 7, 4).[32] Likewise, Averroes says that "being" is a term "used for the true, i.e. that which being *in mente* agrees with what is *extra mentem*", and is used also "for that which has quiddity and essence *extra mentem*, irrespective as to whether this essence is conceived or not". "Hence the term 'being' is reducible to these two senses, i.e. the true and that which is *extra mentem*" (*Epitome*, ed. v.d. Bergh, p. 7; cf. *Met.* VI, 4).

Moses of Narbonne makes the point that Maimonides' failure to distinguish between the uses of the term "is" in the sense of "being true" on the one hand and of the being of the categories on the other prevented him from realizing the essential character of categorial being. For only when using the term "is" in the sense of "being true" do we separate being from essence, whilst in the other case essence and existence are inseparable. Aristotle does indeed say that "existent man" and "man" are the same thing.

[31] Cf. H. A. Wolfson, *JQR*, N.S., VII.

[32] Cf. Franz Brentano, *Von der mannigfachen Bedeutung des Seienden nach Aristoteles* (1862), p. 85: "Die Kategorien sind verschiedene Bedeutungen des ὄν." See also Sir W. D. Ross, *Aristotle's Metaphysics*, I, 307: "Thus Being is not a genus common to the various senses of being but has a different meaning in the various categories."

The duplication in the statement "He is a man and an existent man" yields no fresh meaning (*Met.* IV, 2, 7). Essence has intrinsic being. But Maimonides nowhere disputes this view. He is not concerned with the mode of being that attaches to essence but with the existence of concrete things.

(3) Asher ben Abraham Crescas, in his *Commentary* on the *Guide* (I, 57), identifies Maimonides' view with Avicenna's and quotes Averroes' refutation of it. "Avicenna supposed existence to be an accident, his argument being as follows: If existence signified the essence (*ᶜaẓmūt*), the statement, 'substance exists' would be equivalent to the statement, 'substance is substance'. Averroes, however, argued against him that 'existence' is spoken of in regard to essence and to being true, as e.g. in the statement, 'The man is existent or non-existent', as well as in the sense of the copula (*ḳesher*), as e.g. in the statement 'The man is (*nimẓaʾ*) righteous. Hence 'being' applies to substance essentially (*bĕ-ᶜaẓmūt*) and to the other categories *secundum prius et posterius* (*bi-ḳĕdīmah we-ʾiḥūr*); not homonymously (*bĕ-shitūf*) nor as a *nomen appelativum* (*bĕ-haṣkamah*) but *secundum prius et posterius*. It applies to substance absolutely (*bĕ-ʾamitūt*) and to each other category according to the nature thereof."

Avicenna's argument quoted in the above context occurs, as Dr. Rahmann was good enough to inform the present writer, in the *Kitāb al-Shifāʾ*, *Met.*, Maḳala, 1, Faṣl, 5, and reads as follows: "It is certain that the peculiar essence of everything is different from its being, i.e. its determinate existence. This is the case because if you say, 'such and such an essence exists' . . . your statement yields a definite and intelligible meaning; but if you say (which you *would* say if you equated essence and existence), 'essence is essence', it would be a superfluous and unprofitable talk.' What Avicenna means to convey is, according to Dr. Rahman, the following. (1) In asserting existential propositions of individual objects, we add nothing to the subject of which existence is asserted, and hence any such affirmation is "unprofitable". (2) If, however, we assert existence of quiddities such as "elephant" by saying, "elephant exist", the affirmation of existence is "profitable" because it yields some fresh information about reality. The proposition, "elephant exists" is equivalent to the proposition, "there exists an instance (or there exist instances) of elephant". Existence in such cases means "instantiation". The distinction between essence and existence does, however, not imply that existence is an accident in the logical sense of accident as opposed to substance and attached to it, as it were, from the outside.[33]

While Crescas offers a correct version of Avicenna's argument, Averroes seems to present it in a slightly different form. In the *Epitome* of Aristotle's *Metaphysics* (ed. S. van den Bergh, p. 8) we read as follows: "It was argued that if the term 'being' signified the essence, the statement, 'substance exists' would be self-contradictory". The same version of the argument occurs also in Moses Ibn Tibbon's Hebrew translation,[34] from which Jacob Mantinus made his Latin translation in the sixteenth century. Unfortunately, the present writer was unable to consult the editions of the two Arabic mss. (Cairo and Madrid) used by Dr. van den Bergh. It is, however, generally agreed that the Hebrew translation is more reliable than the Cairo ms.[35] It broadly corresponds with the Madrid ms. This would lead us to assume that the text before us is genuine, and that Averroes in fact misrepresented the true meaning of Avicenna. On the other hand, the statement by Asher Crescas of Avicenna's and Averroes' respective arguments appears to be a paraphrase of the relevant passages in the *Epitome* (cf. pp. 8, 28–29 in van den Bergh's edition). This would indicate that he had before him an Averroes text offering the correct version of Avicenna's argument.

Crescas also presents a brief summary of Averroes' statement that existence applies to substance essentially and to the other categories *secundum prius et posterius*, i.e. *analogice* as distinct from *aequivoce* and *univoce* (*Epitome*, p. 28). This view goes back to Aristotle who, speaking of the senses of "being" as related to the categories, made it clear that that which *is* primarily and absolutely is substance, and that the "being" of the other categories, whilst still essential, is not primary. How then was it permissible to use the term "being" in such a variety of senses? Aristotle's answer is that "we use the terms neither equivocally nor in the same sense, but just as we use the term 'medical' in *relation* to one and the same thing; but not *of* one and the same thing, nor yet

33 The above summary of Dr. Rahman's interpretation follows closely the text of his paper on "Essence and Existence in Avicenna".

34 Cf. Bodleian Library, ms. Can. Or. 63 (Neubauer 1377. 3), fol. 154a.

35 Cf. *Philosophical Essays* by Isaac Husik, ed. by Milton C. Nahm and Leo Strauss (1952), pp. 162–163.

equivocally. The term 'medical' is applied to a body and a function and an instrument, neither equivocally nor in one sense, but in relation to one thing" (*Met.* VII, 4, 12–16; IV, 2, 2). Essential being thus has "ten ultimate meanings or colourings answering to the ten ultimate kinds of things" (cf. Sir W. D. Ross, *ibid.*). But it has to be borne in mind that whilst "to be a quality' is indeed an essential mode of being, "to be white" is accidental being. Likewise, the concrete individual thing, with which Maimonides is concerned, has not essential but accidental being.

(4) Shemtob ben Joseph, in his *Commentary* on the *Guide* (I, 57), mentions four arguments which, in his view, induced Maimonides to hold the opinion that existence is an accident:

(*a*) We conceive the quiddity of things and may still remain in doubt as to their existence. Hence existence is something additional to essence. This argument reflects a line of thought pursued by Alfārābī in his *Ringstones of Wisdom* (ed. Dieterici, pp. 108–109).

(*b*) Essence is not caused, but we say *that* man exists, and ask *why* he exists. Hence existence cannot belong to essential things. In other words, the questions "why?" and "whether?" do not properly belong to essence. They apply only to existence. It follows that existence cannot be essential. This argument reflects Aristotle's distinction as to the four possible questions: *Whether* a thing is such and such; *why* it is such and such; *whether it exists*; and *what* it is (*Anal. Post.* 2. 1). "After the existence of a thing is known to us, we enquire as to its whatness in asking, e.g. 'What, then, is God?', or, 'What is man?'" (*loc. cit.*). Here Aristotle himself distinguishes between essence and existence as related to two different kinds of questions.[36] But in the same way in which Aristotle fails to draw the inference that existence must be accidental, Maimonides, too, may have left it at that.

(*c*) "Existence" is a term which can be used neither as a *nomen appelativum*, i.e. *secundum prius et posterius*, nor homonymously. Hence it must be used as a hybrid term (i.e. one denoting common accidental characteristics).[37] But seeing that hybrid terms denote accidental characteristics, and no accidental characteristics

[36] This fourfold division is used by Gabirol for a fourfold classification of ontological levels. Cf. *Fons Vitae*, V, 24. [For a discussion of Aristotle's four types of inquiry in early Arabic and Jewish philosophy, see now A. Altmann and S. M. Stern, *Isaac Israeli*, pp. 10–23.]

[37] Cf. Maimonides' *Treatise on Logic*, ch. 13; *Guide*, Introduction.

apply to God, it follows that the term "existence" which is applied to all beings cannot be used of God. This argument need not be taken seriously at all, since it begs the question. It pre-supposes the accidental character of existence instead of proving it. On the other hand, it does reflect Maimonides' view that the term "existence" cannot be used *analogice* of God and all other beings. But Maimonides describes the term as a homonymous one, and not merely as a hybrid.

(*d*) "Know thou that every agent, especially one endowed with intellect, must necessarily conceive the essence of the thing (i.e. which he produces) before it comes into existence. Take, e.g., a house which existed in the mind of the architect: it is the cause of the existence of the house existing *extra mentem*. Now, since all things exist by virtue of the First Cause who knows them, it follows that the quiddity of the thing exists prior to its existence. Hence existence is an accident to quiddity." This argument merely proves that the essences of things, i.e. the universals exist in the Mind of God, a view which is totally different from the one which describes existence as an accident. That the Platonic Forms exist in the Mind of God was already stated in Middle-Platonism, Neo-Pythagoreanism and Philo of Alexandria. But it did not there carry the connotation of existence as a mere accident of essence.

Shemtob completely fails to produce evidence that the above arguments had in fact weighed with Maimonides. He himself brushes these arguments aside by declaring that essence and existence are one. Like his predecessors, he joins the camp of Averroes. Like them, he seems to have misunderstood the real purport of Maimonides' concept. As we have seen, Maimonides remains firmly planted on Aristotelian ground.

In his *Aristotle, Fundamentals of the History of his Development* (Oxford, 1934), Werner Jaeger has suggested that there are three different conceptions of the nature of metaphysics underlying the different strata of the corpus of Aristotelian writings to which, probably by Andronicus, the name of *Metaphysics* was given in some complete edition in the Hellenistic age. They are (1) the earliest "theological" concept which replaces Plato's super-sensible Forms by the unmoved Mover, and sees the problems of metaphysics against a Platonic background; (2) the concept of metaphysics as the science of Being as such in the sense that it enquires into the kinds of Being uncritically assumed by the sciences; (3) metaphysics as ontology, describing the various senses of Being, including sensible as well as supersensible substance, and aiming at a morphology of Being (*loc. cit.*, p. 387).

The medieval definitions of the aims of metaphysics faithfully reflect these levels of meaning. Thus Alfārābī's "Catalogue of Sciences" (*Iḥsā᾿ al-ulūm*)[38] subdivides metaphysics into (1) the science which investigates Being *qua* Being; (2) the science which investigates the principles of the particular sciences; and (3) the science which investigates the supersensible beings. Similarly, Averroes assigns to metaphysics the threefold task of examining (1) the sensible beings *qua* beings; (2) the supersensible beings, including God; and (3) the principles of the particular sciences (cf. *Epitome*, pp. 4–5). Amongst Jewish authors, Shemtob ibn Falaquera lists the same three branches of metaphysics (cf. *Reshit Ḥoḵmah*, ed. M. David, Berlin, 1902, p. 53).[39] Maimonides, on the other hand, divides metaphysics into two parts only: (1) into an investigation of all beings which are supersensible, i.e. God and the angels; (2) into an inquiry into the principles (lit. remote causes) of the sciences (cf. *Treatise on Logic*, ch. 14). He entirely omits the ontological task of metaphysics, i.e. the investigation of Being *qua* Being. Whilst Aristotle had moved away from the theological concept of metaphysics towards the ontological one, Maimonides, in common with most of the Jewish metaphysicians, is primarily concerned with the theological aspect of metaphysics. The ontological elements of Aristotle's *Metaphysics*, in so far as they are made use of, now serve the purposes of theology. The concepts of matter and form, potentiality and actuality are employed to this end. But Maimonides seems entirely to ignore Aristotle's investigation into the manifold senses of essential being. This central part of the Aristotelian ontology is left out of account altogether. It is here that Maimonides parts

[38] Quoted in L. Gardet-M. M. Anawati, *Introduction à la Théologie Musulmane* (Paris, 1948), p. 103.

[39] This definition of the objects of metaphysics forms part of the classification of sciences introduced into Arabic philosophy through the translation of John Philoponus' Commentary on Porphyry's *Isagoge*. Sometimes, the Aristotelian scheme is mixed with the Platonic classification which identifies metaphysics with logic. Cf. H. A. Wolfson, *The Classification of the Sciences in Medieval Jewish Philosophy*, HUCA Jubilee Volume, 1925; Leo Strauss, *Farabi's Plato*, Louis Ginzberg Jubilee Volume, American Academy for Jewish Research (New York, 1945), pp. 389ff.

company with Aristotle. He does not repudiate the notion of a gradation of being according to the categories, but, being interested primarily in the theological angle, the different shades of being in all created beings are neutralised, as it were, and reduced to one single level compared with the totally other Being of God. The only ontological distinction which matters from the theological point of view is the one between created and uncreated being. All created existence is caused, actualized from potentiality, and willed by God. The term "being" is therefore used homonymously of God and the created beings. Maimonides makes no use whatever of Aristotle's concept of the analogy of being on which Averroes laid such great stress, and which Alfārābī had already used to theological advantage. Both Alfārābī and Averroes had conceded the admissibility of applying the term "being" to God and created existence *secundum prius et posterius*. They held that God has being primarily and essentially while all other beings possess existence only in a derivative sense, i.e. derived from God. Alfārābī's view is clearly stated in his "The political Governments", a work well known to Maimonides and highly praised by him in his Letter to Samuel Ibn Tibbon.[40] It is all the more remarkable that Maimonides refrained from using Aristotle's concept of the analogy of being and insisted on the homonymous nature of the term. The reason for this attitude must be sought in his neoplatonic orientation which he shared with Avicenna. It was left to his more radically Aristotelian successor Gersonides to introduce the analogical concept of Being into Jewish theology, and thus to follow the lead given by Averroes. But even then the issue was not fully settled, as is apparent from Ḥasdai Crescas' attack on both Avicenna and Averroes, and his compromise suggestion that existence is neither accidental to essence nor identical with it but "essential" to it.

[40] Alfārābī's "The political Governments" was edited in Hyderabad in 1346, and appeared in a German translation ("Die Staatsleitung von Alfarabi") by Brömle (Leiden, 1904). We possess the work also in Samuel Ibn Tibbon's Hebrew translation under the title, *Sefer Hatĕḥalōt Ha-Nimẓaʾōt* (ed. Ẓĕḇi Filipowski (Leipzig, 1849), in *Sefer Ha-ʾAsīf*). The passage referred to in the text is found on p. 16 of this Hebrew edition. As to the significance of the work for an appraisal *of* Maimonides, cf. Leo Strauss, *Farabi's Plato*, pp. 357ff.

5

A NOTE ON THE RABBINIC DOCTRINE OF CREATION

The impulse for cosmological speculation by the Palestinian rabbis of the first three centuries C.E. came chiefly from two sources: Plato's *Timaeus* mediated by Philo of Alexandria, and Gnostic writings of various kinds. The reaction to Gnosticism expressed itself not only in tart replies to attacks but also in the formation of a rabbinic Gnosis of its own (designated as *maᶜaseh bereshit*), only remnants of which have survived.[1] Plato's cosmology has left traces in the more popular and less esoteric rabbinic Haggadah, the most notable instance being R. Oshaᶜya's adaptation of Tim. 29a ("The artificer looked for a pattern to that which is eternal") in Gen. R. 1:1 ("God looked to the Torah and created the world").[2] It also engendered speculation on whether the world was created out of primordial matter or out of nothing.

In Hellenistic Judaism we meet both views. The Wisdom of Solomon (11:18) speaks of creation as an act of shaping the world "out of unformed Matter" (*ex amórphou húlēs*), which goes back to Tim. 50d and Posidonius' description of matter (*hulē*) as "without quality and form" (*ápoios kai ámorphos*).[3] 2 Macc. 7:28, on the other hand, clearly formulates the doctrine of *creatio ex nihilo* in

[1] Cf. G. Scholem, *Major Trends in Jewish Mysticism*, Revised Edition, pp. 42, 73 *et passim*; A. Altmann, "Gnostic Themes in Rabbinic Cosmology", *Essays in Honour of the Very Rev. Dr. J. Hertz* (1942), pp. 19–32.

[2] For the literature on the subject, cf. *Bereshit Rabba*, ed. J. Theodor, p. 2, to which is to be added L. Baeck, "Zwei Beispiele midraschischer Predigt", *MGWJ* (1925), pp. 258f.; H. A. Wolfson, *Philo*, I, pp. 204ff.; I. Baer, *Zion*, XXIII–XXIV (1958–1959), pp. 141ff.

[3] Cf. I. Heinemann, *Poseidonios' Metaphysische Schriften*, Vol. I (1921), p. 140. Philo likewise teaches creation out of prime matter. See *De opificio mundi*, 7–9.

opposition to the Platonic view: God made the world *ex ouk óntōn*. As has already been noted,[4] this is the first literary record of the Jewish doctrine of creation out of nothing. It is re-echoed in some of the Pseudepigrapha such as Slavonic Enoch 24:2 ("I called all things from non-being into being") and 4 Ezra 4:38–54 ("Thy word accomplished this work"),[5] where the stress on the creative power of the "word" implies the doctrine of *creatio ex nihilo*.[6]

In rabbinic Judaism opinion oscillated for some time between accepting and rejecting the notion of primordial matter or elements. The discussion between R. Gamliel II and a philosopher recorded in Gen. R. 1:9 (p. 8, Theodor) shows that the doctrine of *creatio ex nihilo* was considered the sound orthodox view towards the end of the first century C.E. But as late as in the third century, R. Yoḥanan could still uphold the view that God created the world by taking two coils (*peqiᶜot*) of elemental fire and snow and joining them one to the other, a theory reminiscent of Plato's account of the creation of the world soul out of the elements by dividing the compound into two parts and joining them at the centre like the letter X.[7]

The present paper is not concerned with tracing either of the two cosmological trends we have briefly referred to, i.e. the Gnostic and the Platonic ones. Its object is to draw attention to what one might describe as a third point of departure different from both the Gnostic and Platonic. As we shall see, the doctrine concerned is the one of emanation.

A number of midrashic sources[8] record a conversation between R. Simeon ben Jehoṣadaq and R. Samuel ben Naḥman, the famous haggadic teacher of the third century. "As I have heard that you are a master of Haggadah, tell me whence the light was

[4] By Prof. Scholem in his *Eranos* lecture, "Schöpfung aus Nichts und Selbstverschränkung Gottes", *Eranos—Jahrbuch*, XXV, (1957), p. 97. See also D. Neumark, *Geschichte der jüdischen Philosophie*, Vol. II, 1 (1910), p. 345; J. Cohn, "Die Weltschöpfung in der Sapienz", *Festschrift zum siebzigsten Geburtstag Jakob Guttmanns* (1915), p. 25.

[5] See also *Sib. Oracle*, III 20.

[6] In the Slavonic *Book of Enoch* we meet both the doctrine of *creatio ex nihilo* (see above) and a reference to the creative Word (24–30).

[7] D. Neumark's interpretation of this passage in the sense of emanation (*loc. cit.*, Vol. I, 1 (1907), pp. 81–83) seems far-fetched.

[8] See J. Theodor, *Bereschit Rabba*, p. 19 (on Gen. R. 3, 4), where all the parallels are listed. Cf. also W. Bacher, *Die Agada der pal. Amoräer*, Vol. I (1892), p. 545.

created",[9] R. Simeon asked. R. Samuel's reply was: "The Holy One, blessed be He, wrapped himself in a white garment,[10] and its splendour[11] shone forth from one end of the world to the other." He gave his answer "in a whisper" (*bi-leḥishā*). R. Simeon retorted with astonishment, "Is there not a Scriptural verse which says so explicitly, namely Ps. 104:2 ("He covereth himself with light as with a garment"), to which R. Samuel replied, "As I have heard it in a whisper, I told it to you in a whisper." R. Berekhyah, a Palestinian *Amora* of the fourth century, offers an alternative suggestion in the name of R. Isaac: "The light was created from the place of the Temple."

Obviously, the doctrine contained in R. Samuel's rather cryptic statement goes much beyond a recapitulation of the Psalmist's poetic metaphor. It ostensibly reads into it some meaning which could be revealed only to the initiated. Speaking "in a whisper" is a technical term for the communication of esoteric teaching.[12] The doctrine concerned is said to represent a tradition received from R. Samuel's teacher, most probably R. Jonathan the Elder, and possibly going back to a still older source. The question put by R. Simeon ben Jehoṣadaq must likewise be considered one of old standing. It pre-supposes that the plain meaning of Gen. 1:3 ("And God said, Let there be light, and there was light") was no longer considered as self-evident. In fact, the reply given by R. Samuel ben Naḥman implies that the light was not created by a Divine *fiat* or the Word of God but as an effulgence from the splendour of the Divine glory or from the "garment" in which God wrapped himself, as the mythical image describes it. We may see in this doctrine of emanation a decisive breaking-away from the cosmology of the Word as a creative power, preparing the ground for the more elaborate theories of emanation which were

[9] Some recensions read, "Tell me how God created the world." As Bacher, *loc. cit.*, has pointed out, this version cannot be regarded as the original one. The question obviously concerned the creation of the light. The two different formulations of the question are discussed by Sverre Aalen, *Die Begriffe 'Licht' und 'Finsternis' im Alten Testament, im Spätjudentum und im Rabbinismus* (Oslo, 1951), pp. 262–264. Aalen suggests that there is no real difference between them, seeing that the creation of the world is a result of the creation of the light. We cannot accept this facile interpretation.

[10] Other readings: "as in a garment"; "in a garment".

[11] Other readings: "the splendour of His majesty".

[12] Cf. W. Bacher, *Die exegetische Terminologie der jüdischen Traditionsliteratur* (1905), I, p. 94; II, 96, where, however, our passage is not listed, and the esoteric character of doctrines communicated "in a whisper" is not clearly stated. [For a Zoroastrian parallel see Jean Doresse, *The Secret Books of the Egyptian Gnostics* (1960), p. 196.]

to emerge, under neoplatonic influence, at a much later stage of Jewish cosmological speculation.

An analysis of R. Samuel's *midrash* has to start from the fact that the light, the origin of which it seeks to explain, is obviously not the physical light of which we hear in Gen. 1:3. The plain text in Genesis suggests that the creation of light took place only after heaven and earth had been called into being; that the earth was unformed and void, and that there was darkness, the deep and the spirit of God hovering over the face of the waters. Light is the last creation of the first day. This tradition is upheld in Philo's *De opificio mundi* (§§26–29), the *Book of Jubilees* (2, 2) and *Midrash Tadsheh* (6), where we hear of seven things that were created on the first day, viz. heaven, earth, darkness, the abyss, the spirit, water, and, to crown it all, the light.[13] (It makes no difference that in Philo's account only the incorporeal essences of these things were created on the first day.) We meet with a different view in Philo's *De somniis* (I, 75) where the *Logos* is identified with the light which was created in the beginning. God himself, it is pointed out, is the archetype of all light, the model of the model, and the *Logos* is the model or pattern, the Word which contains the fullness of God "light in fact". "For God said, 'Let light come into being'." From this it is clear that the Light which is the *Logos* was the first creation, God's First-born as it were, and the ideal world described in *De opif. mundi* as the work of the first day may be interpreted as the *Logos* or Light spoken of in *De somniis*. Similarly, the cosmogony of *Poimandres* describes the universe which exists within the light as the archetype of the visible universe as yet uncreated.[14] The Slavonic *Book of Enoch* (25A) also sees in the coming forth of the Light from Adoil the first act of creation, preceding the creation of heaven and earth.

That the light preceded heaven and earth in the order of creation is a view also held by several rabbinic teachers, notwithstanding the plain meaning of the Genesis text. At about the middle of the second century, R. Jehuda ben ʿIlaʾi, a Tanaitic teacher of the third generation, upheld this doctrine against R. Neḥemiah, his contemporary. An anonymous midrash states that there are things

[13] In *b. Ḥagigah* 12a ten things are said to have been created on the first day, viz. heaven, earth, *tohu*, *bohu*, light, darkness, spirit, water, the quality (*middah*) of day and the quality of night. Similarly in *Schatzhöhle*, ed. C. Bezold (1883), 1, 3.

[14] See C. H. Dodd, *The Bible and the Greeks* (1935), p. 109.

which Moses left unexplained in the Torah and which were later expounded by King David in the Psalms. Thus, according to the Torah, God created the world first and the light afterwards. But David came and told us in Ps. 104:2 that, in fact, the light was created first, for it is said, "He covereth himself in light as in a garment, and stretcheth out the heavens"—first the light and then the heavens (Ex. R. 15:22). Similarly, R. Jehuda ben Simeon ben Pazzi, a Palestinian *Amora* who lived one generation after R. Samuel ben Naḥman, expresses the view that several things which appear "deep and veiled" in the Genesis account of creation were expounded in later books of Scripture. Thus, he declares, the creation of the light which was left unexplained in Genesis was explained more fully in Ps. 104:2 (Gen. R. 1:6).

The question, "Whence was the light created?" which was put to R. Samuel ben Naḥman makes sense only on the assumption that the light was in fact the first creation. The questioner obviously followed the tradition which we have traced, and was anxious to learn what the famous Haggadist had to say about the origin of the light. There is no need to read into this question anything related to the Gnostic attacks on the Jewish God who created the world. Origen repudiates in his *Contra Celsum*[15] two Gnostic heresies concerning the verse, "Let there be light." The one, reflecting the opinion of Tatian, interpreted the words as a prayer for light uttered by the demiurge. The second expressed astonishment at the great God having lent the light to the "accursed God". Here we have a clear echo of Marcion whose teachings were well known to Celsus and against whom Origen made such a determined stand.[16] We know that the Rabbis of Palestine in the third century were engaged in a great deal of polemics against the Gnostics, and that the defence of Judaism which in an earlier period had been the concern of the Patriarch and his Academy had now been left to individual teachers. R. Samuel ben Naḥman records a trenchant reply to a Gnostic interpretation of Gen. 1:26 in the name of his teacher, R. Jonathan.[17] But there is no warrant for reading into our *midrash* and the question which prompted it any attempt to answer the Gnostic *innuendo* that the

[15] Edited Henry Chadwick (1953), p. 368, VI, 52.

[16] See Chadwick, *loc. cit.*, pp. XXVIII, 369, n. 2.

[17] Gen. R. 8:8. See A. Büchler, "Über die Minim von Sepphoris und Tiberias im zweiten und dritten Jahrhundert", *Judaica: Festschrift für Hermann Cohen* (1912), pp. 282, 294–295.

creation of the light must have been embarrassing to the demiurge. The question, "Whence did God create the light?" is but a natural corollary to the view that before all other things, including heaven and earth, God created the light.

The question does, however, imply that the light which was the first creation was something different from the physical light we know. The reference is undoubtedly to the primordial light of which R. Jehudah ben Simeon ben Pazzi said that in it Adam could see "from one end of the world to another".[18] It should be noted that R. Samuel ben Naḥman uses the same phrase when saying in his reply that by God's wrapping himself in a garment, a splendour shone forth "from one end of the world to the other". There is, moreover, some inner connection between the concept of the primordial light and that of primordial man, as I have tried to show elsewhere.[19] We have to recognize that in haggadic thought the two motifs overlap in the same way in which Philo's *Logos* is described both as the light of the first day and as the heavenly man.[20] It should then be clear that in posing the question, "Whence did the light come into being?", R. Simeon ben Jehoṣadaq referred to the primordial light, and that this notion carried certain undertones of a highly mystical nature.

We have now to consider the answer given by R. Samuel ben Naḥman. What is the meaning of the statement that God wrapped himself in a garment? Robert Eisler has furnished us with a wealth of information on the theme of the "Weltenmantel", and quoted our *midrash* as evidence of the survival of pagan myths of oriental origin in rabbinic Judaism.[21] But this does not lead us very far. It does not explain why Ps. 104:2 was considered innocuous, whereas R. Samuel ben Naḥman's *midrash* had to be communicated in a whisper. V. Aptovitzer's interesting study on our

[18] Gen. R. 11:2; Ex. R. 35:1; Num. R. 13:5. In *b. Hag.* 12a the statement is attributed to R. Eleazar. The spiritual nature of the primordial light is also stressed in patristic literature. Basil the Great (b. *c.* 330; Bishop of Caesarea after 370) refers to it in his first homily on the Hexaëmeron as "a spiritual light" (*phōs noētón*), preceding the genesis of the world. Cf. Basile de Césarée, *Homélies sur l'Hexaeméron*, Text Grec, Introduction et Traduction de S. Giet (Paris) (in the series, *Sources Chrétiennes*, ed. de Lubac-Daniélou).

[19] *loc. cit.*, pp. 28–32.

[20] Cf. E. R. Goodenough, *By Light, Light* (1935), pp. 366, 381, 383. No specific reference to the Light motif is made in H. A. Wolfson's account of Philo's interpretation of the story of the six days of creation. See his *Philo*, I, 310, 393.

[21] Cf. R. Eisler, *Weltenmantel und Himmelszelt*, I (1910), pp. 224–225.

subject[22] is vitiated by the untenable theory that R. Samuel ben Naḥman regarded the light as a kind of prime matter ("Urstoff"), and that R. Isaac similarly used the term "place of the Temple" as a metaphor for light in the sense of prime matter. Aptovitzer ignores the fact that our *midrash* is not concerned with the origin of the world but with the question whence the light was created. Nor does he make any definite suggestion as to the meaning of the mythical image describing God as wrapping himself in a garment.

It may be noted, in the first place, that R. Samuel ben Naḥman speaks in another context of ten garments of God.[23] This particular statement is based on a number of Biblical passages in which God is depicted as clothing himself in majesty, power, justice, etc.[24] It hardly goes beyond the purpose of homiletical edification but clearly illustrates the author's fondness of the motif of God's garment. It also points to the intrinsic meaning of the term "garment" as denoting an "attribute" or "aspect" of God. "Putting on the garment" must therefore be tantamount to manifesting a hidden aspect of the Divine. We suggest that the "garment" of God mentioned in our *midrash* is identical with God's Wisdom (*Ḥokhmah*) or *Logos*, and that the splendour shining forth from it is the primordial light. The image reflects a widespread theme of hellenistic thought, and can be fully appreciated only against its background. Thus the god Aion, representing the dimensions of time and space, is said to contain the five elements or realms of light which are his "garment". As H. Junker has shown, this conception is of Iranian origin, and Aion stands for the god Zarvan.[25] It becomes prominent in the Manichean myth of creation, and is also reflected in the Mandaean Ginza.[26] A faint echo of Zarvan-Aion as the bearer of light can be found in the Slavonic *Book of Enoch* (25A), which was probably written by an Alexandrian Jew of the first century. It depicts the first act of creation as the bursting of the belly of Adoil and a "great light" coming out. Born of that light, there came forth a "great Age" showing all creation which

[22] Cf. V. Aptowitzer, "Zur Kosmologie der Agada. Licht als Urstoff", *MGWJ* (1928), pp. 363–370.

[23] Cf. Cant. R. 4:10; *Pesikta R. K.* (B), p. 147b–148a; Deut. R. 2, end.

[24] The passages concerned are Ps. 104:1; 93:1; Dan. 7:9; Isa. 59:17; 63:2.

[25] Cf. H. Junker, *Über iranische Quellen der hellenistischen Aion-Vorstellung, Vorträge der Bibliothek Warburg* (1921–1922).

[26] Cf. R. Reitzenstein, *Das Iranische Erlösungsmysterium* (1921), pp. 39; 41; *Ginza*, ed. Lidzbarski, p. 7.

God had harboured in his Mind.[27] The "great Age" is obviously identical with the god Zarvan or Aion who is the son of Light and a kind of *Logos*. The idea of Zarvan-Aion-*Logos* being clothed in light as in a garment and containing all creation is closely akin to Philo's *Logos* doctrine. In a passage quoted by Aptovitzer, but not analyzed by him, Philo describes the *Logos* as "illuminated by a brilliant light" and as "putting on the garments", the symbolism being allegorically derived from the Biblical description of the High Priest, his anointment with oil, and his putting on the garments of office (*De fuga*, 110). The garments, Philo explains, are the cosmos, "for he[28] arrays himself in earth and air and water and fire and all that comes from these". This statement strikingly recalls the conception of Aion containing the five elements or realms of light which are his garment. In a sense, Philo's *Logos* is a demythologized Zarvan-Aion. There is no trace in Philo of the Gnostic interpretations (found in later writings, notably in the *Chuastuanift* and *Acta Archelai*) of the "garment" of Zarvan-Aion as "armour" in the battle against the demons of darkness. That the motif of the five elements as garment is older than its interpretation as armour has been shown by Reitzenstein.[29] We suggest that R. Samuel ben Naḥman's description of God putting on a garment of light is modelled on the Philo passage we have quoted. It portrays God as clothing himself in the *Logos* or Wisdom or primordial Light, the garment being the *Logos* itself, not, as in Philo, the cosmos or the elements. Putting on the garment of light is another way of saying that God revealed his *Logos* by the light which radiated from it.

There can be little doubt that the effulgence of the primordial light from the garment of God, i.e. the Divine *Logos* or Wisdom is regarded in terms of radiation or emanation. The use in our text of the phrase, "its splendour shone forth" (*hiḇhīq ziwō*) clearly

[27] See R. H. Charles, *The Apocrypha and Pseudepigrapha of the Old Testament in English*, Vol. II, p. 445. Charles explains the name *Adoil* as a malformation of Yad-El.

The "garments of glory" mentioned in Enoch 62:15 signify the eternal life in the new Aeon. Cf. H. Bietenhard, *Die himmlische Welt im Urchristentum und Spätjudentum*, Tübingen (1951), pp. 226–227.

[28] I.e. the *Logos*, not God, as Colson and Whitaker, *Philo*, Loeb Classical Library, V, p. 69, suggest by their spelling of "he" with a capital H.

[29] *Loc. cit.*, p. 41. For the identification of primordial man with Ormuzd, son of Zarvan, cf. Reitzenstein-Schaeder, *Studien zum antiken Synkretismus* (1926), pp. 276, 281.

indicates this. We have therefore before us a somewhat veiled but unmistakable form of the doctrine of emanation. It does not suggest an emanation of the *Logos*-Wisdom from the Divine essence but is content to allude to the emanation of the primordial light from the Divine *Logos*, mythically described as God's garment. As to the precise nature of the primordial light, we may say that it partly coincides with the *Logos* as the pre-figuration of all creation, as a *κόσμος νοητός* in the Philonic sense, and partly represents the physical light as well. In the hellenistic tradition, even the physical light of the sun is considered as on the border-line between spirit and matter. As A. H. Armstrong has shown, Plotinus' theory of emanation is largely modelled on this concept of the nature of light. In a passage of the *Hermetica* the light of the sun, the source of all being and life in the visible world, is said to be the receptacle of "intelligible substance" (*noētē ousia*).[30] There is, therefore, nothing intrinsically difficult about R. Samuel ben Naḥman's doctrine of the effulgence of light—even physical light—from the Divine *Logos*. The theory made perfect sense in the hellenistic climate of thought.

R. Samuel ben Naḥman's *midrash* became, however, unintelligible to medieval Jewish philosophers who had lost the tradition offering the key to its symbolism. As is well known, Maimonides (*Guide* II, 26) confesses his utter bewilderment in the face of the strange view of creation propounded by our *midrash* in the form given to it in *Pirqē de-R. Eliezer* (ch. 3). He is inclined to see in it a reference to creation from light as prime matter (as Aptovitzer did after him), and emphatically rejects the doctrine implied. In contrast to him, R. Isaac the Blind and the mystics of Gerona upheld the *midrash* by interpreting it in conformity with their emanationist doctrine of creation. Their comments on our *midrash* are found in three places, viz. R. Ezra's *Perush ᶜal Shir ha-shirim* (falsely attributed to Naḥmanides), Altona, pp. 5b–6a; R. Ezra's letter to R. Abraham ben Isaac, Hazan of Gerona and known as a Qabbalist, in reply to a question put to him; published by G. Scholem in *Sefer Bialik*, pp. 157–158; and in R. ᶜAzriel's *Perush ha-Agadot*, ed. Tishby, pp. 110–111. The ᶜAzriel passage is somewhat corrupt but can easily be restored on the basis of the text in R. Ezra's *Perush ᶜal Shir ha-shirim*. The importance of this passage lies

[30] Cf. A. H. Armstrong, *The Architecture of the Intelligible Universe in the Philosophy of Plotinus* (1940), pp. 54–58.

in the fact that it mentions R. Isaac the Blind (*Rabbenu he-Ḥasid*) as author of the interpretation offered.

The passage in R. Ezra's *Perush* links the Comment on our *midrash* with Cant. 3:9 ("King Solomon made himself a palanquin of the wood of Lebanon"), interpreting "Lebanon" as a mystical symbol of the "clear wisdom" (*ḥokhmā melubenet*), a reference to the "white garment" (*simlah lebhanah*) mentioned in some of the variant readings of our text.[31] The passage reads as follows:

> "King Solomon made himself a palanquin of the wood of Lebanon." This means to say that from the emanation and radiance of Wisdom the light shone forth, and emanated from Him (?). This is meant by what is said in Gen. R.: "Whence was the light created? The Holy One, blessed be He, wrapped Himself as in a garment, and its splendour shone forth from one end of the world to the other." The "garment" is the preparing of the emanation of the all-encompassing Wisdom. "He wrapped himself" means that He (?) received a splendour from that emanation, and light in the true sense shone forth.
>
> This is likewise the opinion of R. Eliezer the Great, who said: "Whence were the heavens created? He took part of the light of His garment, put it on like a robe, and they (sc. the heavens) were extending continually, as it is written, He covereth himself with light as with a garment, He spreadeth the heavens like a curtain. From which place was the earth created? He took part of the snow under the Throne of His glory and threw it, as it is written, He saith to the snow, Be thou earth" (Job 37:6). This follows Plato's view who said that it was absurd (to think) that the Creator should produce something out of nothing, and that there is a (pre-) existent matter. It stands to Him in the same relation as for comparison's sake clay to the potter and iron to the blacksmith, who form it as they please. The Creator, blessed be He, likewise forms from matter heaven and earth and sometimes something different. His inability to create something out of nothing does not indicate any deficiency on his part, even as it does not indicate any deficiency on his part that He is unable to produce what is logically absurd, e.g. creating a square the diagonal of which is equal to its length or combining two contraries at the same instant. Just as this does not imply any deficiency in His power, in the same way no short-coming on his part is indicated by his inability to effect an emanation of something from nothing. For this belongs to the logically absurd. King Solomon in his pure wisdom and correct thinking meant this (when he said) in (an utterance inspired by) the Holy Spirit: "Of the woods of Lebanon"—thence everything

[31] Cf. *Teʿudā ḥadashā le-toldot reʾshit ha-qabbalā, Sefer Bialik*, pp. 155–162.

> emanated. The essences existed before, but the emanation was "innovated". To this they referred—be their memory for a blessing—when saying, "Let there be light, and there was light." It is not written, "and light came to be", but, "and light was", i.e. had already emanated from the supernal Light, since it had been in the supernal Power.

Some of the notions expressed in R. Ezra's *Perush* are further expanded in the letter to R. Abraham:

> Where does our teacher Moses (sc. ben Maimon) come into conflict with the Qabbalah? Know thou that the words of R. Eliezer the Great are absolutely correct in saying "Whence were the heavens created, and whence was the earth created?", for he follows the opinion of Plato who said that it is impossible to assume that God produced anything from nothing; but matter has always been in existence. It stands to Him in the same relation as e.g. the clay to the potter, or the iron to the blacksmith who do with it what they please, God likewise one time forming of it heaven and earth, at another time forming of it something else. All this is exactly as our Teacher Moses wrote in the *Guide to the Perplexed* (II, 13) where he speaks of the various theories concerning the question whether the world is eternal. With regard to this King Solomon said, "King Solomon"—i.e. the Holy one, blessed be He, unto whom peace belongeth—"made himself a palanquin of the wood of Lebanon" (Cant. 3:9)—i.e. from the emanation of the splendour of Wisdom which is his garment. Likewise, our Sages of blessed memory, said, "Lebanon denotes the supernal Holy of Holies" (Cant. 3:19). By the "palanquin' is meant His "glory" or Name or Throne, and it emanates from the Wisdom which is in the "Nought". But we must not ask whence the light of his garment was created, for we must not break through the barrier and search for the hidden and that which thought cannot grasp. Likewise our Sages said "Whence was the world created?" The Holy One, blessed be He, wrapped himself in a white garment, and its splendour radiated from one end of the world to the other, as it is written, "Who coverest thyself with light as with a garment" (Ps. 104:2), i.e. with the Splendour of Wisdom. For this reason, Wisdom is called *Lebanon*. The truth is that the essences (*hawayot*) had been in existence before, whereas the emanation was "innovated", for it is written, "He uncovereth deep things out of (the) darkness (of the Nought of Thought)" (Job 12:22), "And bringeth out to light the shadow of death" (*ibid.*): "And God said, Let there be light." "He revealeth the deep and secret things; He knoweth what is in the darkness, and the light dwelleth with Him" (Dan. 2:22). He brought the light out from the darkness. The "deep" denotes the Chariot

(*Merkabā*) and the "secret things" denote the work of Creation (*maᶜaseh bereshit*). "He knoweth what is in the darkness" means that He caused the emanation of the essences which were in the darkness; and "the light dwelleth with Him" means that He brought out the light from the darkness, as it is written, "And darkness was upon the face of the deep . . . and God said, Let there be light."

The doctrine delineated in these passages goes far beyond the meaning of R. Samuel ben Naḥman's *midrash*. It postulates the Divine Nought (*ᵓAyin*) as the hidden source of the supernal Wisdom. It expresses itself in favour of the Platonic doctrine of pre-existent matter, and it differentiates between the pre-existence in the Divine Mind of the essences of things and their actual "innovation" (in time) as a result of a process of emanation. Moreover, the background of this doctrine is no longer hellenistic philosophy and mythology but a certain type of Neoplatonism such as we find in Isaac Israeli, the tenth-century Jewish philosopher, whose "Chapter on the Elements" is quoted by R. ᶜAzriel.[32] There is a direct line from Israeli's concept of supernal Wisdom to the one we find in the incipient Qabbalah of R. Isaac the Blind and the Gerona mystics. But notwithstanding all these differences, the essential element of R. Samuel's *midrash* has been preserved: The light is an emanation from the Divine *Logos* or Wisdom, which contains the totality of creation within it. Creation is a process of emanation. It was not by pure chance, therefore, that the thirteenth-century mystics of Spain found it possible to connect their doctrine with the *midrash* of the third-century teacher of Palestine.[33]

[32] Cf. Tishby, *loc. cit.*, p. 110, n. 19.

[33] Cf. my article, "Isaac Israeli's Chapter on the Elements", *JJS*, Vol. VII (1956), pp. 31ff. [For a subsequent treatment of the subject discussed here see G. Scholem, *Jewish Gnosticism, Merkabah Mysticism, and Talmudic Tradition* (1960), pp. 58–64.]

6

SAADYA'S THEORY OF REVELATION: ITS ORIGIN AND BACKGROUND

The view seems to be commonly held that Saadya's doctrine of the "created Glory" (*Kāḇōd niḇrā*) and "created Word" (*dibbūr niḇrā*), which sums up and formulates his theory of Revelation, was borrowed from the well-known Muᶜtazilite concept of the *Created Kalām* of *Allāh*. J. Guttmann was the first to suggest, "diese ganze Anschauung scheint mutazilitschen Ursprungs zu sein". S. Horovitz expressed himself in exactly the same words. I. Goldziher stressed the view of Saadya's dependence on the *Muᶜtazila* with regard to his *dibbūr niḇrā*-doctrine only. Both Guttmann and Horovitz assumed that the Ḳaraites too adopted the theory from the *Muᶜtazila*. Whereas they held Saadya to be directly influenced by the Muᶜtazilites, S. Munk took it for granted that the theory was first adopted by the Ḳaraites, who in turn influenced Saadya.[1]

Before entering into a discussion of the alleged Muᶜtazilite influence on Saadya, we should first like to state that no evidence has been produced of the assertion that the doctrine with which we are concerned was originally adopted by the Ḳaraites, as Munk suggested. Japhet b. ᶜAli, who in his *Commentary on Ex.* (19:20) interprets the manifestation of God in terms of *created Glory*, was younger than Saadya. He wrote in Jerusalem from about 950–980,[2] and shows himself to be influenced by Saadya in

[1] Cf. Jacob Guttmann, *Die Religionsphilosophie des Saadia* (1882), p. 119, n. 2; S. Horovitz, *Die Prophetologie in der jüdischen. Religionsphilosophie* (1883), p. 41; I. Goldziher, *Le dogme et la loi de l'Islam*, pp. 92–93, and "Mélanges", *REJ*, 60, pp. 32–33; S. Munk, *Guide des Égarés*, I, p. 286. Cf. also M. Ventura, *La philosophie de Saadia Gaon* (1934), pp. 162–163, 183.

[2] Cf. M. Steinschneider, "*Arabische Literatur der Juden*", pp. 81f.

several respects.[3] It can be assumed that his explanation of Ex. 19:20 is taken from Saadya. Benjamin al-Nahāwandī, who is referred to by Guttmann as a contemporary of Saadya's, lived in the middle of the ninth century, but his doctrine of Revelation, which coincides with the one held by the Maghāriya and is centred in the idea of the Angel, has nothing to do with Saadya's theory of the created Word and created Glory. The passage from Judah Hadassi's *Eshkol ha-Kofer* (25b), quoted by Guttmann, contains no evidence that Benjamin Nahāwandī held the theory of *Kaḇōd niḇrā*. It merely records that in the opinion of Nahāwandī as well as the Muᶜtazilites and the Greek philosophers[4] the Divine Glory, its throne, all other manifestations of Glory and the angels were created on the First Day together with the Heavens.[5] This view of Nahāwandī, provided it is authentic, opposes the Rabbinic doctrine of the pre-existence of the Divine Throne of glory.[6] But it does not consider the problem of Revelation. Hadassi, who enlarges upon Nahāwandī's view, employs the term *Kāḇōd ha-bāruʾi* in order to interpret this doctrine.[7] From this it cannot be inferred that Nahāwandī himself used the term. Guttmann's proof for Nahāwandī's acquaintance with the doctrine of the *Kaḇōd niḇrā* thus falls to the ground. Consequently, no support can be given to Munk's thesis from this quarter. So far as we can see, no Ḳaraite author before Saadya held the theory of the created Word and created Glory. This applies both to ᶜAnan and Nahāwandī as well as to al-Ḳumīsī, though the latter's view differed somewhat from Nahāwandī's.[8] Josef al-Baṣīr, the author of the *Muḥtawi*, who represented the *dibbūr nibrā* doctrine in a pure Muᶜtazilite

[3] Cf. S. Poznański's review of the edition of Japhet b. 'Ali's "Com. on Proverbs", in *JQR*, 13 (1901), p. 341.

[4] By the *ḥaḵmē ha-daᶜat* apparently the Muᶜtazilites are referred to, by the *ḥaḵmē hayĕwanim*, the philosophers. Similarly, Aaron b. Elia calls the Muᶜtazilites *ḥaḵmē has-seḵel* in opposition to the *ḥaḵmē yawan*. Cf. *ᶜEṣ ḥayyim*, ed. Franz Delitzsch, p. 165.

[5] *U-ḇinyamin . . . amar ki ḳōdem kol bĕriyā barāʾ elohi[m] ha-kaḇōd ve-kissʾō u-ḵelal ha-keḇōdōt ve-ha-malʾaḵim ba-ᶜōlamōt ve-ḵen ḥaḵmē ha-daᶜat ve-ḥaḵmē ha-yĕvanim be-malḵutenu ōmrim ki bĕ-emōr bĕ-reshit barāʾ elohi[m] et ha-shamayim ve-et ha-areṣ bĕʾūrō et kĕḇōdō ve-ḵitotav ᶜim ha-shamayim ha-ᶜelyōnim ve-aḥar ken ve-et ha-areṣ ve-ḵitōteha.*

[6] Hadassi quotes also other views on this problem. Some hold the Throne of Glory to have been created on the Fourth Day, others (Japhet b. ᶜAli) on the Second Day. Hadassi decides in favour of Nahāwandī.

[7] *Ibid.: le-ḇarrerenū ki ha-kaḇōd ᶜim kisʾō ve-ha-malʾaḵim niḇrĕʾū ᶜim ha-shamayim ha-ᶜelyōnim bĕ-yōm riʾshōn shel yeṣirōt elohi[m] ḥefṣō hū ha-kaḇōd ha-baruʾi.*

[8] Cf. M. Ventura, *op. cit.*, p. 70.

form,[9] lived in the eleventh century, as is now unmistakably established.[10] Moreover, his *Maḥkimat Peti* (the Hebrew paraphrase of the *Muḥtawi*) shows in some respects the influence of Saadya's *Sefer Ha-Emūnōt ve-Ha-Deʿōt*.[11] It can, therefore, safely be assumed that, before the time of Saadya, the Ḳaraites were unacquainted with the term and theory of the created Word and created Glory. Saadya could not then have borrowed this doctrine from the Muʿtazilites through the agency of the Ḳaraites.

We have now to come back to the question whether Saadya's theory is due to Muʿtazilite influence, and if so, how far this is the case. It is noteworthy that, according to Aaron b. Elia,[12] one part of the doctrine, namely the theory of the *dibbūr niḇrā* is identical with the Muʿtazilite conception of the "created Speech" of Allāh. It is, however, important to note that he attributes the other part of the doctrine, namely the conception of the *Kāḇōd niḇrā*, entirely to the Jewish Rabbinic tradition. He admits that this concept was originally alien to the Ḳaraites and came to them only through the agency of the Rabbanites. He frankly reports that the earlier Ḳaraites used to take the angels for corporeal beings.

With regard to the prophetic visions of God they believed, he states, that "something created" manifested itself. They did not, however, use the term *Kāḇōd niḇrā* in order to explain the prophetic visions of God.[13] This statement, in itself, suffices to dispose of the theory advanced by Guttmann, Horovitz and Munk that both

---

[9] Cf. P. F. Frankl, *Ein Muʿtazilitischer Kalam aus dem 10. Jahrhundert*, in: *Sitzungs-Berichte der Philosophisch-Historischen Klasse der kaiserlichen Akademie der Wissenschaften*, Vienna, 71 (1872), pp. 197, 181, 217–218, n. 2.

[10] Not he, but Abū Yūsuf Yaʿḳūb al-Ḳirḳisānī, the author of the *Kitāb al-anwār wal-marāḳib* (in Hebr. quoted as *Sefer ha maʾor ha-gadol*), was a contemporary of Saadya's. Cf. A. E. Harkavy, *Studien und Mitteilungen*, III, pp. 7, 44; Steinschneider, *Hebräische Übersetzungen des Mittelalters*, pp. 449, 452f.; *Arabische Literatur*, §50.—A. Geiger, *Wissenschaftliche Zeitschrift für jüdische Theologie*, V, p. 271; and Delitzsch, *ʿEṣ ḥayyim*, pp. 313–314, held already substantially the same view, whereas S. Pinsker, *Liḳḳuṭe Ḳadmoniyot*, pp. 193f., mistook their identity and held Josef al-Baṣir to be the older one and contemporary with Saadya. The confusion regarding the two Josefs seems to date back as far as the twelfth century. See Steinschneider, *Hebr. Übers.*, p. 449.

[11] Cf. I. Markon, *Encylopaedia Judaica*, V, p. 325.

[12] Cf. *ʿEṣ ḥayyim*, p. 165.

[13] *Ibid.*: *she-ḥakmē ha-ḳaraʾim tafsum kulam ʿal pi peshuṭam milḥad ḳol hasagōt ḥushiōt ... she-maśēʾum meṣurafim el ha-shem hoṣiʾum mi-mashmaʿam ve-yaḥasum lĕ-daḇar niḇrāʾ ... u-ḳěḇar yadaʿta shĕ-ḥakmē yisraʾel hōdū shĕ-yesh daḇar niḇrāʾ ve-ḳarʾum keḇod ha-shem yarʾēhu ha-shem lĕ-mi shĕ-yaḥpōṣ.*

the *dibbūr nib̲rā* and *kāb̲ōd nib̲rā* conceptions owe their origin to the Muᶜtazilite pattern. Aaron b. Elia clearly states that the concept of the created Glory originated from the Rabbanite tradition, not from the *Muᶜtaẓila*. In a similar statement Mordecai b. Nisan records that until the time of Aaron b. Josef (1250 [1260]–1320) and Aaron b. Elia (about 1300–1369) the Ḳaraites believed in the corporeal appearance both of the *Shek̲inā* and the angels.[14] The above two statements are borne out by our knowledge that Daniel al-Ḳumīsī, the Ḳaraite contemporary of Natronai Gaon (ninth century), believed in the corporeal nature of the angels whom he classifies under the same category as fire, clouds and winds, etc.[15] It, therefore, appears that the earlier Ḳaraites combined a Muᶜtazilite outlook[16] with an anthropomorphic view of the *Shek̲inā* and the angels.[17]

There is further evidence that the Muᶜtazilite doctrine of Revelation did not contain the theory of *Kab̲ōd nib̲rā*. Josef al-Baṣīr, a

14 Cf. *Dōd Mordekai*, ed. J. Chr. Wolf (1714), 26ff.: *u-k̲ĕmō ḳen bĕ-ᶜinyan ha-malᵓak̲im ve-ha-shek̲inā ha-shōrā ba-mishkan u-b̲ĕ-b̲ēt ḳōdĕshē ha-ḳōdashim sab̲rū ḳadmonē ḥak̲amenū shĕ-hem mitlabbĕshim bĕ-geshem u-mitnoṣeṣim la-ᶜenayim ha-gashmiim lĕ-ẓakē ha-nefesh mā shĕ-kak̲ heᵓemīnū gam ḥak̲mē ha-rabbanim ab̲al bāᵓū ḥak̲amenū ha-aḥarōnim kĕgon ha-ḥak̲am r*[*abbi*] *aharōn baᶜal ha-mib̲ḥar ve-ha-ḥak̲am r*[*abbi*] *aharōn baᶜal keter torā ve-harsū daᶜtam ve-amru ki ha-malᵓak̲ ᵓī efshar she-yēraᵓē laᶜenayim ha-gashmiim ki hū rūḥani ve-ēn lō meḥiṣat ha-geshem.*

15 Cf. W. Bacher, *JQR* (1894), p. 708, quoted by Ventura, *loc. cit.*, pp. 70, 131. Despite his materialistic conception of the angels, al-Ḳumīsī rejected the anthropomorphic view of God. Cf. A. Marmorstein, *Journal Asiatique* (1916). Marmorstein's assertion that Saadya was indebted to Al-Ḳumīsī has already been disputed by Ventura, *loc. cit.*

16 Their Muᶜtazilite outlook is attested by al-Makrīzī, al-Maᶜsūdī, and Maimonides. Cf. H. Graetz, *Geschichte der Juden*, V, n. 18, p. 469.

17 It is, therefore, not entirely unjustified if al-Shahrastānī (*Milal*, p. 164) compares the Ḳaraites with the anthropomorphists in Islam and the Rabbanites with the Muᶜtazilites. The above view seems to solve the difficulties to which Graetz, *loc. cit.*, has called attention. His suggestion, which is followed by D. Neumark, *Toldot ha-pilosofīa bĕyisraᵓel*, I, p. 123 (cf. Ventura, *loc. cit.*, pp. 66–67), is that at the time of Shahrastānī the Ḳaraites had deteriorated, whereas the Rabbanites had assumed spiritual leadership. But this construction is hardly acceptable in view of the fact that Shahrastānī lived from 1086–1153 (54) (cf. Haarbrücker in the Introduction to his edition, pp. ix f.), which is between the time of Josef al-Baṣīr (first half of the eleventh century) and Judah Hadassi and Aaron b. Josef (twelfth century), all of whom followed the *Muᶜtaẓila*. Our view agrees with Mordecai b. Nisan's statement that at the time of Shahrastānī the Ḳaraites believed in some kind of anthropomorphism (conception of *Shek̲inā* and angels). Shahrastānī compares the Ḳaraites, to quote him more precisely, to the "fatalists and anthropomorphists" in Islam. We suggest that this phrase is meant as a characterization of orthodox Kalam *en bloc*, but that he did not mean to say that the Ḳaraites shared the belief in fatalism. [See below, p. 184.]

typical representative of the *Muʿtazila*,[18] knows the doctrine of created Speech only. In Ḳaraite literature, where he is frequently quoted on account of his high reputation,[19] he is regarded as an authority on the problem of the *dibbur niḇra*.[20] No mention is made of any view he might have held on the *Kāḇōd niḇrā*. From Frankl's analysis of the *Muḥtawi* we learn the reason why Josef al-Baṣīr would not hold the view of the *Kaḇōd niḇrā*. With the rest of the *Muʿtazila* he emphasised that God who is incorporeal cannot be perceived with the senses. Only bodies (substances) and the accidents which are inherent in them can be perceived. The passages in the Bible which record certain manifestations of God must, therefore, be interpreted in a metaphorical sense (*taʾwīl*). He states that even in the after-life God cannot be perceived.[21]

This is exactly the Muʿtazilite standpoint in the great controversy as to whether Allāh will be seen by the Faithful in Paradise. The radical among the anthropomorphists held that seeing Allāh is possible even in this world. Hishām ibn al-Ḥakam went so far as to describe Allāh as a body. A more moderate view was taken by the large majority of the Mutakallimūn who believed that the vision of Allāh will happen, not in this, but in the next world. Official Christianity of the early Middle Ages also believed in the *Visio beatifica* of the blessed in Paradise. The Muʿtazilites, however, denied that this was possible. If God could be seen, al-Djubbāʾī argued, he would fall under the category of visible objects.[22] It has been suggested that the discussions concerning anthropomorphism in Islam started from this problem of the *Visio beatifica*.[23]

[18] Cf. Steinschneider, *Hebr. Übers.* §267.

[19] Cf. the passage in Aaron b. Josef's *Sefer ha-miḇḥar*, *Par. Yetro*. Cf. also Frankl, *loc. cit.*, p. 172.

[20] Both in the *Sefer ha-miḇḥar* and in *ʿEṣ ḥayyim* he is quoted as having formulated the concept of *dibbur niḇrā* in a manner intended to exclude anthropomorphism. The passage in the *Sefer ha-miḇḥar* reads: *vĕ-rabbenū yosef ha-maʾor zikrōnō liḇĕrakā amar ki yitḥaddesh dibbūrō mi-lĕ-panav vĕ-im taḇīn maʾamar mi-lĕ-panav vĕ-lō amar mimmenu tēda kavvanatī*. Very similar in *ʿEṣ ḥayyim*, p. 165: *ha-ḥakam r*[*abbi*] *yosef n*[*oah*] *n*[*efesh*] *bēʾarō bĕ-millā moḥleṭet bĕ-maʾamarō ki dibbūrō yit*[*barak*]*shĕmō yitḥaddesh mi-lĕ-panav bĕ-ōmrō mi-lĕ-panav vĕ-lō amar mimmenu hinē lō yasigenū heseg gashmi vĕ-hĕyot ha-dibbūr bāʾ mimmenu yit*[*barak*] *bĕlī emṣaʾūt kelim*.

[21] Cf. Frankl, *loc. cit.*, pp. 192–193.

[22] Cf. A. J. Wensinck, *The Muslim Creed* (1932), pp. 64–68; M. Horten, *Die philosophhischen Probleme der spekulativen Theologie im Islam* (1910), pp. 274–275. Saadya uses a similar argument. Cf. *Emūnōt*, pp. 54–55; Guttmann, *loc. cit.*, pp. 124–125; Ventura, *loc. cit.*, p. 193.

[23] Cf. Wensinck, *loc. cit.*, p.

If this is the case, the method of *ta'wīl*, which was the Muʿtazilite answer to anthropomorphism,[24] was primarily directed against the literal sense of the prophetic visions in which the Godhead was described. Allāh sitting on his Throne—the Islamic parallel to the Jewish conception of the *kissē ha-kāḇōd*—was explained in an allegorical manner, just as anthropomorphic expressions like Allāh's face and hand were taken in the allegorical sense of bounty and knowledge.[25] The allegorical interpretation of all these expressions including the prophetic visions was naturally bound to rule out any such conception as that of *Kāḇōd niḇrā*. The Muʿtazilites were rather inclined to interpret the experience of Divine manifestations in the sense of an inner vision than to admit their outward reality. Al-Ashʿarī reports that the Muʿtazilites are unanimously of the opinion that Allāh cannot be seen by eyesight; they differ regarding the question whether He can be seen by our hearts.[26] Similarly, the notion of *Sakīna* (*Sheḵinā*) which Islam had taken over from Judaism and which originally was conceived of as a real, objective and externally visible phenomenon, assumed, in Islamic mysticism, the meaning of an inner illumination of the soul (*nūr fī-l-ḳalb*).[27] It is, therefore, impossible to assume that the *Muʿtazila* should have furnished Saadya with the idea of the *Kāḇōd nibrā*, which stresses the real and sensual character of the prophetic visions.

This view is supported by the fact that Saadya was by no means entirely free from Muʿtazilite influence in the way he interpreted the Divine manifestations related in Biblical and post-Biblical literature. In some of his writings he betrays a certain tendency to fall back upon the Muʿtazilite method of *ta'wīl* even with regard to passages describing Divine manifestations. This is not surprising in view of the fact that he adopted the method of

[24] Another answer was the *Maḏhab al-balkafah* of the old Imāms who rejected both anthropomorphism and allegorism. Cf. M. Schreiner, *ZDMG*, 52 (1898), pp. 528–529, 531. About Aḥmad ibn Ḥanbāl, who, in the middle of the ninth century, tried to avert the crisis of Islam by insisting that Ḳur'ān and Sunna must be taken in their literal sense, without asking questions (*bilā kaifa*), cf. Wensinck, *loc. cit.*, pp. 85–86. Different from the Muʿtazilite conception of *ta'wīl* is the doctrine of the *Bāṭiniya* which stresses the *inner* meaning underlying the words of the Ḳur'ān.

[25] Cf. Wensinck, *loc. cit.*, pp. 66–68; M. Schreiner, *Der Kalam in der jüdischen Literatur*, pp. 12–13.

[26] Cf. Wensinck, *loc. cit.*, p. 64.

[27] Cf. I. Goldziher, "La Notion de la Sakîna chez les Mohamétans", in: *Revue de l'histoire des Religions*, XXVIII (1893), pp. 7–12.

ta'wīl with regard to anthropomorphic expressions in general. As is well known, his exegetical canon provides that whenever the literal meaning of Scripture is contradicted by either sensual perception, Reason, another passage in Scripture, or Tradition, the allegorical method has to be employed.[28] He is the first Jewish philosopher to make a systematic attempt to interpret the whole phraseology of Biblical anthropomorphism in an allegorical sense.[29] He was, of course, preceded by the Targum Onkelos and is quite aware of the fact that he merely continues its tradition.[30] But there can be no doubt that the example of the Muᶜtazilites exerted an influence upon him, as Schreiner (*Kalam*, p. 13) emphasized. On account of this influence, he was not entirely unwilling to extend the method of *ta'wīl* even to the prophetic visions of God, according to the Muᶜtazilite pattern. The verse, Dan. 7:19, which in *Emūnōt*, I, p. 51, is explained in the sense of the *Kāḇōd nibrā* theory, is considered in his *Commentary on Daniel* (Cf. N. Porges, *MGWJ*, 1885, p. 63) to admit of an allegorical explanation.[31] Another instance: In the fragment of Saadya's *Refutation of Ibn Sākawaihi*, discovered and published by Harkavy (*JQR*, 13, 1901, pp. 662ff.), the answer given to the Ḳaraite assertion that the Rabbis considered the Creator to be corporeal, reads: Moreover, all those passages [i.e. of midrashic, liturgical and mystical literature] have a figurative meaning just as much as the analogous passages of the Bible (p. 667). Whereas here the allegorical method is preferred, another polemical passage quoted by Judah b. Barzilai in his *Commentary on the Sefer Yeṣirā* (*ed.* Halberstam, 1885, pp. 20–21; cf. S. D. Luzzatto in *Halīḵōt Ḳedem*, ed. G. Polak, pp.

[28] Cf. *Sefer Ha-Emūnōt ve-Ha-Deᶜōt*, ed. D. Slutzki (Leipzig, 1864), VII, p. 109; II, p. 49. Ibn Ḥazm in his exegetical canon enumerates sensual perception, another passage and consensus of tradition, but not the case of a conflict between Scripture and Reason. Cf. Goldziher, *Die Zahiriten* (1884), pp. 122–123, 142–145. The difference between Saadya's and Ibn Ḥazm's canons reflects the controversy between the *Muᶜtazila* and the orthodox school of thought.

[29] Cf. *Emūnōt*, II, pp. 48–57. Cf. Guttmann, *loc. cit.*, pp. 116–130; D. Kaufmann, *Geschichte der Attributenlehre* (Gotha, 1877), pp. 55–77; Ventura, *loc. cit.*, pp. 187–195. It is to be noted that Saadya, interpreting Gen. 1:27, takes *ṣelem* not in an allegorical sense (cf. Maimonides, *More Neḇuḵim*, I, 1; Aaron b. Elia, *ᶜEṣ ḥayyim*, § 22, pp. 49–51), but literally, the idea being that God calls man's image affectionately (*ᶜal dereḵ ha-yiḥud vĕ-ha-sĕgulā*) his own *ṣelem* (I, 49). Judah Hadassi accepts the interpretation and elaborates it. See *Eshkol ha-Kofer*, 25b.

[30] Cf. *Emūnōt*, pp. 49–50; *see* also A. Schmiedl, *Saadya und Onkelos*, *MGWJ*, 46 pp. 84–88.

[31] Cf. Ventura, *loc. cit.*, p. 190.

69ff.) explains the Divine manifestations in the sense of the *Kāḇōd niḇrā* doctrine.[32]

It is, therefore, obvious that Saadya was staggering between two ways of explaining the anthropomorphic passages concerning Divine Revelation: the Muᶜtazilite method of *taʾwīl* which he unhesitatingly employed in all other respects, and the doctrine of the *Kāḇōd niḇrā*. In view of the persistent attacks of the Ḳaraites against the alleged anthropomorphism of Rabbinic theology,[33] Saadya was faced with a very urgent problem. His final answer was the *Kāḇōd niḇrā* doctrine. With regard to this doctrine he was, as we hope to have shown, in no way indebted to the *Muᶜtazila*.

We now turn to the alleged influence of the *Muᶜtazila* on Saadya's conception of the *dibbūr niḇrā*. Let us first examine the Muᶜtazilite view regarding the Speech of Allāh. The doctrine of the created Speech of Allāh, in which is summed up the Muᶜtazilite theology of Revelation, was formulated in opposition to the orthodox Muslim creed which proclaimed that the Speech of Allāh was uncreated and eternal. It is unnecessary to give a detailed account of the well-known controversy between the factions in Kalām on this question which caused so much speculation and excitement in the Islamic world.[34] The depth of feeling aroused in this discussion can be assessed and understood only if we realise that the eternal Speech of Allāh (and the eternal Ḳurʾān with which it was identified) was the Islamic parallel to the Logos as understood by the Christians. There can be little doubt that it was actually inspired by the Christian doctrine. "The problem Christianity had to solve was closely akin to that which troubled Islam. For both religions the question was whether the highest revelations of the Godhead—the incarnation of Christ and the communication of the Ḳurʾān—were signs of Divine action only,

[32] The difference of opinion between the passage of the Harkavy fragment and the one quoted by Barzilai seems to rule out the possibility that the latter, too, is taken from the *Refutation of Ibn Sākawaihi*, to which Poznański was inclined to assign it. H. Malter (*Saadia Gaon* (1942), pp. 383, 385) already emphasized the conjectural character of Poznański's opinion.

[33] Cf. Bacher, *JQR*, 8, p. 695 (quoted by Ventura, *loc. cit.*, p. 67); as for Salmon b. Yeruḥim's attacks against the Talmudic Aggada, cf. Pinsker, *loc. cit.*, p. 18, against the *Shiᶜūr Ḳomā*, cf. Poznański, *JQR*, 8, p. 686. [For a further discussion of the Ḳaraites' (and Muslims') attacks upon the anthropomorphism of the *Shiᶜūr Ḳomā*, see below, pp. 183–185.]

[34] Cf. Goldziher, *Vorlesungen über den Islam* (1910), pp. 112ff.; *Zahiriten*, pp. 138–142; Horten, *loc. cit.*, pp. 250–252; Wensinck, *loc. cit.*, pp. 75, 87, 127, 149–151, 189, 207.

or manifestations of its own essence" (Wensinck, *loc. cit.*, p. 150). John of Damascus, the spokesman of Eastern Christianity, taught that Divine Revelation was a manifestation of God's essence, the Son (Logos, Word) having proceeded from the Father and being *homoousios* with Him. He insisted that this coming forth (*genesis*) must be kept apart from the idea of time; otherwise it would imply a change in the hypostasis of the Father. Thus "The eternal God creates his own Word, perfect, without beginning, without end, *gennētos*, but *agenētos*.[35] The Christian position is reflected in the orthodox Islam notion of essential attributes, with this difference that the place of the Logos is taken by the eternal Word of Allāh by which is meant the Speaking, the Speech and the Ḳurʾān of Allāh.[36] The Muʿtazilites combated the doctrine of essential attributes because of its Christian implications. Josef al-Baṣīr argues against it on these very grounds.[37] It is possible that the Muʿtazilite stress on the unity of Allāh and their doctrine of the created Ḳurʾān was inspired by Jewish influence. There exists a tradition to this effect.[38] In Talmudic and Midrashic thought the pre-existent Torah was considered to be a creation of God, but was never taken to be an eternal entity in the sense of Logos.[39]

It is natural that Saadya should endorse the Muʿtazilite opposition to the Logos doctrine both in its Christian and Islamic forms. Like the Muʿtazilites, he denied all distinct attributes of God, and even outbid the *Muʿtazila*, as Kaufmann (*loc. cit.*, pp. 33–38)

[35] Migne, XCIV, col. 809ff. (*De fide orthodoxa*, I, viii). Cf. Wensinck, *loc. cit.*, pp. 150, 72, 75.

[36] Cf. the *Waṣīyat Abī Ḥanīfa*, art. 9; *Fiḳh akbar*, II, art. 3. See Wensinck, *loc. cit.*, pp. 127, 149ff., 189, 207; H. A. Wolfson, "The Muslim Attributes and the Christian Trinity", *The Harvard Theological Review*, XLIX (1956), pp. 1–18; "Philosophical Implications of the Problem of Divine Attributes in the Kalam", *JAOS*, 79 (1959), pp. 73–80.

[37] Cf. Frankl, *loc. cit.*, p. 194. Vice versa, the same argument is used by al-Shahrastānī (Haarbrücker, I, p. 49) against Abū-l-Huḏail who, differently from the other Muʿtazilites who denied all eternal qualities, considered the three attributes of Knowledge, Power and Life as distinct expressions of God's essence. Cf. Kaufmann, *loc. cit.*, p. 37.

[38] Cf. Schreiner, *Kalam*, p. 3. Djahm b. Ṣafwān (died 745), who is the first representative of the doctrine of the created Ḳurʾān about whom we possess some definite knowledge, combines this theory with a denial of Divine attributes. (Cf. S. Pines, *Beiträge zur islamischen Atomenlehre* (1936), p. 124.) This clearly indicates that, from the outset, the Muʿtazilites combated the idea of the eternal Ḳurʾān for the reason of safeguarding Allāh's unity.

[39] Cf. Schreiner, *Kalam*, p. 4, who makes this point against Sprenger's contrary assertion. On the Jewish conception of the pre-existent Torah, cf. L. Ginzberg, *The Legends of the Jews*, VI, p. 63; H. A. Wolfson, *Philo*, I. 21, 183.

has shown, in his effort to avoid the doctrine of essential attributes. In the course of his elaborate refutation of the doctrine of Trinity he showed himself not only well acquainted with the various schools of thought of Christian theology,[40] but also determined to reject the Logos doctrine in every shape and form. It is important that in this connection he refuted the exegesis of Prov. 8:20 in the sense of the Logos doctrine.[41] He pointed out that the passage which speaks of the pre-existent Wisdom must be taken in an allegorical sense. There was no need for God, he argued, to employ an instrument in order to create the world. The passage merely expresses the idea that from the created universe, its order and perfection, we may infer that a wise Creator has designed it (*Emūnōt*, II, p. 47). Both in his *Commentary on the Sefer Yeṣirah* (ed. Lambert, p. 31) and in his *Commentary on Proverbs* (ed. Derenbourg, p. 49) he moves on the same lines. He strongly emphasizes that the pre-existence of Wisdom in the sense of a separate entity is incompatible with the notion of God's unity. The term *ḳānānī* (Prov. 8:22) is interpreted in the sense of creation.[42] This means that so far as the opposition to the Logos doctrine (eternal Speech of Allāh, eternal Ḳurᵓān, eternal Logos) is concerned, Saadya shares the Muᶜtazilite view.[43]

But does Saadya also share the Muᶜtazilite concept of "created

[40] Cf. *Emūnōt*, II, pp. 47–48. On the question as to which Christian sects are referred to in this passage, cf. Kaufmann, pp. 48–52, Guttmann, pp. 107–113, Ventura, pp. 184–185. [See now H. A. Wolfson, "Saadia on the Trinity and Incarnation", *Studies and Essays in Honour of Abraham A. Neumann* (1962), pp. 547–568.]

[41] *U-maṣāᵓti ḳeṣatam ḥōshēḇ ᶜinyan h*[*a-shem*] *ḳanāni rēᵓshit darkō shě-la-borēᵓ millā ḳedumā lō sarā běrūᵓā* (I, 46f.). That this passage refers to the Christian Logos doctrine is clear from the context.

[42] Cf. *Emūnōt*, II, p. 47. In I, pp. 23–24, the term is further explained with reference to Job 40:19, *hū rēshit darkē ēl*, the idea being that God's Wisdom was not pre-existent in the sense of Logos, but manifested by the first act of creation. Judah Hadassi (*Eshkol ha-Kofer*, 26a) took it in this sense, as is apparent from his interpretation of Prov. 8:22 in conjunction with Job 40:19. In developing Saadya's exegesis he points out that God's Wisdom became manifest only from the sixth Day onward after Man was created.

[43] By explaining Prov. 8 and Job 28 in allegorical fashion, Saadya not only rejects the idea of a pre-existent Logos, but also, indirectly, abandons the conception of the Torah as a pre-existent entity, since in Midrashic thought Torah was substituted for Wisdom. Judah Hadassi actually drew this implication of Saadya's exegesis. He opposes the Rabbinic doctrine that the Torah preceded the Creation of the world by 2,000 years. He adds the argument that prior to creation there was no Time to measure duration (*ki ḳōdem ha-běriyᵓā ēḵ hāyā ẓěman*). This argument, which was later developed in Jewish philosophy (cf. H. A. Wolfson, *Crescas' Critique of Aristotle* (1929), pp. 663–664), has its basis in Saadya's *Commentary on Prov.* (ed. Derenbourg, p. 49).

Speech" in the positive sense they attach to it? Does the influence of the Muᶜtazilites go so far as that?

The above-quoted scholars who take this influence for granted base their view on the assumption that the term "created speech" which the *Muᶜtazila* used means the same as Saadya's *dibbūr nibrā*. Guttmann (p. 119, n. 2) quotes a passage of Shahrastānī (Haarbr. I, p. 42) to which also Goldziher (*REJ*, 60, p. 32) seems to refer. The passage reads: "They [i.e. the Muᶜtazilites] further agree that His Word is something generated and created in a substratum, i.e. letter and sound, the image of which is written down in the [sacred] books as records thereof; and [they agree] that whatever exists in a subject is an accident and perishes at once." Guttmann does not comment on this passage, but apparently takes it in the sense of Saadya's concept of a voice created in the air. Goldziher distinctly says so. Neither Guttmann nor Goldziher go into the question as to whether the substratum mentioned by Shahrastānī really means a material substratum, such as the air, or something different. Goldziher completely identifies the created Speech of the Muᶜtazila with the *dibbūr nibrā* which, from Saadya onward, we meet in both Rabbanite and Ḳaraite theology.[44] But from some further passages of Shahrastānī, which so far have found little attention, it becomes obvious that Goldziher's interpretation is unjustified. Shahrastānī (I, 81) reports that al-Djubbāʾī and his son Abū Hāshim conceived of God as speaking through the Word which he creates in a substratum. According to their opinion, he says, the true nature of the Word consists of articulate sounds and letters arranged in a fixed order. Finally, they hold, that the one who has made the Word is the speaker, not the one in whom the Word abides. The last remark makes it perfectly clear that the substratum mentioned before is identical with the person in whom and out of whom the Word of God speaks, not any external substratum such as the air. The subsequent paragraph (I, 81) corroborates this interpretation. "Al-Djubbāʾī differed from his companions only in so far as, according to him, God creates a Word, whenever a person reads [the Ḳurʾān,], in the subject of the reader . . ." Al-Djubbāʾī thus applies the conception of the created Speech not only to the Prophet in whom it is first created, but to

[44] In his *Vorlesungen über den Islam*, p. 114, Goldziher gives the same account of the Muᶜtazilite conception of the created Speech: "*Gott lässt, wenn er sich phonetisch kundgeben will, an einem materiallen Substrat, durch einen besonderen Schöpfungsakt, die* Rede *entstehen.*"

the reader of the Ḳur'ān as well. The Word of God co-exists with the human voice of the reader, a notion which seemed absurd to Shahrastānī, because it implied the simultaneous existence of two words in one subject.[45] From this it can be inferred that in the act of God's speaking to the prophet, one word only, namely the created Word of God speaks out of the mouth of the prophet.[46] The underlying idea of the Muᶜtazilite conception seems to be that, in the case of the prophet, the human action of speech has a superhuman origin. The Muᶜtazilite definition of the Word of God as "the quality of an action which God creates in Time",[47] must be understood in this sense. Further evidence that the substratum in which God creates His Speech is identical with the human person, is produced by the analogous view of the *Ashᶜariya*. While retaining the idea of an eternal Word of Allāh, of which every single act of revelation is a reflex (*ᶜibāna*), the Ashᶜarites believed that in that single act of revelation God creates a spiritual reality (idea, thought) in the soul of the prophet.[48] Abū Muḥammad records that, according to the *Ashᶜariya*, Gabriel revealed to the "heart" of the prophet the Word of God.[49] The difference between *Muᶜtazila* and *Ashᶜariya*, so far as the single acts of Revelation are concerned, therefore amounts to this: the former insisted on God's Word being actual speech (sounds and letters), whereas the latter regarded God's Speech as a mental process in the mind of the prophet. The Muᶜtazilites' argument was that an idea or thought could not be called a speech; for, otherwise, they argued, one who is silent could also be called a speaker (cf. Horten, p. 252). But some of them (Abū Hāshim) agreed that an idea which unexpectedly comes to one's mind is a kind of inner word which God creates in the heart of a person or which an angel puts in his breast (Horten, p. 65). It is clear from the line of discussion that the created speech of Allāh in the Muᶜtazilite view is in no way an audible voice created in an external substratum, but an act of speech created in the prophet.

There is evidence that Saadya, too, understood the Muᶜtazilite

[45] I, 81; cf. M. Horten, *loc. cit.*, p. 251.

[46] Goldziher, *La Notion de la Sakīna*, p. 12, quotes the phrase, "The Sakīna speaks with the tongue of Omar", from al-Bagawī, *Masābīḥ al-sunna* (1924), II, p. 196.

[47] Cf. Goldziher, *Zahiriten*, p. 138; Horten, p. 250: "*Gott erschafft eine Handlung des Redens im Menschen, deren Eigenschaft ist, dass sie akustisch vernehmbar ist.*"

[48] Cf. Wensinck, p. 151; Horten, p. 252.

[49] Cf. Goldziher, *Zahiriten*, p. 139.

doctrine in the sense of God's word put in the mouth of the prophet. In his polemic against the Christian Trinity (*Emūnōt*, II, p. 46) he explains that the terms *rūaḥ* and *millā*, used in 2 Sam. 23:2 ("The spirit of God spoke unto me and His Word is on my tongue"), do not denote eternal and separate qualities, but created things. They are, he says, "the [articulate] words which the Creator puts in the mouth of the prophet."[50] This echoes the above-quoted passage of Shahrastānī in which emphasis is laid on the articulateness of the words God creates in the substratum. Saadya makes it clear that by the substratum is meant the mouth of the prophet.[51] Goldziher defeats his own argument by quoting this passage as proof for his assertion that Saadya's theory of created Speech is based on the Muᶜtazilite conception. On the contrary, it shows that the Muᶜtazilite theory as Saadya understood it is different from his own doctrine as he developed it later. Saadya used the Muᶜtazilite formula on this particular occasion, but it is clear that it does not represent his exact view on the matter. His own theory is uninfluenced by the Muᶜtazila.

The preceding analysis has shown that neither the *Kāḇōd niḇrā* nor the *dibbūr niḇrā* doctrine are due to Muᶜtazilite influence. We have to find their origin and background elsewhere. What, then, are the decisive factors which account for this complicated theory? Any judgement has to base itself on a clear exposition of what Saadya actually meant by *Kāḇōd niḇrā* and *dibbūr niḇrā*, and what he conceived to be their mutual relationship.

I. KĀḆŌD NIḆRĀ

Saadya rejects not only the metaphorical interpretation of the anthropomorphic passages concerning Divine Revelation, as suggested by the Muᶜtazila; he also refuses to accept the Ḳaraite view that these passages refer to an angel. He holds that wherever God is said to have revealed Himself, either in the likeness of man or in a manifestation of light without a specified form, the idea is that His Glory (*Kāḇōd*) appeared, not He Himself, nor an

[50] On the correctness of the Hebrew text, cf. Goldziher, *REJ*, 60, pp. 32–33.

[51] Kaufmann, *loc. cit.*, p. 46, suggests that the passage reflects the view of al-Ashᶜari. But the passage quoted by him (Shahrastānī, Haarbr. I, p. 101) makes mention of the tongues of the angels only, not of the tongues of the prophets. According to the *Ashᶜariya*, the angel reveals the word of God to the heart of the prophet, whereas the *Muᶜtazila* stresses the articulateness of God's Speech. There can be no doubt that Saadya quoted the Muᶜtazilite view.

angel. He clearly distinguishes between the notion of *Kāḇōd* and that of angel. Both are created and both are of light. But *Kāḇōd nibrā* ranks above the angels. The intensity of its light surpasses that of the angels.[52] There exist various degrees of light, Saadya suggests. *Kāḇōd* in its highest degree may be perceptible by the angels only.[53] He is inclined to explain the gigantic measurements of *Shiʿur Ḳomā* with reference to this highest form of *Kāḇōd nibrā*.[54] *Kāḇōd* is identical with the Rabbinic conception of *Sheḵinā*.[55] This corroborates the view that *Kāḇōd* and angel do not coincide. *Kāḇōd* is also mentioned together with the Throne of God and the angels who are carrying it.[56] From this it appears that it stands for the manifestation of God's Glory as understood in the Jewish mystical tradition of *maʿăsē merkāḇā*. M. Sachs has shown that the term *Kāḇōd* actually covers the conception of *maʿăsē merkāḇā* in the Talmudic tradition.[57] Moreover, according to this tradition, and following upon Ez. 1:26, the angels who are carrying God's Throne do not behold the *Kāḇōd* upon the Throne. Hence they exclaim, "Where is the place of His *Kāḇōd*?[58] The distinction between *Kāḇōd* and angel could not be brought out more strikingly. But, at the same time, Saadya does not always adhere to this distinction. In speaking of *Kĕḇōḏōt* in the plural, he occasionally includes the angels whom, as he explains, God has created for his own glory (*Kāḇōd*).[59] Furthermore, he admits that a prophetic Revelation might take place through the medium of an angel instead of *Kāḇōd*,[60] although he realizes that hearing and seeing an angel does not make a person into a prophet.[61] In view of the fact that both *Kāḇōd* and angel are created beings of light, Saadya's failure to draw a strict demarcation line between them is not surprising. The remarkable thing is that he deemed it necessary to differentiate between the two as he did.

[52] Cf. *Emūnōt*, p. 51: *Vĕ-hī ṣurā yeḳarā min ha-malʾaḵim ʿaṣumā bi-ḇĕriʾatah baʿalat hōd vĕ-ōr vĕ-hī niḳreʾt keḇōd h[a-shem]*.

[53] Cf. Barzilai, *loc. cit.*, where Saadya is reported as having used this idea as an argument against Ḥiwi al-Balkhi. Cf. I. Davidson, *Saadia's Polemic against Ḥiwi al-Balkhi*, pp. 82–84.

[54] Cf. Barzilai, *ibid.*

[55] *Emūnōt*, p. 51; *Commentary on the Sefer Yeṣirā*, ed. Lambert, p. 89; cf. also p. 61 where the light of the angel is distinguished from the light of *Sheḵinā*.

[56] *Emūnōt*, p. 51; cf. also *Comm. Yeṣirā*, p. 95.

[57] Cf. *Kerem Ḥemed*, VII, p. 275, quoted by Senior Sachs in *Ha-Tĕḥiyā*, p. 22; cf. also A. Jellinek, *Beiträge zur Geschichte der Kabbala*, I (1852), p. 55, n. 3.

[58] *Sifrā* 2. 12; Ex. R. 23:15; *Pesiḳta r.* 20; *Ḳĕdushā Mussaf.*

[59] Cf. Barzilai, *loc. cit.*

[60] *Emūnōt*, p. 51.

[61] Barzilai, *loc. cit.*

The reason which prompted Saadya to distinguish between the conceptions of *Kāḇōd* and angel, though both are materially the same, must be sought in his reaction to Nahāwandī's Angel doctrine. He distinctly rejects it because of its dualistic implications. His own theory of *Kāḇōd* is intended to replace the Angel doctrine both in the form given to it by Nahāwandī (and the *Maghāriya* sect) and by Jewish mystics who identified the Angel mentioned in Ex. 23:20 with *Yah Ḳāṭan* (*Meṭaṭron*).[62] The Angel doctrine of Nahāwandī and the *Maghāriya* are closely akin to the Logos of Philonic tradition. The "Alexandrian" whose writings Ḳirḳisānī records among the books of the *Maghāriya* is identical with Philo.[63] Like Philo's Logos, the Angel of Nahāwandī and the *Maghāriya* was a *deuteros theos* in the sense of Demiurge and Mediator.[64] The Jewish mystical tradition of *Yah Ḳāṭan* (*Meṭaṭron*) was likewise bordering upon dualism in the Gnostic sense. Saadya, therefore, eliminated the conception of angel as intermediary of Revelation and reserved it for the lower form of prophecy. Instead of the Angel, he introduced the term *Kāḇōd* with its associations with *Merkāḇā* mysticism. Judah Hadassi who is largely influenced both by Saadya and Nahāwandī attributes the appearance of angels to all stages of prophecy—the highest angel having appeared to Moses only—but, at the same time, opposes the *Yah Ḳāṭan* tradition with the argument that even the highest angel (the one referred to in Ex. 23:20 and, according to his interpretation, in Moses' vision, Ex. 23:17–23) is only a created being and not entitled to be designated by the *Tetragrammaton* which implies eternity.[65] He identifies the *Kāḇōd* of Biblical tradition with the

[62] Cf. *Comm. Daniel*, ed. N. Porges, *MGWJ* (1885), p. 63 (quoted by Ventura, p. 190) *ad* Dan. 8:9: *vĕ-ḵol ha-omēr ki raʾah mal'aḵ hū min ha-shōnim ve-hū min ha-omēr ḳaṭan vĕ-gadōl lĕ-maʿan ki ēn shōfeṭ ba-ʿōlam ki im ha-ḳadōsh bāruḵ hū*. On the *Yah Ḳaṭan* (Meṭaṭron) doctrine see H. Odeberg, 3 Enoch (1928). It goes back to the *Bar Enosh* of Jewish apocalyptic literature. For Mandaean parallels cf. *Ginza*, ed. Lidzbarski, pp. 251, 264, 267. [See now G. Scholem, *Major Trends in Jewish Mysticism*, Revised Edition, p. 366, and *Jewish Gnosticism, Merkabah Mysticism and Talmudic Tradition* (1960), pp. 43–55.]

[63] Cf. W. Bacher, *JQR*, 7 (1894), p. 703; S. Poznański, *REJ*, 50 (1905), pp. 12–23. [See, however, now H. A. Wolfson, "The Pre-Existent Angel of the Magharians and al-Nahāwandī", *JQR*, N.S. LI (1960), pp. 89–106, where the view of the Philonic origin of the angel doctrine of the sect and of Nahāwandī is refuted and the doctrine is traced back to the earliest Christian Gnostics. On the question of the relationship between the Maghāriya and the Qumrān Covenanters see N. Golb, *The Journal of Religion*, XLI (1961), pp. 38–50.]

[64] Cf. Poznański, *loc. cit.*, p. 12.

[65] *Eshkol ha-Kofer*, fol. 26a–b.

angels.[66] The degree of prophecy he holds to depend on the rank of the angel who appears.[67] Saadya, who assigns the appearance of *Kāḇōd* to all ranks of prophecy, has another way of explaining the difference between Moses' and the other prophets' vision of *Kāḇōd*. He points out that whereas the prophets, in general, were unable to endure the sight of *Kāḇōd* for any length of time, because of the strength of its radiance, Moses was granted the privilege to look at it for a while, after his eye had time to accommodate itself to its splendour. This, he says, is implied in the words (Ex. 33:23), "And I will take away my hand, and Thou shall see my back."[68]

2. DIBBUR NIḆRĀ

The Biblical phrase, "God spoke", means, according to Saadya's definition, that God created a speech which, through the medium of the air, reached the ear of the prophet or the people.[69] The creation of the *dibbūr* does not involve any anthropomorphic conception of God since creation, generally, is produced by the will of God.[70] Nor does it presuppose a hypostatic Logos as an instrument of the creation of the Word.[71] Whereas the *Kāḇōd* is created only in the sense of not being eternal, but has a permanent existence, the *dibbūr* is created at the actual moment of Revelation and has no continued existence. Saadya makes this point perfectly clear by contrasting the Speech of God with God's silence. He emphasizes, against the *Mutakallimūn*, that God's silence is not a positive act, but, like all privations, a refraining on the part of God from acting in the way of speech.[72]

What is, according to Saadya, the relation between *Kāḇōd* and

66 *Ibid.: kěḇōdō hū᾿ mal᾿aḵav yarad vě-nir᾿ah li-ḵěḇōd adōnō u-malkō kě-meleḵ asher lě-panav hōlěḵim sarāv vě-gibborāv li-ḵěḇōdō.* Judah Hallevi quotes both theories of Kābōd, viz. (a) *u-kěḇōd h[a-shem] hū᾿ ha-guf ha-daḳ* . . ., which signifies Saadya's *Kāḇōd*; (b) *kělal ha-mal᾿aḵim*, which sums up the Ḳaraite view (*Kuzari*, IV, 3). 67 *Ibid.*

68 *Emūnōt*, p. 55; Barzilai, *loc. cit.* In the *Bhagavatgītā* (cf. R. Garbe, *Die Bhagavatgītā* (1905); R. Otto, *Das Heilige*, ch. 2) Kṛṣna-Viṣnu tells the prophet who wishes to see him, "Thou wilt not be able to behold me with Thine own eyes; I give Thee a god-like eye; now behold my power." Cf. H. Kittel, *Die Herrlichkeit Gottes*, *ZNW*, Beiheft 16 (1934), pp. 132–133.

69 *Emūnōt*, p. 54: *vě-ᶜinyan ha-dibbūr shě-hū᾿ barā᾿ dibbūr higiᶜa ba-᾿avīr el shemaᶜ ha-naḇī᾿ ᾿ō ha-ᶜam.*

70 *Emūnōt*, pp. 46, 54. Cf. Kaufmann, *loc. cit.*, p. 46; Guttmann, *loc. cit.*, p. 106. This answers the argument of the *Barāhima* (Brahmins), *mī shě-ēnō guf ēḵ yedabber ᶜim guf*. Cf. Aaron b. Josef, *Sefer ha-miḇḥar*, *Yetro*; Aaron b. Elia, *ᶜEṣ Ḥayyim*, p. 160 (cf. Delitzsch, p. 307). 71 Cf. H. A. Wolfson, *JQR*, 32 (1942), p. 362.

72 *Emūnōt*, p. 54. Cf. Kaufmann, *loc. cit.*, p. 62; Guttmann, *loc. cit.*, p. 123; Ventura, *loc. cit.*, pp. 192–193.

dibbūr? The answer is that in the case of Moses' prophecy and the Sinaitic Revelation the *dibbūr niḇrā* spoke directly, without the intermediacy of *Kāḇōd*, whereas in the case of all other prophets the *dibbūr* spoke out of the *Kāḇōd*.[73] But it is important to realize that even in the latter case it was God who spoke by means of *dibbur niḇrā*, not the *Kāḇōd* which has no voice of its own. This is obvious in a case where the *Kāḇōd* has a formless existence as in Ex 23:10 or Ps. 99:7 (cf. *Emūnōt*, p. 64), but it must also apply to cases where the *Kāḇōd* has a human form. For it is precisely the function of *Kāḇōd* to testify, in the prophet's own mind, to the Divine origin of the *dibbūr*.[74] Judah Hadassi, though he differs from Saadya in his interpretation of *Kāḇōd*, follows him with regard to the nature of *dibbūr*, and strongly emphasizes that "the one who commands and speaks is God, whereas the one who appears is an angel."[75]

The question arises as to the meaning of the distinction between Moses and the other prophets if the *dibbūr* is in any event the *dibbūr niḇrā* which God creates. Why does the addition, in the case of the other prophets, of *Kāḇōd niḇrā* as an accompaniment of *dibbūr*, constitute a lower degree of prophecy? We understand why in Maimonide's prophetology, for instance, the character of vision introduces an element which makes for a lower degree of prophetic clarity. Vision is the product of imagination.[76] But in Saadya's theory it is exactly the function of the visionary element (*Kāḇōd*) to exclude any doubts and to attest the Divine origin of the *dibbūr*. Why should, then, the presence of *Kāḇōd* in the prophecy of all prophets except Moses debase the character of Revelation? Aaron b. Elia, who closely follows Saadya, differentiates between Moses who heard the *dibbūr niḇrā* without *Kāḇōd* and the other prophets who heard it speak out of *Kāḇōd*.[77] But he does not offer any satisfactory interpretation.[78]

---

[73] Cf. *Emūnōt*, pp. 51, 55; Barzilai, *loc. cit.*

[74] Cf. *Emūnōt*, p. 51: ḥiddēsham ha-borē' mē-'or lĕ-ammēt eṣel nĕḇi'ō ki hū shalaḥ dĕḇarāv 'ēlāv; p. 55: vĕ-her'ēhū la-nĕḇi'im li-hĕyōt re'ayāh lahem kol diḇrē ha-nĕḇu'ā ăsher yashmi'um hem me-'ēt ha-borē'. Cf. also Barzilai, *loc. cit.*

[75] *Eshkol ha-Kofer*, fol. 26b: ki ha-mĕṣavveh vĕ-ha-mĕdabbĕr hū' ha-elohi[m] vĕ-ha-shoḵēn bēn yisra'el hū' ha-mal'aḵ.

[76] Cf. Leo Strauss, *Philosophie und Gesetz* (1935), pp. 92–97; Z. Diesendruck, "Maimonides' Lehre von der Prophetie", in *Jewish Studies in Memory of Israel Abrahams* (1927), pp. 129f.; E. I. J. Rosenthal, "Maimonides' Conception of State and Society", in *Moses Maimonides*, ed. I. Epstein (London, 1935), p. 197.

[77] *'Eṣ Ḥayyim*, p. 168: ha-ma'alā ha-ri'shonā peh el peh shĕ-mosheh 'a[lāv] h[a-shalōm] masig ha-ḳol ha-niḇrā' bĕli 'emṣa'i bĕ-haḳiṣ u-masig kēḇōd ha-shem hasagā hergashit . . . u-ma'alatō shĕl shemu'ēl shĕ-shama' ha-dibbūr bĕ-haḳiṣ min ha-kaḇōd.

[78] Horovitz, *loc. cit.*, p. 41, calls attention to the difficulties involved in Saadya's conception, but fails to suggest any solution.

We believe that the difficulty just mentioned points to an inner complication of the whole theory and its composite nature. Saadya's interpretation of *Kāḇōd* as a criterion[79] must be regarded as a rationalistic interpretation of a fundamentally independent and mystical conception. As we have seen, the *Kāḇōd* belongs to the tradition of *Merkāḇā* mysticism. Although it is used by Saadya with the idea of combating the Angel and *Meṭaṭron* doctrines and their dualistic implications, the fact must not be overlooked that the conception of *Kāḇōd* contains a certain Gnostic element, namely the idea of Primordial Man. There exists a connection between the "appearance of a man" upon the throne in Ez. 1:26, the "son of man" in Dan. 7:13, and in the apocalyptic literature, the Iranian myth of Primordial Man, and its Gnostic development as reflected in both Jewish and Islamic Gnosis. This is not the place to enter into an elaborate exposition of this theme.[80] It should, however, be clear that the conception of *Kāḇōd* echoes this Gnostic tradition both in its stress on the human likeness of *Kāḇōd* in the higher forms of Revelation and in the interpretation of *Kāḇōd* as primordial light.[81] As we have shown in another study,[82] the Rabbinic concept of the "primordial light which is stored up for the righteous in the future world", is intimately connected with the motif of Primordial Man (*Adam Ḳadmōn*). Saadya leaves no doubt that the *Kāḇōd* of prophetic Revelation is identical with the primordial light which the righteous will see in the future world.[83] It can, therefore, be assumed that the concept of *Kāḇōd nibrā* is part of this whole mystical tradition. But whereas Nahāwandī and some Jewish adepts of the *Meṭaṭron* doctrine allowed dualistic implications to enter their theology, Saadya is emphatic that *Kāḇōd* is not co-existent with God in the sense of *Yah Ḳāṭan*, but is a creation, though the first Creation of God.

As regards *dibbūr nibrā*, we suggest that it, too, has a mystical background, namely that of the targumic *Memrā*. Saadya mentions

[79] He even goes so far as to say that *Kāḇōd* was created with this purpose of serving as a criterion of Divine Revelation. Cf. *Emūnōt*, p. 51.

[80] Cf. R. Reitzenstein and H. H. Schaeder, *Studien zum antiken Synkretismus*; H. H. Schaeder, "Die islamische Lehre vom vollkommenen Menschen", in *ZDMG*, 79 (N.F. 4) (1925), pp. 192ff.; R. Bultmann, *ZNW*, 24 (1925).

[81] Cf. Barzilai, *loc. cit.*: *wĕ-hū ha-ʾōr ha-baruʿy tĕḥilat kol ha-bĕriyōt vĕ-ha-nōṣarōt.*

[82] "Gnostic Themes in Rabbinic Cosmology", in *Essays Presented to J. H. Hertz, Chief Rabbi* (London, undated), pp. 28–32.

[83] Cf. Barzilai, *loc. cit.*: *ki ha-ḳadōsh barūḵ hūʾ marʾeh la-ṣaddikim ba-ʿolam ha-bāʾ ʾōr ʿaṣū ... vĕ-emmet hūʾ ki kol mal ʾaḵ vĕ-kol ṣurā ʾōr baruy.*

memrā as the targumic equivalent of the Biblical "Word of God" and makes an allusion to its importance.[84] We do not propose to enter here into a discussion of the nature of *memra.*[85] It seems, however, pretty clear, as J. Abelson has shown, that *memrā* is closely akin to *Shekinā* in so far as it serves as a medium of Revelation and Providence in a deeply mystical sense.[86] But whereas *Shekinā* certainly has a hypostatic nature like *Kābōd, memrā* is merely the Word of God as it flows from the encounter between God and Man. It has no hypostatic character.[87] It, therefore, corresponds exactly to what Saadya calls *dibbur nibrā.* As to its historical background, it represents the Jewish answer to the Logos doctrine. As R. Reitzenstein has shown, the Logos concept itself, in its Hermetic, Stoic and Philonic form, combines the elements of speech and light. It is the *phōteinos logos.*[88] Moreover, it was merged with the conception of Primordial Man. The amalgamation of *Logos* and *Anthropos* dates back to the early Hellenistic period.[89] The *Shiᶜur Ḳomā* is a blend of the Logos doctrine with *Adam Ḳadmōn* mysticism.[90] Saadya's *Ḳābōd nibrā* out of which the *dibbūr nibrā* speaks is likewise an amalgam of the two elements *Logos* and *Anthropos.* It is, therefore, not surprising that Saadya identified the *Shiᶜur Ḳomā* with the *Kābōd nibrā.* On the other hand, *memrā* and *dibbūr nibrā,* according to Saadya's interpretation of Moses' prophecy, seem to isolate the phenomenon of the Word (Logos) from its associations with the *Adam Ḳadmōn* idea. In Saadya's statement that in the case of Moses' prophecy no *Ḳābōd,* but only *dibbūr* was present, this idea is fully expressed. Maimonides, who strongly objected to the *Shiᶜur Ḳomā* and the

[84] *Emūnōt,* p. 50: *ki ēleh ha-millōt ha-mugěshamōt raṣah ba-hem ᶜinyanim gědōlim vě-yěkarim tirgemūm ka-ăsher hitbarrēr lahem.*

[85] Cf. Strack-Billerbeck, II, 302ff.; J. Abelson, *The Immanence of God in Rabbinical Literature* (1912); F. Aber, "Memrā und Schechina", in *Festschrift z. 75jährigen Bestehen des Jüd.-Theol. Seminars Breslau* (1929), II; C. F. Burney, *The Aramaic Origin of the 4th Gospel* (1922); R. D. Middleton, "Logos and Shekinah in the 4th Gospel", *JQR,* 29; A. Marmorstein, "Iranische u. jüdische Religion", *ZNW,* 26 (1927), pp. 231ff.

[86] Cf. Abelson, *loc. cit.,* pp. 150–173. The mystical character of *memrā* was stressed, in opposition to Maimonides' view (*Moreh,* I, 27), by Naḥmanides (Gen. 46:4). Cf. also *Sefer Bahir,* §§32, 94, 95, 96.

[87] Cf. Abelson, *loc. cit.*; Marmonstein, *loc. cit.,* pp. 235–236.

[88] Cf. R. Reitzenstein, *Zwei religionsgeschichtliche Fragen* (1901), pp. 83–92.

[89] Cf. Schaeder, *ZDMG,* 79, pp. 218–219.

[90] Cf. M. Gaster, *Das Schiur Komah, MGWJ,* 37 (1892), reprinted in *Studies and Texts,* V, pp. 1330–1353.

mystical tradition of *Kāḇōd* in general[91] was still able to retain Saadya's theory of *dibbūr niḇrā* as an interpretation of the Sinaitic Revelation.[92]

Whereas Saadya separated, in principle, the *dibbūr* from the *Kāḇōd* in his *Emūnōt*, he combined them into one inseparable whole in his earlier *Commentary* on the *Sefer Yeṣirā*. He interprets the *ruăḥ elohim ḥayyim* (IV, 1), from which, according to the *Sefer Yeṣirā*, all things emanated, as a subtle, rarefied air which he calls "Second Air" (*awīr shēnī*).[93] Next to it, the element of air was created. Saadya calls it the "visible air". The functions of the *awīr shēnī* are of special interest with regard to our problem. They are twofold: (1) In it the *dibbūr niḇrā* is produced; it proceeds from there into the "visible air", and, finally, to the ear of the prophet. (2) It is the medium of the *Kāḇōd niḇrā* in the sense that the visionary manifestations of Divine Revelation are created in it (p. 94). Saadya identifies the *awīr shēnī* with the Biblical *Kāḇōd*, the *Throne of God*, *Sheḵinā* and *Ruăḥ ha-Ḳōdesh*.[94] The conception of *awīr shēnī* thus binds together *Kāḇōd* and *dibbūr*. Both share in the same substratum. Even the Sinaitic Revelation is here interpreted as a combined action of visible and audible manifestations. Saadya bases his idea on *Mekilta*, Ex. 20:15 (*Yetro*, 9; Weiss, p. 79), in which R. Akiba explains that the people both saw and heard the visible.[95] He explains in similar manner the nature of Ezekiel's visions, the light of the *Ḥayyō*t and *Ofanīm*, as well. The *dibbūr* itself

[91] Cf. my article, "Das Verhältnis Maimunis zur jüdischen Mystik", in *MGWJ* (1936), p. 316. See also below, pp. 186–189.

[92] Cf. *Morē Neḇukim*, II, 33.

[93] Cf. *Com. Yeṣirā*, p. 94. Guttmann (*loc. cit.*, p. 47) suggested that it signifies the ether as a fifth element. But it is not regarded as such by Saadya, as Ventura (*loc. cit.*, p. 119) has shown.

[94] Cf. pp. 94–95. *Sheḵinā* and *Ruăḥ ha-Ḳōdesh* are indeed interchangeable to a large extent. They cover the Biblical conception of *Kāḇōd*. Cf. Abelson, *loc. cit.*, pp. 377–382. Cf. also Kittel, *loc. cit.* pp. 39–42.

[95] Saadya explains that God caused a great fire to descend upon the mount (Ex. 19:18) and surrounded it with black clouds. Then He created, in the fire, the Voice which vibrated in the air. The Voice emanated from the fire, and its shape appeared in the cloud according to the impulsion caused by the vibrations in the air. The people saw this shape, and then knew that it was caused by the vibrations of the fire in the black air.

He tries to make this explanation plausible by the following comparison: "If somebody speaks on a cold day and the articulation of the sound traverses the air, it produces in it certain shapes" (p. 27).

Aaron b. Josef in his *Sefer ha-miḇḥar* (*Yetro*) adopted this explanation. For the Philonic origin of this theory, see H. A. Wolfson, *Philo*, II, 38f.

produces in the *awīr shēnī* certain forms of *Kāḇōd* (p. 63). The motive for this conception thus lies deeper than in the *Mekilta* passage. It lies in the tendency to harmonize *dibbūr* and *Kāḇōd*, *Logos* and *Adam Ḳadmōn*.

The influence of Saadya's concept of the *awīr shēnī* can be traced in the theology of the German Ḥasidim who differentiate between two types of *Kāḇōd*, an "inner Glory" (*Kāḇōd pĕnīmī*) which has no form, but a voice, and a "visible Glory" which appears on the throne of the *Merkāḇā* and is identical with the *Shiᶜur Ḳomā*.[96] The first corresponds to the Logos, the second to the Anthropos mysticism. The fact that the Logos (*dibbūr*), too, is called *Kāḇōd* clearly shows that the German Ḥasidim are influenced, not only by Saadya's *Emūnōt*, where the *dibbūr niḇrā* is only the counterpart of *Kāḇōd*, but also by his *Yeṣirā Commentary*, where both are inseparably interwoven.

[96] Cf. G. Scholem, *Major Trends in Jewish Mysticism*, Revised Edition, pp. 112–113.

7

ELEAZAR OF WORMS' SYMBOL OF THE MERKABAH

One of the principal sources of the Zoharic doctrine of the "shells" (*qelipoth*) is to be found in the writings of Eleazar of Worms (*c.* 1160–1238), which were most certainly known to Moses de Leon.[1] Like his teacher Judah the Ḥasid, Eleazar endeavoured "to give a new interpretation to the *Merkabah*",[2] and to this end elaborated in a number of places the mystical significance of the nut as an image of the *Merkabah*: "He who knows the science of the nut (*ḥokhmath ha-ʾegoz*) will know the depth (*ʿomeq*) of the *Merkabah*."[3] The interpretation of the nut as a symbol of the Divine Chariot is suggested by the biblical phrase, "I went down into the garden of nuts" (Cant. 6:11), which was held to refer to the contemplation of the realm of the *Merkabah*. In the terminology of the *Yordey Merkabah* the mystic had to "descend" to that visionary experience, and the expression, "I went down" (*yaradeti*) fitted the situation very well indeed.[4] The "garden of nuts" could easily be identified with the "garden" (*pardes*) *par excellence* by which the object of mystical contemplation is commonly designated in *Merkabah* mysticism. To what extent the *Yordey Merkabah* made actual use of the symbol of the nut is difficult to establish. The tannaitic homilies on Cat. 6:11 as preserved in *Shir Ha-Shirim Rabbah* contain no allusion to the *Merkabah*. It is not unlikely that the detailed symbolism of the nut as found in the

[1] Cf. G. Scholem, *Major Trends in Jewish Mysticism*, Revised Edition, pp. 226, 239.

[2] *Ibid.*, p. 103.

[3] Cf. below text 4, end. Similarly text 3: "And anyone who does not know the mystical meaning of the nut (*sod ha-ʾegoz*) does not know the *maʿaseh merkavah* . . ."

[4] Cf. *Zohar* ii, 15b: "'I went down' is used in the manner in which it is said, 'So-and-so went down to the *Merkabah*'."

writings of Eleazar of Worms is a novelty introduced by himself.[5] The motif of the "shells of the nut" plays an important part in that symbolism, and is taken over, albeit in a changed and much more complex form, in the *Zohar* and Moses de Leon's Hebrew writings.[6]

It is not the purpose of this paper to trace the influence of Eleazar of Worms' *ḥokhmath ha-ʾegoz* on the *Zohar*. The whole problem of the sources of the Zoharic concept of *qelipoth* will be dealt with elsewhere. Here we are concerned with the treatment of the theme in the various writings of Eleazar. We shall therefore present the relevant passages and discuss the place of the *ḥokhmath ha-ʾegoz* within the larger conspectus of Eleazar's mystical doctrine.

The mystical symbolism of the nut occurs in the following writings of his:

(1) In the *Sodey Razayya* as printed in *Sefer Raziʾel*, Amsterdam, 1701, fol. 11a: "And beneath the Throne of Glory is a space (*ḥalal*), like a nut which has a space beneath it[7] . . . This is referred to in the verse, 'I have gone down into the garden of nuts'. A gloss (*hagahah*): This is the depth (*ᶜomeq*) of the *Merkabah*."

(2) In his *Commentary on Canticles and Ruth* (Lublin, 1608), on 6:11: "*Into the garden of nuts*: this refers to Jerusalem or the Congregation of Israel[8] or Abraham . . . and furthermore the 'garden of nuts' refers to *maᶜaseh merkabah*."

[5] On the nut in Jewish folklore cf. M. Gaster-B. Heller, *Beiträge zur vergleichenden Sagenkunde*, *MGWJ*, 80, N.F. 44 (1936), p. 40 and M. Grunwald, *Mitteilungen zur jüdischen Volkskunde* (1927), p. 29. *Idem*, *Zur vergleichenden Sagenkunde*, *MGWJ*, 76, N.F. 40 (1932), p. 31, mentions the Christian motif of the "cross in the nut", quoting G. Graber, *Sagen aus Kärnten* (1914), pp. 32, 82, where there is, however, no real evidence of this theme. It would, if traceable, represent an interesting Christian parallel to the nut as an image of the *Merkabah*. Patristic homilies on *Canticles* do not seem to connect the nut with the cross. But the matter needs further investigation.

[6] Cf. e.g. *Zohar* ii, 15b; 140b; 233b; a clear echo of Eleazar's term *ᶜomeq ha-Merkabah* is found in *Zohar* i, 19b: when king Solomon went down into the depth of the nut—*le-ᶜomqa de-ʾegoza*; Moses de Leon's *Sefer ha-Nefesh ha-ḥakhamah* (Basle, 1608), I, o, c, refers to the *sod ha-ʾegoz* as the *sod ha-Merkabah* and to the shells of the nut as a symbol of the shells round the *Merkabah*; in his great commentary on Ezekiel, ch. 1, Moses de Leon likewise mentions the symbolism of the nut. Cf. *Shaᶜar Yesod ha-Merkabah*, ms. Cambridge University Library Dd. 3.5, fol. 6r.

[7] Cf. Cant. R. 6:11: "Just as a nut has four compartments (*meguroth*) and a space (*sirah*) in the centre, so Israel were encamped in the wilderness, four standards, four camps and the tent of assembly in the middle." Eleazar of Worms uses the term *ḥalal* for space. His mystical interpretation obviously prefers its own terminology.

[8] Most homiletical interpretations in Cant. R. on 6:11 refer to Israel: R. Joshua b. Levi compares Israel to a nut-tree; R. Azariah likens the ignorant among Israel who support the scholars to the protecting shells of the nut, etc. See also *B. Ḥag.* 15b.

(3) In his *Ḥokhmath ha-Nefesh* the symbolism of the nut is treated at first in homiletical fashion but in the end given its mystical value. The passage amply illustrates the fascination which the image of the nut held for the author's mind. Our translation is based on the printed edition (Lemberg, 1876, fols. 11a–11b, and ms. British Museum Add. 27, 199 (Margoliouth 737, iv), fols. 516*r*–517*r*):

"*I went down into the garden of nuts*: A nut has four segments (*ṣelaᶜoth*) and a ridge (*ḥod*) in its centre. Likewise, there are four camps of Israel and one of the mixed multitude (*ᶜerev-rav*). And the entire subject-matter (*ᶜinyan*) of the Torah is like the nut: The numerical value of א״ג according to the method of א״ת ב״ש is 600, and that of ו״ז in the normal way is 13, totalling 613. Even as the nut has an external bitter shell surrounding it, so were the Scroll of the Torah and the sword handed down wrapped together.[9] Beneath the bitter shell are two other shells dry as wood. Likewise, two brothers, Moses and Aaron, guard Israel and act as its guides. Beneath those shells is a soft shell in the centre of the kernel divided in four directions, corresponding to the captains over thousands, hundreds, fifties and tens who judge Israel at all times. Finally, there is a shell which clothes (*malbesheth*) the kernel, corresponding to the clouds of glory and the Levites and priests. The kernel is shaped like four double-columns (*deyomedin*)[10] corresponding to the four camps; and the four double-columns of the kernel are round about its stalk (*ᶜōqeṣ*), and the stalk is in the centre, corresponding to the sons of Kohath, the sons of Gershom, the sons of Merari in three directions, and those encamped in front of the sanctuary Moses and Aaron and his sons, the sanctuary being in the centre. Moreover, the uppermost bitter shell corresponds to the heaven which encompasses everything, and [also] corresponds to the salty ocean (*yam ᵓoqyanos*). And the colour of the water in the sea is like the colour of the shell of the nut which is green, and like 'the green line which encompasses the whole world',[11] and corresponds to the admonitions and punishments which are bitter like the shell of the nut. And even as the shell of the nut, because it is bitter, protects the kernel against worms, seeing that worms are found only in sweet things, so do the

[9] *Sifrey*, ᶜ*Eqev*, §40 end; Lev. R. 35:6; Deut R. 4:2, and further parallels.
[10] Cf. *B.* ᶜ*Erub.* 18a, 19b.
[11] *B. Ḥag.* 12a.

admonitions and punishments protect the commandments . . . And anyone who does not know the mystical meaning of the nut (*sod ha-ᵓegoz*) does not know the *maᶜaseh merkabah* and the *ḥayyoth* and the 'fire' that 'flashed up and down' and 'out of the fire went forth lightning'. The nut has four segments (*ṣelaᶜoth*) like the four *ḥayyoth*, and the middle one is raised at its ridge (*be-ḥuddo*), corresponding to the Throne. And the eatable fruit is white even as *His throne was flames of fire* (Dan. 7:9). It should have read, 'fire from the throne' but it speaks about how the throne was created[12] . . ."

(4) The mystical meaning of the nut is more fully described in yet another text which is extant in the following recensions:

(*a*) In a passage entitled *Shaᶜar Sod ha-Merkabah* which is contained in Eleazar of Worms' *Shaᶜarey ha-Sod we-ha-Yiḥud we-ha-ᵓEmunah*, published by A. Jellinek in *Kokhebey Yiṣḥaq*, ed. M. E. Stern, Vol. 27, Vienna, 1862, p. 13.

(*b*) In a passage quoted in the name of Eleazar (of Worms) by R. Abraham b. R. ᶜAzriᵓel (thirteenth century) in his *Sefer ᶜArugath ha-Bosem*, published by E. E. Urbach, Vol. ii, Jerusalem, 1947, pp. 168–171.

(*c*) In a passage recorded in a marginal gloss in one of the mss. of the work mentioned under (b) and reproduced by Urbach, *loc. cit.*, pp. 168–170.

(*d*) In a passage headed *Hilkhoth ha-Kisseᵓ* in Eleazar's *Hilkhoth ha-Kabod*, published under the erroneous title *Sodey Razayya* by Kamelhar (Bilgoria, 1936), p. 21a.

Texts (*a*), (*c*) and (*d*) represent a recension different from the one found in (*b*). Unfortunately, text (*a*) breaks off in the middle (noted by Urbach, p. 169, n. 6), and text (*d*) omits the first part (noted by Urbach, p. 169, n. 8). All the texts are in a bad condition,

[12] In Eleazar's view the throne of glory (and the angels) arose from the reflection of the Divine light of the *Shekhinah* in the cosmic waters. That light produced a radiance which became a fire and thus caused the throne (and the angels) to come into being. Cf. Scholem, *op. cit.*, pp. 113 and 376, n. 115. To the passages quoted there should be added *Sodey Razayya*, ms. Brit. Mus. Add. 27, 199 (Margoliouth 737), fols. 126*v*–127*r* on *Hilkhoth ha-Kisseᵓ*: "How was it (sc. the Throne) created from the beginning of the world? The Holy One, blessed be He, made his splendour (*zohoro*) appear upon the waters, and from the radiance (*nogah*) of his limitless light his splendour shone (*higgiah*) from amid the waters; and by the force of this splendour fire arose from the water, and from that fire He formed (*ḥaqaq*) and devised (*ḥashav*) the throne of glory and the ᵓ*Ofannim* . . ." Eleazar makes the point that there is only *one* throne (against the view of *Midrash Shemuel* which ascribes a throne to every one of the heavens), and quotes in support the verse from Daniel (7:9) cited in our text.

but it is possible to establish correct readings in a number of cases by comparing the parallel recensions.[13] The following is a translation of the relevant part of the recension extant in (*a*), (*c*) and (*d*), which has to be considered the better one:[14]

"*I went down into the garden of nuts*: The *gematria* of אל גנת אגוז is identical with that of זו עומק המרכבה.[15] *Of nuts*: Know thou that the nut has a green and bitter shell, and beneath this green shell which is cast off[16] it has a wooden shell like two cups in which the fruit is placed. It (i.e. the fruit) has four compartments (*ṣelaᶜoth*), of which two are within one shell and two within another,[17] and between the compartments there stands a soft shell.[18] And there is towards the broad end of the nut a kind of window in the fruit between two of its compartments, and below on the ridge of it there issues from its compartments a kind of *membrum virile*, and there[19] it (i.e. the fruit) sucks from the bitter shell, hence no worms are found in a nut. For the kernel sucks from the bitter shell. In case, however, one removes the bitter shell before the kernel has ripened and whilst it is still on the tree, worms will be found to develop in the kernel.[20] There are nine leaves to every twig of the nut.

Now I have opened unto thee a door to understand in thy heart this [verse], *I went down into the garden of nuts*, and to see that His great fire[21] is, like the nut, thick at its top and thin towards the

[13] The present writer was not in a position to consult the ms. Paris, B.N. *héb.* 850, which contains the *Sodey Razayya* (fols. 46–145). But according to information kindly supplied to him by Prof. G. Vajda, the section of this ms. describing the *Hilkhoth ha-Kabod* (fols. 84–93*v*) offers no parallel to the texts concerning the *ḥokhmath ha-ᵓegoz* listed above.

[14] A critical Hebrew text of this recension is published at the end of this paper [omitted in this Volume]. The first three letters of the Hebrew alphabet used as sigla in the textual notes refer to texts a, b, and c, respectively. Unfortunately, text d was not available to the present writer. It represents in any case only a minor section of the text. [See *Journal of Jewish Studies*, XI (1960), pp. 111–113.]

[15] =501.

[16] *Infra* in the text: "which drops off".

[17] Cf. *infra* in the text: "the soft shell attached to the fruit". Text b refers to it as "the soft shell in the cavity (*be-ḥeqo*) of the nut" (p. 170, line 1).

[18] Cf. *infra*: "the shell which is placed in between the four heads of the nut".

[19] Text b: "And it (i.e. the external bitter shell) enters into the kernel through a hole above."

[20] Text b adds some medical advice how to cure children who are suffering from worms in their intestines (p. 169, lines 6–8).

[21] This term denotes in Eleazar's terminology the "great fire" of the *Shekhinah* as distinct from the lesser fire produced by the radiance of the *Shekhinah* in the cosmic waters. The throne and the angels arose from the lesser fire. See *Shaᶜarey ha-sod*, etc., *Kokhevey Yiṣḥaq*, 27, p. 13, line 36; p. 14, line 1; Scholem, *loc. cit.*, p. 113.

earth.[22] Like the green external shell on its outside, *there was brightness to the fire* (Ez. 1:13) *from the brightness before Him* (2 Sam. 22:13; Ps. 18:13), *like the appearance of torches* (Ez. 1:13): A white flame seen from afar will give one the appearance of a wax-like green, like the external shell.[23] This is the shell which drops off, corresponding to *And behold, a whirlwind came* (Ez. 1:4). Beneath the green one are two shells which are separate, but stick together when the nut is dry: the *great cloud* (Ez. 1:4), *fire and hail* (Ps. 148:8), *And He made darkness pavilions round about Him* (2 Sam. 22:12). [When the nut is] wooden[24] the pavilion[25] is but one, but when the nut is fresh, there are two pavilions—*gathering of waters, thick clouds of the sky* (2 Sam. 22:3)—corresponding to the two shells in which the fruit is placed. *And out of the midst thereof the likeness of four ḥayyoth* (Ez. 1:5): the four compartments of the nut, two of which are in one shell and two in another. *Four faces* (Ez. 1:6): the four heads of the kernel. *Four wings* (*ibid.*): the four segments (*ḥulyoth*) of the nut beneath them (i.e. the heads). *And their feet were straight feet* (Ez. 1:7): likewise in the nut. *And their wings were unfolded* (Ez. 1:11): each segment is bipartite like wings. One stalk: this is the square-shaped throne occupying the centre. The cut in the stalk corresponds to the throne of judgment and the throne of mercy. And *It* (i.e. the appearance of fire) *flashed up and down among the ḥayyoth* (Ez. 1:13): this is the shell which is placed between the four heads of the nut. The four heads of the upper segments are the four *ḥayyoth*, and the four lower ones are the four *cherubim*.[26] And the nut is round: *The appearance of the wheels* (*ᵓofanim*) *and their work was like unto the colour of a beryl* (Ez. 1:16).[27] The soft shell attached to the fruit: *wheel within wheel* (*ibid.*). The side of the kernel facing towards the outer shell is red, green and yellow like the [*rain*]*bow* (Ez. 1:28). The nut has five segments

[22] Text b adds "Likewise the cherubim of the upper fire" (p. 169, lines 10–11), and quotes in support *B. Ḥag.* 13a describing the proportional increase in the magnitude of the limbs of the *ḥayyoth* from bottom to top.

[23] The green colour of the external shell is but the appearance of the "brightness" (*nogah*) or of "torches" (*lappidim*) as seen from the distance.

[24] I.e. dry, and the two inner shells stick together.

[25] Which corresponds to the image of the inner shell, and symbolizes surrounding darkness.

[26] In the *Hekhaloth* literature the *cherubim* occupy a higher place than the *ḥayyoth*. Cf. H. Odeberg, 3 *Enoch* (Cambridge, 1928), pp. 148–149. Eleazar's view seems to be different.

[27] Text b has a further reference to the roundness of the nut: "The circumference (*heqef*) of the *ḥayyot* is like a round nut" (p. 168, lines 12–13).

[altogether], four which are female and one being the *membrum virile*. Correspondingly, there are four *ḥayyoth* and one *ḥayyah* above them.[28] Similarly, it is said in *Genesis Rabbah*:[29] Four times the firmament (*raqia*ᶜ) is mentioned on the second day, and once the firmament is called heaven (*shamayim*) . . . *As the appearance of splendour, as the colour of ḥashmalah* (Ez. 8:2): this is the whiteness of the kernel as such. The *Kavod*[30] has nine colours: each twig of the nut-tree has nine leaves. It is therefore dangerous to plant a nut-tree.[31] The two outer shells[32]: The throne is placed in the centre[33] between *darkness of waters* (Ps. 18:12) and *gathering of waters* (2 Sam. 22:12), and a black shell divides the kernel from the head of the *membrum virile*: this is the strap of the *tefillin*[34] upon the head of the *Kavod*,[35] blessed and exalted be He for ever and in all eternity. And beneath the kernel is a space: beneath the throne of glory is a space[36] like an ark, and in it are the souls of the righteous. He who knoweth the science of the nut will know the depth of the *Merkabah*."

[28] The existence of one *ḥayyah* above the four *ḥayyoth* may be suggested by the use of the singular instead of the usual plural in Ez.1:22, 10:15, 20. This would represent an analogy to Eleazar's doctrine of the "special cherub" (*ha-kerub ha-meyuḥad*) which Scholem traced to the use of the singular in Ez. 10:4 (cf. *Major Trends*, p. 113). On the other hand, the angelology of the *Hekhaloth* literature already knows Ḥayliᵓel, prince of the four *ḥayyoth* and Kerubiᵓel, prince of the *cherubim* (see Odeberg, *ibid.*).

[29] Urbach, *op. cit.*, p. 169, n. 7, quotes Gen. R. 4:2 and *Pirqey R. Eliezer*, 4 for reference, but in neither place anything even remotely resembling our passage can be found. Eleazar makes the point that in its description of the second day of creation the Torah (Gen. 1:6–8) uses four times the word *raqia*ᶜ on its own and once in proximity to the word *shamayim*, thus suggesting a fifth *raqia*ᶜ above the four. He infers from this that a special significance attaches to the numbers four *plus* one: the quaternity is presided over by a fifth being. The theme is illustrated in a variety of ways by scriptural quotations in texts c and d but, having no bearing on the symbolism of the nut, it has been omitted here.

[30] I.e. the "visible glory" (*kabod nirᵓeh*) as distinct from the "inner glory" (*kabod penimi*) which has no shape, only voice. Cf. Scholem, *op. cit.*, pp. 112ff.

[31] On the dangerous properties of the nut in Jewish folklore cf. Gaster-Heller, *loc. cit.*, quoting *Sefer Ḥasidim*, ed. Bologna, fol. 119b, 1160 (not contained in the Parma recension, ed. Wistinetzki) and *Yalquṭ Ḥadash*, fol. 89a, no. 52: the nine leaves are the abode of evil spirits. Eleazar of Worms possibly alludes to this belief. For the phallic significance of the nut see Manhardt, *Wald- und Feldkulte* I, 184 (quoted by Gaster-Heller).

[32] I.e. as distinct from the one clothing the kernel.

[33] I.e. of the nut, between the surrounding darkness of the cosmic waters. As we have noted above (n. 21), the throne actually arose from the fire produced in the cosmic waters.

[34] Which must, according to rabbinic tradition, be black.

[35] See note 30. The haggadic motif of God wearing *tefillin* (*B. Ber.* 6a), which plays an important part in Jewish mysticism, is here applied to the "visible glory".

[36] Cf. the reference to the *ḥalal* in text (1).

The text we have quoted is not conspicuous for either clarity or beauty of its style. It is obscure and abstruse in the extreme, and yields no spiritual insight. Yet it is interesting as an attempt to condense the vast and amorphous material of *Merkabah* mysticism into a succinct pictorial representation of manageable proportions. It gives the whole of the *Merkabah* as it were "in a nutshell". Considering the unrestrained hymnic descriptions of the realm of the *Merkabah* in the *Hekhaloth* literature,[37] it has at least the merit of a certain discipline and systemic order which the limited scope of the image of the nut imposes. Instead of an almost unending series of concentric circles round the throne of glory[38] we find here not more than four circles, corresponding to the four shells of the nut. In his *Sodey Raẕayya* Eleazar still faithfully copies the ecstatic portrayal of the celestical realms in the *Hekhaloth*: "Behind the fearful throne is the wind surrounding it; and light surrounds the wind; and brightness surrounds the light; and fire surrounds the brightness"; etc.[39] In our passage a slightly more rational principle is clearly at work. Its literary form is a twofold one: Eleazar offers a kind of running commentary on certain verses in Ezekiel, ch. 1, and does so in the light of the doctrine of the *Merkabah* which he took over from Judah he-Ḥasid. On the other hand, he takes his cue from the image of the nut (which, it appears, he did on his own)[40] and gives a symbolic interpretation of the nut by relating its anatomy to the text of Ezekiel and other Scriptural passages, again in the light of the new *Merkabah* doctrine. The two approaches, viz. the exegetical and the contemplative one, often intermingle, as can easily be seen from a perusal

[37] Cf. Odeberg, *loc. cit.*, pp. 114–115, especially the quotation from *Midrash Konen.*

[38] *Ibid.*

[39] Cf. ms. British Museum, Add. 27, 199 (Margoliouth 737), fol. 126*r*. The hymnic description of the concentric circles is also retained in the *Shaʿarey ha-Sod we-ha-Yiḥud* itself (*Kokhebe̱y Yiṣḥaq*, 27, p. 15). Eleazar quotes there (in another passage, p. 11) the *Baraita de-maᶜaseh bereshith*=*Midrash Konen* (see Jellinek, n. 6).

[40] In a passage in the *Sodey Raẕayya* (ms. Brit. Mus., fol. 3*v*) which is omitted in the editions (cf. Margoliouth, III, p. 5) Eleazar describes his own part in the elaboration of the *sod ha-Merkavah* as follows: *vĕ-aḥar-kak̲ ek̲tob̲ lek̲a sod ha-merkab̲ah ka-asher qibbalti mi-pī rabbenu yehudah he-ḥasīd ka-asher qībbel mē-ab̲iv rabbenu shemuᵓel he-ḥasīd vĕ-gam qibbalti anī mi-pī abba morī yehudah anī elᶜaẕar ha-qaṭan vĕ-gam ka-asher binōti ba-sĕfarim u-b̲a-midrashim vĕ-ek̲tob lek̲a dab̲ar dab̲ur ᶜal ofnav vĕ-ᶜeẕrat shaddai ᶜimadī li-k̲ĕtob ka-asher ᶜim leb̲āb̲i vĕ-elohey yisrael yōrēnī vi-yĕgal ᶜeynay bi-meᵓōr torato . . . vĕ-aᵓalefk̲a ḥok̲mah le-ahab̲ah et yy'* [*adonai*] *vĕ-la-lek̲et bi-dĕrak̲av u-le-dob̲ka bō*. The expression *li-k̲ĕtob̲ ka-asher ᶜim leb̲ab̲ī* seems to claim a measure of originality.

of the text. Sometimes, he starts by quoting the scriptural text—a method which he uses e.g. in other sections of the *Shaʿarey ha-Sod we-ha-Yiḥud*[41]—and sometimes he proceeds from a contemplation of the nut. The result is in either case an exposition conforming, at least in broad outline, to his theosophical doctrine.[42]

The most important link between our text and Eleazar's teaching concerning the *Merkabah* is provided by the term "His great fire", which clearly indicates the radiance of the *Shekhinah* or "inner glory".[43] It is difficult to understand the reference to its being "thick at its top and thin towards the earth", because it has no shape according to Eleazar's explicit teaching. It may, however, be an allusion to its diminishing radiance. That radiance or *brightness before Him*, etc. is symbolized by the green external shell of the nut, the explanation being offered that a white flame assumes a wax-like green colour when seen from a far distance. The two shells beneath the green outer shell seem again to reflect features known from his doctrine of the *Merkabah*. They symbolize the cosmic waters in which the radiance of the "great fire" is reflected. Eleazar identifies them with *gathering of waters*, *darkness of waters*, *thick clouds of the sky*, and also with *fire and hail*, a reference perhaps to the lesser fire which the radiance of the *Shekhinah* produces in the waters, and out of which the throne and the angels are created. The fire *flashing up and down among the ḥayyoth*, which is symbolized by the intermediate shell dividing the fruit itself, is probably that lesser fire, since it is related to the *ḥayyoth*. Of the throne, too, it is said in our text that it is placed in the centre and surrounded by *darkness of waters and gathering of waters*, a likely reference to the cosmic waters out of which it arose. Moreover, our text mentions the *kavod* in the context of the throne, undoubtedly a reference to the "visible glory" or "cherub on the throne" as distinct from the "inner glory" which is associated with the "great fire". It looks as if this figure is symbolized by the protuberance of the kernel of the nut described as "a kind of *membrum virile*". But the matter remains obscure in view of the fact that one would expect the *kavod* to occupy the throne, and the location of the throne is somewhat at variance with the description of the place of its occupant. Strangely enough, the throne is

[41] Cf. p. 12 where he expounds verses from *Canticles*.
[42] For a full description of his doctrine cf. Scholem, *op. cit.*, pp. 111–116.
[43] Cf. *supra*, n. 21.

visualized in the image of the stalk of the nut. There are, to be sure, other obscurities such as the two references to colours, the meaning of the one *ḥayyah*, and the unexplained symbolical significance of the "window" in the kernel. Most probably, there are *lacunae* in the text which are partly responsible for the riddles it presents. But the fact remains that our passage reflects the authentic teachings of Eleazar concerning the *Merkabah* in a highly novel form.

One point stands in need of further clarification. As we have noted, the four shells of the nut are interpreted as symbols of (1) the "great fire" of the *Shekhinah*; (2) and (3) as the cosmic waters; and (4) *the fire flashing up and down*, i.e. the lesser fire out of which the throne and the angels are created. The soft shell attached to the fruit is explained as a *wheel within a wheel*, i.e. as representing the angelic class of *ᵓofanim*, whilst the four compartments of the fruit itself stand for the four *ḥayyoth*. A somewhat different line of interpretation is taken in text *b* (p. 170, lines 2–4) where the first three shells are said to symbolize the elements of the theophany in Ez. 1:4 and its parallel in 1 Kings 19:11–12: The outer green shell stands for the *stormy wind* (Ez.) or *wind* (1 Kings). The first inner shell corresponds to the *great cloud* (Ez.) or *earthquake* (1 Kings). The second inner shell represents the *fire flashing up and down* (Ez.) or the *fire* (1 Kings), whereas the shell attached to the kernel symbolizes again a *wheel within a wheel*. There is no mention here of the "great fire", although the green external shell is additionally interpreted as the appearance of the surrounding brightness from a distance, as in the other recension. Conversely, there is a trace of that other interpretation also in our main text. Interspersed in the exposition of the theme and unconnected with it there occurs the sentence: "This (i.e. the external shell) is the shell which drops off, corresponding to *And behold, a stormy wind came*." But this line is not here pursued further. It is possible that the two recensions were conflated or that the original text contained already both ways of interpretation. According to one the shells symbolize elements of Eleazar's doctrine of the *Merkabah*, whereas according to the other they represent the paraphernalia of the theophanies as set out in the biblical texts. As it happens, it was the second line of interpretation which was adopted by Moses de Leon. He obviously had little use for the first, which was so closely linked with a theosophy no longer subscribed to. Interestingly enough, the symbolism of the nut was disregarded by all pre-Zoharic kabbalists.[44] Isaac b. Jacob Ha-Kohen's Commentary on Ezekiel's vision of the Merkabah (*Mirkebet Yeḥezq'el*)[45] elaborates on the *stormy wind*, the *great cloud*, etc. without using the imagery of the shells of the nut. This is all the more remarkable, in that the author was in many ways not uninfluenced by Eleazar of Worms.[46] It was left to Moses de Leon to re-introduce the *sod ha-'egoz* into Jewish mystical thought. But far from representing Divine potencies of a positive character, the *qelipoth* now assumed demonic aspects not foreseen by Eleazar of Worms.

[44] It is all the more noteworthy that Abraham b. ʿAzri'el (thirteenth century) quoted it in full in his *ʿArugath ha-Bosem*, a commentary on the *Piyyutim*.

[45] Cf. the edition of this text (with a most informative commentary) by Scholem, *Le-ḥeqer qabbalath* R. *Yisḥaq ha-Kohen* (Jerusalem, 1934), pp. 1–30.

[46] Cf. Scholem, *Le-ḥeqer* etc., pp. 44–45.

8

THE MOTIF OF THE "SHELLS" IN ᶜAZRIEL OF GERONA

In the imagery of the *Zohar* the symbol of the "shells" (*qelipoth*) surrounding the "kernel" (*moḥa*ᵓ) plays a major role.[1] As is well known, the theme won increasing importance in Lurianic Kabbalah,[2] and eventually became one of the most popular (and even hackneyed) notions in Jewish mystical thought. One of the sources from which Moses de Leon, the presumed author of the *Zohar*, drew this concept is undoubtedly Eleazar of Worms' allegorical interpretation of the shells and kernel of the nut (*Ḥokhmath ha-ᵓEgoz*, cf. Cant. 6:11), as has already been recognised by G. Scholem.[3] A detailed analysis of Eleazar's treatment of the theme has been given by the present writer elsewhere.[4] In this paper research into the antecedents of the Zoharic concept of the *qelipoth* is carried a stage further by the attempt to trace yet another, hitherto unsuspected, literary source. ᶜAzriel of Gerona, a younger contemporary of Eleazar's, is known to have influenced Moses de Leon in certain respects.[5] We suggest that ᶜAzriel's notion of *qelipah* had a share in the evolution also of Moses de Leon's

[1] It also occurs in Moses de Leon's Hebrew writings. Cf. *Sefer ha-Nefesh ha-ḥakhamah* (Basle, 1608), I. o, c; *Shaᶜar yesodh ha-Merkabhah*, ms. Cambridge University Library, Dd.3.5, fol. 6r; *Sheᵓeloth u-teshubhoth*, ed. J. Tishby, *Qobheṣ ᶜal yad, Meqiṣey Nirdamim*, V (XV) (Jerusalem, 1950), p. 21, line 50; p. 25, line 44; p. 26, line 53. For an analysis of the concept in the *Zohar* see J. Tishby, *Mishnath ha-Zohar*, I (Jerusalem, 1949), pp. 298–301.

[2] Cf. J. Tishby, *Torath ha-raᶜ we-ha-qelipah be-qabbalath ha-ᵓAri* (Tel Aviv, 1942).

[3] Cf. *Major Trends in Jewish Mysticism*; Revised Edition, p. 239.

[4] [See the preceding essay, which was originally scheduled to appear in the Eightieth Anniversary Volume of the Jewish Theological Seminary of Budapest (projected, yet never published), and which was subsequently printed in the *Journal of Jewish Studies*, XI (1960).]

[5] Cf. Scholem, *loc. cit.*, p. 173.

complex doctrine of the "shells". To prove the fact of such influence presupposes a full analysis of the Zoharic concept and lies beyond the scope of this paper. Our present purpose is confined to an elucidation of ᶜAzriel's position only, and it is hoped to deal with the wider aspects of Moses de Leon's dependence on his sources in a later study.

ᶜAzriel's *Perush ha-ᵓAggadoth* (ed. J. Tishby, Jerusalem, 1945), p. 105 contains the following passage:

> And because *tohu* surrounds *bohu* and encompasses it, the shell (*qelipah*) of every creature surrounds it (sc. the creature); and everything interior (*penimi*) in living beings is precious (*mibhḥar*), and all fruits have a shell outside, and darkness encompasses the light. To this Scripture alludes: "The wicked walk on every side" (Ps. 12:9); and it is written, "And turn ye not aside; for then ye go after vain things (*ha-tohu*) which cannot profit nor deliver, for they are vain (*tohu*)" (1 Sam. 22:21); and it is written, "He created it not a waste (*tohu*), He formed it to be inhabited" (Isa. 45:18); and it is written, "And turn aside a just with a thing of nought (*bha-tohu*)" (*ibid.* 29:21).

The background of this passage is a highly complicated cosmogony in which rabbinic and neoplatonic elements are curiously blended.[6] Although it is hardly possible to co-ordinate ᶜAzriel's various descriptions of the cosmogonic process in all their details, the following aspects stand out more or less clearly. The uppermost triad among the *Sefiroth*, viz. *Kether* (also *raṣon*, *ᵓayin*, etc.), *Ḥokhmah*, and *Binah*, is identified with the "three creations" which according to Ex. R. 15:22 preceded the world, viz. water, spirit and fire. *Kether* corresponds to spirit, *Ḥokhmah* to water,[7] and *Binah* to fire. According to the same midrashic source, "The water conceived and gave birth to darkness, the fire conceived and gave birth to light; and the spirit conceived and gave birth to wisdom." ᶜAzriel interprets this to mean that from *Kether* = spirit (also called

[6] For ᶜAzriel's neoplatonic sources see now A. Altmann, "Isaac Israeli's 'Chapter on the Elements' (ms. Mantua)", *JJS*, VII (1956), pp. 32–33; *idem*, *JJS*, VII, pp. 203–206; A. Altmann and S. M. Stern, *Isaac Israeli, A Neoplatonic Philosopher of the Early Tenth Century* (Oxford, 1958), pp. 131–132.

[7] "The paths (*nethibhoth*) of all essences (*hawayoth*) are in water". In Abraham bar Ḥiyya's *Hegyon ha-Nefesh* (p. 3) it is similarly said that the water represents universal Form.

ᵓawir she-ᵓeyno nithpas)[8] there emanated the *Sefira Ḥokhmah*, from *Ḥokhmah*=water darkness, and from *Binah*=fire light (pp. 88–89). He distinctly uses the term "emanation" in describing the process: "And from spirit and water and light and fire which emanated one from another (*ha-neᵓeṣalim zeh mi-zeh*) and from that which emanated from them, everything . . . was created." It is, then, clear that *Ḥokhmah* emanated from *Kether*. We also have a straightforward explanation for the statement that light emanated from fire: *Binah*=fire which represents the hypostasis 'Intellect' (*sekhel*) of ᶜAzriel's neoplatonic source[9] contains "all essences" (*hawayoth*) or forms. They are the "lights" which emanate from it.[10] But what is implied in the emanation of darkness from *Ḥokhmah*=water? The answer to this question holds the key to the understanding of the meaning of the passage quoted earlier on.

ᶜAzriel mentions in several places the *Baraitha B. Ḥag.* 12a: "*Tohu* is the green line which encompasses the whole world, from which darkness went forth; for it is written, 'He made darkness His hiding place round Him' (Ps. 18:12). *Bohu* is the wet stones

[8] Cf. *Perush ha-ᵓAggadoth*, p. 107. The term is adopted from *Sefer Yeṣirah*, 2:6. On its Stoic background see Scholem, *MGWJ* (1927), p. 121, n. 1. Cf. also G. Margoliouth "The Doctrine of the Ether in the Kabbalah", *JQR*, O.S. XX (1908), pp. 825ff.

Both the *ᶜIyyun* circle and the mystics of Gerona describe it as the "source of all essences". In the writings of the *ᶜIyyun* circle it is also called *ᵓawir qadmon* (derived from *Sefer Yeṣirah* and Saᶜadya's Commentary on it) and in both the *ᶜIyyun* and Gerona circles it is referred to as *ha-ᵓOr ha-Mithᶜallem*. Cf. Scholem, *ᶜIqebhothaw shel Gebhirol be-Qabbalah*, Meᵓassef Soferey Ereṣ Yisrael (1940), pp. 168, 173. For the use of the term *ᵓawir she-ᵓeyno nithpas* by Moses de Leon see *Zohar* III, 2a; *Nefesh ha-ḥakhamah, Sodh Shabbath*; *Sheqel ha-Qodesh*, ed. Greenup, pp. 109–110.

[9] Scholem, *ᶜIqebhothaw shel Gebhirol*, etc. (pp. 173–174) has shown that the ontological scheme quoted by ᶜAzriel from the neoplatonic pseudepigraph incorporated in the Mantua text came to be adapted to the kabbalistic system in writings of the Gerona school and the *ᶜIyyun* circle. ᶜAzriel's cosmogony is a case in point. Another striking example is provided by the *Sodh ha-Sefiroth we-sodh ha-gawwanim* (quoted by Scholem), where the neoplatonic triad of universal matter—universal form—intellect re-appears in a paraphrase.

[10] "The paths of all essence are in the Fire which shines forth (*ha-mithnoṣeṣ*) one from another. This is meant by our saying that Fire conceived and bore light." ᶜAzriel (*Perush ha-ᵓAggadoth*, p. 89) links the expression *be-heytibho ᵓeth ha-neroth* (Ex. 30:7) and its rendering in Targum Onqelos (not in our version nor in A. Berliner's edition of the Sabbionetta text) by *be-ᵓadliqutha* with the passage Gen. 1:4 ("And God saw the light that it was good"). The "goodness" referred to in the two Biblical phrases mentioned is said to denote the emanation of the light one from the other. This passage is quoted in Ṭodros Abulafia's *ᵓOṣar ha-Kabhod* (Satu Mare, 1925), p. 37b, as noted by Tishby, *Perush ha-ᵓAggadoth*, p. 35. It occurs also in Ezra's *Com.* on Cant. 1:1.

immersed in *tehom*, from which water goes forth; for it is written, 'And He shall stretch over it the line of confusion (*qaw tohu*) and the plummet of emptiness (*we-ʾabhene bohu*)' (Isa. 34:11)." He also quotes the comment of *Sefer Bahir* (§2), according to which the earth pre-existed as *tohu*, i.e. "something which astonishes men", and then became *bohu*, i.e. "something in which there is 'reality' (*mammash*), for it is written *bo-hu*".[11] As G. Scholem pointed out, ᶜAzriel in his *Commentary* on *S. Yeṣirah* (I: 11) was the first to interpret this *Bahir* passage in terms of the distinction between "matter" and "form": "*Tohu* is the potentiality of the essences in which there is no form (*reshimah*); *bohu* is the potentiality of the essences in which there is form."[12] (The *Bahir* pas age is based on *S. Yeṣirah* ii: 6: "He formed from *tohu* reality (*mammash*) and made the non-existent existent.") It should, however, be noted that the interpretation of *tohu* and *bohu* as matter and form respectively, and the etymology of *bohu* as *bo-hu* occur already in Abraham bar Ḥiyya's *Hegyon ha-Nefesh* (2b-3a).[13] The members of the Gerona circle undoubtedly knew the interpretation offered by Abraham bar Ḥiyya. Apart from the testimony of ᶜAzriel there is a passage in Ezra of Gerona's *Commentary* on Canticles: "*Tohu* is something without form, and *bohu* is that which clothes *tohu* so that there is formed a formation (*ṣiyyur*) subtler than air."[14]

It should be noted that according to this imagery *bohu* (form) clothes *tohu* (matter). The metaphor is reversed in the ᶜAzriel passage quoted at the opening of our discussion. There it is said that *tohu* surrounds *bohu* and encompasses it like a shell. This conception arises from a combination of the *Bahir* passage with the *Baraitha* which describes *tohu* as the "green line which encompasses the whole world". According to ᶜAzriel, the green line is not identical with *tohu* but arises within it, and causes darkness to go forth from it. The following passages will help to clarify his meaning:

"And *tohu* is the green line: from it (sc. *tohu*) is the encompassing

[11] *Perush ha-ʾAggadoth*, p. 92, lines 2–5, 12–13; see also p. 89, line 17; p. 103, lines 1–2.

[12] *Das Buch Bahir* (Berlin, 1923), p. 4, n. 1.

[13] Quoted by Tishby, *Perush ha-ʾAggadoth*, p. 92, n. 6. It is possible that the *Sefer Bahir* took this interpretation from Abraham bar Ḥiyya. On the latter's influence on the latest parts of the *Bahir*, cf. Scholem, *Le-ḥeqer qabbalath Rabbi Yiṣḥaq ben Yaᶜaqobh ha-Kohen* (Jerusalem, 1934), pp. 73–74.

[14] Cf. Altona edition (which ascribes the *Commentary* to Naḥmanides), 1764, p. 27a.

line from which darkness comes forth" (p. 103, lines 1–2; see Tishby, n. 2). "And *tohu* is that in which there is no reality (*mammash*): because in it all essences (*hawayoth*) were without limitation (*hagbalah*) and without form and matter . . . When *from it* a green line arose encompassing and darkening (*maḥshikh*), the elements, which are forces (*koḥoth*) one within another, were established . . . and these elements . . . are called 'stones of *bohu*' (Isa. 24:11), in which there is reality (*mammash*) that is recognizable (*nikkar*) and conceivable (*nithpas*) in its limit (*gebhul*), and the essence of everything is recognizable in them" (p. 89, lines 14–20).

"And *tohu* is the root (*ᶜiqqar*) of the essences . . . and its appearance is green, drawn as a line marking the limitation of space in which the essence cannot be recognized; and it is subtle, deficient and confused like something wiped out and deleted, the form of which cannot be recognized and the reality of which cannot be conceived . . ." (p. 92, lines 19–21).

"And before the limit was imposed, He stretched over it (sc. the limitless) the line of right measure (*qaw ha-yosher*) to fix even limits" (p. 89, line 14).

It is obvious from these and similar passages that *tohu* denotes the hylic Wisdom (*Ḥokhmah*) in which the essences are still undifferentiated, and that the green line symbolises the darkening, and hence limiting, power by which *bohu*, i.e. the totality of Forms emerges, thus giving rise to the *Sefirah Binah* or Intellect. This is how ᶜAziel understands the midrashic phrase, "Water conceived and gave birth to darkness." The interpretation of "water" as hylic or universal matter in a neoplatonic sense corresponds to Abraham bar Ḥiyya's interpretation of it as universal form.[15]

The correctness of our interpretation is borne out by the *résumé* of ᶜAzriel's doctrine offered in Ṭodros Abulafia's (*d.* 1298) *ᵓOṣar ha-Kabhod* (Satu Mare, 1925, fol. 37a–b). But it is interesting that Ṭodros Abulafia does not mention the motif of *qelipah* which ᶜAzriel uses as a symbol of *tohu* surrounding *bohu*. This symbol does not organically connect with the theme, and it is indeed surprising that ᶜAzriel should have introduced it in this context. For seeing that *tohu* stands for *Ḥokhmah* and *bohu* for *Binah* one does not expect to find *tohu*, which is the higher principle, compared to a shell protecting the "precious" kernel within. It may well be that this incongruity was felt by Ṭodros Abulafia. On closer inspection

[15] See above, n. 7.

one is, however, able to detect in ᶜAzriel another line of thinking which fully explains his choice of metaphor. For in the passage subsequent to the one mentioning the *qelipah* he describes the process of creation as one of sifting the light out of the darkness, identifying the surrounding *tohu* (darkness) with the refining of metals and, in another simile, with the disposal of refuse and dregs. "And all is revealed from the depth of *tohu*, and out of darkness the forms become visible . . . And the conclusion of the matter is that all that is refuse (*pesoleth*) and dregs (*shemarim*) and something evil is called by the name of the surrounding darkness (*ha-ḥoshekh ha-maqqif*), and all that is pure, sifted and tried and every good thing is called by the name of light" (p. 105, lines 11–17). This view of creation is suggested by a midrashic tradition (see Gen. R. 10:2) quoted by ᶜAzriel (p. 103, lines 20–25) which sees in *tohu* and *bohu* the "dross" which had to be sifted out in order to establish creation. His interpretation of *tohu* as *qelipah* follows in this tradition, but ill accords with his previous view of *tohu* as denoting the *Sefirah Ḥokhmah*.

A comparison of the concepts of *qelipah* in Eleazar of Worms[16] and ᶜAzriel shows the following points of difference: In Eleazar the "shells" are part of the world of the *Merkabhah* whilst in ᶜAzriel the *qelipah tohu* is, according to one interpretation, identical with the *Sefirah Ḥokhmah*, according to another with the "dross" of creation. Moreover, in Eleazar the shells bear no evil or demonic connotation, whereas ᶜAzriel's second view does imply this. ᶜAzriel's use of the term *qelipah* as a symbol of dross, refuse, darkness, etc., goes back to neoplatonic, notably pseudo-Empedoclean writings. According to al-Shahrastānī,[17] (pseudo-)Empedocles described the vegetative soul as the "shell" (*qishr*) of the animal soul; the latter as the shell of the rational soul; and the latter as the shell of the intellectual soul: Everything lower is shell for the higher, and the higher is its kernel (*lubb*). Al-Shahrastānī adds that sometimes (pseudo-) Empedocles uses the terms "body" (*jasad*) and "spirit" (*ruḥ*) instead of "shell" and "kernel". The same imagery occurs also in the *Rasāʾil ikhwān al-safāʾ* in the Iraqi's claim, "We are the kernel (*lubb*) of mankind, and mankind is the kernel of the animals, and the animals are the kernel of the plants, and the plants are the kernel of the minerals . . ."[18] Yehudah Hallevi's claim

[16] See above, pp. 170–171. [17] *Kitāb al-milal wa-l-niḥal*, ed. Cureton (1842), p. 262.
[18] Cairo, 1928, Vol. II, pp. 235–236.

that Adam's aptitude for receiving the gift of prophecy was transmitted to the descendants of Sheth, Noah and Abraham because they were the "kernel" and all the others merely the "shell" of mankind (*Kuzari*, i: 95) derives from this source. ᶜAzriel echoes this passage in a sentence contained in the *Perush ha-ᵓAggadoth* (p. 97, lines 13–14): ". . . so are the Israelites like the kernel (*lebh*) of the tree, and all the other nations like the shells". In the *Sefer ha-Yashar* the same theme is slightly varied: "Even as the fruit has a shell (*qelipah*) and what is precious (*ha-mibhḥar*) is within the shell, so are the devout the fruit of the creation of the world, and the wicked are like the shells."[19] It is clear from the context of this passage that "shell" is synonymous with "refuse" (*pesoleth*), "filth" (*refesh*) and similar terms of inferiority and worthlessness. Here as in the ᶜAzriel passage (p. 105) the *qelipah* represents not merely something inferior to the kernel which it protects but something positively evil.[20] The Scriptural passages quoted in support ("The *wicked* walk on every side", etc.) clearly illustrate this point. This usage of the term *qelipah* derives from the same neoplatonic tradition which was mentioned before. Pseudo-Empedocles' *Book of the Five Substances*[21] employs the term *qelipah* as denoting the sensual and evil as opposed to the spiritual: "The senses grasp only the shells, i.e. the visible, not the hidden aspects of things" (ed. Kaufmann, p. 19; see also pp. 34, 42). "Evil is the shadow of the good even as the body is the shell of the simple substance" (pp. 30, 50). One has to "cast away the shells of these senses" in order to "become intellectual" (*sikhli*); the pleasures obtained through the body are but "shells of the shells" (p. 34). The *Theology of Aristotle* (ed. Dieterici, p. 94) says likewise: The "sensual things" are "but shells of the substances". One "cannot penetrate to the substances . . . except by piercing the shells". This neoplatonic view is more radically expressed in al-Shahrastānī's account of Proclus as implying a division of the world into two parts, viz. "the world of purity and kernel, and the world of

[19] If the work was written by Jonah Gerondi as suggested by J. M. Toledano, Moses de Leon could have known and used it. Jonah Gerondi died in 1263. But his authorship is far from being accepted. See G. Vajda, *L'Amour de Dieu*, etc. (Paris, 1957), p. 181, n. 1.

[20] An interesting usage of the motif of the shells of onions as denoting hypocrisy is found in the Talmud; cf. S. Lieberman, *Louis Ginzberg Jubilee Volume*, II, p. 245.

[21] Hebrew Fragments of it were published by D. Kaufmann in his *Studien über Salomon Ibn Gabirol* (Budapest, 1899), pp. 17–51. On its influence on medieval Jewish Neoplatonism, cf. A. Altmann, *Tarbiṣ*, 27 (1958), p. 505.

filth and shell" (*loc. cit.*, p. 341). Isaac Israeli's *Book of the Elements* frequently speaks of the corporeal or sensual aspects of things as "darkness and shells" (ed. Fried, pp. 54ff.).[22] A Kabbalist like ᶜAzriel, who was well-acquainted with some of the neoplatonic pseudepigrapha current in his time,[23] could, therefore, easily adopt the simile of *qelipah* when speaking of the "surrounding darkness" in the sense of "refuse" and "dross".

Joseph Giqatila's pre-Zoharic work *Ginnath-ᵓEgoẓ* (written in 1274) is still untouched by either Eleazar of Worms' treatment of *sodh-ha-ᵓegoẓ* or ᶜAzriel's cosmogony. In explaining the title of the book he quotes Cant. 7:11 and also uses the familiar imagery of the shell and the fruit but without any dualistic flavour: "In the nut you find the hidden and the open (*nistar we-nigleh*), the outer to guard the inner which is concealed. For the ways of the Torah are (both) open and hidden . . . And you will find the mystery (*sodh*) hidden in the shell . . . like the nut: its fruit is within and the shell surrounds the fruit" (Hanau, 1614, p. 3b). The concept of *qelipah* in its radical neoplatonic sense as a symbol of the power of evil occurs only in his later writings.[24] It appears that Giqatila adopted this motif from the *Zohar*.

[22] Cf. Altmann-Stern, *Isaac Israeli*, etc., pp. 136–137.

[23] Cf. above, nn. 6 and 9. See also Scholem, *Kithebhey yad be-Qabbalah* (Jerusalem, 1930), pp. 4–5.

[24] E.g. in his *Shaᶜarey ᵓOrah*, Riva di Trento, 41bff.; *Shaᶜarey Ṣedeq*, Riva di Trento, 2b, 10a, 14b, 18a, 49a; *Sodh ha-ḥashmal*, *ᵓArẓey Lebhanon* (Venice, 1601), p. 41a; *Sodh ᵓarbaᶜ kosoth*, ms. Cambridge University Library, Dd. 4.2.2, fol. 80r.

9

MOSES NARBONI'S "EPISTLE ON *SHIᶜUR QOMĀ*"

An Introduction*

Among the documents of anthropomorphism in religion the *Shiᶜur Qomā*[1] ("The Measure of the [Divine] Body") may certainly claim pride of place. Drawing on the rapturous descriptions of the body of the beloved in the Song of Songs and assuming this poem to be an allegory of the love between God and Israel, the *Shiᶜur Qomā* unashamedly portrays the limbs of the Creator in terms of gigantic measurements and secret names. Yet if, in Edmund Burke's phrase, "greatness of dimension is a powerful cause of the sublime",[2] this attribute hardly applies in this case. The impression created by the fantastic numbers and *nomina barbara* is one of stupefaction rather than elevation, relieved only by the hymns of the *Hekalot* type thrown in at the end. Still, there can be no doubt that the vision of the *shiᶜur qomā* stems from the same mental climate which produced the *Hekalot* and their hymnody: that of Merkabā mysticism.[3] The vision is associated with the Creator's

* A critical edition of the Hebrew text of the "Epistle" and an annotated English translation of it were published, in addition to this Introduction, in *Jewish Medieval and Renaissance Studies* (see "Source References" n. 9 at the end of this Volume). References to lines of the text found in the present essay relate to the critical text edition.

[1] See Gershom G. Scholem, *Major Trends in Jewish Mysticism* (New York, 1946), pp. 63–67; *Idem*, *Jewish Gnosticism, Merkabah Mysticism, and Talmudic Tradition* (New York, 1960), pp. 36–42.

[2] Edmund Burke, *A Philosophical Inquiry into the Origin of our Ideas of the Sublime and Beautiful*, 6th ed. (London, 1770), p. 127.

[3] This has been conclusively proved by Scholem, *Jewish Gnosticism*, pp. 36–42, and corroborated by Saul Lieberman in Appendix D of the same work, pp. 118–126. Scholem follows Moses Gaster, "Das Schiur Komah", *Monatsschrift für Geschichte und Wissenschaft des Judentums*, N.F., 1: 179–188, 213–230 (1893), reprinted in Gaster, *Studies and Texts*, II, 1330–1353. Both Gaster and Scholem rejected Heinrich Graetz's assumption that the book originated in the Geonic period under the influence of Islamic anthropomorphism.

appearance on the throne,[4] and the angel Meṭaṭron plays a notable part in it.[5] What lends a colour of its own to this bizarre tract is the use it makes of Canticles rather than of Ezekiel's theophany. The very term *qomā* (meaning here "body", not "stature") is taken from Canticles (7:8).[6] Hence some of the sanctity attached, according to Rabbi ᶜAqiba's famous *dictum*,[7] to the canonical text of that book was claimed for this esoteric *midrash* on its descriptions of the body of the beloved: "Rabbi Yishmael said: 'When I recited this before Rabbi ᶜAqiba, he said to me: Every one who knows this measure of our Creator [*yoẓerenu*] and the glory of the Holy One, blessed be He, Who is hidden from the creatures, is assured to be a son of the world-to-come.'"[8] It is, perhaps, this emphatic promise, more than anything else, which secured the hold of this strange text on the imagination and loyalty of posterior generations.

That the crude anthropomorphism of the *Shiᶜur Qomā* proved a severe stumbling block to its acceptance can, however, scarcely be in doubt. The Targum on Canticles may indeed contain "rejoinders" to some of the passages in *Shiᶜur Qomā*, as has recently been argued.[9] The history of the reactions evoked by this tract from the tenth century onward is one of disquiet—even where belief in its authenticity prevailed—alternating with open rejection. The Geonim Sherira and Hai (tenth century) sought to allay the misgivings of certain Jews of Fez who wanted to know whether Rabbi Yishmael, the presumed author of the book, was supported

[4] See the text (opening of the second version) in *Merkabā Shelemā*, ed. Shelomo Mussajov (Jerusalem, 1921), 36a.

[5] See *Merkabā Shelemā*, 32a; 34a; 36a; 39b–40a.

[6] This was noted by the Kabbalists. See below, p. 192. The statement by Raphael Loewe, "The Divine Garment and Shiᶜur Qomah", *The Harvard Theological Review*, Vol. 58, number 1, p. 153 (1965), that "the term *qomah* does not occur in the original text itself" seems to admit only Cant. 5:10–16 as the basic text for *Shiᶜur Qomah* mysticism.

[7] *Mishnā Yadayim*, III, 5.

[8] *Merkabā Shelemā*, 38b. This statement is immediately followed by another one to his disciples, which is the one most frequently cited in kabbalistic and other medieval works: "I and Rabbi ᶜAqiba pledge our word that everyone who knows this measure of our Creator and the glory of the Holy One, blessed be He, will be a son of the world-to-come, provided he studies this mishnā every day." Both statements occur also in the version contained in *Sefer Raziʾel* (Amsterdam, 1701), fol. 38a. The first version in *Merkabā Shelemā* (34b) has simply: "Every one who knows this mystery [*raz zē*] is assured that he will be a son of the world-to-come and will be saved from the punishment of hell . . ."

[9] By Raphael Loewe, "The Divine Garment and Shiᶜur Qomah", p. 155.

by an accredited tradition or had written it "out of his own head", in which latter case he had obviously violated the Mishnaic injunction against discoursing on esoteric matters in a manner irreconcilable with the honour of God (*Ḥagigā* II, 1). They explained that far from expressing a merely personal view, Rabbi Yishmael had written down profound mysteries the meaning of which could be revealed only to the select few possessed of the requisite qualifications; the questioners, though held in high esteem, did not belong to that group; at any rate, the literal meaning of the anthropomorphic terms was out of question, since God had no limbs nor measures, and "what likeness will ye compare unto Him" (Isa. 40:18).[10] In contrast to Sherira and Hai, Saᶜadya Gaon admitted the possibility of the spuriousness of the *Shiᶜur Qomā*. There was, he pointed out, no agreement among scholars as to its origin, and hence no compelling need to refute the objections raised against it. He remarked, however, that "were we to attribute the book *Shiᶜur Qomā* to Rabbi Yishmael, we could find in his words many aspects [that is, of an acceptable character] and could explain that they do amount to the way of the Faith and the Unity, namely, that . . . the Creator creates a splendid light for all his prophets to serve as a sign and proof and testimony of His Glory and Divinity so that they may know that the word which is audible to them comes at the command and behest of God".[11] In other words, Saᶜadya applied to the vision of the Divine Body reported in the *Shiᶜur Qomā* his well-known theory of the "created glory" (*kabod nibra*ʾ), which explains the prophetic theophanies as visions not of God Himself but of a luminous substance created by God. According to his theory, God creates this light (*kabod; shekinā; ruaḥ ha-qodesh*) in order to assure the prophet of the Divine origin of the verbal revelation which he receives.[12] It should be noted that Saᶜadya makes no attempt to read into the *Shiᶜur Qomā* an allegorical meaning which would make its descriptions symbolic of Divinity itself. It is also significant that he offers his interpretation only on the hypothetical assumption that the book is authen-

[10] *Ozar Ha-Geʾonim*, ed. B. M. Lewin, *Ḥagigā*, pp. 10–12.

[11] Quoted by Jehuda b. Barzilay of Barcelona in his *Perush Sefer Yeẓirā*, ed. Solomon Zalman Ḥayyim Halberstam, with additional notes by David Kaufmann (Berlin, 1885), pp. 20–21, from "one of the books of our teacher Saᶜadya, of blessed memory, in refutation of the claims of a certain heretic [*min*] . . ." (reproduced in *Ozar Ha-Geʾonim*, *Berakot*, reponsa section, 17).

[12] See my article, "Saadya's Theory of Revelation", *Saadya Studies*, ed. Erwin I. J. Rosenthal (Manchester, 1943), pp. 4–25; [pp. 140–160 in the present Volume].

tic. He would, however, rather disclaim any concern with this text "since it is not found in either Mishna or Talmud, and since we have no way of establishing whether or not it represents the words of Rabbi Yishmael; perhaps someone else pretended to speak in his name".[13]

Saᶜadya's embarrassment was all the more acute because the Karaites had fastened upon the *Shiᶜur Qomā* as evidence of the theological backwardness of the Rabbanites. The *Sefer Milḥamot Adonai*, by the Karaite Salmon ben Yeruḥim, contains in its last three chapters (15–17) lengthy quotations from the *Shiᶜur Qomā* interspersed with violent attacks upon Rabbis Yishmael and ᶜAqiba.[14] Saᶜadya's statement on the *Shiᶜur Qomā* cited above is probably a direct answer to this particular Karaite assault. The work embodying his reply seems to be his *Kitāb al-radd ᶜalā Ibn Sāqawaihi*, of which only fragments have survived,[15] and Ibn Sāqawaihi, against whom it is directed, may be identical with Salmon ben Yeruḥim, as Abraham Geiger and Israel Davidson maintained.[16] The Muslims, likewise, charged the Rabbanites with anthropomorphism (*tashbih*: literally "likening", specifically, of God to man) on account of the *Shiᶜur Qomā*, and this may have lent a special urgency to Saᶜadya's rebuttal of the Karaite attack. There is an explicit reference by Ibn Ḥazm (944–1063/4) to the *Shiᶜur Qomā* in the chapter on the Jews in his *Kitāb al-milal wa ᶜl-niḥal*:[17]

> In one of their books called *Shiᶜr Toma* [sic][18] which forms part of the Talmud (the Talmud being their trusted foundation in their jurisprudence and in the minutiae of their religion and revealed Law) and which in their unanimous view forms part of the dicta of their

[13] See Jehuda b. Barzilay, *Perush Sefer Yeẓirā*, p. 21.

[14] See *Sefer Milḥamot Adonay*, ed. Israel Davidson (New York, 1934), pp. 114–132.

[15] See Henry Malter, *Saadia Gaon, His Life and Works* (Philadelphia, 1942), pp. 265, 382–384.

[16] See Davidson's introduction to *Sefer Milḥamot Adonay*, pp. 21–28.

[17] The chapter is reproduced in both the original text and in a German translation by Ignaz Goldziher, "Proben muhammedanischer Polemik gegen den Talmud", *Jeschurun*, ed. Joseph Kobak, VII, 4 (Bamberg, 1872), pp. 76–104. The passage quoted here is found on pp. 87–98. See also Miguel Asín Palacios, *Abenházam de Córdoba y su Historia Crítica de las Ideas Religiosas*, II (Madrid, 1928), 385–386.

[18] M. Asín suggests that *shiᶜr* for *shiᶜur* may be a deliberate arabism by the editor so as to give the title of the book the meaning: "Poem of Toma". Goldziher, "Proben muhammedanischer Polemik", p. 87, n. 28, records the reading found in the manuscripts.

> rabbis,[19] [it is said] that the extension of the face of their Creator (Who is exalted above their speech) from its extreme altitude down to his nose amounts to 5,000 ells. There be far from God any shape, measure, limits and extreme points.

Ibn Ḥazm obviously quoted only from hearsay, since this particular measure does not occur in the text, but he certainly caught the gist of the book and correctly reproduced the term "Creator" which is characteristic of it.[20] In the twelfth century, al-Shahrastānī repeated the charge of crude anthropomorphism against the Jews in general, without, however, referring specifically to the *Shiᶜur Qomā.*[21] Al-Maqrīzī (fifteenth century) still maintained the well-worn accusation but differentiated between various Jewish groups. The relevant passage in his *Khiṭaṭ* reads: "The *ᶜAnaniyya* upholds the unity and justice [that is, of God] and rejects anthropomorphism [*tashbīh*]; the *Ashmaᶜath* admit *tashbīh*; the *Djālūtiyya* carries *tashbīh* to excess."[22] From the motley list of Jewish sects offered by al-Maqrīzī in the same context it is clear that by *ᶜAnaniyya* he designates not the Karaites in general (to whom he refers as *al-Qarā* in contradistinction to the Rabbanites, *al-Rabbaniyya*),[23] but merely one of the many Karaite groups.[24] The *Ashmaᶜath*, who are said to admit *tashbīh*, denote most probably the Talmudists or adherents of tradition (*shemuᶜā; shemuᶜatha*), as has been plausibly suggested by de Sacy.[25] Finally, the *Djālūtiyya*, who are described as radical anthropomorphists, are probably the

19 M. Asín's Spanish translation obscures the point made here that the *Shiᶜur Qomā* forms part of the dicta of the rabbis. Goldziher's German translation, though clear on this point, does not cover the parenthetical clause.

20 Ibn Ḥazm was in personal contact with Samuel ha-Naggid, who was his compatriot, and may have derived some of his knowledge of *Judaica* directly from him. Cf. Goldziher, "Proben muhammedanischer Polemik", pp. 76–77.

21 *Kitāb al-milal wa l-niḥal,* ed. Curton, pp. 164, 169–171. Al-Shahrastānī contrasts the allegorism of certain sects with the anthropomorphism of the Jews in general.

22 Quoted from Antoine-Isaac Silvestre de Sacy, *Chrestomathie arabe*, I (1826), text, p. 116; French translation, p. 307. The full title of the work is *Al-Mawāᶜiẓ wa l-Iᶜtibār fī Dhikr al-Khiṭaṭ wa l-Āthār*, paraphrased in the title of the French translation by U. Bouriout and P. Casanova (in six volumes, 1893–1920): "Description topographique et historique de l'Egypte."

23 See de Sacy, *Chrestomathie*, text, pp. 90f. On p. 106 Rabbanites and Karaites are referred to as *banū mishnō* and *banū miqrā*, respectively.

24 De Sacy, *Chrestomathie*, pp. 116–117.

25 *Ibid.*, pp. 213, 351, 356. Al-Maqrīzī cites a passage from al-Masᶜūdī, *Kitāb al-tanbīh wa l-ishrāf*, in which the Ashmaᶜath are said to comprise the majority of the Jewish nation, and Saᶜadya, among others, is called an Ashmaᶜathī. The passage mentions Abū Kathīr as Saᶜadya's teacher, and is referred to by Malter, *Saadia Gaon*, p. 32.

Babylonian Jewish mystics who adhered to the *Shiᶜur Qomā.*[26] At any rate, the reference to anthropomorphism carried to excess can apply only to the *Shiᶜur Qomā.* To these Muslim condemnations of the book may be added an instance of Christian polemics. In his letter to the Emperor Ludwig the Pious, Bishop Agobard launched an attack against Jewish anthropomorphism. The letter (*De judaicis superstitionibus, c.* 829) was based either on the *Shiᶜur Qomā,* as was suggested by Graetz,[27] or on an Anglo-Saxon writing of the eighth century, which had drawn on the book, as Gaster proposed.[28]

Saᶜadya's tentative interpretation of the *Shiᶜur Qomā* along the lines of his theory of "created glory" was not followed up by subsequent Jewish philosophers. (As we shall note, it played an important role in the mystics' treatment of the theme.) Abraham ibn Ezra dealt with the subject briefly in his *Yesod Moraʾ* and at some length in an excursus on the passage in his Long (Standard) Commentary on Exodus explaining Ex. 33:21. In *Yesod Moraʾ* he says: "Our ancients, of blessed memory, knew the mystery of the *Merkabā* and of *Shiᶜur Qomā,* and God forbid that they compared a likeness unto Him; but their words are in need of interpretation, as are the words of the Tora, 'Let us make man in our image after our likeness', and as [the words] in Ezekiel's prophecy (1:26–27) 'a likeness as the appearance of a man upon it above' and 'from the appearance of his loins and downward'."[29] These hints are elaborated in the final chapter of the work:

> Now consider that One is the foundation [*yesod*] of all number, while itself no number; it subsists in itself, and has no need for what follows it. Every number too is composed of ones . . . Hence it is written in the *Shiᶜur Qomā:* "Rabbi Yishmael said: Every one who knows the measure of the Creator (*yoẓer be-reʾshit*) is sure to be a son of the world-to-come, and I and ᶜAqiba vouch for this." In this way the intelligent will be able to know the One in so far as the All is attached to it, whereas to know it in so far as its total good is concerned is beyond the power of a created being . . . Being attached to

[26] See de Sacy, *Chrestomathie*, text, p. 90: *al-djālia bi-bābil*; p. 191: *ᶜAnan rās al-djālūt*. For the term *rās al-djālūt* (*resh galuta*) see also al-Shahrastānī, *Kitāb al-milal*, p. 167; Goldziher, "Proben muhammedanischer Polemik", p. 77. Graetz (*Monatsschrift*, 8:117–118 [1895]), derives the term *Djālūtiyya* from the "Chaldaic" *galiyyata* in the sense of "revelation of mysteries", which is hardly plausible.

[27] *Monatsschrift*, 8:110ff. (1859).

[28] *Monatsschrift*, N.F., 1:226ff. (1893).

[29] *Yesod Moraʾ*, ed. M. Creizenach (Frankfurt a.M.-Leipzig, 1840), pp. 10–11 (Hebrew section).

> the total good is like [the vision of] the face; and being attached to the created [things] is like [the vision of] the back. This is meant by "And thou shalt see My back" . . .[30]

It would appear from these cryptic remarks that Ibn Ezra saw in the *Shiʿur Qomā* an allegory of the macrocosm. He distinctly mentions in this context the notion of man as a microcosm (identified by him with the "mystery" of Meṭaṭron, the Prince of the Presence). The created beings are attached to God in a way analogous to the presence of the root number One in all numbers. The measures listed in the book *Shiʿur Qomā* would, therefore, seem to signify to Ibn Ezra the dimensions of the created world. The limbs of the figure described in the book are, no doubt, the parts constituting the universe. This interpretation of Ibn Ezra's view of the book is borne out by the more explicit (though far from plain) remarks offered in his Commentary on Exodus (lines 32–38 of our text). The reverence in which Ibn Ezra clearly holds the book reflects a tradition which, in spite of an undercurrent of misgivings, surrounded it with the halo of a deep mystery.[31]

Maimonides, too, was in his youth affected by the same outlook, as is attested to by his reference to the *Shiʿur Qomā* in the Introduction to *Sanhedrin* XI (*Pereq Ḥeleq*) of his *Commentary on the Mishna.* Speaking about the difficulty of doing justice, in the present context, to such subtle subject matters as Moses' prophecy, the existence and hierarchical order of the angels, and the faculties of the soul, he adds:

> The circle would have to be extended to include a discourse on the forms (*fī al-ṣuwar; ba-ẓurot*) which the prophets mentioned in connection with the Creator and the angels; into this there enters the *Shiʿur Qomā* and its subject-matter. For [a treatment of] this subject alone, even if shortened to the utmost degree, a hundred pages would be insufficient . . .[32]

The authenticity of the brief sentence referring to the *Shiʿur Qomā* cannot be doubted.[33] Nor is there any doubt that Maimonides

[30] *Ibid.*, pp. 50–51.

[31] On this tradition see Lieberman, Appendix D to Scholem's *Jewish Gnosticism*, p. 124, particularly the references given in nn. 29–30.

[32] *Maboʾ le-Pereq Ḥeleq*, ed. J. Holzer (Berlin, 1901), p. 24 (Arabic–Hebrew section).

[33] Such a doubt was expressed by M. Gottlieb in his edition of Maimonides' Commentary on *Mishnā Sanhedrin* (Hanover, 1906), pp. 97–98. Lieberman, Appendix D to Scholem, *Jewish Gnosticism*, p. 124, n. 32, lists four manuscripts which contain the sentence. He takes the authenticity of the entire passage for granted.

subsequently deleted this sentence. The Manuscript (295) of the Edward Pococke Collection in the Bodleian Library (Neubauer 404), which is Maimonides' autograph[34] of the Commentary on the Mishna Order *Neẓiqin*, carries both the sentence and the bold stroke of deletion.[35] As in many other instances, Maimonides changed his mind on the subject.[36] Strangely enough, he even went so far as to deny that he had ever considered the *Shiᶜur Qomā* as an authentic work, and he used the harshest language possible in its condemnation:

> I never thought [*lam arā qaṭṭ; lo ḥashabti me-ᶜolam*] that it was one of the works of the Sages [*ḥakamim*], of blessed memory, and far be it from them that this [book] should have come from them. It is but a work of one of the Byzantine preachers, and nothing else. Altogether, it is a great *miẓwā* to delete this book and to eradicate the mention of its subject matter; "and make no mention of the name of other gods" (Ex. 23:13), etc., since he who has a body [*qomā*] undoubtedly is [to be classed among] "other gods".[37]

The severity of Maimonides' attack accords with his well-known stand against anthropomorphism in religion, and chimes also with his known attitude to mysticism.[38] His earlier approval of the *Shiᶜur Qomā* was probably facilitated by Ibn Ezra's allegorical interpretation of the work. Since Maimonides used the allegorical method in his treatment of Biblical and Midrashic anthropomorphism, he might have found it possible to adhere to his

34 See the careful weighing up of all the evidence to this effect in Solomon D. Sassoon's introduction to *Maimonides Commentarius in Mischnam* (Copenhagen, 1956), Vol. I, chs. ii–vi.

35 See the facsimile of Maimonides' autograph in Sassoon's edition referred to in the preceding note, Vol. II, which reproduces the Commentary on *Seder Neẓiqin* from ms. 295 of the Edward Pococke Collection.

36 Sassoon, introduction to *Maimonides Commentarius*, I, 33, n. 4, thinks that the deletion of the passage by Maimonides need not be taken as evidence for a change of mind but merely as an indication of anxiety lest the anthropomorphic language should occasion misunderstanding. This interpretation is, however, untenable since it ignores the complete disavowal of the *Shiᶜur Qomā* in the *responsum* (see next note).

37 R. *Moses b. Maimon Responsa*, ed. Yehoshuᶜa Blau (Jerusalem, 1957), I, 200–201. Lieberman's interpretation (Appendix D . . ., p. 124) of Maimonides' reply is based on Freimann's translation and cannot be maintained in the light of the Arabic text and Blau's more exact rendering of it. Maimonides' words *lam ʾarā qaṭṭ* (Blau: *lo ḥashabti me-ᶜolam*) clearly indicate a denial of ever having attributed the work to the *ḥakamin*. This is a statement difficult to explain, but it has to be accepted as textually incontrovertible.

38 See my article, "Das Verhältnis Maimunis zur jüdischen Mystik", *Monatsschrift*, 80, N.F., 44 (1936), 305–330.

original approach to the book. It seems, however, certain that he was repelled by its basic features (measurements, *nomina barbara*) and was forced to the conclusion that it was a spurious work. To what extent his repudiation of the *Shiʿur Qomā* became known in wider circles and in later periods is a matter still to be determined. We note a certain disdain for the work among some of the rationalists of the thirteenth century.[39] Interestingly enough, Moses ben Ḥasday Taku (1250–1290), though a strict literalist and fierce opponent of philosophy, also cast serious doubts on the authenticity of the book.[40]

Ibn Ezra's positive evaluation of the *Shiʿur Qomā* was shared by his contemporary, Jehuda Ha-Levi, although perhaps to a smaller degree and on different grounds. "One should not reject", he said in his *Kuzari* (IV, 3, end), "what has been said about 'And the image of God did he behold' (Num. 12:8) and 'They saw the God of Israel' (Ex. 24:10) and the *maʿasē merkabā*, and [one should not reject] even the *Shiʿur Qomā* since it helps to produce the fear of Him in the souls, even as it is said, 'and that His fear may be before you' (Ex. 20:17)." The possible effect of the vision of God described in the *Shiʿur Qomā* is here considered a sufficient reason not to reject "even" this strange book. Jehuda Ha-Levi need not, of course, have expressed here his entire view of the work. Close as he was to Jewish mysticism, he might have regarded it as a repository of profound mysteries.

Ibn Ezra's approach to the *Shiʿur Qomā* will, as we shall see, reassert its influence in the fourteenth century. Before, however, proceeding with our account of the reaction to this book among the philosophers, we might glance at the way in which the mystics related themselves to it. It may be noted at the outset that there is no trace to be found, among this group, of the critical attitude that had led others to doubt or deny the authenticity of the work. Yet it is obvious that there was considerable concern among the members of this group too about the description of the *qomā* in terms at variance with the notion of God's unity and incorporeality. Eleazar of Worms (*c.* 1160–*c.* 1230), the theologian of German Hasidism, took issue with this problem in his *Shaʿarē ha-Sod we-ha-Yiḥud we-ha-ʾEmuna*.[41] What he did in order to remove any flaw

[39] See the reference to the book *Shiʿur Qomā* in one of Zeraḥya Gracian's letters to Hillel b. Samuel of Verona, published in *Ozar Neḥmad*, 2:142 (1857).

[40] See the passage in his *Ketab Tamim*, published in *Ozar Neḥmad*, 3:61–62 (1860).

[41] Ed. A. Jellinek, *Kokebe Yizḥaq*, 27:7–15 (1862).

from the concept of God was to separate the notion of *shi*ᶜ*ur qomā* from that of the Creator. He resorted to this radical step in spite of the fact that it contradicted the very text of the *Shi*ᶜ*ur Qomā*, which distinctly portrays the figure and its measures as belonging to the Creator (*yoẓer be-re*ʾ*shit*). According to Eleazar's theory, the vision described refers not to the Creator but to something created: the "visible glory" (*kabod nir*ʾ*ē*), also called the "special cherub" (*kerub meyuḥad*), which is created by way of emanation from the invisible "inner glory" (*kabod penīmī*) representing the Creator. Eleazar applies to both the visible and inner glory the term *shekinā*, calling the former *shekinā of His greatness* and the latter *shekinā of His holiness*. The *Shi*ᶜ*ur Qomā* does indeed speak about the *shekinā*, but only in the qualified sense of the lower, created *shekinā*. One will notice that this doctrine is a revival, albeit in a more complicated fashion, of Saᶜadya's tentative interpretation of the *shi*ᶜ*ur qomā* as a vision of the "created glory" or *shekinā* (see above, p. 182).[42] Eleazar takes the text much more seriously than Saᶜadya did, seeing that its authenticity was for him undisputed. Yet just because of this he had to render it theologically innocuous. The context in which he explains the *Shi*ᶜ*ur Qomā* is an eloquent and moving plea for faith in the infinite Creator who "fills all worlds and yet transcends them", and to whom no measure or similitude may be applied. Rabbi Yishmael's statement promising the bliss of the next world to everyone who "knows the measure of the Creator" is given a meaning opposite to what it originally implied: only he who has faith in the infinity of God will inherit the world-to-come.[43]

Eleazar's view of the *Shi*ᶜ*ur Qomā* was challenged by Menaḥem Recanati (*c.* 1300)[44] on the ground of its incompatibility with the text. According to Recanati, the "Measure of the Body" is to be

[42] See particularly pp. 10, 13–14. On Eleazar's concept of the *merkabā* see Gershom G. Scholem, *Major Trends in Jewish Mysticism*, pp. 111–116, and my article "Eleazar of Worms' Ḥokhmath Ha-ʾEgoz", *Journal of Jewish Studies*, 11:101–113 (1960); [renamed and reproduced in the present Volume, pp. 161–171].

[43] Jellinek, *Kokebe Yiẓḥaq*, p. 10. Eleazar's interpretation of the *Shi*ᶜ*ur Qomā* is quoted by Naḥmanides in his letter to the French rabbis (see *Qobeẓ Teshubot ha-Rambam we-Iggerotav* (Leipzig, 1859), section *Iggerot Qanaʾut*, 10a; for a critical text see F. Perles' article in *Monatsschrift*, 9:192 (1860).

[44] In a passage said to be taken from Recanati's *Sefer Ta*ᶜ*amē ha-Miẓwot* by Jehuda Ḥayyat in his commentary (written *c.* 1494–1500) on the *Sefer Ma*ᶜ*areket ha-Elohut* (Ferrara, 1557), fols. 33b–34a. The printed editions of Recanati's *Ta*ᶜ*amē ha-Miẓwot* do not contain the lengthy quotation (fols. 33a–41b) offered by Ḥayyat. It appears, however, as Professor Scholem informs me, in the extant mss. of the work, where it is part of the preface.

identified with the *Sefirot* spoken of by the Kabbalists. Yet there is a rider to this statement. Recanati is careful to point out that in his view (which, he knows, is not shared by his fellow Kabbalists) the *Sefirot* are not of the same nature as the Divine essence but distinct from it: they are but the organs or instruments (*kelim*) thereof.[45] Hence, the descriptions of the measures found in the *Shi*ᶜ*ur Qomā* have no bearing on the essence of Divinity. They relate merely to its *modus operandi*, and even so must be understood in a figurative, non-quantitative sense. Recanati suggests that the *parsa*ᵓ*ot* (parasangs) mentioned in the book are not to be taken in their literal meaning but stand for articulations, in the form of letters, of the Divine power or "divisions" (as in Dan. 5:28: *peres perisat malkutek*) defining its various operations.[46] He lays down the following canon of interpretation[47]:

> Know thou that whenever the Sages, of blessed memory, speak about the *Sefirot* and say something that is fit to be said only about the Creator, blessed be He, they do, in fact, speak about the Creator Who dwells in them . . . Finally, whenever you find them saying about the *Sefirot* things which are not fit to be said about the Creator, blessed be He, as, for example, "the measure of the body" [*shi*ᶜ*ur qomā*] and suchlike matters, it all refers to the *Sefirot* . . .[48]

The sense of uneasiness about the *Shi*ᶜ*ur Qomā* felt by Recanati is only too plain from this passage. He admitted, indeed, openly that he had to draw a line between the *Sefirot* and the Creator in order to accommodate the *shi*ᶜ*ur qomā* in a de-Divinized realm, as it were.[49] He was conscious of thereby violating the concept of Sefirotic Divinity as firmly held by other Kabbalists but saw no other way of safeguarding the notion of the unity of God.[50] His way of dealing with the problem follows the earlier pattern of Eleazar's. While the latter assigned the *shi*ᶜ*ur qomā* to the "visible glory" as distinct from the Creator, he related it to the *Sefirot* as

45 *Ma*ᶜ*areket ha-Elohut*, 34aff. In taking this view of the *Sefirot*, Recanati followed Azriel of Gerona. See A. Jellinek, *Beiträge zur Geschichte der Kabbala*, II (Leipzig, 1852), 38–40.

46 *Ma*ᶜ*areket ha-Elohut*, 41b–42a.

47 *Ibid.*, 39b.

48 This passage and the subsequent statement about the meaning of the measurements are reproduced as a gloss by the editor in the printed text of *Tiqqunē ha-Zohar*, no. 70, fol. 121b, in the name of Jehuda Ḥayyat. The editor had obviously failed to notice that Ḥayyat was quoting Recanati. A printed marginal gloss (*ibid.*) laconically states: "This text is not by Rabbi Jehuda Ḥayyat, of blessed memory", without referring to Recanati.

49 *Ma*ᶜ*areket ha-Elohut*, 40a.

50 *Ibid.*

distinct from the essence of God. He, therefore, hardly improved on Eleazar in so far as adherence to the text was concerned.

Later Kabbalists seem to have taken a more relaxed view of the *Shi*ᶜ*ur Qomā.* Since the very concept of the *Sefirot,* in whatever way interpreted, already amounted to a kind of fragmentizing of the absolute unity of God, the ice had been broken or, to use the Talmudic phrase adduced in this connection by Jehuda Ḥayyat at the end of the fifteenth century: "the strap was untied" (*hutera ha-reẓu*ᶜ*ā*): that is, there really was no further reason for excessive restraint, provided one took great care to shun all literalness and, in particular, to interpret the quantitative measures of the *Shi*ᶜ*ur Qomā* along the lines suggested by Recanati.[51] Viewed in this light, Recanati's separation of the essence of God from the *Sefirot* no longer seemed necessary. Jehuda Ḥayyat, who considered the emanation (*aẓilut*) of the *Sefirot* as a process within Divinity, could say: "If we ascribe a measure [*shi*ᶜ*ur*] to them, this refers to their power; for He [sc. God] set an end and limit to their power in order that the emanation should not expand in its operations beyond the pre-established plan."[52] In other words, the measure and limitation of the *Sefirot* or *shi*ᶜ*ur qomā* do not indicate any finitude in the Divine world per se but express a Divinely imposed finitude of operations of the *Sefirot.* "What emerges from this is [the realization] that there is a necessity on high for a distinction between the Divine powers operating upon the created beings in order that one should not intrude into the domain of the other; and this is indicated by the letters [viz., each having its clearly defined articulation]; and the parasangs [*parsa*ʾ*ot*] which are mentioned are Divine powers."[53] Once this position is reached, the *Shi*ᶜ*ur Qomā* no longer presents a serious problem. Jehuda Ḥayyat is able to refer to various interpretations of the book conceived on this level. What is common to them is the duplication of the *shi*ᶜ*ur qomā* into a male and female aspect or figure. This new departure is not a capricious overloading of an already highly charged concept but the logical conclusion of the step taken in identifying it with the *Sefirot.* The bisexual character of the Sefirotic system was now transferred to the *shi*ᶜ*ur qomā.* This procedure had also the advantage of making complete the correspondence of this ancient midrash on Canticles to the text. Since Canticles contains descriptions of the bodies of the lover and the beloved, it

51 *Ma*ᶜ*areket ha-Elohut,* 108b. 52 *Ibid.,* 160b. 53 *Ibid.,* 161a.

was natural to think in terms of a two-fold or two-faced (*du-parẓufim*) *shiᶜur qomā*. The very name of the book borrows the term *qomā* from the verse *ẓoᵓt qomatek* . . . (7:8), where the reference is to the female partner. Ḥayyat speaks, accordingly, of a *shiᶜur* of the *arik anpin* or male aspect, and of a *shiᶜur* of the *ẓeᶜir anpin* or female aspect of the *Sefirot*.[54] According to the *Tiqqunē Zohar*, the male *Sefirā Ẓaddiq* is called "measure" (*shiᶜur*) and the female *Sefirā Binā* is termed *qomā*.[55]

Of particular interest is the link established by the Kabbalists between the *shiᶜur qomā* concept and the Biblical story of the Tower of Babel. It is not clear to which original source this connection is to be assigned. From Naḥmanides' guarded remarks in his *Commentary on the Tora* (Gen. 11:2) it would appear that he was alluding to a mystical interpretation well understood by the Kabbalists. It involved the secret meaning of the word *shem* (name) in the verse, "Let us make ourselves a name" (Gen. 11:4), the "measure" (*shiᶜur*) of the tower designed, and the sin of "cutting off the plants", or heresy. Naḥmanides' remarks were explained by Isaac of Acco in his *Meᵓirat ᶜEnayim*,[56] and by Recanati in his *Commentary on the Tora*, where the language is rather terse and obscure.[57] A reference to this theme occurs also in the *SeferMaᶜareket ha-Elohut* (*c.* 1300) on which Jehuda Ḥayyat in his commentary on this work based his interpretation.[58] According to his explanation, the heresy of the generation of the Tower consisted in their attempt to build a miniature image of the *shiᶜur qomā*—that is, of the *Sefirot*—by employing the gigantic measurements of the *qomā* on a proportionate small human scale. This way of using inadequate substitutes is said to be alluded to in the words, "And they had brick for stone, and slime had they for mortar" (Gen. 11:3). They tried to imitate the structure (*binyan*) of the *Sefirot* by building a "city" (a kabbalistic synonym for the last *Sefirā ᶜAtarā* or *Malkut*) and a "tower" (synonymous with the *Sefirā Tifᵓeret*). In this way they sought to procure the influx upon them of the

[54] *Ibid.*

[55] *Ibid.*, 160a. The reference, as Professor Scholem has pointed out to me, is to *Tiqqunē Zohar* 19, fol. 38b.

[56] Quoted by Jehuda Ḥayyat in his commentary. See *Maᶜareket ha-Elohut*, 158a.

[57] See the text in *Lebushē Or Yeqarot* (Jerusalem, 1960/61), fol. 20a, and the slightly different recension quoted by Ḥayyat, *Maᶜareket ha-Elohut*, 158a–b. Ḥayyat assumed that Recanati had plagiarised from some kabbalistic scholar (158b).

[58] *Maᶜareket ha-Elohut*, 158b–159a. On the question of the authorship of the *Maᶜareket ha-Elohut*, see Scholem, *Kiryat Sefer*, 21:248ff. (1944–45).

Divine Power so as to be unified and safe against dispersal and separation. Their intention was good in so far as it was directed against succumbing to the power of the stars which threatened to disperse them all over the earth. It was, however, evil in that their secret aim was to break away from the worship of the *Sefirot* as a whole and to seek their unity under the aegis as it were of the last *Sefirā* alone. Hence they said, "Let us make ourselves a name": that is, let us make the *Sefirā ᶜAtara* (which is called "name") our only object of worship.[59] This act constituted heresy.[60]

The ingenious interpretation of the Biblical story just mentioned obviously rests on the assumption that the *shiᶜur qomā* has to be identified with the *Sefirot*. As we have noted, the *Sefer Maᶜareket ha-Elohut* subscribes to this interpretation. There is, therefore, every reason to believe that the author of this work shared also the view of the identity of *qomā* and *Sefirot*. He does not make an explicit statement to this effect, and from his various utterances on the subject of *shiᶜur qomā* Jehuda Ḥayyat drew the inference that the other author's view approximated to that of Eleazar of Worms. One will remember that the latter saw in the "measure of the body" the prophetic vision of the created "visible glory". The author of *Maᶜareket ha-Elohut* also repeatedly identifies the *shiᶜur qomā* with "prophetic vision",[61] but he makes it clear at the same time that the prophetic vision—of a human figure on high—finds its true explanation in the light of what he had pointed out as to the structure (*binyan*) of man.[62] The reference is to his treatment of the theme in the chapter on man,[63] where it is stated, and elaborated in great detail, that man is created in the image of the *Sefirot*. The prophetic vision can, therefore, only refer to the *Sefirot*, in whose image man is made. According to Ḥayyat, the author saw in the *shiᶜur qomā* not the *Sefirot* but Meṭaṭron.[64] He based his view undoubtedly on a statement in the chapter on man[65] in which the author pronounces his agreement with

59 Cf. Mordecai Jaffe's commentary *Eben Yeqarā* in *Lebushē Or Yeqarot*, 20a.

60 The designation of the exclusive worship of the tenth *sefirā* as idolatry (*ᶜabodā zarā*) par excellence is a widespread kabbalistic motif. It is pronounced in the *Sefer Taᶜamē ha-Mizwot* attributed to Isaac ibn Farḥi, a work which was, however, written toward the end of the thirteenth or at the beginning of the fourteenth century. (On its authorship see my article in *Kiryat Sefer*, XL, no. 2 [1965], 256–276). The term *harisā* used in *Maᶜareket ha-Elohut* (see *shaᶜar ha-harisā*, fols. 138a–177b) for "heresy" is probably a deliberate coinage in imitation of the Latinized Greek word haeresis.

61 *Maᶜareket ha-Elohut*, 157b; 191b.

62 *Ibid.*, 190a; 191b.

63 *Ibid.*, 178a; 180bff.

64 *Ibid.*, 159a.

65 *Ibid.*, 213a.

Rabad's notion of Meṭaṭron as a power emanated from God ("the first cause") in whose image man was created and who appeared unto Moses and Ezekiel in the form of a man; and with regard to whom it was said, "He who knows the measure of the Creator . . ." The author admits that at first blush he had considered this view of Rabad's contrary to his own (which we take to mean the view of the identity of *qomā* and *Sefirot*). "And he who undertands the prophetic vision to which I have alluded [*videlicet*, that of *shi*ᶜ*ur qomā*] will be able to understand that his words are like mine, something profound and true." This can only mean that the author regards the supernal Meṭaṭron spoken of by Rabad as identical with the *Sefirot*, and not merely as "the body of the *shekinā*", as Ḥayyat suggested. According to him, Rabad and the author of *Ma*ᶜ*areket ha-Elohut* assumed the existence of the "great Meṭaṭron" or "Meṭaṭron of the [world of] emanation" (*aẓilut*), also called "body of the *shekinā*", who is of a Divine nature, in contradistinction to the "small Meṭaṭron", who is created. There is, however, no warrant in the text to confine the concept of the supernal Meṭaṭron according to the *Sefer Ma*ᶜ*areket ha-Elohut* to the "body of the *shekinā*". It would rather seem that there was unanimity among the Kabbalists of the thirteenth and fourteenth centuries that the *shi*ᶜ*ur qomā* referred to the *Sefirot*.

The account we have given of the various ways in which the *Shi*ᶜ*ur Qomā* was received and interpreted will serve to place in its proper setting a fourteenth-century *opusculum* on this theme by an eminent Jewish philosopher. We are referring to the *Iggeret* ᶜ*al Shi*ᶜ*ur Qomā* ("Epistle on the Measure of the Body") by Moses ben Joshua ben Mar David of Narbonne (Moses Narboni), also called Maestre Vidal Bellsom Narboni.[66] The work, which we present (see prefatory note) in a critical edition accompanied by an annotated English translation, was completed in Perpignan on the Eve of Sukkot, 5103 (15th September, 1342),[67] when the author had already composed his commentary on al-Ghazālī's *Maqāṣid al-Falāsifa* ("The Intentions of the Philosophers" [to be cited in Notes as CIP])[68]

[66] For biographical details see S. Munk, *Mélanges de philosophie juive at arabe* (Paris, 1859), pp. 502–506; M. Steinschneider, *Catalogus Libr. in Bibliotheca Bodleiana*, cols. 1967–1977; *idem*, *Die Hebr. Übersetzungen des Mittelalters*, pp. 311–319; Ernest Renan and A. Neubauer, *Les Ecrivains juifs français du XIVe siècle* (Paris, 1893), pp. 320–355.

[67] See the *explicit* of the text, where, however, the place is not given. It is certain that Narboni was in Perpignan (his native town) at the time, since he did not emigrate to Spain until 1344.

[68] It is referred to in our text, line 62.

and a commentary on Lamentations.[69] The great bulk of his literary production then still lay ahead. His commentary on Averroes' treatise on *The Possibility of Conjunction with the Agent Intellect* [cited as CPC] was written in 1344, when he was still in Perpignan.[70] Most of his works, however—and they number twenty, according to Steinschneider's list[71]—were produced in Spain. His magnum opus, the commentary (*biʾur*) on Maimonides' *Guide of the Perplexed* [cited as CG], was commenced in Toledo and finished, after seven years of labour, at Soria in 1362, the year in which he probably died.[72]

What moved Naboni, who is known as a radical Averroist and who on this account incurred the opprobrium of many orthodox thinkers,[73] to concern himself with the *Shiᶜur Qomā*, the most obnoxious document of Jewish mysticism? Was he unaware of Maimonides' stern repudiation of this text? The answer to the last question is definitely: yes. In his view Maimonides himself had offered a kind of commentary on the subject of *shiᶜur qomā* (more precisely, he had "alluded" to it) in his description of the universe as a *makroanthropos* and of man as a microcosm in the *Guide* (I, 72).[74] He obviously had not heard of Maimonides' responsum (see above, pp. 187f.) nor of his deletion of the passage in the Introduction to *Pereq Ḥeleq*.[75] He shared, moreover, the prevalent view that the *Shiᶜur Qomā* was an authentic work. He states in two places in our text (lines 13, 160) that it was written by "the Sages of Israel" and makes the specific point (not made before him) that the Sages found it necessary to write the book in order to elucidate, at a time of diminishing understanding, the prophetic visions of God in human form (lines 12–13). His acceptance of the *Shiᶜur Qomā* as authentic does not yet, however, explain his motivation in offering an elaborate commentary on it. Two factors have to be taken into account in answering the question we have posed. The first concerns Narboni's relation to Ibn Ezra, the

69 See Steinschneider, *Cat. Bodl.*, col. 1975.

70 *Ibid.*, col. 1971.

71 *Ibid.*, col. 1969ff.

72 *Ibid.*, cols. 1967, 1977.

73 See Joseph Solomon Delmedigo's letter to Zeraḥ b. Nathan in: Abraham Geiger, *Melo Chofnajim* (Berlin, 1840), Hebr. section, p. 18; German section. pp. 65–68, n. 70; Steinschneider, *Hebr. Übersetzungen*, p. 313.

74 See lines 13–14 of our text. The reference to ch. 70, instead of 72, is obviously due to a slip of the pen.

75 The unexpurgated version is still extant in a number of manuscripts. See Lieberman, Appendix D . . ., p. 124, n. 32.

second his interest in Kabbala. We shall elaborate these two points.

(1) Narboni's *Epistle* takes the form of a commentary on Ibn Ezra's excursus in the *Long Commentary on Exodus* (33:21), which deals with the *Shiᶜur Qomā* (see above, p. 185). He quotes most of the Ibn Ezra passage verbatim (lines 16–38) and interprets it word by word in two large sections (lines 39–55; 186–226), separated by a relevant metaphysical disquisition (lines 55–95), a quotation from Averroes (95–109) on which he amplifies (110–134), another quotation from Averroes (135–156), and his comments (157–185). There follows a reference to the final part of Ibn Ezra's excursus with his comments (227–249) and a concluding paragraph (250–265) with the *explicit* (266–268). The *Epistle* is thus clearly structured around the Ibn Ezra text. Ibn Ezra is presented as having explained the *Shiᶜur Qomā* more fully than Maimonides did in his allusions to the subject in *Guide*, I, 72 (13–14), but not as fully as required: "[His words] are . . . in need of elucidation if his intention is to be perfectly understood" (line 40). Here, then, is a clear statement explaining the motivation of the *Epistle*. "I, Moses son of Joshua son of Mar David of Narbonne, therefore decided to comment on this subject and enlarge on its presentation" (40–42).

What enabled Narboni to make Ibn Ezra's rather cryptic remarks the basis of his interpretation of *Shiᶜur Qomā* was his view that they are the words of a man "who faithfully reflects the metaphysical science" (line 39). In other words, Narboni believed that Ibn Ezra, the "perfect scholar" (*ibid.*), expressed in his allusive way notions that accord with the truths of metaphysics—that is, of Averroes' metaphysics—and that a proper exegesis of his comments will show the very text of *Shiᶜur Qomā* to represent "the fruit of metaphysics" (line 56). Unfortunately, the text of the sentence in which this rather startling pronouncement occurs is somewhat corrupt, but the essential meaning seems clear. In what way the claim is made good will be seen later. At this stage we may simply note the fact that Narboni holds Ibn Ezra in high veneration as a spokesman for metaphysics, and that he feels justified in projecting his own Averroist concepts upon the twelfth-century Neoplatonist. This attitude fits very well into what one might call the fourteenth-century Ibn Ezra renaissance. Leon Jehuda Mosconi, a contemporary of Narboni's who wrote (between 1362 and 1370) a supercommentary on Ibn Ezra's commentary on the Tora,[76] reports having seen nearly thirty supercommentaries on Ibn Ezra's works on his extensive journeys.[77] Joseph Solomon Delmedigo of Kandia (Crete) (1591–1655) was shown twenty-four such supercommentaries in Constantinople.[78] As Steinschneider observed, "none of the authors [of supercommentaries on Ibn Ezra] known to us goes as far back as the thirteenth century, while in the fourteenth one follows upon the heels of the other".[79] The fascination which Ibn Ezra held for the fourteenth century may have been partly due to the rising interest in astrology.[80] It may also reflect the then growing impact of Kabbala, since Ibn Ezra appeared to be closer to the mystical approach than any other Jewish philosoper. Yet there were also those who regarded Ibn Ezra simply as a profound metaphysician. Joseph ibn Waqār, who was the outstanding representative of the fourteenth-century attempt at reconciling philosophy and Kabbala,[81] recommended Ibn Ezra and Maimonides as the two philosophers to be studied.[82] Joseph Kaspi (1279–*c.*1340), who was perhaps closest in spirit to Narboni, wrote a commentary on the obscure passages in Ibn Ezra's commentary on the Tora.[83] It contains an interpretation of the excursus on Ex. 33:21 treated in Narboni's *Epistle*,[84] and has certain points of contact with the latter. How much Narboni himself was attracted by Ibn Ezra may be gauged also from the fact that he wrote yet another Epistle (which, unfortunately, is lost) commenting this time on Ibn Ezra's allegorical interpretation of the Genesis account of paradise.[85] From the references to this work in the Commentary on the *Guide*[86] it appears that he interpreted the "garden" (*gan*)

[76] See Steinschneider, *Hebr. Übersetzungen*, pp. 313–314; and *Magazin für die Wissenschaft des Judentums*, ed. A. Berliner and D. Hoffmann, III (Berlin, 1876), pp. 94–100; 140–153; 190–205; Hebr. section, 24–25, contains Mosconi's supercommentary on the Ibn Ezra passage treated by Narboni in our text.

[77] See Berliner, *Magazin*, III, 44–45; Hebr. section 7.

[78] See Geiger, *Melo Chofnajim*, Hebr. section. p. 20.

[79] See Steinschneider, "Supercommentare zu Ibn Esra", *Jüdische Zeitschrift für Wissenschaft und Leben*, ed. A. Geiger, VI (Breslau, 1868), p. 123.

[80] See Steinschneider, *Hebr. Übersetzungen*, p. 318.

[81] See Steinschneider, *Gesammelte Schriften*, ed. H. Malter and A. Marx (Berlin, 1925), I, 171ff.; G. Vajda, *Recherches sur la philosophie et la kabbale dans la pensée juive du moyen âge* (Paris–La Haye, 1962), pp. 115–297.

[82] See the text published by G. Scholem in *Kiryat Sefer*, 20:155 (1943).

[83] Edited by Isaac Last in *Zehn Schriften des* R. *Josef Ibn Kaspi*, II (Pressburg, 1903), 145–196.

[84] Last, *Zehn Schriften*, II, 160–162.

[85] Listed as no. 20 in Steinschneider, *Cat. Bodl.*, col. 1975.

[86] Ed. Jacob Goldenthal (Vienna, 1853), 41a.

as a symbol of man or microcosm, and the "tree of life" as man's intellectual conception of all beings in the sublunar sphere. In this context too the term *shiᶜur* occurs, denoting here the "measure" of the tree of life which equals the measure of Jacob's ladder, and being tantamount to the measure of man's intellect.

(2) Narboni's second motivation in writing the *Epistle* on the theme of *shiᶜur qomā* was his interest in Kabbala. Although a staunch Averroist, he was, at least in his younger years, captivated by the then somewhat fashionable tendency to bring about a reconciliation between philosophy and Kabbala. His commentary on Ibn Ṭufayl's *Ḥayy ibn Yaqẓān*, written in 1349 (only seven years after he had written the *Epistle*), contains an elaborate passage on the *Sefirot*, the separate intellects, and the spheres[87] which clearly shows the extent to which he had become a follower of Joseph ibn Waqār's effort of harmonization. We do not know in which year Ibn Waqār's great work *Al-Maqāla al-jamīᶜa bayna l-falsafa wal-sharīᶜa* was completed. It would appear that it was already known by the time when Narboni wrote his *Epistle* (1342).[88] When he met him personally in Toledo many years later (1355–1358),[89] Ibn Waqār was already a very old man.[90] At any rate, his outline of the reconciliation of the Sefirotic system with the philosophical bears, for all its oddities, unmistakable traces of Ibn Waqār's influence. The important thing is that this harmonized system is presented not on behalf of either the Kabbalists or any other group[91] but as his own view: "I shall reveal to you a wonderful mystery . . ."[92] When, toward the end of his life, in the commentary on the *Guide* he refers to certain of these very same matters, he does so by quoting them in the name of the Kabbalists,[93] which seems to indicate that he had moved away from his earlier position. In fact, the commentary on the *Guide* abounds in open or veiled

[87] Quoted and analyzed by Vajda, *Recherches*, pp. 396–403.

[88] According to Vajda, *Recherches*, p. 118, Ibn Waqār approached his task *c.* 1340. In fact, Narboni's commentary on the *Maqāṣid al-falāsifa* (written prior to the *Epistle*) already shows the influence of Ibn Waqār (see below in the text and n. 97).

[89] See CG (ed. Goldenthal), 4a. On Narboni's stay in Toledo see *Cat. Bodl.*, cols. 1967, 1975.

[90] Narboni calls him (CG, 4a) *ha-ḥakam ha-ẓaqen*.

[91] As is the case at the beginning of the passage (Vajda, *Recherches*, p. 396), when Narboni refers to a view held by some "adepts of the Law" (*toriyyim*), viz. the Kabbalists (designated by him also as *toraniyim* or *ha-mequbbalim min ha-toraniyim* or *baᶜale ha-qabbala*). For his use of *toriy* in the general sense of "religious" see Vajda, *Revue des Etudes Juives*, 3(120):391 (1961); Charles Touati, "Dieu et le monde selon Moïse Narboni", *Archives d'Histoire Doctrinale et Littéraire*, 21:194 (1954).

[92] Vajda, *Recherches*, p. 399.

[93] CG, 62a.

criticisms of the Kabbalists. Thus, under the cloak of rigid objectivism befitting a mere commentator, Narboni refuses to be drawn into the controversy about Maimonides' theory of the purpose of the sacrificial cult but clearly dissociates himself from the kabbalistic notion that it was meant to bring about the unification of the *Sefirot*.[94] He openly rejects the kabbalistic view, which regards the *shekinā* as "being not outside the essence of the Creator". In his opinion, the *shekinā* is identical with the *Merkabā* and as such created.[95] He ironically calls the Kabbalists, who allegedly interpret the rabbinic reference to God as the "Place" of the world in a semi-literal sense, "the Kabbalists who dwell in the light", which obviously is intended as a euphemism for darkness.[96] There is, then, sufficient warrant for assuming that some change of heart had taken place.

What was Narboni's harmonistic view at the earlier stage, and how is it reflected in the *Epistle*? Broadly speaking, Narboni adopted Ibn Waqār's principle of co-ordination between the *Sefirot*, the separate intellects of the philosophers, and the spheres, or celestial souls, of the astronomers and astrologers. In his commentary on al-Ghazālī's *Maqāṣid*, which precedes the *Epistle*, he relates the special attributes (*middot*) of each of the *Sefirot* to the corresponding qualities of the celestial souls. "For it is in accordance with the action that comes from the sphere that the power and quality of the soul of the sphere and of the *Sefirot* is specified."[97] In the commentary on Ibn Ṭufayl's *Ḥayy ibn Yaqẓān* he offers a full list of correspondences. It starts with the first three *Sefirot*—*Keter* (also named *reʾshit*, *rom*, *ʾayin*), *Ḥokmā*, and *Binā*—which are correlated with the all-encompassing, starless sphere, the sphere of the stars, and Saturn, respectively.[98] Exactly the same co-ordination was offered in one of Ibn Waqār's tentative proposals, the assumption being that this scheme implies also the correlation of the separate intellects or movers of the spheres. The assignment of the first *Sefirā* (*Keter*) to the outermost sphere presupposes the non-identity of *Keter* and *En-Sof*, or, in philosophical terms, of the prime mover and the First Cause.[99] Ibn

[94] *Ibid.*; similarly in the case of the kabbalistic interpretation of *teqiʿat shofar*, CG, 63b.

[95] CG, 49a; see also 62a.

[96] *Ibid.*, 14b.

[97] CIP, Vatican ms. 260, fol. 54*r*. In this connection Narboni identifies Samaʾel (to whom the scapegoat is offered) with the soul of Mars.

[98] See Vajda, *Recherches*, pp. 399–401.

[99] *Ibid.*, pp. 400, 265.

Waqār discusses also an alternative scheme based on the notion of the identity of *Keter* and *En-Sof*,[100] and it seems that in the *Epistle* Narboni takes this view when referring to God as being called *Keter*.[101] It accords with his philosophical position in the great controversy about the identity or non-identity of God and first mover.[102] As far as the remaining seven *Sefirot* are concerned, Narboni's scheme deviates from Ibn Waqār's outline of alternative possibilities.[103] It does not adopt even the standard denominations and order of the *Sefirot* (which are accepted by Ibn Waqār). He has the following list of *Sefirot* 4–10: (4) *Tifᵓeret* or *Ḥesed*, corresponding to Jupiter, (5) *Neẓaḥ*, corresponding to Mars, (6) *Hod*, corresponding to the sun, (7) *Malkut* corresponding to Venus, (8) *Meᶜon Ẓedeq*, corresponding to Mercury, (9) *Yesod*, corresponding to the moon, (10) *Kallā* or *Keneset Yisraᵓel*. There is nothing in Ibn Waqār resembling this strange assortment, except that he too, in his first scheme, has a *Sefirā* (in his case, *Yesod*) which is unrelated to any specific sphere, and which (as in the case of Narboni's last) has the function of transmitting the influx from above to the sublunar world. Ibn Waqār identifies it with the agent intellect, the last of the separate intellects.[104] Narboni does not mention the agent intellect in this context but he does so in the *Epistle*, where he approvingly mentions the kabbalistic designation *Keneset Yisraᵓel* for the agent intellect.[105] Whatever Narboni's source for the compilation of his list of *Sefirot* 4–10, his basic concept of co-ordination could only have been Ibn Waqār's treatise. For while he may have adopted the identification of the *Sefirot* with the separate intellects from other Kabbalists,[106] their correlation with the astrologically conceived souls of the spheres or stars could only have come from Ibn Waqār.

[100] *Ibid.*, pp. 266ff.

[101] Line 161 of our text.

[102] On this controversy see Vajda, "Un Champion de l'avicennisme", *Revue Thomiste*, XLVIII, No. 3 (1948), 480–508. Narboni clearly sides with Averroes. See CPC, Bodleian ms. Michael 119, fol. 139(i)*v*.

[103] See Vajda, *Recherches*, p. 266.

[104] *Ibid.*, p. 265.

[105] Lines 88–89 in our text.

[106] Thus Jacob b. Sheshet and Abraham of Cologne identified the *sefirā ḥokmā* with the agent intellect (cf. Scholem, *Tarbiẓ*, 2:215. n. 96 [1930–31]); Abraham Abulafia equated the latter with the *sefirā malkut* (Scholem, *Major Trends*, p. 143), Jacob Ha-Kohen, in a text representing a late recension, with the *sefirā reshit*: viz., *keter* (Scholem, *Madaᶜē Ha-Yahadut*, II, 227, text b, lines 4–13). See also Scholem, *ᶜIqbotav shel Gabirol ba-qabbala*, in *Meᵓassef Sofrē Ereẓ Yisraᵓel* (1940), p. 174, where an anonymous Spanish Kabbalist is quoted who sought to reconcile Maimonides with the Kabbala and, to this end, identified the separate intellects with the *sefirot*.

Since by the time of Narboni's literary activity all Kabbalists were practically agreed in identifying the *shiᶜur qomā* with the *Sefirot*, it is not difficult to see why he was attracted to this theme. It held out the prospect of a philosophical treatment once the *Sefirot* were correlated or equated with the separate intellects, a position which Narboni had already embraced in his commentary on the *Maqāṣid*. The sophisticated manner in which the Kabbalists themselves had dealt with the *Shiᶜur Qomā* must have heightened the respectability of this previously embattled tract and may have served as a challenge to a philosopher like Narboni to try his hand at commenting on it. This and the fact that in Ibn Ezra's exposition he found a precedent combined to arouse his desire to write on the subject. The way he tackled it, however, owed its inspiration to Averroes.

In the *Epistle*, he quotes two passages from Averroes[107] which are taken from the Long Commentary on *Metaphysics* and from the *Tahāfut al-Tahāfut*, respectively.[108] The first of these makes the point that each of the separate intellects recognizes the First Cause (God) under different aspects and that the totality of motions of the spheres forms a harmonious whole owing to the unifying principle provided by God as the common object of the intellects' cognition. The second enlarges on this theme by showing God to be the principle and cause of the hierarchy of existents. The key notion of the entire passage is found in the statement that in thinking Himself God thinks the existents in their noblest mode of existence. In other words, God's self-intellectualization, far from implying ignorance of the other existents, is a thinking of the very same forms which are found at the various levels of existence below Him; but He thinks them in a way in which no other being can think them: in their noblest mode and order. The various levels at which forms exist are, starting from the bottom, forms-in-matter, or material forms; forms as conceived by the human intellect; forms existing in the agent intellect and, in a rising scale of excellence, the forms in the other separate intellects, and, finally, the forms existing in the First Cause or God. Again, Averroes stresses the corollary of this view: "So it has become evident . . . that there is one single order and act in which

107 Lines 96–109 and 135–156 in our text.

108 See nn. 63 and 74 on the Translation, where we have identified these passages. Narboni gives no reference.

all existents participate in common." Narboni takes this to mean that God is in fact "identical with His conceiving the existents in their most perfect and most glorious mode".[109] Quoting Averroes' saying that God was in some respect all existents,[110] he feels justified to apply to God Ibn Ezra's term "Image" in the sense of His being the imageless "universal aspect of all images".[111] In a subsequent passage he explains in the same way the verse (Num. 11:8), "and the image of God doth he behold": "All existents are the image of God, seeing that they are in Him in the most noble [way of] existence."[112] The Averroean formula describing God as the most noble existence of the forms—as the existence of the forms "in perfect and simple unity"[113]—is linked by Narboni with Maimonides' concept of God as the "principle" (*al-mabdaʾ*) of all existent things (*Guide*, I, 16). It means, according to Narboni, that "He thinks the forms in the most glorious existence possible."[114] It is, then, clear that for him the essence of God consists in the simplicity and unity in which the forms exist in God or, to put it differently, the most glorious level of existence of forms is tantamount to God's essence or existence, both being the same. In this view, which is reminiscent of Leibniz' concept of God as the central Monad,[115] God, while distinct from all other beings and transcending them, is yet intimately linked with them. He is their existence in its most superb mode, and there is, in Averroes' words, "one single order and act in which all existents participate in common".

It is this notion which struck Narboni as offering a key to the understanding of the allegorical meaning of *shiᶜur qomā*. Immediately after the quotation of the second Averroes passage, which, toward the end, contains the sentence just referred to, he comments: "It should be clear from all this that the sensible existents are abstract forms in the First Cause, and that it thinks them in the most noble way. This being the case, we may call the [confining] measure of the existents *shiᶜur qomā* ["measure of the body"] in accordance with the dictum of theirs (*Ḥagiga* 12a): 'The world went on expanding until the Holy One, blessed be He, rebuked it.'"[116] As he immediately explains, the totality of existents (which

[109] Lines 210–211 in our text. [110] Lines 162–163. [111] Lines 161–162.
[112] Lines 237–238. [113] Lines 120–121. [114] Lines 123–127.
[115] See Leibniz, *The Monadology And Other Philosophical Writings*, trans. by Robert Latta (1898), p. 243, n. 75. The relevant paragraphs in the Monadology are nos. 57, 60, 62–63. [116] Lines 157–160.

we take to mean all beings except God) is designated by the term *qomā*. He might have added that God is symbolically called its "measure" (*shiᶜur*). Yet the meaning is plain from the previous sentence as such, since it differentiates between the measure and the body, and by quoting the passage *Ḥagiga* 12a, identifies God with the measure.[117] God, then, is the "measure" (*shiᶜur*) of the existents (*qomā*). The term "measure" is taken here in analogy to Aristotle's use of it, as has already been noted in Charles Touati's excellent study on Narboni.[118] According to Aristotle, the measure (*metron*) or principle (*archē*) is some invisible unit (*Metaphysics*, X, i, 1052b, 32), and it is always akin to the things measured. Thus, the measure of magnitude is magnitude; of sounds, a sound; and so on (1053a, 25ff.). Narboni is able to apply the term "measure" to God in relation to the world because he has adopted Averroes' notion of God as the existents in their most glorious mode of being, a notion which implies a certain kinship between God and the existents. It is this kinship which justifies the use of the term "measure", in the sense of "principle", with regard to God. In the commentary on *Ḥayy ibn Yaqẓān* he says distinctly that God is the measure of everything in a manner comparable to the one and indivisible unit which is the principle and measure of the beings entering into that particular category.[119] Reflecting Aristotle's remark (*Metaphysics*, X, ii, 1053b, 29ff.) about white as the unity of colour, he says in the commentary on the *Guide*: "Even as the white which is the measure of colours neutralizes vision, so that glorious substance [namely, God] which is the measure of all substances neutralizes the faculty of the intellect so as to make it incapable of comprehending Him on account of the power of His manifestation."[120] He bases this analogy on the fact that God is the principle of all substances in the way in which there is a principle in every genus such as sound, colour, et cetera.

The reference to God as the "measure of all existents" is paralleled, in the Commentary on the *Guide*,[121] by the interpretation

117 In the same Talmudic passage Resh Laqish interprets the Divine name *Shadday* as denoting the measure: *ani she-ᵓamarti la-ᶜolam day*. On the possibly Platonic background of the rabbinic concept see Manuel Joel, *Blicke in die Religionsgeschichte*, I (Breslau–Leipzig, 1880), 147, n. 1; for the motif of the "limit" (*horos*) in Gnosticism see Jean Doresse, *The Secret Books of the Egyptian Gnostics* (New York, 1960), 28.

118 "Dieu et le monde selon Moïse Narboni" (see n. 91), 195ff.

119 Quoted by Touati, *op. cit.*, 195–196, from a manuscript of the Bibliothèque Nationale, Paris. Narboni distinctly refers to the discussion in book 10 of the *Metaphysics*.

120 CG, 10a–b (on I, 59).

121 CG, 14b (on I, 70).

of the rabbinic designation of God as the "Place of the world". This term, Narboni explains, simply means that God is the "Form of the world" in the sense in which the form perfects and, at the same time, limits a thing. As in the *Epistle*, he quotes in this connection the rabbinic dictum describing God as having called a halt to the expanding universe by His "rebuke". He sees in it an allegorical reference to the limitation of the world by virtue of its formal principle (namely, God). "The Mover has a relation to the moved, or the Form to the formed", and in this sense limitation is a necessary corollary of the concept of God as the form-giving principle. It may, however, be noted that Narboni does not revert here to his interpretation of *shiᶜur qomā* in the dual sense of God (measure)—world (body) but takes it as a single term denoting the limited universe: "'The heaven for height, and the earth for depth' (Prov. 25:3)—this is the *shiᶜur qomā*." In his *Epistle* on Ibn Ezra's allegorical interpretation of the "garden" (see above, p. 197) he similarly speaks of the *shiᶜur* of what is between earth and heaven, and of the *shiᶜur* of Jacob's ladder.[122] The dual-term theory seems to be confined to the *Epistle on Shiᶜur Qomā*. It is reminiscent of the division of the term which we found in the *Tiqqunē Zohar*[123] where, however, the order is reversed in that *shiᶜur* denotes the lower, and *qomā* the higher principle. In our *Epistle*, *qomā* stands definitely for the total order of the existents, excluding God, who is the "measure". Unlike the kabbalistic view, which sees in the *shiᶜur qomā* a reference to the *Sefirot*, Narboni does not confine the *qomā* to the separate intellects (which, as we have seen, he equated with the *Sefirot*). In his interpretation the term covers all levels of existence: the three worlds of sublunar, celestial, and separate forms.[124] In this respect he follows Ibn Ezra, while the interpretation of *shiᶜur* as referring to God is entirely his own and based, as we have seen, on Averroes' concept of God as well as on Aristotle's notion of measure. There is, however, an echo of the Kabbalists' view in his identification of the *qomā* of the "perfect man", who is obviously a symbol of the macrocosm (see above, p. 186), with "what the adepts of the *Sefirot* call the 'Tree'."[125] This equation is repeated later in the text when the macrocosm is said to be allegorized in Jacob's ladder and in the Kabbalists' tree.[126] Narboni obviously confused

[122] CG, 41a. [123] See above, p. 192.

[124] Cf. line 186 of our text: *we-hinē hezib ha-qomā*; line 189: *we-ᵓaḥar she-heᶜemid gobā ha-qomā*. [125] Line 207. [126] Lines 251–252.

here the kabbalistic notion of the *shiᶜur qomā* as *Sefirot* with Ibn Ezra's view of it as the macrocosm or Meṭaṭron. His *lapsus* is an involuntary testimony to the challenge which the kabbalistic treatment of the theme had presented to him. In spite of his own involvement in Kabbala (see above, pp. 198–201), he did not, however, pursue this line but interpreted the *Shiᶜur Qomā* philosophically on an Averroean basis. The *shiᶜur qomā* is but the figurative expression of Averroes' notion of "one single order and act in which all existents participate in common".

The detailed exposition of this theme is modelled on Ibn Ezra's allegorical treatment of it. Significantly, Narboni introduces his philosophical disquisition (followed by the two quotations from Averroes) when a comment is called for on Ibn Ezra's reference to the "length" between the two extreme points: between the "Prince of the Presence" and the "end of the power".[127] It is this reference which serves as a cue prompting him to enter into the philosophical aspect of the matter. The upshot of his discussion is that the *qomā* as interpreted by him is what Ibn Ezra meant by the "length" from the highest but God to the lowest, and that God is the measure and principle of it. His detailed interpretation of the *shiᶜur qomā* begins by resuming the thread where he had left it off: "He [Ibn Ezra] established the *qomā*, saying: 'length is [the extension] between two points'—is the *qomā*", and so on.[128] Ibn Ezra, he repeats a few lines below, has set up the "height of the Body" (*goba ha-qomā*).[129] It is visualized in the form of the human figure. It has a right side and a left, a front and a back. Narboni explains that right and left indicate high and low in the order of beings.[130] (The meaning of front and back will be discussed below.) Following Ezekiel's description of the division of the body into a part from the loins downward and a part from the loins upward (1:27), he allegorically interprets the soles of its feet, which are the very lowest part, as the accidents inherent in the sublunar bodies; the parts from the soles up to the knees as the sublunar bodies; the thighs as the celestial bodies; the upper part as the separate intellects, the head representing the first intellect[131]; and the face as God's essence.[132] The part from the loins upward is

[127] See nn. 21 and 22 on the Translation.

[128] Line 186.

[129] Line 189. The term *gobā ha-qomā* ("the height of the body") clearly shows that Narboni understood *qomā* in the sense of "body", and not of "height" or "stature", as Touati assumes (p. 198, n. 4).

[130] Lines 190–196.

[131] See n. 100 on the Translation.

[132] Lines 220–223.

described by Ezekiel also in terms of "an appearance of splendour, as the colour of electrum"; and the lower part as "the appearance of fire" (1:27; 8:2). Narboni sees here a symbolic reference to the separate intellects and the bodies (celestial and sublunar), respectively, and applies to the division thus indicated the terms "flame" (*shalhebet*) and "coal" (*gaḥelet*) in the sense in which they are used in the *Sefer Yeẓirā* (I, 7): as symbols of an indivisible unity.[133] In the commentary on the *Guide* the symbolism is slightly changed in that both the splendour and the fire (the flame and the coal) are applied to the realm of the separate intellects, higher and lower. They are all unified by virtue of the concept of God which they form (albeit from different aspects), and the denial of this unity is tantamount to what the mystics mean by "cutting the plants" (the term for heresy).[134] In the *Epistle*, where he is concerned with establishing the concept of the single and unified order of the *qomā* as the totality of existents, he applies the two divisions of the body to the entire universe.

Of special interest is the distinction between front and back. It stems from the famous Exodus passage (33:23) on which Ibn Ezra's treatment of the theme is based. The front or face of God is "His true essence which cannot be perceived".[135] This interpretation, which goes back to Philo,[136] is specified by the statement that God's Face stands for His way of conceiving the existents, while His Back stands for the manner in which the existents necessarily follow from Him. That the Face cannot be seen thus means that we are unable to know the quiddity of the concept which God has of the existents.[137] The Face of God is also said to stand for the existence of all things in Him[138]: namely, for the most glorious mode of the existence of forms. In other words, the Face is identical with the absolute and simple unity of intellect, intelligent, and intelligible which is God.[139] It is distinct from the "head" of the *qomā*—that is from the first intellect[140]—and having no image, it is the "universal aspect of all the images".[141] The term *Keter* which Narboni applies to God fits the concept of the Face as the supreme level of the existence of forms, since it has the connotation of that which "surrounds" and thereby limits *qua*

133 Lines 215–216. 134 CG, 48b.
135 Line 223; see also 198–199, 239–240.
136 *De Specialibus Legibus*, I, 8, 43–46; *De Fuga et Inventione*, 166.
137 Lines 164–169. 138 Line 210. 139 Lines 120–127.
140 Line 223. 141 Lines 161–162.

form-giving principle.[142] Although in Narboni's outline of the *Sefirot* (see above, p. 200) *Keter* is identical with *En-Sof* and hence is not below God, he uses here this term probably to indicate the concept of God as the highest in the series of existencies. The symbol of the Face serves the same purpose. For although the Face is distinctly unknowable and transcendent, it is not separable from the figure designated as the Body (*qomā*). Being its measure and principle, it is akin to it. It is the eternally veiled Face of the Body. The Averroean notion of the single order and act in which all existents participate is thus maintained in the simile of the Face. In this sense Narboni can say toward the end of the *Epistle*[143] that all existents are the "image of God" since they are in Him in the most noble way.[144]

Narboni was conscious of the fact that the concept of God as expressed in the *Epistle* meant a radical departure from the prevalent (neoplatonic) theology which had stressed the total otherness of God. His epilogue clearly indicates the sense of reluctance he felt in committing his interpretation of *shiᶜur qomā* to writing. His decision to take that step, he tells us, was motivated by his awareness that the time in which he lived was ripe for a bolder disclosure of the truth that, until then, had been concealed in the form of allegory. Now "all Israelites" were to share in the "light" of truth and in the "true felicity" vouchsafed by its possession.[145]

142 In his outline of the *sefirot* in the commentary on *Ḥayy ibn Yaqẓān* the first *sefirā* is said to be called *keter* "because it surrounds everything" (see Vajda, *Recherches*, p. 400).

143 Lines 234–240.

144 The identification of the "Face" with the Self-thinking or essence of God, though based on the Exodus passage and its treatment in medieval Jewish philosophy, may also owe something to the prominence which the concept of the "Face [*wajh*] of Allāh" acquired in the Koran (see *Shorter Encyclopaedia of Islam* [Leiden, 1953], p. 36) and the significance attached to it by al-Ghazālī. The phrase "Everything perishes, except His Face" (*Koran*, XXVIII: 88) is explained by him to mean: "For everything other than Allāh is, when considered in and by itself, pure not-being; and if considered from the 'aspect' [*wajh*, lit. 'face'] of existence flowing from the First Being, it is viewed as existing, but not in itself; solely from the 'aspect' which belongs to Him who gives it existence . . . All existence is, exclusively, His Face" (see W. H. T. Gairdner, *Al-Ghazzali's Mishkāt Al-Anwār* [London, 1924], p. 104). The closeness of Narboni's interpretation of the "Face" to al-Ghazālī's is striking. Interestingly enough, the reproduction of God's answer to Moses' request (Ex. 34:21) in the Koran (VII: 135) makes no mention of the "Face". It reads: "Said He, 'Thou shalt not see Me; but behold the mountain—if it stays fast in its place, then thou shalt see Me.' And when his Lord revealed Him to the mountain, He made it crumble to dust." An inexact rendering of this Koran passage is found in Narboni's CPC (ms. Michael, 126*r*), as noted already by Munk (*Mélanges*, p. 453, n. 1).

145 Lines 259–265. See also CG, 34a.

This is the authentic language of *Aufklärung*, and the truth propounded is tantamount to a radical reversion, under the influence of Averroes, to the Aristotelian concept of God as the Self-thinking supreme Intellect. Plotinus had rejected this concept as incompatible with the absolute unity of the One.[146] Maimonides, following Avicenna,[147] had admitted it (*Guide*, I, 68) but adhered, at the same time, to the negative theology of Neoplatonism. God's intellect, he insisted, has nothing in common with ours (*Guide*, III, 20). The ambivalence of this position did not escape severe criticism.[148] There were two alternative ways to avoid it: either to adopt the classical neoplatonic view, which denied intellect to the One, or else to return to the Aristotelian concept of God, at the price of giving up negative theology. This alternative had been clearly formulated in an early neoplatonic work: Damascius' (fifth-century) *Dubitationes et solutiones de primis principiis in Platonis Parmenidem*,[149] where the first aporia reads: "Whether the so-called unique principle of all is beyond all things, or a certain one out of all; for example, the highest point of the class of things proceeding from it."[150] Averroes opted for the second alternative. He rejected the negative interpretation of the term "intellect" as applied to God: "for this is not true—on the contrary, it is the most special appellation for His essence according to the Peripatetics, in contrast to Plato's opinion that the intellect is not the First Principle and that intellect cannot be attributed to the First Principle".[151] Narboni sides with Averroes, as we have seen, and by describing God as the "measure" (*shiᶜur*) of the "body" (*qomā*)—that is, of the hierarchy of existents—affirms exactly what Damascius had pointed out as the Aristotelian alternative; he makes God into "a certain one out of all, for example, the highest point of the class of things proceeding from it". The corollary of this view is a doctrine

[146] See *Enneads*, III.8.8; V.3.12–13; V.6.2.

[147] Cf. S Munk, *Le Guide des égarés . . . par Moïse ben Maimoun*, I (Paris, 1856), 301–302, n. 4; for Maimonides' indebtedness to al-Fārābī see my article "Maᵓamar beyiḥud ha-Boreᵓ", *Tarbiz*, 27, nos. 2–3 (1958), p. 301, n. 2.

[148] Such criticism is offered in the *Maᵓamar be-yiḥud ha-Boreᵓ* (anonymous) published by me (see preceding note).

[149] Ed. C. A. Ruelle (Paris, 1889), Vol. I, p. 1, 1–2. See Ronald F. Hathaway, "Hierarchy and the Definition of Order in the Letters of Pseudo-Dionysius" (unpubl. diss., Brandeis University, 1965), p. 30, n. 63.

[150] Damascius, of course, adopted the neoplatonic viewpoint. The Platonic phrase *epékeina tōn pántōn* is frequently used by him. See Hathaway, *loc. cit.*

[151] Averroes, *Tahāfut al-Tahāfut*, ed. Maurice Bouyges (Beirut, 1930), p. 310. We are quoting Simon van den Bergh's translation, I (London, 1954), 186.

of attributes which substitutes the principle of analogy (*per prius et posterius*) for that of homonymity. Narboni's fears lest Jewish susceptibilities be offended by his departure from negative theology were unfounded. His view had already been anticipated by Gersonides, and it was to be reiterated by even so staunchly an orthodox thinker as Abraham Bibago in his *Derek Emunā* (written toward the end of the fifteenth century). In formulations which echo Narboni's, Bibago says that God "comprehends Himself and thereby comprehends all beings; for they are Himself in an infinitely more glorious form of existence". God is said to be "the Form of the world in an infinitely glorious sense" (ch. ii, 12d–13a). "All things are, in a sense, the 'Face of the Most High' [*penē ᶜelyon*]" (13a), a statement which seems to elaborate Narboni's view of the "Face" of God. It should also be noted that Bibago lists the *Shiᶜur Qomā* among other mystical treatises (*Hekalot*, *Sefer Bahir*) which are said to contain metaphysics (*ḥokmā ʾelohit*) of the highest order. This, again, appears to reflect Narboni's interpretation of the *Shiᶜur Qomā* in the *Epistle*.

The concept of God offered in the *Epistle* reappears in the *Treatise on Free Will* (*Ha-maʾamar ba-beḥirā*), written by Narboni at the very end of his life, and representing another valuable document of his personal faith.[152] What distinguishes the treatment of the theme in the *Epistle* is the wealth of symbolism employed in the service of explicating his notion of God and God's relation to the world. God is the *shiᶜur* and the "Face", while the world is the *qomā*, the sanctuary (*mishkan*), the perfect Man or Man, Jacob's ladder, the image (*temunā*) of God, and, up to a point, the Kabbalists' tree. There is a superb concrescence of symbols and motifs in this unifying vision of his. The challenge presented by the kabbalistic interpretation of the *shiᶜur qomā* is fully met on philosophical ground but not without some reverberations of kabbalistic influence.

[152] See *Cat. Bodl.*, col. 1977. The treatise is published in *Sefer Dibre Ḥakamim*, ed. Eliezer Ashkenazi (Metz, 1849), pp. 37–41. It is briefly analyzed in Yiẓḥaq Julius Guttmann, *Ha-Pilosofia shel ha-Yahadut* (Jerusalem, 1951), pp. 190–191.

10

WILLIAM WOLLASTON: ENGLISH DEIST AND RABBINIC SCHOLAR[1]

In the year 1724, there appeared in London an anonymous book called "The Religion of Nature Delineated" which was to become one of the most successful works of English Deism. It took the form of a letter addressed to "A. F. Esq.", and was signed by N. N., to which cryptic signature was appended the equally unrevealing Hebrew *notarikon mkʾ vtl*. The treatise comprised 218 pages and was written in pellucid and graceful language, setting out its theme under nine main heads. But not content to develop his subject logically and systematically, the author clinched his arguments by innumerable quotations from Latin, Greek, and Hebrew sources in their original texts. He was obviously extremely well versed in the languages and literatures on which he so lavishly drew, and apparently expected his readers to be sufficiently at home in the three learned tongues to appreciate the relevance of the passages quoted.

In the very year of the publication of this book, its author died. Anonymity was lifted a year later when a second edition of the work appeared under his full name—William Wollaston.[2] The book achieved rapid fame which was to last for over half a century, and spread far beyond the British Isles. We are told that 10,000 copies of it were sold in the course of a few years. In all, eight editions appeared, the last one coming out in 1759. As early

[1] Paper read before the Jewish Historical Society of England on 1st November, 1948.

[2] For biographical information see Samuel Clarke's Preface to the sixth, seventh, and eighth editions of the work (1738, 1750, 1759); *Dictionary of National Biography* (1909), Vol. XXI; *Nouvelle Biographie Générale*, ed. Firmin Didot Frères (Paris, 1866), Vol. 46.

as 1726, a French translation was published by Garrigue at the Hague under the title "Ebauche de la Religion Naturelle par Mr. Wollaston", to be followed, in 1756, by a fresh edition in three volumes. In the Preface to the work the translator speaks of "l'applaudissement extraordinaire, que le Public a donné à ce livre", and greatly eulogizes the author. The two editions contain also a translation into French by de la Faye, Professor of Oriental Languages at the Hague, of Wollaston's copious Latin, Greek, and Hebrew notes, and supplementary notes by the translator. At the end, three supplementary chapters offer an evaluation of Wollaston's work. In England, a similar service was performed by John Clarke, Dean of Salisbury, a younger brother of the famous Samuel Clarke and translator of Hugo Grotius. He not only wrote a "Preface containing a General Account of the Life, Character and Writings of the Author", which was added to the last three editions (1738, 1750, and 1759) of Wollaston's work, but also published an English translation of the Latin, Greek, and Hebrew notes, which appears, side by side with the original texts, in the last two editions (1750 and 1759).[3] In a prefatory note dated 17th April, 1750, he explains that "The Religion of Nature being a Book in great Esteem with her late Majesty Queen Caroline, she was pleased to command me to translate the Notes into English for her own use; And there being a Demand for a new Edition, it was thought proper to publish this Translation." Queen Caroline, it may be noted, expressed her admiration for Wollaston in yet another way. In 1732 she placed a marble bust of him, along with Newton's, Locke's, and Samuel Clarke's, in her hermitage in the royal garden at Richmond. Unfortunately this marble bust has disappeared, and so has the fame of Wollaston's book of which it could be said as late as 1866 (in the *Nouvelle Biographie Générale* published in that year) that it still enjoyed celebrity. History has failed to confirm Queen Caroline's gracious gesture of putting Wollaston on the same level of importance as Newton and Locke. But the Queen was at least in good company so far as her judgment is concerned. John Conybeare, Rector of Exeter College, Oxford, in his "A Defence of Reveal'd Religion" (1732), sees in Wollaston's theory of morals a decided advance

[3] Hugh James Rose, in his *New General Dictionary* (1844), Vol. VI, p. 337 (also in the following editions) makes the mistake of attributing the Notes to John Clarke.

upon Locke's,[4] and Christian Garve, in his "Übersicht der vornehmsten Prinzipien der Sittenlehre" (1798), describes as the most noteworthy representatives of new principles in morals Samuel Clarke, Wollaston, and the man to whom his book is dedicated—Immanuel Kant.[5]

Within the compass of the present study only the barest outline can be given of Wollaston's place in the history of moral philosophy. In the great eighteenth-century controversy between sense and reason in morals, Wollaston, like Samuel Clarke, Richard Price, and Thomas Reid, bases morals on reason, whilst Shaftesbury, Hutcheson, Adam Smith, and Hume stand on the side of sense and feeling.[6] One may agree with Conybeare's summing up of Wollaston's main thesis when he says that it "is the most complete system of moral principles which hath yet been given us on the mere foot of natural reason".[7] By connecting the notions of truth and rightness, he shows that the good resolves itself into the true. One can contradict truth by one's actions as much as by any proposition or assertion. To treat things as being what they are not is the greatest possible absurdity. To talk to a post as if it

[4] Clifford Griffeth Thompson, in his *The Ethics of William Wollaston* (Boston, Mass., 1922), p. 4, quotes Conybeare as saying of Wollaston that his theory was a discovery in morals "fit to be placed beside the discoveries of Newton in astronomy". In actual fact, the words alleged to be a literal quotation do not occur in Conybeare's treatise though their meaning may be inferred from the context. Conybeare recalls that, in his famous Essay, Locke had made bold "to think Morality . . . capable of Demonstration, as well as Mathematics". Yet in his letter to Molineux he wrote, "Whether I am able to make it out, is another Question. Every one could not have demonstrated what Mr. Newton's Book hath shewn to be demonstrable." Conybeare adds on p. 239 (the reference quoted by Thompson), "We have lately indeed had a Noble Performance much in the Way which Mr. Locke propos'd; and the Design hath been so well executed by Mr. Wollaston that however some objections may be made against certain Parts of his Book, yet it hath been receiv'd, in the general, with the highest Applause."

[5] Cf. also Drechsler, *Über William Wollaston's Moralphilosophie* (Erlangen, 1801). Thompson (*loc. cit.*, p. 39) remarks that the Germans, guided by Garve's and Drechsler's interpretation, regarded Wollaston's system of morals as a precursor of Kant's. It should, however, be noted that Garve made a slightly different point. He felt that the Kantian principle, if strictly and consistently applied, was bound to lead to the doctrine of Wollaston, not vice versa. Cf. *loc. cit.*, p. 172. On his failure to do full justice to Kant, cf. Albert Stern, *Über die Beziehungen Chr. Garve's zu Kant* (Leipzig, 1884), p. 86.

[6] Cf. D. Daiches Raphael, *The Moral Sense* (1947), p. 2; Erdmann, *Geschichte der neueren Philosophie* II, p. 107; W. Windelband, *History of Philosophy*, p. 504.

[7] *Loc. cit.*, p. 239; Conybeare himself disagrees with Wollaston's thesis. In his view, neither morality nor religion can be reduced to Reason. Deism, he points out, is bound to lead to atheism. His treatise is mainly directed against Tindal's *Christianity as old as Creation* (1730).

were a man must be reckoned an absurdity. Conversely, to treat a man as a post, as if he had no sense and felt no injuries is likewise a denial of truth and therefore morally wrong. A more religious turn is given to this argument by introducing God as the Author of nature: to own things as they are is to submit to His Will as revealed in the books of nature. In other words, to act against truth is to contradict the truths as they have always subsisted in the Divine Mind. Wollaston thus links together morals and natural religion.[8] But whereas Clarke founded the obligations of natural religion upon *a priori* truths concerning God,[9] Wollaston established them on the basis of the concept of truth as such. Morality merges into natural religion, both being founded upon reason.

The radical rationalism of Wollaston's theory was bound to provoke attack. In 1725, "A Defence of Mr. Wollaston's notion of moral good and evil" appeared in answer to a letter by T. Boll which claimed to have refuted it. In the same year, John Clarke, Master of the Public Grammar School in Hull,[10] wrote "An Examination of the notion of moral good and evil advanced in a late book by W. W., entitled *The Religion of Nature Delineated*". He criticizes Wollaston as "a person of considerable parts, who might have made a fine book of it, had he set out upon a right bottom: but unluckily falling upon a whimsical notion of morality, and perhaps too much tickled with the novelty of it, and a desire to support and leave it as a legacy to the world, has so leavened his treatise with it as must render it disagreeable to the most judicious readers, and at the same time expose morality instead of recommending it".[11] Of greater historical interest is Hume's devastating attack upon Wollaston in his "A Treatise of Human Nature", which proceeds from the assumption that actions do not derive their merit from a conformity to reason, nor their blame from a

[8] Cf. Wollaston, *The Religion of Nature Delineated*, pp. 14–15.

[9] Cf. Samuel Clarke, *A Discourse concerning the unalterable Obligations of Natural Religion, and the Truth and Certainty of the Christian Revelation.* Being eight Sermons preached in the year 1705, at the Lecture founded by the Hon. Robert Boyle, pp. 110ff.

[10] Not to be confounded with John Clarke, Dean of Salisbury (1682–1757), who wrote the Life of Wollaston and translated the Latin, Greek, and Hebrew parts of his Notes. This John Clarke (1687–1734) was a classical scholar, and wrote, in addition to the books mentioned in the text, *The Foundation of Morality in theory and practice considered in an examination of Dr. S. Clarke's opinion concerning the original of Moral Obligation* (1730?).

[11] *Loc. cit.*, pp. 2–3.

contrariety to it. Actions may be laudable or blameable; but they cannot be reasonable or unreasonable. Moral distinctions are not the offspring of reason. For reason is wholly inactive, and can never be the source of so active a principle as conscience or a sense of morals. "One might think", he says, "it were entirely superfluous to prove this if a late author, who has had the good fortune to obtain some reputation, had not seriously affirmed that such a falsehood is the foundation of all guilt and moral deformity." Like John Clarke, Hume calls Wollaston's doctrine a "whimsical system", and endeavours to disprove it from its own premises.[12] But it was Kant who gave the *coup de grâce* to the intellectualist theory of morals (and religion) by his distinction of pure reason and practical reason.

Whilst Wollaston's position in moral philosophy is clear beyond doubt, his place in the history of English Deism stands in need of some clarification. When *The Religion of Nature Delineated* appeared in 1724, English Deism had already attained to a mature age. Exactly a hundred years earlier, in 1624, Herbert of Cherbury, the "father of English Deism", had published his *Tractatus de Veritate*, in which the five *communes notitiae* of Natural Religion—God, worship, virtue and piety, repentance, and the future life—were derived from the natural reason instead of from Revelation. In 1652, Nathaniel Culverwell, one of the earliest Cambridge Platonists, had published a treatise on the Light of Nature in which he described Reason as "the candle of the Lord", without, however, disputing the necessity of Revelation seeing that Reason had been weakened by the Fall of Man. Like Leah, it was blear-eyed, but not on that account to be despised. Religion must not be considered a bird of prey come to peck out our natural eyes.[13] There is a great deal of anti-clerical rebellion alive in this assertion of the autonomy of reason, yet one may also discern in some protagonists of Natural Religion a tendency to provide a rational foundation for the belief in Revelation. As Hunt observes, the men who first discoursed of the certainty of Natural Religion did so with a good Christian object in mind. They wished to establish the reliability of our natural faculties against the sceptic, and assumed that when this was done, the certainty of the Christian Revelation would follow as a matter of course.[14] In this they

[12] David Hume, *A Treatise of Human Nature*, Vol. II (1890), pp. 235–239.
[13] Cf. John Hunt, *Religious Thought in England*, Vol. II (1871), p. 335.
[14] *Loc. cit.*, p. 333.

were mistaken. In 1704, Toland had published his *Letters to Serena* from which Bishop Berkeley derived the conclusion that Natural Religion inevitably led to materialism, and which provoked his violent reaction to Deism.[15] In the following year (1705), Samuel Clarke, in his Robert Boyle Lectures, presented his famous description of the Four Sorts of Deists, which reflects the variety of view-points into which Deism had shaded off by this time. The Deist of the first type believes in an eternal, infinite, intelligent Being but denies the Divine government of the world. The second subscribes to belief in Providence, but does not allow any difference between the morally good and evil. The third has faith in the just government of the world but denies the immortality of the human soul. The fourth, described as the only "true Deist", believes in God, Providence, and the immortality of the soul without, however, admitting a Divine Revelation. It is this fourth type of Deist that Clarke hopes to convert.[16]

William Wollaston belongs to neither of the four types of Deists listed by Clarke, notwithstanding the fact that Lord Bolingbroke, himself an unsparing critic of the belief in Revelation, identifies him with the fourth.[17] He believes in God, Providence, and Immortality—articles of faith which he most emphatically underpins by rational arguments in his book on the Religion of Nature—and he does not deny Revelation. On the contrary, he confesses, towards the end of his book, when discussing the future life, that "Here I begin to be very sensible how much I want a guide." But seeing that "the religion of nature is my theme, I must at present content myself with that light which nature affords; my business being, as it seems, only to show what a Heathen philosopher, without any other help, and almost *autodidaktos*, may be supposed to think". He expresses the hope, "that neither the doing of this, nor anything else contained in this *DELINEATION*, can be the least prejudice to any other *true* religion". He makes the point that "whatever is immediately *revealed from God*, must, as well as anything else, be treated as being *what it is*: which cannot be, if it is not treated with the highest regard, *believed* and *obeyed*. That, therefore, which has been so much insisted on by me, and is, as it were, the burden of my song,

[15] Cf. F. F. Heinemann, "Toland and Leibnitz," *The Philosophical Review* (1945), Vol. LIV, p. 438.

[16] *Loc. cit.*, pp. 115–123.

[17] Cf. Lord Bolingbroke, *Works*, Vol. V (1777), p. 363.

is so far from undermining true *revealed religion*, that it rather paves the way for its reception."[18] In spite of Wollaston's protestations of belief in Revelation, his contemporaries felt a measure of uneasiness about the nature of his belief. It hardly reflected the Christian view-point, and seemed to give credence to "any other true religion", as he put it. Moreover, it treated Revelation as a mere historical fact without due regard to the necessity attached to it owing to the corruption of natural reason. Whilst Samuel Clarke had emphasized the aspect of the fall,[19] Wollaston had failed to do so. He had, on the contrary, stressed the self-sufficiency of Reason, and had constructed a system of morality without recourse to Revelation. This, again, was very different from what more orthodox Deists such as Clarke had done. The latter, in his "A Discourse concerning the unalterable Obligations of Natural Religion, and the Truth and Certainty of the Christian Revelation" (1705), had founded morality not so much on the idea of Truth as on rational theology and Revelation. How offensive Wollaston's method must have been to the orthodox may be gauged by the fact that in 1737 the Glasgow Presbytery prosecuted Hutcheson for teaching the heresy that we can have knowledge of good and evil without, and prior to, a knowledge of God.[20] This is what Wollaston, too, had implied by choosing to demonstrate the nature of the good before demonstrating the nature of God.

No wonder then that Wollaston's position had to meet attack from orthodox quarters. So much had his book incurred suspicions of unorthodoxy that John Clarke, the author of his biography and translator of his notes, felt it necessary to vindicate the good name of Wollaston. "It is scarce worthwhile", he remarked at the end of his biographical introduction, "to take any notice of an idle or malicious reflection which has been cast by some over-zealous persons upon this gentleman's memory, as if he had put a slight upon Christianity by laying so much stress upon the obligation of Reason, and Virtue. Or as if he could not have believed alright, because he did not think it necessary to digress from his subject in order to insert his creed. Surely, a suspicion thus founded can

[18] *Loc. cit.*, p. 211.

[19] Revelation is necessary "to recover mankind out of their generally degenerate estate, into a state suitable to the original excellency of their nature", *loc. cit.*, p. 113.

[20] Cf. Rae, *Life of Adam Smith* (1895), pp. 12–13, quoted by Norman Kemp Smith, *Hume's Dialogues concerning Natural Religion* (Oxford, 1935), p. 42, n. 1.

deserve no regard."[21] A similar motive guided the editor of an abridged version of Wollaston's book, which appeared in 1726 (and in a second edition in 1737), under the title "A Compendious View of the Religion of Nature Delineated". From the Preface to this edition we learn that Sir Richard Steele had inspired the compiler to undertake the work as an apologia for Wollaston seeing that one could "not in the least suspect the Author not to have been a Friend to the Christian Institution". In an "Appendix concerning the Christian Religion" (pp. 129–154), the suggestion is put forward that Wollaston must have believed in "some farther light than that which Nature affords". But whilst it is true that he expressly confessed to faith in Revelation, his position can hardly be described as being in harmony with orthodox Christian sentiment. His biographer, John Clarke, says of him that "The love of Truth and Reason made him love Free Thinking, and, as far as the World would bear it, Free Speaking too." He adds that Wollaston "stressed the essential points of Natural Religion and the Christian Revelation".[22] But, in fact, Christianity plays no part whatever in Wollaston's *Religion of Nature*. One may describe his place in English Deism as a position intermediate between the more radical Deists, like Bolingbroke, who attacked Revelation, and the orthodox, like Clarke, who saw in Natural Religion a mere prelude to Revelation.

We suspect that the deeper reasons for Wollaston's remarkable independence from Christian theology lie not so much in his "Free Thinking" as in the influence which Jewish theology exercised upon him. We have so far studiously refrained from making any distinct reference to his intimate acquaintance with Hebrew literature, and endeavoured to place Wollaston within the general setting of English Deism. Let us now turn from Wollaston the Deist to Wollaston the Rabbinic scholar, and see whether the latter may not shed some light on the former. It may be observed that our author has so far escaped the attention of students interested in the subject of Hebrew scholarship among English divines of the period. None of the several studies in the field so much as mentions his name.[23] Nor do we find any

[21] *Loc. cit.*, pp. xxix–xxx.

[22] *Loc. cit.*, pp. xvi–xvii.

[23] Cf. Cecil Roth, *Maimonides and England*, in "Moses Maimonides", ed. I. Epstein (1935), pp. 209–214; S. Levy, *English Students of Maimonides*, in *Miscellanies* IV of the Jew. Hist. Soc. of England; G. H. Box and Leon Roth in their respective essays in *The Legacy of Israel*, ed. Edwyn R. Bevan and Charles Singer.

reference to Wollaston's indebtedness to the Hebraic legacy in any history of English Deism.[24] The present paper may therefore be said to break new ground in tracing the scope and historical significance of Wollaston's Hebrew learning. It may also be considered a tribute, at this late hour, to the scholarship of this once so popular and now almost forgotten philosopher.

Wollaston's *The Religion of Nature Delineated* contains in its footnotes nearly 150 Hebrew quotations and references. They are drawn from an extraordinarily wide range of Hebrew literature, and bear eloquent testimony to the author's Biblical and Rabbinic scholarship. John Clarke, his biographer, did not exaggerate when saying of Wollaston that he had "made himself Master of the Sentiments, Rites, and Learning of the Jews".[25] His interest and proficiency in the Hebrew tongue dates from his early days at Cambridge. Born, in 1659, as a member of an ancient family in Staffordshire, he entered Sidney Sussex College, Cambridge, in 1674, and left it as Master of Arts in 1681. The story is told that at the college he gained some reputation as a scholar, but made an enemy of the College Dean by ridiculing him in an exercise at the schools. The Dean is said to have avenged himself by spreading scandals about his pupil. Once the don told him to write a copy of verses which it was intended to ridicule, but he evaded the issue by writing in Hebrew which no one understood. Naturally, he lost any chance of a fellowship.[26] It may be surmised that Wollaston's interest in Hebrew was stimulated by the great reputation which Cambridge had achieved in the domain of both Biblical and Rabbinic literature. John Lightfoot, who has rightly been described as "the greatest of the Christian Rabbinical scholars",[27] became Vice-Chancellor of Cambridge University in 1653. When Wollaston entered Sidney Sussex College he was still alive, but died a year later (1675). The young undergraduate could therefore hardly have come under his personal influence but may have, none the less, profited from the atmosphere of Hebrew studies created by Lightfoot. Nor could Wollaston have been in personal touch with Isaac Abendana, the noted Anglo-Jewish scholar, who was commissioned by Trinity College to translate the entire

[24] Cf. John Hunt, *loc. cit.*; Leslie Stephen, *English Thought in the Eighteenth Century*.

[25] *Loc. cit.*, p. xv.

[26] Cf. *DNB*, article *William Wollaston.*

[27] Cf. G. H. Box in "Hebrew Studies in the Reformation Period and After" in: *The Legacy of Israel*, p. 356.

Mishnah into Latin. Having completed the manuscript of the work in 1675, he left Cambridge soon afterwards.[28] It is most unlikely that young Wollaston should have made his acquaintance. Who his teachers at Cambridge were is nowhere recorded.[29] The late Dr. Travers Herford suggested the possibility that in Hebrew he was self-taught.[30] However this may be, his familiarity with Rabbinic literature is truly amazing and has about it a natural ease and sureness of touch rarely to be found in non-Jewish writers. Though Wollaston is equally at home in Latin and Greek, his chief interest seems to have lain in Hebrew. In 1690 he published a Paraphrase of *Ecclesiastes*, and among his literary remains were found a Hebrew Grammar; a Specimen Vocabularii Biblico-hebraici; a work entitled "Judaica sive Religionis et Literaturae Judaicae Synopsis"; and a "Treatise relating to the Jews, their Antiquities, Language, etc."[31] It may also be considered characteristic of his fondness for Hebrew that he concludes his *magnum opus* with the Hebrew *notarikon mkʾ vtl*, which John Clarke interpreted to

[28] Cf. Israel Abrahams, *Trans. Jew. Hist. Soc. of England*, VIII, pp. 98–122, quoted by Box, *loc. cit.*, pp. 361–362.

[29] The late Wilfred S. Samuel, in a letter to the present writer, dated 2nd November, 1948, raised the question of Wollaston's possible Jewish contacts in Cambridge. "I like to think", he writes, "that W. W. knew Haham David Nieto in London, but I cannot guess at his Jewish contacts in his early days at Cambridge. He was too late, I fancy, for Isaac Abendana and too early for the Revd. Solomon Lyon. Nor can I call to mind any Jewish converts to Christianity who were scholars whom he is likely to have known."

[30] In answer to an inquiry by the present writer dated 13th December, 1948, as to the possible teachers from whom Wollaston learned his Rabbinics, the late Dr. Travers Herford wrote: "Now about the chief subject of your letter, i.e. the possible teachers from whom Wollaston learned his Rabbinics. I have not been able to search my library as thoroughly as I should have done when I was younger and physically less infirm. I can only, therefore, offer you a few suggestions in the hope that you might find them useful. In the first place, is it likely that Wollaston had any Jewish teachers at all? At the time of his mature life there were (so I have always understood) very few Jews in England outside London and what there were, including those in London, were principally engaged in trade and commerce. There may have been a teacher or teachers among them, but I have never heard of one. It seems much more likely to me that Wollaston was self-taught. The works of John Lightfoot, the most distinguished Hebraist and Rabbinist of Wollaston's contemporaries, were accessible to him. So also were the earlier works of the Buxtorfs and others. If Wollaston wished to master Rabbinics as of course he did, he could, by using such helps as these, learn a great deal without any living teacher. I speak with some experience, for that is how I learned what I know of Rabbinics. I never had a teacher except for elementary Hebrew, and even that I learned mostly by myself. I think that Wollaston may have been in a similar case."

[31] Cf. John Clarke's *Life of Wollaston*. Unfortunately, Wollaston's literary remains are no longer extant. Sidney Sussex College, as Dr. Erwin I. J. Rosenthal of Cambridge informs me, has preserved no mss. of his.

stand for the laudatory phrase, *mī ḵamoḵa ʾēl u-ṭĕhilā la-ʾēl*, "Who is like unto God? And praise unto God." It is also noteworthy that the last letters following upon the Latin inscription which he composed for his own epitaph form another *notarikon*, *ʾʿḥ vʾzʾ*,[32] which may stand for the words *ʾōdeh ʿal ḥasadeḵa ve-ʾazkir ʾamiteḵa*, "I render thanks for all Thy mercies, and shall recall Thy Truth."

Wollaston's unpublished literary remains are, unfortunately, no longer available to us, but we possess ample evidence of his wide Hebrew reading in the footnotes of his *The Religion of Nature*. One may reconstruct, from the numerous Hebrew references which they contain, the Rabbinical library on which Wollaston was able to draw. It is, however, not always easy to determine the source of a quotation seeing that in many instances all reference to either the title of the book or the name of the author is omitted.[33] Even when a reference is given, it mentions, as a rule, only the bare title or the author's name without troubling to quote "chapter and verse". Only in three cases out of almost 150 is the reference a precise one.[34] Again, in quoting names of books or authors, Wollaston employs the utmost economy. Such names as are given appear in but the scantiest abbreviation.[35] One sympathizes with

[32] John Clarke records in his Preface to the seventh and eighth editions of Wollaston's book the epitaphs composed by him for his and his wife's memorials.

[33] A few examples will illustrate Wollaston's strange method of quoting. As to the omission of book titles: R. Gedalya ben Solomon Lipschütz' Commentary, *Ez Shatul*, on Albo's *Sefer Ha-Ikkarim* is quoted as "R. Gedal" ; Joseph Moscato's Commentary, *Kol Jehudah*, on Jehudah Ha-Levi's *Kuzari* is referred to as "Muscatus"; the Biblical Commentaries by Rashi, Abraham Ibn Ezra, Kimhi, Alshek, and Abrabanel are quoted simply by their authors' names. That in itself should occasion no misgivings, but one begins to feel a little anxiety when left in doubts as to the source of quotations given in the name of Abrabanel and Ibn Ezra. Does Wollaston refer to Abrabanel's Commentary on the Bible or to its frequently quoted Commentary *Nahalat Abot* on the *Pirke Abot*? As to Ibn Ezra, which of his works is the source of the quotation, the Biblical Commentary or some other work?

As to the omission of authors' names: Elijah de Vidas' *Reshit Hokmah* is invariably quoted without giving the author's name. A reference to the author occurs once when the name of the book is in turn omitted. As a rule, Wollaston is content to mention either the name of the book or of the author. He regards it obviously as a waste of time to mention both. In most cases, the identity of the author is, of course, apparent from the name of the book quoted.

[34] On p. 69, n. a: Albo b.2.c.19; on p. 71, n. h: *Mor. nebok*. 3.12; on p. 176, n. a: Rashi, *Gen*. XLIV, 10.

[35] A few examples will suffice: *S.B.* (p. 13, n. a) obviously stands for "Sefer Bereshit"; *S. Hhas*. for *Sefer Hasidim*; *Nahh. Ab.* for *Nahalat Abot*; *Qab. ven.* for *Kab we-Naki*; *Men. hamma.* for *Menorat Ha-Maor*; etc. etc. As for the abbreviation of authors' names: Ab. Ez. stands for Abraham Ibn Ezra; R. Is. Abuh. for R. Israel Aboab; etc. Unfortunately the identity of the author referred to as "Is. Lev." (p. 213, n. b) could not be established.

the French and English translators of the notes who made hardly any attempt to trace and check Wollaston's cryptic references.[36] One has to realise that the notes were insufficiently prepared for the press,[37] and that the severe criticism they met from several quarters is largely deserved.[38] At the same time, there is a disarming

[36] Whilst Clarke leaves Wollaston's references to Hebrew sources in their abbreviated and often abstruse manner of quotation, de la Faye, the orientalist responsible for the translation of the notes in Garrigue's French edition, at least spells, in many cases, the names in full and in footnotes of his own, at times, indicates the author. Thus he gives Joseph Albo as the author of "Le Livre des Articles", Saadias Gaon as author of "Le livre Emunah", Abouaf as author of "Menorat hamaor". To Rashi he applies the name "Rabbi Salomon Jarchi", a mistake which was rather common and dates back to the sixteenth century (see JE, Vol. X, p. 324). Occasionally he also indicates the chapter from which Wollaston derived his quotation. Thus, he correctly indicates Mishnah Berakot IX as the source for Wollaston's reference on p. 104 (p. 177 in Garrigue's edition of 1726). He seems to be particularly at home with Maimonides' *Moreh Nebukim*, seeing that he is able to trace Wollaston's frequent quotations from that work. But apart from this, no serious effort is made to check the Hebrew references in Wollaston's Notes.

[37] In fairness to the author, it has to be pointed out that the book was not originally intended for a wider public. According to the "Advertisement" prefixed to the 1724 (anonymous) edition, "A few copies of this book, tho not originally intended to be published, were printed off in the year 1722, but, it being transcribed for the press hastily, many *errata* and mistakes got into it, which could not all be presently observed." In view of "some talk of a piratical design" upon the extant copies of the book, the author "thought fit to reprint it himself, more correctly". Cf. also the concluding paragraph of the work (p. 218) where it is said distinctly, "I have also printed a few copies of this Sketch, not with any design to make it public, but merely to save the trouble of transcribing."

It has also to be borne in mind that the book is addressed to one who had expressed a desire to hear the author's thoughts on the subject, and was likely to appreciate the notes even in their incomplete state. Wollaston is quite explicit on this point when addressing his friend in these terms: "At the foot of the page I have in some places subjoined a few little strictures principally of antiquity, after the manner of annotations: such as, when I came to revise these sheets, I could recollect upon the sudden (in a footnote: Some more were added in the second impression); having no commonplace book to help me, nor thought of any such thing before that time. They may serve sometimes a little to explain the text; and sometimes to add weight; but chiefly to divert you, who know very well how to improve any the least hint out of the Ancients, and I fear will want to be diverted."

[38] One need not take too seriously the rude remarks made by John Clarke, Master of the Public Grammar School in Hull, in his *An Examination of the Notion of Moral Good and Evil* (pp. 2–3): "The Latin and Greek Quotations are generally very little to the purpose. But what he could mean by his frequent Quotations from the Rabbinical Writers, especially upon such a subject, unless it was to make a Parade of his great Reading in a sort of Authors remarkable for nothing but Stupidity and Lying, must be the Wonder of every Man of Sense that reads him. He knew very well what kind of Character the Rabbis have amongst the learned, and how well they deserve it, and must be sensible, tho' their Character was the reverse of what it is, how little to the Purpose of his Readers it was to trouble them with Quotations, they would none of them, or not one in ten thousand understand."

Garrigue (*loc. cit.*, pp. 411–412) quotes this malicious attack and takes up the cudgels

charm about the informality and almost privacy of these notes in which Wollaston's associative memory rather than purposive research is at work. Though meant for the sake of illustration rather than argument, they reveal, at the same time, the sources and background of his thinking. Above all, they make it strikingly clear how deeply he is steeped in Rabbinic literature, and how familiar he is with its very idiom of expression. Sentences in the vernacular are freely interspersed with Rabbinic phraseology and, in one case, the whole note consists in the curt yet allusive formula *maskīl yaḇīn*, employed in the manner of Abraham Ibn Ezra.[39] Fortunately, we have been able to trace the exact sources of the greater part of Wollaston's Hebrew references,[40] and thus to make possible a correct estimate of his Rabbinic scholarship and its influence on his thinking.

WOLLASTON'S HEBREW REFERENCES

There is nothing particularly striking about Wollaston's quotations from the Hebrew Bible of which there are altogether twelve, drawn from Genesis, Deuteronomy, Kings, Jeremiah, Psalms, and Proverbs. But our interest is immediately aroused when we find him quoting on two occasions the *Targum Onḳelos* and, in many instances, some of the medieval commentators on the Bible. He is familiar with Rashi, and also knows the Commentaries of Abraham Ibn Ezra, David Kimḥi, Levi ben Gerson, Isaac Abrabanel, and Moses Alshek. He quotes Ibn Ezra's interesting observation "that *aḇah* in Hebrew is to will, in Arab, to nill (though in Arab the word is written *aḇī*): and in another place, that the same word even in the same language sometimes signifies *daḇar vě-hofěḵō*, a thing and its contrary". The quotation is given in support of his theory that "Words are but arbitrary signs of our ideas" whereas facts (i.e. actions) "are the very conception of the mind brought forth", and therefore, "the most natural and express

[39] Page 120, n. c.

[40] A table of Wollaston's Hebrew References and, where traceable, of their sources is set out in an Appendix to the present paper [not reproduced in this Volume].

---

on behalf of Wollaston and the Rabbis. His apologia will be referred to in another context. But even he could not help criticizing the Notes as partly useless, almost in their entirety badly digested, and lacking in preciseness of quotation. He complains that passages are cited without naming their sources, and that furthermore, authors' names are almost in every instance unrecognizable through abbreviation.

representations of them".[41] One single quotation is from Kimḥi's Commentary, and another from Levi ben Gerson's interpretation of Ex. 3:17. Abrabanel is cited six times in all. In one instance Wollaston quotes him in support of the idea that the precept of honouring parents is "commonly following, or rather adhering to that of worshipping the Deity". In a footnote he remarks that "We indeed usually divide the two tables of Moses's law so, that the fifth commandment (Honour thy father and thy mother) falls in the second: but the Jews themselves divide them otherwise." After mentioning the views of Philo and Josephus, he continues, "Abrabanel reckons the fifth commandment the last of the first table: and says their *Hhakamin* do so: and in the offices of that nation these commandments are mentioned as written *ᶜal ha-luḥōt ḥamishā ḥasmishā*."[42] From Alshek's Commentary he quotes a brief remark on Gen. 26:8. In addition to the exegetical works mentioned, he cites, in two instances, the commentary on Proverbs called *Kab we-Naḳi* (22:6; 30:19).

From the quotations listed we may draw the inference that Wollaston made use of at least two different editions of the so-called "Rabbinic Bible". He must have had recourse to the first edition of this type which was published by Felix Pratensis at Venice in 1517–1518, and was the only one to contain the commentary *Kab we-Naḳi* on Proverbs.[43] He must also have used one of the Bomberg editions of the Bible which contained Ibn Ezra's *Commentary on the Torah* (absent from the afore-mentioned edition). He may have consulted the Basle edition of 1618–1619, arranged by the elder Buxtorf. Levi ben Gersons' *Commentary on the Torah* he could have known only from the Mantua edition of 1476–1480. For the *Biblia Rabbinica* published at Amsterdam which contains this *Commentary* commenced to appear only as late as 1724, the year in which Wollaston's book was published. Alshek's commentary, called *Torat Mosheh*, he obviously knew in the Venice edition of 1601.

The only grammatical work quoted by Wollaston is Elijah Levita's *Tishbi*, a dictionary of 712 difficult words, which he may have used either in the Basle edition of 1529 or in the Hebrew–Latin one of 1541, arranged by the Christian Hebraist Paul Fagius.

We now turn our attention to Wollaston's quotations from *Mishnah*, *Talmud*, and halakic works.

[41] Pages 12–13. [42] p. 164. [43] Cf. *JE*, Vol. III, pp. 158–160.

Being familiar with Rabbinic Hebrew, he had no need to resort to the Latin translation of the Mishnah which Surenhusius had brought out in Amsterdam (1698–1703). He seems to have been quite at home with the tractate *Abot*, which by its very nature was able to supply him with the type of ethical maxims required in support of his statements of moral truths. Thus he cites the injunction, "Judge not thy neighbour until thou art come into his place" (*Abot* 2, 5) in corroboration of his thesis that "Whatever is either reasonable or understandable in B with respect to C, would be just the same in C with respect to B, if the case was inverted" whence it follows that a good way to know what is right or wrong in relation to other men is to consider what we should take things to be were *we* in their circumstances".[44] These occur in all six quotations from *Abot*. Wollaston read this tractate—referred to by him as P. Ab(oth)—not only by itself but also with the help of Isaac Abrabanel's lucid commentary, *Naḥalat Abot* (Venice, 1544). He quotes this commentary five times. It served him, incidentally, as a mine of information on Talmudic and Midrashic topics not otherwise accessible to him. Thus the Rabbinic doctrine that "all souls were created in the beginning" is referred to as "an opinion mentioned in *Nahh. ab. & al.* often".[45]

In addition to the afore-mentioned quotations from *Abot*, we meet five more from other tractates of the Mishnah. Having put the case for the efficacy of prayer in spite of "the order of events, proceeding from the settlement of nature", he is confident to have answered the statement of the Mishnah in *Berakot* (9, 3), which calls a man's crying to God over what is past "a vain prayer". To Wollaston it is not vain at all. He holds that "the prayers which good men offer to the All-knowing God, and the neglect of others, may find fitting effect already forecasted in the course of nature".[46] From the Mishnah in *Peah* (5, 4) he quotes the case of a person rendered poor in a certain situation, though in fact a rich man (*ᶜanī bĕ-ōtā shaᶜā*), which serves him as an illustration of the principle that "In order to judge rightly what any thing is . . . the whole description of the thing ought to be taken in."[47] That the rather intricate and technical tractate *Peah* should have yielded Wollaston this apt and felicitous quotation testifies to a high degree of familiarity with the Mishnah. Other quotations are taken from *Ḳiddushin* (1, 1), *Soṭah* (9, 9), and *Abodah ẓarah* (4, 7).

[44] Page 129. [45] Page 89, n. c. [46] Page 104. [47] Page 19.

The fact that Wollaston quotes a fair number of Talmudic sayings cannot be taken as evidence of his direct acquaintance with the Talmud. More than once he mentions such *dicta* in the name of medieval authorities in whose works he found them cited and discussed. In other instances he vaguely refers to them as sayings of "The Jews" or of "The Jewish Doctors". Sometimes no reference to any source is given. We must assume that in all these instances his knowledge of Talmudic lore is derived from medieval sources. Thus, the Talmudic discussion of the problem of Divine Justice—summed up in the phrase *ẓaddīq ve-rāᶜ lo*—is quoted not in the name of the Talmud (*b. Berakot* 7*a*) but of no less than six medieval authors.[48] Certain Talmudic sayings about disciplining one's tongue and "other sayings of this kind" he found collected in the work of a medieval moralist.[49] Probably his knowledge of the Talmudic phrase *ăbaq lĕshōn ha-rāᶜ*—cited in another context[50] without any reference—is derived from that particular work. He translates it, "To *throw dust* upon a man's reputation by innuendos, ironies, etc.", which is not far removed from the original meaning of the phrase, and has the advantage of happily preserving the metaphor. The Talmudic *dictum*, "God sitteth and feedeth all, from the horns of the unicorn even unto the eggs of insects" (*b. Shabbat* 107*b*)—quoted with the accompanying reference, "as the Jews speak"—[51] is obviously known to him from a chapter of a medieval work from which other quotations occur on the same page in the subsequent footnote. We meet with about twenty second-hand citations of Talmudic phrases and statements in Wollaston's book. He is not always impressed with the Rabbinic point-of-view, and does not withhold occasional criticism. Thus he described the severity with which the Talmudic sages condemn every kind of idle talk as "superstitious preciseness which carries things too far".[52] In another context he approves of the rabbinic principle of "erecting a fence around the Law", but proceeds to qualify his approval: "To appoint things as the Jewish Doctors have done, to be *sĕyyag la-torā*, or *kĕdē le-harḥīq et ha-ᵓadam min ha-ᶜaberā*, would be right if they were judiciously chosen, and not so very particular and trifling." He admits, however, that "some of their cautions are certainly just", and adduces as an example those bearing on sexual relationships.[53]

[48] Page 110, n. a. [49] Page 171, n. b. [50] Page 143, n. g.
[51] Page 95, n. a. [52] Page 171, n. b. [53] Page 175, n. a.

Of halakic works Wollaston knows Moses Maimonides' great code, the *Mishneh Torah*, and Joseph Karo's *Shulḥan ᶜAruk* with Moses Isserles' *Supplements*. He is particularly interested in the former work which must have appealed to him as a systematic and lucid presentation of the entire body of Jewish Law and doctrine. He quotes from it on six occasions: once from *Hilkot Deᶜot* (6, 8); twice from *Hilkot Teshubah* (3, 14; 5, 1, 3); three times from *Hilkot Tefillah* (4, 15; 5, 5; 5, 9); once from *Hilkot Berakot* (1, 7) and, again, once from *Hilkot Ishut* (14). It is worth observing that he allows his own views on certain matters of practical import to be influenced by halakic rules which he found laid down in Maimonides' Code. Thus, he suggests that private prayer should be spoken no louder "than just to make it audible to our selves", and remarks in a footnote: "This we find often among the *Dinim* of the Jews." He quotes in support of this statement two passages from Maimonides. The first one (*Hilkot Berakot*, 1, 7) he finds cited and insisted upon by a medieval moralist (R. Eliezer Azikri); the second (*Hilkot Tefillah* 5, 9) he ventures slightly to amend on the basis of its quotation in the *Shulḥan ᶜAruk* (*Oraḥ Ḥayyim* 101, 2).[54] His other references to the latter work are to *Oraḥ Ḥayyim* 98, 1 (concerning devotion in prayer[55] and Eben Ha-ᶜEzer (concerning Jewish marriage laws).[56]

Of particular interest is Wollaston's acquaintance with the literature of the medieval Jewish moralists. Here he proves himself at home in a region least known to Christian students of Jewish lore. No more convincing evidence of his proficiency in Jewish learning could be found than the fact that he was sufficiently equipped to explore this difficult terrain in which the ethics and ritual of *Halakah* join hands with mysticism. He is well versed in R. Judah the Hasid's *Sefer Ḥasidim* which so faithfully reflects the asceticism and mystical bent of the circle from which it sprang. Of its two recensions—the one printed in Bologna in 1538, the other preserved in a Parma ms. and published as late as 1891–1893 by Wistinetzki—he knew, of course, only the first one, possibly in the Cracow edition of 1639, or in David Grünhut's Frankfurt edition of 1713. Though an avowed rationalist and by no means a friend of mysticism, he found in this strange book enough that appealed to him as a moral philosopher. He quotes from it nine times. Most of the passages cited paraphrase Talmudic sayings.

[54] Page 123, n. f. [55] Page 124, n. a. [56] Page 157.

Another medieval moralist known to Wollaston is Isaac Aboab I, whose famous and popular work, the *Menorat Ha-Maʾor*, is referred to twice. A great deal of support for his own moral teachings he found also in Eliezer Azikri's *Sefer Ḥaredim* which expresses the devotional fervour of the mystics of sixteenth-century Safed. In this book the attempt is made to catalogue, as it were, the six hundred and thirteen precepts of the Torah plus Rabbinic Law with reference to the organs of the human body engaged in the performance of the *Mizwot.* This may be a queer idea. But Wollaston seems to be impressed by it. For in connection with his discussion of the "Truth belonging to a Private Man", he makes the following observations: "He must subject his sensual inclinations, his bodily passions, and the motions of all his members to reason", and adds in a footnote: "The author of *S. Hhared* reckons eight, the right use of which comprehends all practical religion: the heart, the eye, the mouth, nose, ear, hand, foot, and *roʾsh ha-gĕviyā*. The duties respecting these are the subject of that (not bad) book."[57] As in the case of the *Sefer Ḥasidim*, he ignores the mystical elements of the book, and draws exclusively on ethical and devotional maxims. There are, apart from the general reference we have just noted, seven quotations from it. They deal with marital relations, respect for parents, the sanctity of truth (permitting a white lie only in the furtherance of peace), and devotion in prayer. Similar in kind are his (five) quotations from another, rather more intricate work of the Safed school, i.e. the *Reshit Ḥokmah* by Elijah ben Moses de Vidas, a book steeped in kabbalistic thought which Wollaston could not have found easy reading. It is all the more remarkable that he should have been able to draw from it a number of references relevant to his own purposes.

We now come to the most important class of Hebrew references in Wollaston's work, i.e. his quotations from medieval Jewish philosophy, a field closely akin to his own domain of rational theology. They clearly prove how intimate was his acquaintance with the major works of that branch of literature. Some of those works had been made available to Christian scholars in Latin translations. Johannes Buxtorf II had rendered into Latin the *Moreh Nebukim* of Maimonides (*Doctor Perplexorum*, Basle, 1629) and the *Kuzari* of Judah Ha-Levi (*Liber Cosri*, Basle, 1660). Wollaston had no need to resort to these translations. Saadya Gaon's

[57] Page 169, n. c.

magnum opus, the *Sefer Ha-Emunot We-Ha-Deᶜot*, must have been known to him in either the Constantinople edition of 1652 or in the rather poor Amsterdam edition of 1647. He quotes this work four times. Baḥya Ibn Pakudah's *Sefer Ḥobot Ha-Lebabot* is cited twice. It is impossible to suggest which of the numerous editions of this extremely popular treatise he may have used. We are in a more fortunate position in regard to the *Kuzari*. From his reference to a remark by Muscatus, we gather that he read the *Kuzari* in the Venice edition of 1594 which contains Jehudah Moscato's commentary, *Ḳol Jehudah*. He quotes two passages from the text of the *Kuzari* itself. Much more frequent are Wollaston's citations of Maimonides' celebrated *Moreh Nebukim*. They number fourteen in all, and cover substantial elements of Maimonides' theology. But honours are almost evenly shared with Joseph Albo whose *Sefer Ha-Iḳḳarim*, the classical work on Jewish dogmatics, is quoted no less than thirteen times. By once referring to "R. Gedal's words", he betrays the fact that he studied the *Sefer Ha-Iḳḳarim* in the Venice edition of 1618 which contains the commentary called *Eẓ Shatul* by Gedalayah ben Solomon Lipschütz. Finally, our author is at home with Manasseh ben Israel's half philosophic, half mystical treatise *Nishmat Ḥayyim*, from which he quotes twice.

There is hardly any important topic in Wollaston's exposition of Natural Religion in which the influence of medieval Jewish philosophy does not make itself felt in some degree. A brief analysis of the quotations referred to will substantiate this point. The first Section of his book deals with the nature of moral good and evil. It will be remembered that its main thesis stresses the essential identity of the good and the true. In this connection he quotes in the name of Elijah de Vidas' *Reshit Ḥokmah* the pregnant formula, "God is called Truth" (*ha-qadōsh bārūḵ hūʾ niqrāʾ emmet*), which goes back to Albo (*Iḳḳarim* II, 27) and, ultimately, to the Talmudic *dictum*, "The seal of the Holy One, blessed be He, is Truth." He finds a kind of parallel to it in Chrysostom who "defines truth in the same words which philosophers apply to Deity".[58] He adduces support for his notion of truth as the basis of morality also from Maimonides' statement that "a good man acts in accordance with the truth for the sake of the truth".[59] and mentions in vindication of the overriding power of truth "a

[58] Page 15, n. a. [59] Page 15, n. f.

passage somewhere in *S. Iqqar*". (Cf. *Iḳḳarim* II, 28), where it is said "that he who worships an Angel *mi-ẓad mā hū' shĕlīaḥ h[a-shem]* (as being what he is, i.e. the messenger of God) is not guilty of idolatry".[60] In asserting yet another fundamental principle of morality, that of Free Will, he quotes from Cicero on the one hand, and from Maimonides and Abrabanel on the other.[61] In another place, he records Albo's view (*Iḳḳarim* IV, 5) that of human actions "some are free, some necessary, and some made up of necessity and freedom".[62] In discussing Aristotle's notion of the good as the middle of two extremes, he seems to be impressed by Albo's criticism of it (*Iḳḳarim* I, 8), but remarks that the difficulty pointed out had been felt by Aristotle himself and that "Therefore R. Albo might have spared that censure."[63]

Of infinitely greater significance than the more or less casual references noted so far are Wollaston's quotations relating to the subject of the existence, attributes, and providence of God. Here the influence of the medieval Jewish authors bears on the very substance of his thought. His proof for the existence of a First Mover is clearly modelled on the medieval Jewish discussion of Aristotle's and Ibn Sīnā's arguments. Having quoted Aristotle and his neoplatonic commentator Simplicius, he remarks that "Not only those Arabian philosophers called Hebr. *mĕdabbĕrim*, Arab. *al-mutakallimūn*, but many of the elder Jews have agreed with the Greeks in this matter, and added arguments of their own." He cites at some length the various forms which the demonstration of the impossibility of an infinite series took in a number of Jewish writers such as Saadya, Jehudah Ha-Levi, Maimonides and Albo.[64] Strangely enough, he omits all reference to the treatment of the subject by the Christian schoolmen, and mentions only an argument adduced by Justin Martyr.[65] In trying to elucidate his point that "an infinite succession of effects will require an infinite efficient, or a cause infinitely effective", he offers for an illustration the case of "a chain hung down out of the heavens from an unknown height", and adds in a footnote: "This matter might be illustrated by other similitudes (even *shalshelet ha-qabbalah* [the chain of tradition] might serve for one): but I shall set down one more . . . It occurs in *Hhob. halleb.* and afterwards in *Resh. Hhokm.* Suppose a row of blind

[60] Page 14, n. b. [61] Page 7, n. e. [62] Page 64, n. c.
[63] Page 25, n. b. [64] Page 66, n. a; 67, n. c. [65] Page 66, n. a.

men, of which the last laid his hand upon the shoulder of the man next before him, he on the shoulder of the next before him, and so on till the foremost grew to be quite out of sight; and somebody asking, what guide this string of blind men had at the head of them, it should be answered that they had no guide nor any head but one held by another, and so went on, *ad infin.*, would any rational creature accept this for a just answer? Is it not to say that infinite blindness (or blindness, if it be infinite) supplies the place of sight, or of a guide?"[66] The simile quoted by Wollaston is taken from Baḥya's *Ḥobot Ha-Lebabot* (1, 2), which, in turn, had borrowed it from Islamic sources.[67] It was used in illustration of the contrast between those whose religion rests on the "blind" acceptance of tradition, and those who profess their faith on the basis of philosophic conviction. The former must be guided by the latter. Wollaston, who obviously relished the simile, turned it to good advantage for his own purpose.

Having demonstrated the existence of a Prime Mover, Wollaston proceeds to interpret it as "necessary existence": "A Cause or Being that has in nature no superior cause, and therefore (by the terms) is also unproduced and independent, must be self-existent: i.e. existence must be essential to him; or, such is his nature that he cannot but be."[68] He derives this concept entirely from medieval Jewish sources, as his references show. After briefly referring to Aristotle, he mentions that "The Arabic philosophers, Maimonides, Albo, & *al. pass.* teach all that God exists *necessarily*." He quotes repeatedly the medieval Hebrew term by which God is designated as *meḥuyyaḇ ha-meẓiʾūt* in contradistinction to created being that is *efsḥar ha-meẓiʾūt*. He records the classical interpretation of the *Tetragrammaton* as indicating God's necessary existence. He cites Philo, Abrabanel and Gersonides to this effect, purposely omitting "others who write after the same manner". As an interesting parallel to the Biblical name of God, he mentions Plutarch's saying that "Thou art" is the most complete appellation of Deity.[69]

[66] Page 67 and n. d.

[67] Cf. F. Dieterici, *Die Philosophie der Araber im X. Jahrhundert*, Erster Teil, Einleitung und Makrokosmos (Leipzig, 1876), p. 90. A. S. Yahuda, in his Introduction to the edition of Baḥya's Arabic text (Leiden, 1912), p. 110, n. 1, points to Luke 6:39, as the source of Baḥya's simile, without noticing the more immediate parallel in the Islamic source mentioned.

[68] Page 68.

[69] Page 68, n. a.

Wollaston does not enter deeply into the medieval discussion of the term "necessary existence" nor does he mention al-Fārābī's and Ibn Sīnā's distinction of essence and existence, which lies at the root of that term. In identifying the *uncaused* existence of the Prime Mover with *necessary* existence, he lays himself open to the criticism which Ibn Rushd levelled against Ibn Sīnā.[70] But he does not seem to be aware of the fallacy of this identification. For him, the argument for the existence of a Prime Mover lays the ground also for God's necessary Being. He adds, however, a second argument which, upon closer examination, reveals itself as a curious combination of Maimonides' third proof for the existence of God, and Saadya's demonstration of the impossibility that the world should have created itself. He argues that there must be such a necessary Being, "For (beside what has been said already) if there was not at least *one* such Being, nothing could be at all."[71] His quotation from Maimonides' third proof makes it clear that the nerve of the argument is ontological rather than cosmological. "Something must be *meḥuyyab̲ ha-meẓiʾūt* otherwise *lōʾ yihĕyeh dab̲ar nimẓāʾ kĕlal.*"[72] But he immediately gives it a new aspect by adding, "For the universe could not produce itself, and then produce the rest: because this is supposing a thing to act before it is." He refers to this latter argument as "a very old one" which he found in Saadya and Baḥya.[73] Unfortunately, it spoils the logical impeccability of the proof to which it is joined. On the other hand, this combining of arguments furnishes striking evidence of Wollaston's familiarity with medieval Jewish authors. Again, the absence of any reference to the Christian schoolmen has to be noted.

From God's necessary existence Wollaston derives the notion of His eternity. But what do we mean by eternity? He makes the point that "Adequate ideas of eternity and infinity are above us", and mentions that "Many philosophers therefore have thought themselves obliged to deny that God exists *in time*."[74] After a reference to Plato and Plutarch, he quotes Maimonides' statement that "there can be no relation between Him and time" (*Moreh* I, 52), and recalls that "Albo has a whole Chapter to show that He

[70] Cf. de Boer, *Die Widersprüche der Philosophie nach Al-Gazzali und ihr Ausgleich durch Ibn Rosd* (1894), p. 42; Fritz Bamberger, *Das System des Maimonides* (Berlin, 1935), pp. 29–31.

[71] Page 68. [72] *Ibid.*, n. b. [73] *Ibid.*, n. c. [74] Page 69 and n. a.

is not subject to time" (*Iḳḳarim* II, 18–19). Again, he does not elaborate details such as the definition of time according to Aristotle, which underlies Maimonides' statement, nor is he aware of Crescas' opposition to it. But he makes an interesting observation on Albo's distinction between two kinds of time, one being "unmeasured duration, which is conceived only in thought and has perpetual existence, having existed prior to the creation of the world", and "time which is numbered and measured by the motion of the sphere". The former is called "abstract time" (*ha-zĕman be-shilūaḥ*), the latter is, in Albo's view, designated by the rabbinic expression, "the order of time" (*seder zĕmanīm*). Albo himself distinctly declares that God is independent of time in both senses, and Wollaston seems to have understood him correctly. But he interprets him to mean that the Rabbis would exempt God only from being subject to the created "order of time", not from participating in "abstract time", which is, after all, not to be considered "true time". Wollaston feels that such a limitation of the use of the term "time" does not help us to clarify the problem of God's relation to time. He finally quotes Albo's saying that "we cannot say of God that He is older to-day than He was in the time of David or when He created the world".[75]

Wollaston's outline of the attributes of God follows in large measure the medieval Jewish pattern. In demonstrating the unity of God, he mentions that Maimonides "having proved that there must be some Being who exists necessarily, or whose existence is necessary *bi-b̲ĕḥinat ᶜazmō*, proceeds from this necessity of existence to derive incorporeity, absolute simplicity, perfection, and particularly unity".[76] Wollaston does likewise. He emphatically states that God is but One, and that his manner of existence is not shared by any other being. "If any other could partake with Him in it, He must . . . be deficient and limited."[77] It is remarkable to find Wollaston repeat the stern rejection of any violation of God's Unity which from Saadya onward forms a recurrent theme in medieval Jewish philosophy. Though there is a solitary quotation from Lactantius[78] in support of monotheism, one can hardly reconcile Wollaston's attitude with his supposed faith in the Christian doctrine of the Trinity. Moreover, in the course of his discussion of the nature of God, he emphasizes the point that "there can be no corporeity in God", and that He "exists in a

[75] Page 69, n. a. [76] Page 70, n. c. [77] Page 70. [78] Page, 70 n. e.

manner that must be uniform, always one and the same, and in nature unchangeable".[79] He also repudiates every kind of pantheism. God is neither infinite space nor infinite duration.[80] He makes a spirited attack on Spinoza, and deplores the fact that "such gross Atheism as this should ever be fashionable".[81] As to the Rabbinic designation of God as "Place" (*Maqōm*), he quotes the saying of "the ancients" which declares that "God is the place of the world, but the world is not His Place". He explains that the sentence merely expresses God's "omnipresence and immensity", though he realizes that "there is a Cabbalistic reason assigned too".[82]

Wollaston agrees with Maimonides in yet another important aspect concerning the doctrine of Divine attributes. He makes the point that "when we speak of the internal essential attributes of God positively, as that He is omniscient, omnipotent, eternal, &c, the intent is only to say that there is no object of knowledge or power, which He does not know or cannot do, He exists without beginning and end, &c. . . . That is, we may speak thus without pretending to comprehend His nature."[83] Here we have clearly a restatement of Maimonides' doctrine of negative attributes, though Wollaston does not distinctly refer to his Jewish source. There are other instances of direct dependence on Maimonides without express acknowledgment. Thus, Wollaston takes care to explain that "When we ascribe mercy to God, or implore His mercy, it must not be understood to be mercy like that which is called compassion in us."[84] This is an echo of Maimonides' words in *Moreh* I, 54. These and other instances only illustrate the fact that Wollaston's mind is deeply and often unconsciously saturated with medieval Jewish thought.

Wollaston's treatment of the problem of Divine Providence—perhaps the most fascinating part of the book—is, again, largely influenced by Maimonides' discussion of the subject. Like Maimonides, who in this respect follows Aristotle, he sees a Divine Providence at work in the "laws and provisions" of Nature.[85] He quotes from *Moreh* III, 17, the Talmudic statement that "God sitteth and feedeth all, from the horns of the unicorns even unto the eggs of insects",[86] which, along with similar Rabbinic sayings, Maimonides explains to mean that Providence takes care

[79] Page 74. [80] *Ibid.* [81] Page 76, n. c. [82] Page 75, n. a.
[83] Page 94. [84] Page 115. [85] Page 95. [86] Page 95, n. a.

of the species of all living creatures, not of their individual members. Wollaston finds no difficulty in associating himself with this interpretation of the purposiveness of Nature as evidence of a general Providence. He is not so sure whether to agree with Maimonides that particular cases relating to inanimate or irrational beings such as "a leaf's falling from a tree, a spider's catching a flie, etc.", are to be regarded as due to pure chance. He wonders how it is possible to separate them in every instance from the cases of rational beings. Moreover, he considers it difficult to comprehend what *miqrē gamūr*, *perfect accident*, is.[87]

Having strongly asserted, and amply illustrated, the "fact" that there is a general Providence at work in the universe, Wollaston poses the question "how to account for that *providence* which is called *particular*; or that which respects (principally) *particular* men".[88] Like Maimonides, he takes it as certain that there is such a Providence, seeing that "rational beings and free agents are capable of doing and deserving well or ill".[89] But while Maimonides makes the degree of providential care dependent on a man's measure of intellectual perfection, and makes allowance, in exceptional cases, for the suspension of natural laws by way of miracle,[90] Wollaston is concerned to explain the operation of particular Providence within the framework of general Providence. "If a good man be passing by an infirm building, just in the article of falling, can it be expected that God should suspend the force of gravitation till he is gone by, in order to his deliverance; or can we think it would be increased, and the fall hastened, if a bad man was there, only that he might be caught, crushed and made an example? . . . In short, may we expect miracles?"[91] Wollaston mentions that "some have talked to this purpose". He quotes Albo and Abrabanel, and records in the name of Isaac Aboab a statement which goes back to Nahmanides: it expresses the view that "the good or evil which happens to a man in this world by way of reward or punishment is in fact due to the operation of a miracle, and represents a mystery, notwithstanding the impression that it happens in the natural course of things."[92] Wollaston does not accept this view-point. He suggests that "It is not impossible that such laws of nature, and such a series of causes and effects may be originally designed that not only general

[87] Page 95, n. b.
[88] Page 98.
[89] *Ibid.*
[90] *Moreh Nebukim* III, 18–19; II, 29.
[91] Page 99.
[92] Page 99, n. e.

provisions may be made for the several species of beings, but even particular cases, at least many of them, may also be provided for without innovations or alterations in the course of nature." He realizes that "this amounts to a prodigious scheme", but considering "what a Being God is, incomprehensibly great and perfect", one cannot deny "such an adjustment of things to be within His power".[93] Again falling back upon Maimonides, Wollaston makes it clear that God's manner of knowing must be "different from and infinitely transcending all the modes of apprehending things, which we know anything of".[94] He quotes Maimonides' words to this effect,[95] and mentions the striking utterance that "To attempt to comprehend the manner of God's knowing is the same as to endeavour to be ourselves God."[96] As to the possibility of God foreknowing things without abolishing the freedom of will, he once more relies on Maimonides' answer to the problem. After quoting from *Moreh* III, 20, he adds, "Much might be inserted upon this subject (out of *Abarb.* particularly) which I shall omit."[97]

Wollaston is at pains to show that his concept of Providence does not preclude the efficacy of prayer. God foreknows the petitions of man, and designs the course of happenings accordingly. "Thus the prayers which good men offer to the All-knowing God, and the neglect of others, may find fitting effect already forecasted in the course of nature."[98] He quotes Albo's statement that Prayer "is a branch growing out of the notion of Providence", and that "Every one who believes in Providence must believe that prayer will help and save him from misfortune."[99] But he also records the saying of the *Sefer Ḥasidim* "that we should not pray for the impossible, or that which is contrary to nature, or the unseemly, or that God should change the world by way of miracle".[100]

Having concluded his arguments for a particular Providence, Wollaston enters into a discussion of the old problem of theodicy. How can belief in a Divine Providence be upheld when we see "that things do not seem to be dealt with according to reason, virtuous and good men very oft labouring under adversity, pains, persecutions, whilst vicious, wicked, cruel men prevail and flourish"?[101] Wollaston mentions that "The Jews, who call this case *ẓaddīq veʾ-rāᶜ lō rashaᶜ vĕ-to\b lo*, have written many things about

[93] Page 103. [94] Page 101. [95] Page 101, n. e. [96] Page 102, n. a. [97] Page 102, n. b.
[98] Page 104. [99] Page 121, n. a. [100] Page 120, n. f. [101] Page 110.

it." He refers to the *Moreh Nebukim*, *Sefer Ha-Iḳḳarim*, *Menorat Ha-Maʾor*, and *Naḥalat Abot.*[102] He adds, "So have the Heathen philosophers too: Seneca, Plutarch, Plotinus, Simplicius." He does not find the answers of either always just. Thus he cannot agree with the Talmudic answer (quoted in the name of *Sefer Ḥasidim* and *Menorat Ha-Maʾor*) which is summed up in the formula *ẓaddiq vĕ-rāᶜ lō ẓaddīq ben rashaᶜ*.[103] He is more in sympathy with the suggestion that sufferings endured by the righteous are in the nature of a test. But he thinks that the way of solving the problem by reference to *gilgul ha-neshamōt* (metempsychosis) or what the Kabbalists call *ᶜibbur* "is worst of all". He quotes this particular solution from Manasseh ben Israel's *Nishmat Ḥayyim.*[104] Among the answers advanced by Wollaston himself is one which he cites in the name of Abrabanel, but which, in fact, derives from the Talmud. He paraphrases the Talmudic statement, *ha-ᶜolam nīdōn aḥar rubō*, by saying that "Men ought to be considered as members of families, nations, mankind, the universe, from which they cannot be separated: and then from the very condition of their being it will appear that . . . the innocent cannot but be sometimes involved in general calamities or punishment, nor the guilty but share in public prosperities."[105] In a previous context he agrees with Maimonides that "There are not more evil than good things in the world, but surely more of the latter."[106]

Wollaston's doctrine of the human soul is, again, indebted to the Jewish philosophers. Having demonstrated the absurdity involved in the assumption of a thinking matter,[107] he examines the suggestion that the soul is a mere faculty of thinking, superadded to certain systems of matter. He dismisses this theory as well, and insists that the soul is a spiritual substance. He argues that if the faculty of thinking were considered inherent in a material substance, that faculty would have to be considered as the substratum of further faculties such as reflecting, comparing, judging, willing, and many more, comprising the sum total of the psychic functions. These latter faculties would thus be in the nature of faculties of a faculty, which cannot be admitted.[108] The reason why this cannot be admitted is not elaborated in the text. But two footnotes illumine the background of Wollaston's thought. One refers to a statement by Locke,[109] the other to one

[102] Page 110, n. a. [103] *Ibid.* [104] *Ibid.* [105] Page 113 and n. f.
[106] Page 71, n. h. [107] Pages 186–9. [108] Pages 189–193. [109] Pages 191, n. a.

by Saadya,[110] who refuted the Kalam doctrine of the soul by using against it the very notion of the Kalam that an accident cannot be the substratum of another accident.[111]

There is reason to believe that Wollaston's treatment of the problem of the soul was greatly stimulated by a perusal of Manasseh ben Israel's treatise on the subject. His insistence on the soul being a substance, not an accident, echoes the elaborate exposition of this theme in the second chapter of the *Nishmat Hayyim*. There is, in addition, a lengthy quotation from the first chapter of that work relating to "that fine body in which the soul is clothed, and from which it is never separated, according to an old tradition".[112] He adds that "Saadya long before him joins to the soul *ᶜeẕem daq*; which he says is *daq* (*yoter ẕak̲*) *min ha-galgalīm*, etc."[113] The Saadya passage referred to also occurs in the *Nishmat Ḥayyim* (II, 4), but does not bear the meaning which Wollaston mistakenly attributes to it. Saadya does not "join" a subtle body to the soul but conceives the soul itself to be a bodily substance, only "finer, clearer, purer, and simpler than the substance even of celestial spheres".[114] Manasseh ben Israel, however, does suggest that the spiritual substance of the soul has for its vehicle a subtle material body which remains united with it even after death. This notion of a "spiritual body" seems to be derived from the neoplatonic concept of *pneuma* as a kind of mediator between body and soul. Wollaston himself quotes a passage from Hierocles, the neoplatonic teacher at the school of Alexandria, who distinguished between our mortal body and the fine, spiritual (pneumatic) body which communicates life to the former.[115] He adopts this notion from Hierocles and, particularly, from Manasseh ben Israel, in whose *Nishmat Ḥayyim* he found "much concerning that *fine body* in which the soul is clothed",[116] and he does so for two reasons. Firstly, it helps him to explain the survival of the soul long after its separation from the body: there still remains, connected with the soul, some kind of body, i.e. that "fine vehicle" which prevents death from reducing the soul to a state of absolute insensibility and inactivity.[117] Secondly, it offers a solution to the problem as to how the soul, being a spiritual substance, can act upon the

[110] Page 192, n. a.

[111] Cf. Saadya Gaon, *The Book of Doctrines and Beliefs*, ed. Alexander Altmann (Oxford, 1946), p. 142, n. 8.

[112] Page 197, n. a.

[113] *Ibid.*

[114] Cf. Saadya, *loc. cit.*, p. 146.

[115] Page 197, n. a.

[116] *Ibid.*

[117] Pages 196–9.

material body. Wollaston seems to disregard both Descartes' theory of "vital spirits" as a medium of contact between body and soul, and the famous doctrine of the "two clocks" which Geulincx had invented and which had been borrowed by Leibniz. He revives, instead, the concept of a "fine body" and interprets it as "some refined and spirituous vehicle, which the soul doth immediately inform; with which it sympathises; by which it acts, and is acted upon; to which it is vitally and inseparably united".[118]

Finally, Wollaston draws on Jewish sources in describing the "difference of human souls with respect to perfection and imperfection". It lies, in his opinion, "in their different degrees and habits of reasonableness or unreasonableness."[119] He remarks that "The Jews, who generally say that by the practice of religion the soul acquires perfection and life eternal, lay such a stress upon *habits* of piety that R. Albo makes the effect of giving 1,000 zuzin in charity at once by no means equal to that of giving one zuz and repeating it 1000 times."[120] His last Hebrew quotation relates to the immortality of the soul achieved by piety and reason. It blends into a strange unity the view-points held by traditionalists and rationalists respectively. Whoever the author may have been to whom Wollaston refers as "Is. Lev.", the sentence he quotes in his name admirably reflects his own attitude of faith in Reason and a godly life. Translated into English, the sentence runs as follows: "He who fulfils the commandment of God will achieve good understanding (*sekel tob*), and the reward of true understanding is the survival of the soul after the body has perished, its attachment to the Active Intellect (!), and the enjoyment of Life everlasting."[121]

It will have become evident from the foregoing account how closely Wollaston, the English Deist, is related to Wollaston, the Rabbinic scholar, and how much the former is indebted to the latter. No other figure in English Deism shows a similar acquaintance with, and appreciation of, the legacy of Jewish thought. Culverwell, in his treatise on "The Light of Nature" (1652), is outspokenly hostile and misinformed. In his view, the Jews, like the sceptics, cast doubt on all the conclusions of philosophy, limiting certainty to what he calls "an oriental tradition, a Rabbinical dream, a dusty manuscript, a remnant of antiquity, a

[118] Page 197.
[119] Page 213.
[120] Page 213, n. a.
[121] Page 213, n. b.

bundle of testimonies".[122] He has obviously never heard of Maimonides. Bishop Butler, in his famous "Analogy of Religion" (1736), speaks of Judaism as a manifestation of "natural religion",[123] but does not draw on Hebrew sources at all. Others seem to disregard Judaism altogether. It was left to Wollaston's great Hebrew learning to introduce the Jewish legacy into English Deism. The peculiar position which he holds within that movement of thought, and which has been analyzed earlier, is in no small measure determined by the Jewish element in his thinking.

While Wollaston's Rabbinic scholarship is a unique phenomenon in English Deism, it should cause little astonishment if viewed against the background of seventeenth-century Rabbinic learning amongst Christian savants and divines. The pioneering work which the Buxtorfs, father and son, had performed in opening up the study of Rabbinics to Christian scholarship had borne rich fruit. It had stimulated research in the rabbinic field not merely as an adjunct to biblical exegesis but for its own sake. The Christian Hebraists of the sixteenth century—men like Sebastian Muenster, Paul Fagius, and Edward Lively—had studied the Hebrew language and the classical rabbinic commentators of the Bible chiefly with the purpose of vindicating the Christian interpretation of Holy Writ.[124]. Others of a more humanistic bent of mind like Joseph Scaliger (1540–1609) and Isaac Casaubon (1559–1614) were interested in medieval rabbinic literature chiefly as a key to Arabian philosophy.[125] But the position is changed in the seventeenth century. The elder Buxtorf's *Bibliotheca Rabbinica*, and his son's Latin translations of Rabbinic classics had focused attention on the rabbinic legacy as such. In France, Jean Plantavit (1576–1651) had composed his gigantic *Thesaurus Synonymus*

[122] Cf. Hunt, *loc. cit.*, Vol. II, p. 336.

[123] Cf. Joseph Butler, *The Analogy of Religion* II, vii, 49 (ed. W. E. Gladstone, Oxford, 1895, p. 306).

[124] Cf. Erwin I. J. Rosenthal, *Sebastian Muenster's Knowledge and Use of Jewish Exegesis*, in "Essays in honour of the Very Rev. Dr. J. H. Hertz" (1942), p. 352; Siegfried Stein, *Phillipus Ferdinandus Polonus*, *ibid.*, pp. 397ff.; Erwin L. J. Rosenthal, *Edward Lively: Cambridge Hebraist*, in "Essays and Studies Presented to S. A. Cook", ed. D. Winton Thomas (1950), pp. 95ff.

[125] Cf. *Isaaci Casauboni Epistolae insertis ad easdem responsibus* (Rotterdam, 1709), Letter 972 (written in 1591), pp. 568–569, where he asks a friend to procure for him the Venice edition of the *Biblia Hebraica* and also Kimhi's "Michlal et Liber Schoraschim" and, at the same time, confesses that his aim in studying these works is not "ut Hebraeos Rabbinos intelligam . . . sed ut harum ope Arabicam intelligere queam".

Hebraico-Chaldaico Rabbinicus, and also published a *Florilegium Rabbinicum*. In Holland, Peter Cunaeus—a disciple of the famous Johann Drusius (1550–1616)—had written an elaborate work, *De Republica Hebraeorum*, which met with widespread interest, was published in several editions, and appeared, with valuable annotations by Johann Nicolai, in a Leyden edition (1703). In Germany, orientalists like Wilhelm Schickard, Johann F. Frischmuth, and Johann H. Majus[126] made their contributions to the elucidation of rabbinic thought. In England brilliant work was done by Edward Pocoke (1604–1691) and John Lightfoot (1602–1675). Pococke's *Porta Mosis* (1655) made Maimonides' Commentary on the *Mishnah* available in the original Arabic text (in Hebrew characters) side by side with a Latin translation. Lightfoot's *Horae Hebraicae et Talmudicae* was another remarkable piece of scholarship. A veritable tradition of Rabbinic Studies had been created at continental and English universities. Already at about the middle of the seventeenth century, scholars were conscious of this tradition. Thus, John Selden, in the Preface to his great treatise, *De Jure Naturali et Gentium Juxta Disciplinam Ebraeorum* (1665), could write with appreciation of the labours of his predecessors in the field of Rabbinics.[127] That tradition had been enriched and greatly enhanced in prestige by the time Wollaston wrote his works at the beginning of the eighteenth century. That he eagerly absorbed its spirit may be gauged by the fact that among his literary remains —unfortunately lost to us—there were manuscript treatises on subjects closely allied to Rabbinics. Though we are not in a position to assess their degree of scholarship, we may, from our knowledge of the book we have analysed, safely assume a high level of achievement.

Wollaston inherited not only the tradition of Rabbinic learning which we have referred to, but yet another tradition closely allied to it. We may call it the tradition of respect for, and even veneration of, Maimonides. When Wollaston's critic, John Clarke, Master of the Public Grammar School at Hull, wrote his scurrilous attack upon the Rabbis,[128] Garrigue was able to rebut it by cata-

[126] Schickard wrote *Mishpat Ha-Melek. Jus Regium Hebraeorum e Tenebris Rabbinicis erutum luci donatum* (Strasbourg, 1625); Johann Frischmuth published *Dissertationes II De Septem Noachi Praeceptis ad Gen. IX*, in "Thesaurus Theologico-Philologicus sive Sylloge Dissertationum Elegantiorum ad Selectiora et Illustriora Veteris et Novi Testamenti loca" (Amsterdam, 1701).

[127] Cf. *loc. cit.*, pp. 34–35.

[128] Cf. above, p. 221, n. 38.

loguing a whole list of Christian scholars who had eulogized Maimonides and other rabbinical authors.[129] "One has to be pretty well a newcomer to the Republic of Letters to ignore the merit of the Rabbis cited by Mr. Wollaston", he scathingly remarks. Clarke had pretended that amongst the scholars the Rabbis had a bad reputation. "I do not know", Garrigue retorts, "to which scholars Clarke refers. If to contemporary ones, I know some of the first order and belonging to several nations respectively, who by no means entertain the notions concerning the Rabbis attributed to them by Clarke. If he wishes to speak of the dead, I will quote for his benefit the testimonies of several famous men of letters who did not write as he did." After describing Maimonides as "the most learned man of the twelfth century", he mentions without actually quoting them the following works in which Maimonides is mentioned: Joseph Scaliger's *Letters*[130]; Casaubon's *Letters*[131]; Cunaeus' *République des Hébreux*[132]; [Christoph] Sontagius' *Titres des Psaumes*[133]; Drusius' *Opuscules*[134]; [Wilhelm] Schickard's *Du Droit des Hébreux*[135]; Solomon Glassius' *Rhétorique Sacrée*[136]; Frischmuth's *Dissertation* 1 of the *Sept Préceptes de Noé*[137];

[129] Cf. Garrigue, *Ebauche de la Religion Naturelle par Mr. Wollaston*, Traduite de l'Anglois, avec un Supplement, et autres, Additions considérables, A la Haye, 1726 pp. 411–412.

[130] Cf. *Iosephi Scaligeri Epistolae*, Lugduni Batavorum (Leyden), Letter 62, pp. 193–197: "*Moreh Ha-Nebukim* non potest satis laudare. Ego non tantum illum librum sed etiam omnia illius Magistri opera tanti facio, ut solum illum inter Iudaeos desiisse nugari dicam."

[131] Cf. Casaubon, *loc. cit.*, Letter 433 (1605), p. 231: "Incomparabilis Rabbenu Mosis Maimonis filii *Moreh Nebukim*." Letter 439 (1605), p. 234: ". . . quam ut in nugis Rabbinorum tempus perdes. E quorum puridissimis scriptis paucos Magistros excipio, et omnium maximum Mosem Rambam, quem ego cum paucis demiror sic, ut nihil supra." Garrigue refers to Letter 24 only. But no mention of Maimonides can be found there.

[132] Cf. Cunaeus, *De Republica Hebraeorum Libri Tres* (Leyden, 1703), Book i, ch. 2, pp. 22–23: "Est in admiratione hominum scriptor maximus, Rabbi Moses Ben Maimon, is, qui Talmudicam doctrinam sepositis nugamentis feliciter complexus est divino illo opere, quod ipse *Mishneh Torah* appellat."

[133] *De titulis Psalmorum*, p. 96.

[134] Cf. Joh. Drusius the Elder, *Opuscula* (1609), ch. 49.

[135] *De jure regio Judaeorum* (1625; 1674).

[136] *Grammatica et Rhetorica sacra*, 1776, Preface.

[137] Cf. Frischmuth, *loc. cit.*, Dissertation I, p. 154: "Praestat tamen hic R. Maimonidem disserentem audire, qui eruditorum diverbio ineptire desiit." In discussing the question whether the Noachian laws—said to conform to the Law of Nature—were given by Divine Revelation or whether they had been implanted in man's reason at his creation, he mentions that the rabbis had assumed the first alternative whilst Maimonides had decided in favour of the second. At least, this is how he

Samuel Petit's *Observations*[138]. A thousand others, he says, could be added to this list.[139] This may be exaggerated, but one could easily find more names of illustrious people further to augment this already impressive galaxy of competent witnesses. In Wollaston's own generation, Robert Clavering, Bishop of Peterborough, was an ardent admirer of Maimonides, from whose *Mishneh Torah* he translated two chapters into Latin.[140] He was confident that the memory of Maimonides which had hitherto flourished "will continue to flourish for ever".[141] Another contemporary of Wollaston's, the great German philosopher, Leibniz, also shared these sentiments. He speaks of Maimonides as one who "fuit in philosophia, mathematicis, medica, arte, denique, sacrae scripturae intelligentia insignis".[142] This high estimation is by no means confined to Maimonides though he certainly occupies the foreground of interest in the tradition which we have traced in brief outline. Other rabbinic writers such as Albo, Abrabanel, and Manasseh ben Israel also enjoy a position of great repute.[143] It should, however, be noted that in many instances admiration for Maimonides and his peers goes hand in hand with ill-concealed disdain for the generality of rabbis. No praise is too high for Maimonides, but it is not infrequently coupled with some derogatory remark about the "pettiness" (nugae) of the rank and file of the rabbis. Maimonides and a handful of others are the exception to the rule, and all the more praiseworthy because they do not conform to the general picture of the Jew. This attitude certainly prevails in Scaliger,[144] Casaubon,[145] and a host of

[138] *Observationes*, Book III, ch. 2.

[139] *Loc. cit.*, p. 412.

[140] Cf. Robert Clavering, R. *Mosis Maimonides Tractatus duo*: *De doctrina legis, sive educatione puerorum*. 2. *De natura & ratione Poenitentia apud Hebraeos* (Oxford, 1705).

[141] Quoted by James Townley, *The Reasons of the Laws of Moses. From the "More Nevochim" of Maimonides* (1827), p. vi.

[142] Cf. A. Foucher de Careil, *Leibniz, la philosophie Juive et la Cabale* (Paris, 1861).

[143] As to Albo and Abrabanel cf. Garrigue, *loc. cit.*, who refers to Bayle's *Dictionary* and Buxtorf's *Bibliotheca Rabbinica*. On Manasseh ben Israel's high reputation cf. *Monatsschrift für die Geschichte und Wissenschaft des Judentums*, Vol. V (1856), pp. 295ff.

[144] Cf. the passage quoted above, p. 241, n. 130.

[145] Cf. the passage quoted above, p. 241, n. 131.

---

interprets Maimonides: "Quanto rectius, silente Scriptura, posterior sensus admitti debere videtur, quem Rabbinorum coryphaeum Maimonidem perspexisse haud obscure ex eo colligere est, dum ait: *ha daʿat noṭah lahen*, Naturalis ratio illuc inclinat. Item *heḵraʿ ha-daʿat*, Naturalis ratio suadet."

others.[146] It is, however, not characteristic of Wollaston. Though his occasional remarks concerning the *minutiae* of Jewish Law[147] seem to echo the old prejudice about the "pettiness" of Judaism, his appreciation of the Hebrew legacy is indeed catholic and profound. The astounding range of rabbinic literature on which he draws, and the sympathetic manner in which he enters into its spirit raise him far above those whose cult of Maimonides was somehow in the nature of a double-edged sword.

The third tradition to which Wollaston is heir goes back to the Renaissance concept of the essential unity underlying all human thought and justifying the hope in a common religion of the future. The essence of the Divine, so that concept implied, manifests itself not in one particular religion but in the totality of revelations granted to mankind. This universal theism is shared by men like Marsilius Ficinus, Erasmus of Rotterdam, Thomas More, and Jean Bodin.[148] It survived into the seventeenth century among a group of thinkers who resisted the revival of theological dogmatism instituted by the Reformers,[149] and many of whom were attracted to Jewish thought as a vehicle of a more "natural" type of religion.[150] Judaism seemed to enter into some pre-established harmony with Natural Law (Hugo Grotius; John Selden; Johann Frischmuth)[151] or with Natural Religion (in some of the Cambridge Platonists).[152] Even a superficial glance at the writings of these men reveals their basic concept of universal truth. For it is indeed symbolic of their belief in the essential oneness of the human mind that they delight in quoting, almost on every page, the classical Greek and Latin authors side by side with patristic and rabbinic authorities. One has to view Wollaston's fondness for trilingual quotations against the background of this seventeenth-century humanist tradition. The similarity is indeed striking when one compares Wollaston's Notes with the copious

[146] Cf. the passage from Cunaeus cited above, p. 241, n. 132.

[147] Cf. above, p. 225.

[148] Cf. Ernst Cassirer, *Die Philosophie der Aufklärung* (Tübingen, 1932), pp. 182–188; Wilhelm Dilthey, *Gesammelte Schriften* (Leipzig and Berlin, 1921), Vol. II.

[149] Cf. Cassirer, *loc. cit.*

[150] Cf. Alexander Altmann, "Judaism and World Philosophy", in *The Jews—Their History, Culture, and Religion*, edited by Louis Finkelstein (New York, 1949), Vol. I, pp. 650–660.

[151] Cf. Hugo Grotius, *The Rights of War and Peace*, Transl. by A. C. Campbell (1814), Book I, ch. 1, 10, 15, 16, 18; Selden, *loc. cit.*; Frischmuth, *loc. cit.*

[152] Cf. Henry More, *The Defence of the Threefold Cabbala* (1662).

annotations in works like Selden's *De Jure Naturali*, etc., or Henry More's *Defence of the threefold Cabbala*. Even the names of authors and books we meet in More's treatise seem to be identical with those familiar from Wollaston's work,[153] although it is true that the latter's range of Hebrew knowledge is incomparably larger. Nor can it be said of Wollaston that he shared the Cambridge Platonists' view that "Pythagoras and Plato had their Philosophy from Moses". That "credible fame"[154] was a legacy from the Middle Ages which, in turn, had inherited it from Jewish Hellenistic and Christian Patristic writers.[155] More was still naive enough to believe that a complete identity of view prevailed between the cabbalist interpretation of the Bible and his own neoplatonic-Cartesian philosophy. "Wherefore the Cartesian philosophy being in a manner the same with that of Democritus, and that of Democritus the same with the physiological part of Pythagoras his philosophy, and Pythagoras his philosophy the same with the Sidonian (cf. Vossius, *De Hist. Graec.* lib. 3; Strabo, lib. 16: Moschus a Sidonian), as also the Sidonian with the Mosaical; it will necessarily follow that the Mosaical philosophy in the physiological part thereof is the same with the Cartesian."[156] One will readily agree that the passion for unity of belief could not be indulged in to greater excess. Here everybody seemed to agree with everybody. Maybe it was the exorbitant price paid for the longing after religious unity in an age split into such a multitude of religious sects. Wollaston is altogether of a different frame of mind. His outlook is sober and factual. His grasp of relationships in the history of philosophy is clear and unbiased. Yet his predilection for putting side by side the classical pagan and the Jewish Christian writers is strangely reminiscent of the more uncritical humanists of the seventeenth century, and betrays his kinship with the Renaissance tradition of which he was one of the last outposts in an age rapidly moving away from the larger vista of the past. His combination of learning and philosophy struck his contemporaries as a little queer, and perhaps they were right. Yet

[153] The following is a short list of such names: Aristotle, *Metaphysic*; Plotinus, *Enneads*; Plutarch, *De Iside et Osiride*; Lucretius, *De Natura rerum*; Philoponus, *Metaphysic*; Philo Judaeus; Justin Martyr, *Protrepticus*; Augustine, *De Civitate Dei*; Lactantius, *Divina Justitia*; Maimonides, *Moreh Nebukim*; Manasseh ben Israel.

[154] More, *loc. cit.*, p. 54.

[155] Cf. Altmann, *loc. cit.*, p. 626.

[156] More, *loc. cit.*, pp. 99–104.

one should not forget that there is more in his Latin, Greek, and Hebrew quotations than meets the eye. It is a silent affirmation of the humanist's faith in the essential oneness of the human race, and does not ill fit a man who was both a Deist and a rabbinic scholar.

11

MOSES MENDELSSOHN ON LEIBNIZ AND SPINOZA

Moses Mendelssohn's first literary effort, the *Philosophische Gespräche* of 1755,[1] was motivated by a desire to rehabilitate the merits of the Leibniz–Wolffian philosophy, then under attack by the Berlin Academy members who were admirers of Voltaire. It was akin in spirit to the essay *Pope ein Metaphysiker*! written jointly by Lessing and Mendelssohn and published in the late autumn of the same year.[2] How deeply Mendelssohn was committed to Leibniz' thought may be gauged from a passage in his *Über die Empfindungen* (which also appeared in 1755) extolling, beside Locke and Wolff, the "immortal Leibniz", who had rescued the writer (Palemon) from his tormenting doubts about the existence and providence of God and had proved his guide to "true knowledge and virtue".[3] The moving tribute put into the mouth of Palemon has all the marks of an autobiographical confession. In the *Gespräche* "our" Leibniz is hailed as "the greatest philosopher" and the Germans are chided for copying the French, who, since Malbranche, had failed to produce a single metaphysician, and for lacking pride in their own Leibniz and Wolff, who had brought philosophy to perfection.[4]

[1] Published anonymously by Christian Friedrich Voss (Berlin, 1755). A revised edition appeared in *Moses Mendelssohns Philosophische Schriften*, Erster Theil (Berlin, 1761; reprinted in 1771). Both editions are reproduced in Moses Mendelssohn, *Gesammelte Schriften*, Jubiläumsausgabe, I (Berlin, 1929) (JubA), 1–39; 335–377. The second edition is contained also in *Moses Mendelssohn's Gesammelte Schriften*, I (Leipzig, 1843) (GS), pp. 191–231.

[2] See Leo Strauss' introduction to this essay in JubA, II, 1931, xv–xx.

[3] JubA, I 64 (Sechster Brief). The letters are republished in Mendelssohn's *Philosophische Schriften* of 1761 (1771), where, however, Palemon is replaced by Theokles. For the passage quoted see JubA, I, 256–257.

[4] JubA, I, 11, 12, 14 (346, 349).

Thus it is Leibniz who claims Mendelssohn's unquestionable allegiance, yet the foreground of the first two dialogues in the *Gespräche* (out of the four) is occupied by another figure whose identity emerges in almost dramatic fashion and whose rehabilitation, rather than Leibniz', seems to be the author's real concern in the first half of the book. This figure is Spinoza. Not that Mendelssohn wishes to divide his loyalty between the two. Spinoza's system is "absurd" and his principles are "mistaken and distasteful". One who has read Wolff's painstaking critique of Spinoza "will, surely, never be tempted to agree with Spinoza".[5] Mendelssohn rejects Spinoza, yet he pleads on his behalf. Having reminded the Germans of their neglected pride in Leibniz and Wolff, Neophil tells his interlocutor Philopon that, in justice, one ought to admit that "also someone other than a German, and, I would add, someone other than a Christian, i.e. Spinoza, has a great share in the improvement of philosophy".[6] It almost seems as if the theme of the Germans' pride in Leibniz and Wolff was introduced merely as a curtain-raiser to the assertion of Mendelssohn's pride in his fellow-Jew Spinoza. He mingles this sentiment with that of pity for the "misfortune" of this man who "lived moderately, withdrawn and blamelessly'; who "gave up all human delights, dedicating as he was his entire life to contemplation, and behold, in the maze of his reflections he went astray and, misled into error, asserted what the most abject knave would desire in order to be free to indulge his evil inclinations".[7] Mendelssohn's sense of pity for Spinoza is not that of Leibniz' deploring Spinoza's *infelix ingenium* which carried the overtone of *esprit malin.*[8] He "went astray from error, not from a wickedness of heart".[9] Nor was he far from truth. "The step from him to truth was but a small one."[10] The "truth" is, of course, the Leibnizian philosophy, and

[5] JubA, I, 9, 10 (344, 345); 15 (350). Christian Wolff's critique of Spinoza is found in his *Theologia Naturalis*, Pars Posterior, no. 672ff., pp. 346ff. in the Verona edition of 1738. Mendelssohn is particularly impressed with Wolff's argument that an infinite number of finite perfections cannot produce an infinite perfection. He quotes this argument in the *Gespräche*, JubA, I, 16 (351); *Morgenstunden*, GS, II, 346–7. In his *Erinnerungen an Herrn Jacobi* (published by Friedrich Heinrich Jacobi in his *Über die Lehre des Spinoza in Briefen an den Herrn Moses Mendelssohn*, Neue Vermehrte Ausgabe (Breslau, 1789), 78–96) he says: 'Die grösste Schwierigkeit aber, die ich in dem System des Spinoza finde, liegt mir darin, dass er aus dem Zusammennehmen des Eingeschränkten das Uneingeschränkte will entstehen lassen' (94–95).

[6] JubA, I, 14 (349). [7] JubA, I, 14–15 (349–350).

[8] See Georges Friedmann, *Leibniz et Spinoza*, 1962, 133.

[9] JubA, 1, 16 (351). [10] JubA, I, 18 (354).

Mendelssohn is anxious to show the proximity between Leibniz and Spinoza. Putting it differently, the development of modern philosophy from Descartes to Leibniz leads *via* Spinoza. The tragedy of Spinoza consists in the role of a mediator in which fate had cast him. "Before the transition from Cartesian to Leibnizian philosophy could take place, someone had to fall into the tremendous abyss lying between them. This was Spinoza's hapless fate. How much one has to regret his destiny! He became a sacrifice for the sake of the human mind; a sacrifice, however, that deserves to be adorned with flowers. Without him, philosophy could never have extended its borders thus far." Hence, "how unjust is the implacable hatred of the learned towards such a hapless one!"[11] The melodramatic manner in which Mendelssohn describes Spinoza's fate reflects the categories of the Greek tragedy. Spinoza is clearly viewed as the hero of a *Trauerspiel.*[12] Moreover, he is portrayed in almost Christ-like fashion as a mediator who is sacrificed or, rather who sacrifices himself. He "falls" into the "tremendous abyss" between Cartesian and Leibnizian philosophy, yet there is only a "small step" from him to the truth.

How does Mendelssohn attempt to substantiate his rather sweeping thesis? He does it in two stages. In the first dialogue he sets out to prove that Leibniz' doctrine of the pre-established harmony was essentially taken over from Spinoza. Leibniz, who was "not only the greatest but also the most cautious philosopher", took care not to reveal his source in order not to incur the odium attached to Spinoza's name.[13] In the second dialogue he offers the ingenuous suggestion that Spinoza's system is identical with the archetypal world which, according to Leibniz, pre-existed in God's mind before it became real (*antecedenter ad decretum*). Thus understood, he argues, Spinoza's pantheism (or acosmism, as we might say) can be reconciled with religion. We propose to deal with this second proposition first.

[11] JubA, I, 14 (349); 15 (350).

[12] In the course of his discussions of the *Trauerspiel* with Friedrich Nicolai in the summer of 1756, Mendelssohn suggested that the tragic hero was not necessarily a virtuous man who is destroyed through an error he has committed; even a rogue who bears a certain semblance of virtue may be a tragic figure. See JubA, XI, 59, and Bruno Strauss' note, p. 409. For a full appraisal of Mendelssohn's theory of tragedy see Robert Petsch, *Lessings Briefwechsel mit Mendelssohn und Nicolai über das Trauerspiel* (Leipzig, 1910).

[13] JubA, I, 11–12 (346–347).

The second proposition is advanced with the clearly expressed intention of showing that "Spinoza's system is compatible with reason and religion".[14] The Leibnizians attribute to the world a twofold existence as it were. It existed first, prior to God's choice, as one of a number of possible worlds in the Divine mind. It was, then, made real and external to God because, being the best, God gave it preference before all other possible worlds. Now Spinoza stopped short at its first existence. He believed that no world ever became real outside God, and that all visible things were to be found in the Divine mind alone. In other words, Spinoza characterizes the visible world in the terms applied by the Leibnizians to the plan of the world as it existed in the Divine mind *antecedenter ad decretum*. According to the Leibnizians God conceived the possibility of accidental things by thinking His own perfections as limited to some degree.[15] Spinoza says the same: "All individual things express the Divine attributes in a certain limited way."[16] In the Leibnizians' view the nature of accidental things in the mind of God consists in this, that they cannot be conceived without attributing to them an infinite series of causes.[17] Spinoza says in almost identical words: "The idea of an individual thing actually existing has God for a cause, not in so far as He is infinite, but in so far as there is found in Him the idea of another thing which also actually exists. God is, likewise, the cause of this latter one in so far there is found in Him the idea of a third, and so on *ad infinitum*."[18] Mendelssohn asks: "What objection can a sound philosopher raise against this doctrine as applied to the world which existed in the Divine mind?" In such a world there was no room for the Leibnizian soul as a "special

[14] JubA, I 17 (352); see also 10 (344).

[15] In the second edition Mendelssohn quotes Wolff's *Theologia Naturalis*, Part II, no. 92: *Deus possibilia prima omni possibili modo limitat, & omnes eorundem limitationes quam distinctissime ac simul cognoscit.*

[16] Mendelssohn gives no reference. Fritz Bamberger, who edited and annotated JubA, suggests that he was possibly referring to *Ethics*, I, 25, corollary: *Res particulares nihil sunt nisi Dei attributa certo et determinato* [in the sense of *limitato*] *modo exprimuntur.*

[17] No reference is given. Wolff's *Theologia Naturalis*, II, no. 154–156 discusses the knowledge of God as embracing the *singularia*, which are said to be determined by the *entire* nexus of causes (unknown to us). The term '*infinite* series of causes' does not, however, occur.

[18] *Ethics*, II, 9: *Idea rei singularis, actu existentis, Deum pro causa habet, non quatenus infinitus est, sed quatenus alia rei singularis actu existentis idea affectus consideratur, cujus etiam Deus est causa, quatenus alia tertia affectus est, & sic in infinitum.* Mendelssohn translates *affectus consideratur* imprecisely by *in ihm . . . anzutreffen ist.*

force"[19] since there existed in it only the idea by which God conceived the human soul. In this noumenal (*verständlichen*) world the distinction between necessary and accidental things does, however, have its place according to Spinoza. The common assumption to the contrary is refuted by Spinoza's statement that the necessary derives from the Divine attributes in so far as He is infinite, while the accidental is explained by reference to God in so far as there exists in Him an infinite series of other accidentals. Hence there was but a "small step" from Spinoza to Leibniz.

Having shown how close Spinoza came to Leibniz, Mendelssohn raises the question: "Yet what may have motivated him to deny freedom to God?"[20] Obviously, no reconciliation is possible between Spinoza's and Leibniz' respective positions on the question of God's freedom. All Mendelssohn can hope to do is explain how Spinoza was misled on this issue. His answer is entirely in the spirit of his *apologia pro Spinoza*. "If ever he committed an error innocently, it was this particular one." He considered as genuine freedom the *aequilibrium indifferentiae* only, viz. the freedom to act from indifference and by a certain absolute will.[21] He shared this concept of freedom with many orthodox philosophers. He was, on the other hand, sagacious enough to understand that the choice made by an intelligent being is invariably determined by motives. Hence he regarded this equilibrium as impossible and denied freedom to all intelligent beings. Leibniz has happily dispelled this error and demonstrated that genuine freedom consists in the choice of the best; moreover, that motives do determine the choice and, while they abolish chance, never bring about necessity.

How firmly Mendelssohn was convinced of the correctness and relevance of the two lines of argument which we have traced is evident from the fact that they re-appear toward the end of his life in his *Morgenstunden* (1785). The occasion is the famous controversy with Friedrich Heinrich Jacobi about Lessing's alleged Spinozism. Mendelssohn is deeply disturbed by Jacobi's disclosures, and in an effort to clear his friend's memory of the charge

[19] JubA, I, 18 (353–354). Mendelssohn interprets Spinoza's notion of *mens idea corporis* (*Ethics*, II, 12–13) to imply that the soul is devoid of a force of its own. Leibniz understood it in the same way. This was, however, not Spinoza's meaning. See below, pp. 271–272.

[20] JubA, I, 18 (354); cf. 9 (343).

[21] JubA, I, 18–19 (354–355); Spinoza; *Ethics*, I, 17, *scholium*.

of rank pantheism he offers the concept of a "purified pantheism" which is innocuous and reconcilable with religion and morality in so far they are practical.[22] This purified pantheism is identical with the Spinozistic system as portrayed in the *Gespräche*, viz. as an intra-deical world which the theist too has to admit, and which the pantheist refuses to recognise as real outside God.[23] Against Spinoza's denial of God's freedom Mendelssohn, again, uses the interpretation he had offered in the *Gespräche*. Spinoza's objection to freedom is valid only if we identify freedom with perfect equilibrium. It does not affect the affirmation of freedom by the determinists, viz. the freedom to choose the morally best.[24] It is remarkable indeed that thirty years after he had written his first work he resorted to the very ideas he had expressed there.

Can these ideas stand the test of scrutiny? Mendelssohn bases his notion of the identity of Spinoza's system with Leibniz' world as it existed in God's mind on two textual comparisons. In both instances he quotes not Leibniz himself but "the Leibnizians', and his one and only direct reference is to Wolff's *Theologia naturalis*. The text quoted (II, no. 92) is supposed to express the same notion as found in Spinoza's statement (*Ethics*, I, 25, cor.) that the *res particulares* are but the modes expressing the Divine attributes in a certain limited way (*certo et determinato modo*). What Wolff does in fact say bears, however, a different connotation. He distinguishes the in-existence in God of the "first possibles" (*possibilia prima*), or "unlimited realities" (*realitates illimitatae*), from the "second possibles" (*primitiva secunda*) or "first principles of finite things" (*prima entium finitorum principia essendi*), which arise from the first possibles by way of limitation and are known by God but do not exist in Him. The point Wolff makes in the paragraph quoted by Mendelssohn is based on this distinction (found in nos. 87, 88, 91–93). It relates to God's knowledge of the second possibles: *Patet adeo Deum omnia possibilia primitiva secunda sive a primis orta quam distinctissime cognoscere* (no. 92). This is also the meaning of the sentence quoted by Mendelssohn: *Deus possibilia prima omni possibili modo limitat, & omnes eorundem limitationes quam distinctissime ac simul cognoscit*. The stress is on God's knowing (*cognoscit*) the second possibles which arise by the limitation of the first. Although God is the *ens perfectissimum* in whom all reality

[22] *Morgenstunden*, chs. XIII–XIV, GS, II, p. 340ff.
[23] GS, II, p. 352.
[24] GS, II, p. 345.

exists *in gradu absoluto summo* (no. 93), He knows the second possibles because they arise from the first by limitation (no. 92). These second possibles are, however, the principles of finite things, and not—as Mendelssohn seems to assume—particular things as such. The "possibility of contingent things" of which, in Mendelssohn's phrase, the Leibnizians speak is something entirely different from the "particular things" which he finds discussed by Spinoza. Nor is it correct to describe the second possibles as the Divine ideas which constitute the "possibility of the contingent things". It would be more correct to define the second possibles as the principles of finite things. At any rate, Spinoza speaks of particular things as modes of the attributes, while Wolff deals with the principles of finite things. What is even more decisive, Spinoza conceives of the particular things or modes as being in God, whereas Wolff differentiates the unlimited realities which are in God from the second possibilities of which God knows. Mendelssohn's identification of Spinoza's system with the Leibnizians' world in God's mind breaks down. While for Spinoza the modes are intra-deical, for Wolff the second possibilities are clearly not.

The second comparison is less fraught with ambiguity but is still unconvincing. Mendelssohn quotes Spinoza's statement (*Ethics*, II, 9) which explains the possibility of the infinite having a knowledge of the finite. Directly, the idea of each individual thing has for its cause the idea of another individual thing, and so on *ad infinitum*. God is the cause of these individual ideas in so far only as they form an infinite whole.[25] The same notion, Mendelssohn asserts, is found in almost identical words in the Leibnizians. He quotes no *locus probans* but might have pointed to Leibniz' *Monadology*, no. 36 where the sufficient reason for the contingent truths of fact is found in an infinite sequence of causes. The point Mendelssohn wants to bring out is the recognition by both the Leibnizians and Spinoza of contingent things as possible objects of God's knowledge, and the definition, by both, of contingent things in terms of an infinite number of causes. But does this help to prove Mendelssohn's main thesis, which equates Spinoza's system with Leibniz' world *antecedenter ad decretum*? Does it imply that the meaning of the infinite series of causes is the same for

[25] Cf. Harry A. Wolfson, *The Philosophy of Spinoza* (Cambridge, Mass., 1934), II, p. 32.

Spinoza and Leibniz? The answer is in the negative. For Spinoza every contingent fact is not only determined but also necessary.[26] For Leibniz, a contingent fact is determined but not necessary.[27] In his commentary on Wachter's *Elucidarius Cabalisticus* (1706), where he criticizes Spinoza *via* Wachter, he makes the point (against *Ethics*, I, 7 and 10, *scholium*) that while essence and existence are one and the same thing in necessary things, this is not the case in individual or contingent things. The latter have no necessary connection with God but are freely produced. *Dieu a été incliné vers eux par une raison déterminée, il n'y a point été nécessité.*[28] Moreover, Spinoza's God is the cause of an infinite series of causes within Himself, whereas Leibniz' God is a transitive, not an immanent cause.[29] In the light of these fundamental differences it is hard to see Mendelssohn's justification for trying to approximate the two thinkers. The distance between them was not as small as Mendelssohn suggested.

Nor can one easily approve of Mendelssohn's effort in explaining Spinoza's denial of God's freedom as an error due to a faulty definition of "genuine freedom". It follows, in the first place, from his definition of the will as "a certain mode of thought, like the intellect" (*Ethics*, I, 32) and from his basic notion of the immanence of all things in God: *quare nihil extra ipsum esse potest, a quo ad agendum determinetur, vel cogatur, atque adeo Deus ex solis suae naturae legibus, & a nemine coactus agit* (I, 17). It is this concept of the necessity from which God acts which constitutes the essential difference between Spinoza and Leibniz. That God acts *sub ratione boni* is a proposition sternly rejected by Spinoza (I, 33, *scholium* 2) and firmly embraced by Leibniz: "The reason why the best of all possible worlds is the world which exists, is that God's wisdom makes him know, his goodness makes him choose, and his power makes him produce, the best possible" (*Monadology*, no. 55).[30] In

26 Cf. Wolfson, *loc. cit.*, I, 188ff., pp. 398–399.

27 Cf. Herbert Wildon Carr, *The Monadology of Leibniz* (London, 1930), p. 75.

28 See A. Foucher de Careil, *Leibniz, Descartes et Spinoza* (Paris, 1862), 197. The text of Leibniz' comments on Wachter appears there (pp. 185–220) under the title "Remarques critiques de Leibniz d'après le manuscrit original de la Bibliothèque de Hanovre". It was published first by Foucher de Careil under the title, *Réfutation inédite de Spinoza par Leibniz* (Paris, 1854). The full reference of the book commented on by Leibniz is: *Elucidarius Cabalisticus sive reconditae Hebraeorum philosophiae Brevis et succincta recensio*, Epitomatore Joh. Georgio Wachterio, philos. Prof. (Romae, 1706).

29 Cf. Friedmann, *loc. cit.*, p. 167.

30 See also Leibniz, *Essais de Théodicée*, I, 8, 173 (Gerhardt, VI, pp. 107, 217). Cf. Friedmann, *loc. cit.*, p. 101.

Spinoza's view there is no distinction between a world in the mind of God before the *decretum* and an actual world after God's choice of the best possible world. *At cum in aeterno non detur quando, ante, nec post: hinc, ex sola scilicet Dei perfectione, sequitur, Deum aliud decernere nunquam posse, nec unquam potuisse; sive Deum ante sua decreta non fuisse, nec sine ipsis esse posse* (*Ethics*, I, 33, *scholium* 2). Leibniz' distinction between the infinite possibilities *antecedenter ad decretum* and the reality of the world chosen by God is the very antithesis of Spinoza's doctrine. No doubt, Mendelssohn was fully aware of this, and yet he tried to present Leibniz as having "happily" dispelled Spinoza's error by re-defining the concept of freedom.

We now turn to the other proposition, viz. the one offered in the first dialogue of the *Gespräche*. It is built up skilfully and with dramatic effect. From an unguarded remark of Neophil's Philopon concludes that in his friend's view Leibniz was not the "inventor" of the doctrine of the pre-established harmony. When pressed to declare himself, Neophil admits that this is indeed his considered opinion. Philopon challenges him to prove what seems an odd proposition since, in Neophil's own words, "no one has as yet contested the fame he [sc. Leibniz] has earned on this score, and that Bayle himself offered him congratulations on this great discovery on behalf of the scholarly world".[31] Neophil is ready with his proof but first defines more clearly the nature of his proposition. All he means to say is that the "essential core" (*das Wesentliche*) of this particular doctrine was discovered first by another philosopher (whose identity remains as yet undisclosed). He admits, moreover, that Leibniz was the first to designate this doctrine by the name "pre-established harmony."[32] After some

[31] JubA, I, 4 (337–338). The point is taken up again later in the discussion, p. 11 (346). It introduces a slightly fictional element into the presentation of the facts surrounding Leibniz, since nothing is known about any "congratulations" offered by Bayle. Cf. Bamberger's note, JubA, I, 615.

[32] JubA, I, 4 (338). Mendelssohn quotes [Johann Christoph Gottsched's] German translation of Bayle's *Dictionnaire historique et critique*, 1702, *art.* Rorarius, n. L, [Gottsched's] n. A, which records Leibniz' refutation of Bayle's remark attributing the invention of the term to Dom François Lamy. The term was used by Lamy in his *La Connaissance de soi-même*, II, 1699, 226. Leibniz replied in his "Extrait du Dictionnaire de M. Bayle article Rorarius . . . avec mes remarques" (Gerhardt, IV, 534): "Je luy avois déja donné ce nom dans ma réponse à M. l'Abbé Foucher mise dans le Journal des savans du 9 Avril de l'an 1696, et le R. P. Lami l'a trouvé convenable." The original text of Leibniz' "Extrait" was first published in C. I. Gerhardt's edition of Leibniz' philosophical writings (1880). A German translation of it appeared,

bantering talk about the trifling nature of this latter point the discussion becomes more serious. What is meant by the pre-established harmony? Philopon offers an account which is carefully designed to fit Mendelssohn's notion of an "essential core" of the doctrine which Leibniz could have taken over from Spinoza. In the ensuing debate the point is made that Leibniz did in fact present his doctrine in two different ways, viz. with and without its monadological aspect, and that Wolff adopted it in the latter sense. This, then, represents the "essential core" of Leibniz' theory which he is said to have borrowed from another philosopher. Who is that other philosopher? Neophil still refuses to name him, but the quotation of a passage from Spinoza's *Ethics* gives him away. "Unless I am mistaken, I believe to be recognizing Spinoza in these words", says Philopon. We are now in the full swing of philosophical argument and more of Spinoza's passages are adduced in proof of the point at issue. The line of argument proceeds roughly as follows: Spinoza (like the Cartesians and Leibniz) assumes that body and soul cannot determine each other; the body follows the natural laws of corporeal motion, and the actions of the soul can arise only from its adequate ideas. How, then, does Spinoza explain the accord between body and soul? The occasionalist theory of the Cartesians could not have been his answer since it presupposes the attribution of free will to God, which he denies. We are driven to the conclusion that he assumed a pre-established harmony between the two realms. This is what, in fact, he says in clear terms: "The order and connection of ideas is the same as the order and connection of things" (*Ethics*, II, 7). Mendelssohn feels he has achieved the rehabilitation of Spinoza. "You have shown me yesterday with much acumen", Philopon attests in the second dialogue, "that Spinoza asserted the pre-established harmony." As a result of the discussion in the first dialogue both friends agree that, notwithstanding the difference of principles, Leibniz and Spinoza arrived at almost the same view; that Spinoza's propositions are incomplete rather than false; and that by the correct principles contained in his system he was

however, as early as 1720 in Heinrich Köhler's *Des Hn. Gottfried Wilh. von Leibnitz Lehr-sätze über die Monadologie . . . wie auch Dessen letzte Vertheidigung seines Systematis Harmoniae praestabilitae wider die Einwürffe des Herrn Bayle* (Jena, 1720). The relevant clause reads in Köhler's version: "Ich hatte dem Systemati diesen Namen schon in meiner Antwort an den Herrn Abt Foucher gegeben . . . und der P. Lamy hat ihn für bequem gefunden." Gottsched copied this sentence *verbatim* from Köhler.

able to discover many other truths. The dialogue ends with an apology on behalf of Leibniz, who for reasons of prudence considered it necessary to conceal his source. He would have courted disaster had he revealed it.

Before we proceed to a closer inspection of Mendelssohn's main thesis, viz. the assertion of the Spinozistic origin of the doctrine under discussion, a minor point has to be cleared up. Mendelssohn presents his view of Leibniz' indebtedness to Spinoza as a brand-new theory. No one, Neophil declares, has ever before contested Leibniz' title to fame as the author of this doctrine. This statement is, of course, historically incorrect. Already in Leibniz' own lifetime the Dutchman Ruardus Andala accused him of having plagiarized Spinoza in putting forward the doctrine of the pre-established harmony as his own.[33] The charge was later renewed with a great deal of venom by Joachim Lange in his attacks against Christian Wolff. Lange sought to discredit Wolff by labelling his and Leibniz' systems as Spinozistic. His *Causa Dei* (Halle, 1723) describes the notion of the pre-established harmony as *adoptatus pseudo-philosophiae Spinozianae foetus, novo potius nomine insignatum [sic] quam alio habitu indutus.*[34] The memorandum written by him as Dean of the Theological Faculty at Halle accuses Wolff, *inter alia*, of propounding a doctrine, viz. the one of the pre-established harmony, which amounted to Stoic and Spinozistic fatalism.[35] Wolff defended himself in his *Erinnerungen wieder diejenigen, die in seiner Metaphysick den Spinozisinum entdecket zu haben vermeinen*[36] and in other writings of his.[37] Mendelssohn might have been unaware of Andala's dissertation, but he could not have been ignorant of the Lange-Wolff controversy and the charge

[33] In his *Dissertatio de unione mentis et corporis physica*, which forms part of his *Pentas dissertationum philosophicarum* (Franecker, 1712). Cf. Ludwig Stein, *Leibniz und Spinoza* (Berlin, 1890), 3. Andala attacked Leibniz also in his *Dissertatio philosophica*, etc., which likewise appeared in the *Pentas*. See Carl Günther Ludovici, *Ausführlicher Entwurff einer vollständigen Historie der Leibnitzischen Philosophie* (Leipzig, 1737), no. 362, p. 393. His attacks on Leibniz were continued by his pupil Bernhardus Jorna. See Stein, *loc. cit.*, 3.

[34] Quoted by Stein, *loc. cit.*, 4. He uses similar terms in his *Modesta disquisitio novi philosophiae systematis de deo mundo et homine et praesertim de harmonia praestabilita*, Halle, 1733, 127, 138.

[35] See C. G. Ludovici, *Ausführlicher Entwurff einer vollständigen Historie der Wolffischen Philosophie* (Leipzig, 1737), no. 252, pp. 196–197; no. 260, pp. 200–201.

[36] Published in *Leipziger gelehrte Zeitungen*, 1723, 527ff.; see Ludovici in the work quoted in n. 35, no. 254, p. 198.

[37] See Ludovici, *ibid.*, no. 57, pp. 44–45; no. 58, p. 45.

levelled against Leibniz. It has been suggested that he actually took his point of Leibniz' dependence on Spinoza from either Lange or Wolff's defence.[38] Whatever the merits of this suggestion, there can be no doubt that he knew about the accusation of plagiarism laid at Leibniz' door. This knowledge on his part is reflected in his apology (at the end of the first dialogue) for Leibniz' failure to acknowledge his debt to Spinoza: "Let it suffice to say that there are people who judge even truths according to a certain genealogy. In order to condemn a doctrine, they only need to know that it occurred in this or that author in bad company with other doctrines . . . Tell me, would those people not have believed to find the refutation of this doctrine in the very name of Spinoza, had Leibniz freely confessed that he had borrowed the essential core of his harmony from Spinoza?" There is a subtle irony in Mendelssohn's defence of Leibniz' silence on his source. He presents his caution as if it had achieved its purpose. Those who know history, he implies, know of course that it availed him nothing. Far from obliterating the memory of the Lange–Wolff controversy which centred around Leibniz, the dialogue presupposes it. The denunciation of Leibniz' doctrine as Spinozistic, which is portrayed as merely hypothetical, actually took place. It is, therefore, obvious that Mendelssohn deliberately uses an element of fiction in what is otherwise a straight philosophical dialogue. This insight into his working method enables us to understand the inaccuracy of his statement that no one had ever before contested Leibniz' title to fame. In the first place, it is in league with the point just discussed. The irony of Mendelssohn's apology for Leibniz could not be expressed unless the historical charge of plagiarism was suppressed. Neophil had to present himself as the first to suggest such a connection, which in the changed intellectual climate of the attempted rehabilitation of Spinoza no longer incriminated Leibniz. In the second place, the disclosure of Leibniz' indebtedness to Spinoza achieves a heightened dramatic effect by its claim to be something entirely novel and daring. We have to make allowance for these fictional ingredients which Mendelssohn could safely assume to be understood by his readers.[39]

38 See below, pp. 268–269.

39 It is possibly the dramatic quality of the *Gespräche* which gave the reviewer in *Göttingische Anzeigen von gelehrten Sachen* (1755), pp. 586–588 (Johann David Michaelis) the impression that Lessing was the author.

Mendelssohn develops his thesis in two stages. In the first, he defines the meaning of what he described as the "essential core" of Leibniz' doctrine of the pre-established harmony. In the second, he offers his arguments in proof of his assertion that this doctrine, in its essential form, derives from Spinoza. His procedure at both stages calls for some closer inspection.

(1) Philopon gives the following account of Leibniz' doctrine of the pre-established harmony:

> A doctrine according to which everything that happens in our soul arises therein, in compliance with the body, by its own original power, and not as the effect caused by another substance; precisely as everything that happens in our body is produced therein, in compliance with the soul, by no other than corporeal, mechanical powers. Should one, then, ask a Leibnizian by which means the union of the body and soul is achieved, he will answer: God has, from eternity, arranged such a harmony between them that certain representations in the soul give rise to certain motions in the body, which have their sufficient reason simultaneously in both; viz. the reason *by which* they arise they have in the mechanical powers of the body, and the reason *why* or *to what end* they arise they have in the state of our soul. Conversely, certain motions in our body give rise to certain corresponding representations in our soul, which have their reason *by which* they arise in the original power of our soul and in its preceding state, while they have the reason *why* they arise in the motions of our body. The Leibnizian simile of the two clocks is well known.

This account contains no reference to the monadological concept with which the doctrine of the pre-established harmony is interwoven.[40] In the course of the discussion Neophil suggests that Leibniz was anxious to show the validity of his new theory,

[40] It is based on Leibniz' doctrine as presented first in the essay entitled "Système nouveau pour expliquer la nature des substances et leur communication entre elles, aussi bien que l'union de l'âme avec le corps" and published in the *Journal des Savans* (June, 1695) (reprinted in J. E. Erdmann's edition of Leibniz' *Opera Philosophica* I (Berlin, 1840), pp. 118ff.). The original draft and a version revised and altered by Leibniz appear in Gerhardt's edition (IV, pp. 471ff.; 477ff.).

The distinction between the reason "by which", and the reason "why" (in other words, between the efficient and the final causes) does not occur in the essay. It appears in the *Monadology* (no. 79) and in the *Théodicée* (I, no. 62, Gerhardt, VI, 137), where, however, acting according to final causes is said to belong exclusively to the soul, and where acting according to efficient causes is attributed exclusively to bodies. See also Leibniz' essay of 1705 (Gerhardt, VI, pp. 539ff.). Mendelssohn's presentation of Leibniz' view is, therefore, incorrect, as far as this particular aspect is concerned.

irrespective of the acceptability or otherwise of his monadological view. For this reason, he further suggests, Leibniz made no use of the monadology in his first presentation of the pre-established harmony nor in his replies to Bayle's criticisms in the *Journal des Savans*.[41] Moreover, he says, the pre-established harmony was accepted by Wolff in the simplified form only in which Leibniz had defended it against Bayle.[42] All this is clearly designed to make plausible Mendelssohn's suggestion that the "essential core" (*das Wesentliche*) of this doctrine can be traced to Spinoza. Mendelssohn is obviously intent upon isolating such an essential element not merely by a logical process of abstraction but also by textual evidence. He wants to show that Leibniz himself offered his doctrine also in its reduced form, and that it therefore makes sense to link this particular form with Spinoza. He admits, on the other hand, that the pre-established harmony is, for Leibniz, inseparable from the monadic system: "In the *Monadology* he showed it as following from his system of monads. It is here that it is revealed in its full splendour."[43] The question, then, arises whether Leibniz did in fact present a simplified version of his doctrine, viz. one shorn of the monadological concept. According to Mendelssohn he did so in his essay *Système Nouveau* and in subsequent *Éclaircissements* in the *Journal des Savans*. Do the texts bear out his contention? We shall deal with the essay first.

It starts from the notion of simple substances endowed with force analogous to feeling and desire and after the manner of souls. This concept is applied to the bodies of animals and other corporeal substances. The rational souls are said to follow much higher laws. The term monad is not used but its meaning is clearly

[41] JubA, I, pp. 5–7 (339–341).

[42] Mendelssohn quotes Wolff's "Latin Cosmology" [viz. his *Cosmologia Generalis* (Frankfurt-Leipzig, 1737)], no. 206, 213. As already noted by Bamberger (JubA, I, 617), the paragraphs referred to do not discuss the subject. Bamberger substitutes a reference to the "German Metaphysics" [viz. Wolff's *Vernünfftige Gedanken von Gott, der Welt und der Seele des Menschen* (Frankfurt-Leipzig)], 1720, no. 765. See, however, *Cosmologia Generalis*, no. 294, and also *Vernünfftige Gedanken*, nos. 215–219. Mendelssohn seems to have conflated the two references. Jacobi (*Über die Lehre des Spinoza*, etc., p. 392, note) quotes both. He likewise describes Wolff as never having adopted Leibniz' monadology "totally and expressly" (p. 380, note). For a similar view see Robert Latta, *Leibniz* (London, 1898), pp. 166ff.

[43] JubA, I, 6 (340). Mendelssohn refers to [Michael Gottlieb] Hansch's discussion of the doctrine in his *Principia philosophiae Leibnitzii geometrico modo demonstrata* (Frankfurt, 1728), which work was based on the Latin version of the *Monadology* published in the *Acta eruditorum Lipsiensium* (Suppl. Vol. VII, 1721, sect. 11, 500–514).

present. Thus, it is said that each of these substances represents the whole universe in its own way and from a certain point of view. Yet Leibniz himself obscures the relevance of this concept for the doctrine of the pre-established harmony by not using it straight as proof for it. For after the initial presentation of his notion of simple substances he continues: "Having settled these things, I thought I had gained my haven, but when I set myself to meditate upon the union of soul and body I was as it were driven back into the deep sea. For I found no way of explaining how the body transmits anything to the soul or vice versa."[44] It could, therefore, have appeared to Mendelssohn that Leibniz' subsequent discussion of the pre-established harmony was not meant to follow from the notion of substance or monad. He was, however, mistaken and, moreover, was simply ignoring Leibniz' own statement in his first reply to Foucher: "With laudable candour you recognise that my hypothesis of harmony or concomitance is possible. But you still have a certain repugnance to it; doubtless because you think that it is purely arbitrary; through not being aware that *it follows from my view regarding unities*; *for everything in my theory is connected together*."[45] Jacobi already drew attention to this statement when questioning the accuracy of Mendelssohn's contention that in the *Journal des Savans* Leibniz did not proceed from a monadological position.[46] He added the remark: "And so I see indeed no material difference between the first essay and the *Principes sur* [*sic*] *la nature & la grâce* or the *Principia philosophiae*[47]; only a difference, according to the author's own remark,[48] in accommodation and way of presentation."[49] This sweeping statement does not, however, correspond to fact. There is a material difference between the view of the monads pre-

[44] Erdmann, I, 121; Gerhardt, IV, 483. The English translation is Latta's (*loc. cit.*, 311).

[45] Gerhardt, IV, 494 (Latta, 322). The italics are mine.

[46] *Über die Lehre des Spinoza*, etc., 389–391, note.

[47] I.e., the writings which, in Jacobi's assumption, represented the French original and the Latin version respectively of what the German translation called the *Monadologie*. See *Über die Lehre des Spinoza*, etc., pp. 387–389. In this assumption he was, however, mistaken. The discovery of the original manuscript of the *Monadology* proved that this work was different from the *Principes de la nature et de la grâce*. Cf. Robert Zimmermann, *Leibnitz' Monadologie* (Vienna, 1847), pp. 7–8; Bamberger, JubA, I, pp. 616–617.

[48] JubA, I, p. 6 (340).

[49] This is a misreading of Mendelssohn, who speaks of *verschiedene Gestalten* in the sense of two variants of the doctrine, viz. one based on the monadological concept and one divorced from this base.

sented in the essay and the one offered in the *Monadology*. Only in the latter work does Leibniz go as far as to reduce the difference between bodies and souls to one of degree, and thereby establish the harmony between them.[50] Mendelssohn's statement nevertheless remains open to criticism. The monadic concept plays a decisive part in the presentation of the doctrine in the essay.

In the three *éclaircissements* published in the *Journal des Savans* in reply to Foucher Leibniz makes but sparing use of the monadology. The first of these refers to it as the premise from which the view of the pre-established harmony necessarily follows.[51] It mentions the notion of substances *douées d'une véritable unité*[52] and, with special reference to the harmony, the endowment of substances with "forces" (*efforts*),[53] but it does so merely in order to clarify, not to prove the doctrine. The second and third *éclaircissements* do not mention the monadic concept at all but introduce, for the first time, the analogy of the two clocks.[54] Mendelssohn was, therefore, right in suggesting that in the *Journal des Savans* Leibniz defended the doctrine with "only such weapons as common philosophy put into his hands". He was, however, mistaken in applying this characterization to Leibniz' defence of it against Bayle. The three *éclaircissements* published in the *Journal des Savans* were in reply to Foucher, not to Bayle. Leibniz' answers to Bayle, on the other hand, are far from conforming to Mendelssohn's description. For both the *Éclaircissement* of 1698 (Gerhardt, IV, 517ff.) and the *Réponse* of 1712 (Gerhardt, IV, 554ff.) are steeped in the monadological theory, as even the most cursory glance will reveal. Mendelssohn knew at least the first of these replies, since he quotes Bayle's argument from the transition from pleasure to pain which occurs in it. He does not, however, mention the *Histoire des ouvrages des scavans* where the *Éclaircissement* appeared, and it may, therefore, be inferred that all he really meant to say was that in the *Journal des Savans* Leibniz defended his theory on grounds other than monadological. His argumentation is, however, anything but a model of accuracy.

[50] Cf. Latta, *loc. cit.*, p. 263, n. 126; p. 324, n. 16.

[51] Cf. the passage quoted above and n. 45.

[52] Gerhardt, IV, pp. 493–494.

[53] Gerhardt, IV, p.496.

[54] For a discussion of this simile see Latta, *loc. cit.*, pp. 46ff.; for the question whether Leibniz borrowed it from Geulincx see the references in Latta, *loc. cit.*, pp. 43–44. Mendelssohn unquestioningly takes it to be Leibniz' invention.

Even though Leibniz did make use of his monadology both in the *Système Nouveau* and in his replies to Bayle, the fact remains that his concept could be neglected by him in his defence against Foucher, and that Wolff adopted the doctrine of the pre-established harmony in a form divorced from Leibniz' understanding of the monads.[55] There was, then, some justification for Mendelssohn's attempt to differentiate between an "essential core" of the doctrine and its fully-fledged form. The question still to be discussed is whether he succeeded in proving his thesis asserting the Spinozistic origin of the essential form of Leibniz' doctrine.

(2) In building up his proof, Mendelssohn first shows that the problem of explaining how body and soul can act upon one another was as acute for Spinoza as it was for Leibniz, since both started out from the Cartesian dualism of extension and thought. He quotes Spinoza's proposition (*Ethics*, III, 2) which states that "The body cannot determine the mind[56] to thought, neither can the mind determine the body to motion or rest or to anything else (if there be anything else)." Two further quotations are offered in corroboration of this point. The first is from the *scholium* on the proposition just cited, and the second from proposition 3 which follows it. In the *scholium* Spinoza points out that "what the body can do no one has hitherto determined, that is to say, experience has taught no one hitherto what the body, without being determined by the mind, can do and what it cannot do from the laws of Nature alone, in so far as nature is considered merely as corporeal". He adds that "no one as yet has understood the structure of the body so accurately as to be able to explain all its functions, not to mention the fact that many things are observed in brutes which far surpass human sagacity, and that sleepwalkers in their sleep do very many things which they dare not do when awake—all this showing that the body itself can do many things, from the laws of its own nature alone, at which the mind belonging to that body is amazed".[57] In *proposition 3* Spinoza says that:"The actions of the

[55] Cf. above, n. 42.

[56] Mendelssohn translates Spinoza's term *mens* by "soul". There is some justification for this, since for Spinoza *mens* includes such *modi cognitandi* as *amor*, *cupiditas*, etc. (*Ethics*, II, *axiomata*, 3). Cf. Heinrich Christoph Wilhelm Sigwart, *Der Spinozismus historisch und philosophisch erläutert* (Tübingen, 1839), 122.

[57] Mendelssohn's German translation is not altogether precise. The English translation quoted above is taken from James Guttmann's edition of the *Ethics* (New York, 1949), pp. 130–131.

mind arise from adequate ideas alone, but the passive states depend upon those alone which are inadequate."[58] Mendelssohn adds:

> He demonstrates this proposition by reference to the fact that the essence of the soul consists in its thoughts. Now, all thoughts are composed of adequate and inadequate ideas. Hence that which follows from the nature of the soul, i.e. that which has the soul for its proximate cause by which it can be explained, must follow from either an adequate or an inadequate idea. Since, however, it has been demonstrated in the third part of the *Ethics* that from inadequate ideas nothing but passions can arise, he draws the conclusion that the actions of the soul can arise from its adequate ideas only.[59]

The radical dichotomy between body and soul having been thus established as Spinoza's view, Mendelssohn shows that for Spinoza the problem of the accord between body and soul could not be solved by invoking God's constant intervention as suggested by the occasionalist theory ("the system of occasional causes"). "Nothing can be more contrary to Spinoza's philosophy than the system of occasional causes. The protagonists of this view must, of necessity, attribute free will to the Being by whose intervention body and soul are connected; and how could Spinoza have admitted this? He who considered intellect and will to be one and the same?"[60] Moreover, he argues, Spinoza stated that all changes that occur in the body can be explained from purely mechanical causes, a view not acceptable to the occasionalists. Finally, he recalls the close similarity between Spinoza's description of the feats which the human body can perform *per se* and the Leibnizians' statements on this subject. "Spinoza even employs all the argumentation resorted to by the Leibnizians. Like them, he invokes our ignorance of the inner structure of our body, and, finally, the fact that no one has as yet shown the impossibility of a machine capable of producing mechanically all those performances which are allotted to this or that individual body." Mendelssohn is obviously referring to Leibniz' discussion of the artfulness of the human body and the possible accomplishments of a superbly constructed automaton, in his *Réponse* to Bayle (Gerhardt, IV, 555–557).

[58] Mendelssohn translates simply: *Die Wirkungen der Seele entspringen aus ausführlichen (ideis adequatis) und die Leidenschaften aus unausführlichen Begriffen* (JubA, I, pp. 8, 342–343).

[59] This is a fair restatement of Spinoza's demonstration.

[60] See above, p. 253.

Since the occasionalist theory was of no avail to Spinoza, we are led to assume that, in his view, the accord between body and soul must be due to an exact correspondence between the two systems. The sequence of ideas in the soul must be an exact pre-established parallel to the sequence of the motions of the body. This is what Spinoza says in effect: "The order and connection of ideas is the same as the order and connection of things" (*Ethics*, II, 7). Mendelssohn considers this proposition as decidedly expressive of the same notion as Leibniz':

> Do you now recall what Leibniz had to say in his defence against Bayle's objection that, without our assuming the action of another substance upon the soul, it would be incomprehensible how the soul can pass on occasion immediately from pleasure to displeasure and from sadness to joy? Did not he too suggest that the changes in the soul can be explained by the very same reason by which the changes in the visible world can be understood? That the states of the soul succeed each other in the very same way in which there is succession in the nexus of things? What else does this amount to than what Spinoza says in the words we have quoted: "The order and connection of ideas is the same as the order and connection of things."

This, then, is Mendelssohn's proof for his thesis that the doctrine of the pre-established harmony is found in essence, though not in name nor in its full expression, in the much-maligned Spinoza, and that Leibniz took it from there.

The validity of this proof does not seem to have been questioned by the reviewers of Mendelssohn's *Gespräche*. "I am surprised", Lessing wrote to Mendelssohn in a letter dated 17th April, 1763, eight years after the publication of these dialogues, "that no one has as yet spoken up for Leibniz and against you."[61] This omission was now being made good by Lessing himself. "I must confess to you that for some time past I have not been too happy with your first dialogue. I believe you were a little of a sophist at the time you wrote it." The gist of his objections is as follows: Spinoza assumed that body and soul are one and the same substance, which is considered now under the attribute of extension and now under that of thought (*Ethics*, II, 7, *scholium*). What kind of harmony had to be established between them? A harmony which the thing has with itself? Is this not playing with words?

[61] GS, V, pp. 168–170.

Leibniz wants to solve by his harmony the riddle of the union between two entities as diverse as body and soul. Spinoza, on the other hand, sees no diverse things, no union, therefore, and no riddle to be solved. Lessing, in other words, denies that the problem which Leibniz wished to solve ever existed for Spinoza. The need for the hypothesis of the pre-established harmony did not arise for him. Lessing quotes Spinoza's proposition (II, 21) which he understands to mean that the soul is united with the body in the same way as the idea of the soul which it has of itself is united to the soul. Now, the idea which the soul has of itself belongs to the essence of the soul, and is inseparable from it. Hence the body too is inseparable from the soul, and it is by virtue of this inseparability or identity that they are united. Lessing admits that the key-passage quoted by Mendelssohn ("The order and connection of ideas is the same as the order and connection of things") and a similar one (V, 1) do have a Leibnizian ring. This, however, he does not consider decisive.

> If, then, both use the same words, do they, at the same time, associate identical concepts with them? Impossible. Spinoza only means to say thereby that everything that follows formally from the nature of God and hence, from the nature of an individual thing, follows also objectively in the same order and connection. According to his view, the sequence and connection of ideas in the soul agrees with the sequence and connection of the changes of the body merely because the body is the object of the soul; because the soul is nothing but the body thinking itself, and the body is nothing but the soul that extends itself. But Leibniz?

Fortunately, we possess Mendelssohn's reply to his friend's criticism.[62] Far from disowning his youthful dialogue and its argumentation, he firmly upholds them. His so-called "sophistry" can, he thinks, be justified. Notwithstanding the fact that for Spinoza body and soul are modifications of one and the same substance, extension and thought are still two different attributes. Each of them is conceived by itself without involving the other (II, 6). Hence motion cannot be understood by reference to thought, nor thought by reference to motion. Ideas follow from ideas and motions follow from motions. Yet they harmonize with each other, i.e., in Spinoza's language, the ideas invariably express *per modum cognitionis* what the motions express *per modum extensionis*. It follows

[62] GS, V, pp. 174–177. Mendelssohn's letter is undated.

that Spinoza regards body and soul as different attributes between which a harmony exists. The fact that they are one substance—in the unusual sense in which he uses the term, there being for him only one single substance—and one individual, does not obliterate the distinctiveness of the attributes. What matters, he sums up, is not this or that expression used by Spinoza nor the concept of substance but whether or not Spinoza subscribed to the following propositions, which constitute the essence[63] of the doctrine of harmony: (*a*) Motion and thought are different things; (*b*) *cognitio* can never be *causa efficiens mutationis extensi*, nor can *extensio* be *causa mutationis cogitationis*; (*c*) *cogitatio* invariably follows *ex cogitatione*, and *motus ex motu*; (*d*) at the same time, the series *motuum et cogitationum* are always in harmony.

Mendelssohn affirms that these propositions, which are the essential elements of the doctrine of the pre-established harmony, were held by Spinoza before Leibniz, who merely fitted them into his system. One may admit that the proposition which reads "The order and connection of ideas is the same as the order and connection of things" is demonstrated in different ways by Spinoza and Leibniz. This, however, Mendelssohn suggests, is irrelevant to our point. What is important is not the systematic framework in which a sentence is embedded but the meaning of the sentence. "Has the proposition as such", he asks, "one meaning in Spinoza and another in Leibniz? Does the latter explain the words differently? Is his understanding of the terms 'things', 'ideas', and 'order' different from that of any one else? Not at all. The meaning of the proposition is thoroughly Leibnizian." This is, clearly, a restatement of the claim made in the *Gespräche*: the "essential core" of Leibniz' doctrine is found in Spinoza. Mendelssohn adds, however, a further thought in this letter:

> You say: "According to his [viz. Spinoza's] view, the sequence and connection of ideas in the soul agrees with the sequence and connection of the changes in the body merely because the body is the object of the soul; because the soul is nothing but the body thinking itself, and the body is nothing but the soul that extends itself. But Leibniz?" . . . I must confess to you that to me Leibniz does not seem to be very far from these thoughts. According to him, the ideas and

[63] *das Wesen der Harmonie* (p. 175); *die wesentlichen Sätze der vorherbestimmten Harmonie* (p. 176). We have here a restatement of the term *das Wesentliche dieser Meinung* in the *Gespräche* (JubA, I, 4; see also 8).

representations are but the changes of the simple things [viz. the monads] *as they are*, and the motions are but the changes of the simple things *as they appear*. The same modifications of the simple things constitute thought on the one hand, when considered as realities, and extension and motion on the other, when considered as phenomena. The soul has representations of the world, i.e. of all changes in the simple things, in accordance with the position of its body in it. Spinoza expresses this by saying: the body is the object of the soul, and the body itself is but the totality of changes occurring in certain simple things and perceived by me as phenomena. This being the case, it is inevitable that the series of phenomena be in harmony with the series of realities, i.e. that the motions of the body harmonize with the ideas in the soul.

Mendelssohn's view may be restated as follows: Spinoza held that the body is the object of the idea constituting the human mind (*Ethics*, II, 12–13, 21), and that the object of our mind is a body existing, and nothing else (II, 13). Spinoza, moreover, considered the body to be nothing but the totality of changes occurring in certain simple things and perceived as phenomena. Similarly, Leibniz saw in the body and all that appertains to it (extension, motion) but *phenomena bene fundata* reflecting the viewpoint of the monad, which alone is real.[64] Hence the difference between the two systems is even further reduced. It seems, however, that Mendelssohn wrongly attributed to Spinoza the view that the body is but the totality of changes in certain simple things (?) perceived as phenomena. For Spinoza the body is not a phenomenon in the Leibnizian sense. He defines "body" as "a mode which expresses in a certain and determinate manner the essence of God in so far as He is considered as the thing extended" (*Ethics*, II, *Def.* 1). He says that "The mind does not know itself except in so far as it perceives the ideas of the modifications of the body" (II, 23). The relation between body and soul cannot be described, therefore, as one between phenomena and reality. Both equally express reality. Mendelssohn's argumentation for a closer resemblance of the two systems than originally suggested by him thus falls to the ground.

Interestingly enough, Lessing's point was restated with even greater emphasis twenty-six years later by Karl Heinrich Heydenreich, an admirer of Jacobi's, in his brilliantly written

[64] See Leibniz' *Éclaircissement* in answer to Bayle, Gerhardt, IV, 523, and his *Réponse*, IV, 562; Latta, *loc. cit.*, 98ff.

Natur und Gott nach Spinoza (Vol. I, Leipzig, 1789, 90–102).[65] The author develops his critique of Mendelssohn (who had died three years earlier) in a dialogue between two philosophers, called rather anachronistically Parmenides and Xenophanes. Parmenides admits not having read a single line of Spinoza's nor having derived any clear view of his system from the accounts of it by Bayle, Lamy and many others. He gratefully acknowledges, however, the help he had received from the most recent writers on the subject, viz. Mendelssohn (in the *Morgenstunden*, 1785) and Herder (in *Gott*, 1787). They had indeed attracted him, and he was convinced that Spinoza, would he rise again, would accept the revisions suggested by them. Xenophanes is not of this opinion. In order to understand the Spinozistic doctrine one ought to read, above all, Jacobi's *Über die Lehre des Spinoza, in Briefen an den Herrn Moses Mendelssohn* (1785). In the ensuing discussion Parmenides recalls Mendelssohn's early *Philosophische Gespräche* in which the agreement of Spinoza's system, if shorn of some unessential points, with the Leibniz–Wolffian philosophy is shown with a delicacy which defies criticism, provided his interpretation of Spinozism is correct. He adds: "It seems to me also highly probable that Leibniz borrowed the basic concept (*den Grund*) of his pre-established harmony from Spinoza, as he [i.e. Mendelssohn] has already shown many years ago." Xenophanes reacts rather sharply to this reminiscence. "It is true, Mendelssohn asserted this, and he did so with such a degree of confidence that one seemed to have done enough for Leibniz' honour if one covered his theft with a few lame excuses. I believe, however, that this philosopher [i.e. Mendelssohn] committed here the same mistake as was made by another long before him." "Was, then, Mendelssohn not the first to offer this particular suggestion?" asks Parmenides. Xenophanes is hesitant to accuse Mendelssohn of plagiarism but his reply tends that way. "I do not know whether he himself knew that this had been done before. I should, however, almost assume that since he took such a great interest in Wolff's philosophy, he turned one

[65] Heydenreich does not seem to have had any knowledge of the objection raised by Lessing in his letter to Mendelssohn. The letter, as well as Mendelssohn's reply, is included in *Gelehrter Briefwechsel zwischen D. Johann Jacob Reiske, Moses Mendelssohn und Gotthold Ephraim Lessing* (I, pp. 290–295; 301–307), which appeared in 1789, the year of the publication of Heydenreich's book. In an earlier treatise entitled *Animadversiones in Mosis Mendelii Filii Refutationem Placitorum Spinotzae* (Leipzig, 1787) Heydenreich had already taken issue with Mendelssohn's interpretation of Spinoza as offered in the *Morgenstunden* (1785).

day, from curiosity, the pages of Joachim Lange's book against Wolff." In that book, viz. in the *Modesta disquisitio*,[66] Xenophanes relates, proof is offered to the effect that Leibniz took the pre-established harmony from Spinoza. The startling fact is disclosed that the very same passages from Spinoza quoted as evidence by Lange re-appear in Mendelssohn's argumentation. Lange has cited, *inter alia*, the passage (*Ethics*, III, 2): *nec corpus mentem ad cogitandum, nec mens corpus ad motum neque ad quietem . . . determinare potest* (which is the very same passage which Mendelssohn adduces as the basis of his proof). Xenophanes challenges, however, the validity of the argument, and he does so on grounds familiar to us from Lessing's objection: Matter and thought are, strictly speaking, one and the same thing according to Spinoza. Hence there are no things requiring harmonization, and there is no scope for the notion of a pre-established harmony. It is different in the case of Leibniz whose system, both in its dualistic and monadological form, poses a plurality of substances in need of harmonization. In other words, Leibniz could not have taken his doctrine from Spinoza for the simple reason that in Spinoza's system the problem of explaining the accord between body and soul does not even arise. Xenophanes shows with a wealth of quotations that this point had already been made by Wolff in his *De differentia nexus rerum sapientis et fatalis necessitatis nec non systematis harmoniae praestabilitae et hypothesium Spinozae* (1724).[67] He assumes that both Lange and Mendelssohn had but a superficial knowledge of Spinoza's system. The former sought to discredit the Leibniz–Wolffian philosophy by labelling it as Spinozistic, while the latter was led into error by the outward resemblance between certain of Spinoza's propositions and the principles which underlie Leibniz' doctrine. Mendelssohn might, however, have considered the possibility that Leibniz was sufficiently capable of producing his doctrine on his own, and sufficiently honest to admit his source had there been one. "But what does one not put out of sight when the possibility of exhibiting oneself as a discoverer is at stake!"[68]

[66] See above, n. 34.

[67] Heydenreich, *loc. cit.*, pp. 96–100. We quote some of Wolff's statements cited here: *Spinoza non admittit duplicem substantiam, adeoque nullum statuit inter mentem et corpus commercium, consequenter iuxta ipsius hypothesin vana quaestio: quomodo commercium illud obtineatur, seu quaenam sit eius causa . . . Vide itaque, quam absonum sit, systema harmoniae praestabilitae in Spinosa quaerere, qui nullo prorsus opus habet . . .*

[68] Heydenreich, *loc. cit.*, p. 96.

Mendelssohn could no longer reply to these charges. He might have admitted that he had read Lange or—as suggested by Jacobi[69]—found Lange's proof in Wolff. As we have ventured to suggest, his presentation of the theory asserting Leibniz' indebtedness to Spinoza contains a deliberate fictional element. What matters, however, is not the (still open) question as to whether or not he had met this theory in Lange or Wolff, but the fact that he made it so thoroughly his own and defended it vigorously against Lessing's objections long after he had first expressed it. If he knew Wolff's rejection of Lange's proof, he certainly disregarded it when writing his *Gespräche* and when replying to Lessing. The impression one gets is that he was unaware of Wolff's line of reasoning. Otherwise, he might have mentioned Wolff's precedence to Lessing. He may have read Lange, but the way he presents the theory is much subtler and interwoven with the point made in the second dialogue. Above all, he offers it from an entirely new viewpoint, viz. that of deep respect for Leibniz and, coupled with it, a desire to rehabilitate Spinoza. The courage which he evinced by taking his stand was not without effect. The change of attitude towards Spinoza which became noticeable in the eighties of his century can be traced back to his little *opus* and the influence which it then began to exercise. Lessing was probably first introduced to an appreciation of Spinoza by Mendelssohn.[70] Jacobi, who had the lion's share in the renaissance of Spinoza starting in Germany, was well aware of Mendelssohn's *Gespräche*. He referred to this work in his historic discussion with Lessing in 1780: "Mendelssohn has publicly shown that the *Harmonia praestabilita* is found in Spinoza."[71] Heydenreich's book gives further evidence of the attention which Mendelssohn's first *opus* commanded in the last decade of his life.

It seems futile to discuss the validity of Mendelssohn's reply to the objections raised by his friend Lessing and, after his death, by Heydenreich, who had discovered them in Wolff's refutation of Lange. For even assuming that Mendelssohn's interpretation of Spinoza was correct, viz. that the two attributes of the one substance involve two distinct orders of existence and, therefore,

[69] *Über die Lehre des Spinoza*, etc., pp. 385–386. Jacobi more or less endorses Heydenreich's critique of Mendelssohn.

[70] Cf. Erich Schmidt, *Lessing* (Berlin, 1884), I, 297.

[71] *Über die Lehre des Spinoza*, etc., p. 34.

call for an explanation of their harmony,[72] we would still be far from proving that Leibniz took his doctrine from Spinoza unless it could be shown that this was also Leibniz' interpretation of Spinoza. In other words: The issue at stake is not, as Mendelssohn asserted, the identity of meaning of certain propositions in the two systems (which represents a purely semantic problem) but whether or not Leibniz actually understood Spinoza after the manner suggested by Mendelssohn (which is a historical question). This historical question admits of an answer in the light of a number of documents which were not available to Mendelssohn since they were published only after his time. All of them make it plain that Leibniz considered Spinozism a monistic system in which the harmonization of the body and soul did not even arise. In his annotations in the margin of his copy of Spinoza's *Oeuvres posthumes* (written *c.* 1678), which were first published in 1830, he comments on the words of the *scholium* to *Ethics* II, 21, *hoc est Mentem et Corpus unum et idem esse Individuum*, etc.: *Ergo revera non differunt mens et corpus, non magis quam urbs diversimode inspecta a se ipsa, sequitur et extensionem a cogitatione revera non differe* (Gerhardt, I, 151).[73] He clearly understands Spinoza's words to mean that body and soul are the same reality conceived under two different attributes but not differing more from one another than a town viewed from here and there differs in itself. This view of Spinoza's doctrine is restated in his *Animadversiones* on Johann Georg Wachter's *Elucidarius Cabalisticus* (1706)[74]:

> Spinoza dit (*Eth.*, p. 3, *schol.*, prop. 2) que l'esprit et le corps sont la même chose, mais seulement exprimée de deux manières, et (*Eth.*, p. 2, *schol.* 5, prop. 7) que la substance pensante et la substance étendue sont une seul et même substance, que l'on conçoit tantôt sous l'attribut de la pensée, tantôt sous celui de l'étendue . . . Je blame tout ceci. L'esprit et le corps n'est pas même chose, pas plus que le principe de l'action et celui de la passion . . .

Leibniz' interpretation of Spinoza's two attributes as *la même chose* accords with his understanding of Spinoza's *mens idea corporis* as implying a concept of soul as mere idea, devoid of force. In his annotations on the *Oeuvres posthumes* (Gerhardt, I, 150–151) he wrote *à propos* proposition 12 of part II: *ideae non agunt. Mens agit.*

[72] Sigwart, *loc. cit.*, pp. 123, 139, 154, interprets Spinoza in this sense.
[73] Cf. Friedmann, *loc. cit.*, pp. 102, 298 (n. 1 *ad* p. 101).
[74] Foucher de Careil, *loc. cit.*, p. 200.

Totus mundus revera est objectum cujusque mentis . . .[75] An over-simplified version of Spinoza's concept of *mens idea corporis* is offered by Leibniz in his *Elementa rationis* (*c.* 1686) along the same lines. According to him, Spinoza considers the soul as bereft of all activity of power since "l'âme n'est rien d'autre que l'idée ou, si vous préférez, la figure abstraite ou la forme mécanique de son corps de même que le cube géometrique est la forme du cube matériel".[76] This is, of course, a misreading of Spinoza who did attribute concrete reality and power to the soul.[77] The fact, however, remains that in Leibniz' view the soul was but the idea of the body and both were the same reality, a view which precludes the possibility of assuming that he took the notion of the pre-established harmony from Spinoza. Wolff's, Lessing's and Heydenreich's interpretations of Spinoza agreed with Leibniz'. Mendelssohn's thesis has, therefore, no *locus standi*, and would most probably not have been proposed had Mendelssohn known of Leibniz' observations on Spinoza.

The question of Spinoza's influence on Leibniz, which Mendelssohn's *Philosophische Gespräche* had set afloat, was not settled by the late eighteenth-century reaction to the claim that had been put forward. Jacobi, who endorsed Heydenreich's critique of Mendelssohn, left the question in abeyance: "How much or how little Leibniz owed to Spinoza—I have no opinion on this nor do I seek to have one."[78] The issue claimed a great deal of attention in the nineteenth century and has not ceased to be debated even today. It was no longer confined to the doctrine of the pre-established harmony but took in the whole range of Leibniz' monadology and other areas as well.[79] Ludwig Stein placed the discussion on a new basis by investigating in great detail and with a wealth of fresh documentary evidence the stages of Leibniz' development. He believed that he had shown, among other things, that Leibniz passed through a Spinozistic phase.[80] This view has, however, since been discarded. Ernst Cassirer rejected it as ill-founded,[81] and Georges Friedmann disproved it more

[75] Cf. Friedmann, *loc. cit.*, pp. 103, 172.
[76] Cf. Friedmann, *loc. cit.*, p. 134.
[77] Cf. Friedmann, *loc. cit.*, p. 134.
[78] *Über die Lehre des Spinoza*, etc., p. 394.
[79] For a survey of the debate up to 1890 see Stein, *loc. cit.*, pp. 1–16.
[80] *Loc. cit.*, pp. 60–110.
[81] Ernst Cassirer, *Leibniz' System* (Marburg, 1902; Hildesheim, 1962), p. 519.

recently in convincing fashion.[82] While Cassirer admits Spinoza's possible influence on Leibniz' moral theory,[83] Friedmann makes the point that Spinoza had no share in the formation of Leibniz' system,[84] and that Leibniz' *Système Nouveau* was offered in radical opposition to previous systems.[85] Leon Roth, to whose memory the present study is respectfully dedicated, expressed a different point of view[86]:

> All that Leibniz says about his many individual things is the same as what Spinoza says about one thing . . . Nor is there any reason why Leibniz should not have made his own use of Spinoza. What he ought not to have done, however, was to go out of his way at every opportunity to discredit the source from which he drew. And he drew and adapted much. His theory of soul, of the pre-established harmony, of liberty, of perfection, depend closely on specific points in Spinoza's doctrine; while his central concept of the fundamental place of activity (*esse=agere*) is one of the most important, although usually neglected, sides of Spinoza's general point of view . . .

It is interesting to find that Leon Roth resumed, on a far larger scale and in far sterner accents, the thesis which the young Mendelssohn had propounded *sine ira*, albeit *cum studio*. Roth was obviously not aware of Mendelssohn's early *opus*, since he quotes only his *Morgenstunden*.[87] His rather sweeping claim is supported by but one single reference, viz. to Stein's "very thorough discussion".[88] In view of the shakiness of Stein's theory, his claim does not stand on firm ground, and one cannot withold sympathy from Herbert Wildon Carr's angry rejection of the charge of plagiarism so repeatedly levelled against Leibniz.[89] Mendelssohn's *opus* 1, we may sum up, made history, and it has its place in the protracted debate on the issue it raised long after Lange's rancorous attack had occurred and fallen into oblivion. It also

[82] Friedmann, *loc. cit.*, pp. 225, 273ff.

[83] Cassirer, *loc. cit.*, p. 520.

[84] Friedmann, *loc. cit.*, p. 218.

[85] Friedmann, *loc. cit.*, p. 137.

[86] Leon Roth, *Spinoza* (London, 1929), p. 205.

[87] See p. 210.

[88] See p. 205, n. 1.

[89] Carr, *loc. cit.* (n. 27), pp. 206ff.—Carr's book appeared in 1930, one year after Roth's, but his strictures do not seem to be directed particularly against Roth's claims. It may be noted that Leibniz himself rejected the charge of plagiarism in his letter to Bourguet quoted by Jacobi, *loc. cit.*, pp. 363–304, and by Friedmann, *loc. cit.*, p. 188.

made history in Mendelssohn's own life, and did so in rather a poignant way. The figure of Spinoza which his very first dialogue had raised from the shades was to haunt him almost like a ghost when, towards the end of his life, Jacobi's disclosure about Lessing's Spinozism upset him in uncommon degree and forced him to re-examine his own relationship with Spinoza. It may well be true, as many of his contemporaries felt to be the case, that the anguish over his shattered peace was a contributory factor to his death. Spinoza had been his first thought as a young writer. Spinoza was also his last.

12

FRANZ ROSENZWEIG ON HISTORY

I

From the autumn of 1908 until the summer of 1912, with one year's interruption, Franz Rosenzweig studied History in Freiburg under Friedrich Meinecke, the celebrated teacher and leader of national liberalism in Germany. Rosenzweig was greatly impressed by Meinecke's *Nationalstaat und Weltbürgertum* which had appeared in 1907 and seems to have formed a topic of discussion in the seminars of the period.[1] The method of *Ideengeschichte* which it had introduced[2] became one of the formative influences in Rosenzweig's thinking. It taught him to see the force and interplay of ideas at the root of history. The book showed the tremendous impact which philosophical ideas had had on nineteenth-century German politics. It brought Rosenzweig close to the fundamental issues in modern political thought and stimulated all kinds of literary plans in his own mind.[3] These projects finally crystallized in his doctorate thesis, the two-volume work, *Hegel und der Staat* (1920), which Meinecke regarded very highly.[4]

[1] Cf. Franz Rosenzweig, *Briefe*, edited by Edith Rosenzweig (Berlin, 1935), pp. 40, 41, 43–44.

[2] Cf. Carlo Antoni, *Vom Historismus zur Soziologie* (Stuttgart), pp. 126ff. Rosenzweig refers to the method of *Ideengeschichte* in *Briefe*, pp. 55, 318.

[3] Cf. *Briefe*, pp. 43–44, 60–61.

[4] In an obituary note on Rosenzweig in *Historische Zeitschrift*, Vol. 142 (München-Berlin, 1930), pp. 219–220, Meinecke described his former pupil as "der Verfasser des bedeutenden und sehr wirksam gewordenen Werkes 'Hegel und der Staat'". "Rosenzweig", he continued, "begann als Historiker mit stärkstem philosophischem Einschlag . . . Der Weltkrieg machte ihn irre an dem zuerst verfolgten Weg, die Höhen der deutschen protestantischen Kultur zu erforschen; darum flüchtete er in die Welt seines Bluts. Aber durch jenes Buch über Hegel hat er der deutschen Geistesgeschichte ein Werk von bleibendem Wert hinterlassen."

Meinecke made another reference to Rosenzweig in a chapter devoted to his pupils

Rosenzweig brought to his historical studies a strong philosophical bent, as his teacher was not slow to recognize.[5] This involved the temptation to "construct" history and in the end led him into paths far removed from historical science proper. Yet the training received in Freiburg served as a salutary check in curbing any flights of pure speculation. He remained conscious of the need to observe philological criteria and to ascertain the empirical facts concerning the ideas assumed to have played a part in individuals and groups.[6] Meinecke's warnings against "speculative constructions"[7] had obviously not failed in their purpose. But whilst Rosenzweig was determined to avoid false or superficial constructions he was equally convinced that historical insight was impossible without the right kind of construction.[8]

The focal point of Rosenzweig's historical thinking is the year 1800 around which cluster the dates of the French Revolution, Hegel and Goethe.[9] The historical perspective offered by these dates suggests to Rosenzweig that the Christian world had entered into its last, Johannine, phase. The notion of Johannine Christianity formed one of the leading ideas of the German idealist movement. It occupied Fichte's mind since 1804, as Hans Ehrenberg has shown.[10] Schelling concludes his lectures on the Philosophy of Revelation with the words, "If I had to build a church in our time, I would dedicate it to Saint John."[11] Peter is the apostle of the Father, Paul of the Son, and John of the Holy Spirit.[12] John

[5] See n. 4.

[6] Cf. *Briefe*, p. 318, and Franz Rosenzweig, *Kleinere Schriften* (Berlin, 1937), pp. 505–507.

[7] Cf. *Briefe*, p. 41.

[8] Cf. *ibid.*, p. 49.

[9] Cf. *Kleinere Schriften*, p. 358: "weil die Unruhe in meinem Denkuhrwerk '1800' heisst ('Hegel' and 'Goethe' . . .). Und also von diesem meinem intellektuellen Mittelpunkt aus muss ich alles sehen . . ." See also *Briefe*, p. 706: "Für uns handelt es sich jetzt um 1789 (1781, 1794, 1806)."

[10] Cf. Hans Ehrenberg, *Disputation. Drei Bücher vom deutschen Idealismus. Fichte. Der Disputation Erstes Buch* (München, 1923), pp. 136ff. The book is dedicated "Dem Freunde Franz Rosenzweig und seinem Werke 'Der Stern der Erlösung'".

[11] Cf. Schelling, *Philosophie der Offenbarung*, Sämtliche Werke, II, iv (1858), p. 332.

[12] *Loc. cit.*, pp. 326–327.

in *Strassburg, Freiburg, Berlin*, 1901–1919, *Erinnerungen von Friedrich Meinecke*, Stuttgart, p. 97: "Ich nenne weiter ein in der Wissenschaft bekannt gewordenes jüdisches Mitglied dieses Kreises, Franz Rosenzweig, der durch das Hegelkapitel in meinem Weltbürgertum angeregt, das subtile Buch über Hegel und den Staat geschrieben hat und nach dem Kriege, erschüttert über diesen, wie er fürchtete, endgültigen Zusammenbruch deutscher Ideale, in einem vergeistigten Judentum seine angestammte Bestimmung wieder zu finden glaubte . . ."

represents the Church of a free, undogmatic Christianity.[13] This concept of a progressive liberalization of Christianity is a modern, secularized version of the revolutionary doctrine of the three Churches which was first propounded by Joachim of Fiore, the twelfth-century abbot, and had paved the way for the Reformation.[14] The hopes which the German Idealists associated with the Johannine form of Christianity had an eschatological ring and were echoed in Jewish circles during the period of emancipation. The messianic fervour which seized the Jewish Reform Movement in the nineteenth century and which is reflected in the philosophical writings of S. Formstecher and S. Hirsch down to Hermann Cohen stems from the idealist concept of Johannine Christianity. Rosenzweig, who took the notion from Schelling,[15] still retains its eschatological flavour but gives it a new interpretation. It arises from a close study of the relationship between Christianity and philosophy, the latter representing the force of paganism, the "wisdom of the Greeks". It also presupposes the acceptance of Hegel's view that having comprehended itself historically, the Mind has reached the full consciousness of itself. Rosenzweig sees in the history of philosophy from Thales to Hegel ("from Jonia to Jena") one sustained pagan effort of idealist thinking which is gradually neutralized by the impact of the

[13] *Loc. cit.*, p. 328: "Johannes ist der Apostel der zukünftigen, erst wahrhaft allgemeinen Kirche jenes zweiten, neuen Jerusalems, . . . jener nichts mehr ausschliessenden Stadt Gottes . . ., in die Heiden und Juden gleich eingehen, . . . die ohne beschränkenden Zwang, ohne äussere Auktorität, welcher Art sie sey, durch sich selbst besteht, weil jeder freiwillig herbeikommt, jeder durch eigne Überzeugung, indem sein Geist in ihr eine Heimat gefunden, zur ihr gehört."

[14] On Joachim of Fiore see Ernst Benz, *Ecclesia Spiritualis* (Stuttgart, 1934), and Karl Löwith, *Meaning in History* (Chicago, 1949), pp. 145ff. and (bibliography), p. 243. A good introduction with selected texts is given in Alfons Rosenberg's *Joachim von Fiore, Das Reich des Heiligen Geistes* (München–Planegg, 1955).

According to I. F. Baer, *Zion*, Vol. V (Jerusalem, 1939), pp. 1–44, the Franciscan Spirituals in the thirteenth century, who were followers of Joachim, influenced the author of the *Raya Mehemna*, a kabbalistic interpretation of the commandments and prohibitions of the Torah. Joachim's doctrine of the correspondence of the three stages of the Church and of the three persons in the Christian Trinity may seem to have had some influence on the book *Temunah* (about 1250) which emanated from the circle around Naḥmanides. It describes the various (7) aeons of the world (*Shemiṭṭot*) as representing the (7) lower aspects (*Sefirot*) of Divinity. Cf. G. Scholem, *Major Trends in Jewish Mysticism*, Revised Edition (New York, 1946), pp. 178–180, where direct influence is, however, considered unlikely. In his *Ursprung und Anfänge der Kabbala* (Berlin, 1962), p. 410 Scholem points out that by the time when Joachim's doctrine had spread to Spain the concept of the *Shemiṭṭot* was already entrenched in the kabbalistic circle of Gerona.

[15] Cf. *Briefe*, p. 706; *Kleinere Schriften*, p. 266.

Jewish-Christian tradition, i.e. Revelation, and spends itself in Hegel. The Christian world *post Hegel mortuum* is identical with the Johannine Church.

The theme is one that engages Rosenzweig's mind from an early period and is worked out in his letters and writings in a variety of shades and emphases yet with a remarkable constancy of construction in fundamentals. Already in his letter to Hans Ehrenberg (dated 11th December, 1913) Rosenzweig outlines the view which was to become characteristic of his entire historical thinking: The separation of Church and science from the Reformation onward means that the Church had by then completed the absorption of Greek philosophy. The pagan Aristotle was no longer a power. Descartes, Spinoza and Leibniz cannot be considered pagans outside the Church but heretics within it. In Kant, Fichte, Schelling, Hegel, the heretics return to the fold of the Church. They regard themselves as Christian philosophers. The philosopher has ceased to be synonymous with freethinking. He is no longer *discipulus Graeciae*, as Tertullian called him, but simply a Christian. Hegel is the last philosopher and the first of the new Church Fathers, i.e. of the Johannine Church.[16] More outspoken is a letter from March, 1916: "The idealist movement is both the end of philosophy (that is of paganism) and the beginning of the Johannine epoch (its patristic age as it were)."[17] The letter also introduces for the first time the recognition of Freemasonry as an expression of the third (Johannine) Church. The theme is more fully elaborated in Rosenzweig's letter to Eugen Rosenstock, dated 30th November, 1916: Since 1789 the Church has no longer any relationship with the state but only with society, the reason being that the Church has now entered into its last (Johannine, to use Schelling's term) epoch. There exists no more Greek wisdom, no more Roman Empire, only Christianity. This is what the Johannites wanted from the start, but it did not happen earlier because wisdom and Empire had not yet fulfilled themselves in time.[18] The emancipation of the Jews is another expression of the Johannine period. Until 1789 the Old Testament was the Book in which the Church had found its typology. Hence its opposition to Israel, the denier of its claim. Since 1789 the Church can look to its own history of the past when the hierarchy and

[16] Cf. *Briefe*, pp. 81–82.
[17] Cf. *ibid.*, p. 91. See also *loc. cit.*, p. 265.
[18] Cf. *Briefe*, pp. 706–707.

the Book had an institutional character, and those earlier, substantive periods now move into the position of the Old Testament. What remains of the Jew and for the first time enters into the horizon of Christianity is the "naked Jew", seen without the prism of the Old Testament.[19]

In his *Star of Redemption* Rosenzweig further elaborates Schelling's idea of the three Churches. They represent the three fundamental virtues of love, faith and hope respectively. In the love of the missionary who goes out to convert those still dwelling in darkness, the Church of Peter created its own Empire and at the same time built in its institutions the visible body of the Church. But throughout the Middle Ages it failed to come to grips with the paganism in its own soul. Paganism had been repressed but not truly converted. Hence the dualism of faith and reason in medieval scholasticism. A new power accrues to Christianity after the revival of paganism in the Renaissance when the Pauline Church of the Reformation could baptize the Christian's invisible, inward soul. But, again, the work remained incomplete. By subscribing to faith alone (*sola fides*) reality had been split into the pure inwardness of faith and an external secular world which no longer owed allegiance to the Spirit. Christianity had lost control of the world. Body and soul had become separated. German idealist philosophy reflects this Protestant error. The Spirit presumes to produce everything out of itself. With Goethe's pagan assertion of individuality, wholeness and personal destiny a new period enters. Now man feels completely at home in the world and becomes fully alive. The nations too discover their individual soul and destiny. In the Petrine Church they had been subject to the Holy Empire. In the Pauline Church they obeyed secular authorities. Now, in the Johannine era they are Christian nations who believe in their own historical destiny. As Rosenzweig put it in one of his letters,[20] nationalism is the "complete Christianizing of the concept of peoplehood". The Johannine Church is historically connected with the Eastern Church but now assumes a universal significance. It can lay claim to no institutional form of its own. It cannot be "built", as Freemasonry mistakenly believes, it can only grow. Its message is one of hope. In this Johannine world, the Christian no longer converts the heathen around him nor the pagan within him. Now the Jew is meant to convert the pagan

[19] Cf. *Briefe*, pp. 707–708. See also *loc. cit.*, p. 282. [20] Cf. *Briefe*, p. 686.

lurking in the Christian soul. For only in the Jewish blood hope lives eternally, and hope is what the Christian needs today more than anything else. This is why the emancipation of the Jew had to happen precisely in this modern age.[21]

Rosenzweig's reading of the history of Christianity is a remarkable blend of *Ideengeschichte à la* Meinecke and theological conceptualism. History is seen as the dialectic of pagan myth and revelation, as the field in which the Kingdom of God grows toward its realization. There is an eschatological urge or *nisus* at work in the history thus constructed. Obviously, Rosenzweig is fascinated by the plenitude of visions which the panorama of the struggles within Christianity evokes in him. From his first excitement in reading Tertullian's *Apologeticus* in 1911 which gave him a vivid impression of Christianity in the Roman Empire[22] down to his no less exciting correspondence with Eugen Rosenstock he learned to see history proper enacted in the Christian centuries. History became to him tantamount to the history of Christianity against the background of Greece and Rome. His theology of creation, revelation and redemption is but the conceptualized application of this historical vision. Creation, the Alpha of history, expresses the pagan world; revelation, though stemming from Judaism, transforms creation only through Christianity, and redemption is the goal towards which the world is moving.

Judaism itself remains essentially outside history. Not only after the year 70 but long before, it had seceded from active participation in the growth of the surrounding world, a view which comes close to the results of Max Weber's sociological analysis of Judaism.[23] Rosenzweig himself acknowledged this affinity and

[21] Cf. Franz Rosenzweig, *Der Stern der Erlösung* (Heidelberg, 1954), III, pp. 25–34. For Schelling's concept of the "growth of the Kingdom" (Mark 4:26ff.) see *loc. cit.*, II, iv, p. 295.

[22] Cf. *Briefe*, p. 59.

[23] Cf. Max Weber, *Gesammelte Aufsätze zur Religionssoziologie*, Vol. III, *Das antike Judentum* (Tübingen, 1921), where post-exilic Judaism is described as the religion of a "Pariah nation". The term "Pariah nation" is not meant in a derogatory sense but is intended to designate the character of post-exilic Judaism as living in a self-imposed social seclusion. In his review of Weber's work, Julius Guttmann interprets the sociological aspects of Jewish exclusiveness in terms which come very close to Rosenzweig's and may have been influenced by him. Cf. *Monatsschrift für Geschichte und Wissenschaft des Judentums*, edited by I. Heinemann, Vol. 69, N.F. 33, 1925, pp. 222–223: "Die messianische Hoffnung des Judentums macht die jetzige Welt zu einem Provisorium, dem die gottgewollte Ordnung erst folgen soll. In den Zeiten ihrer unmittelbaren Aktualität führte diese Hoffnung zu völliger Gleichgültigkeit gegen die gegenwärtige Welt. Eine eigentümliche Haltung musste sich ergeben, als

regretted the fact that at the time of writing the *Star of Redemption* he had not yet known Max Weber's work.[24] His discovery of the ahistorical nature of Judaism first produced a serious crisis in his life. The disquieting question which it posed was: Was there still any room for Judaism in a world in which Christianity was the motive force? It was this question which lay at the root of his intention to leave Judaism and embrace Christianity. The story of his "conversion" to Judaism need not be retold here.[25] What interests us in this context is the fact that his affirmation of Judaism entailed a revaluation of history as such. History, for all its fascination to the historian, becomes a temporary, provisional affair, and the emphasis is shifted to the eschatological realm, the end and goal of history. The significance of Judaism lies in the fact that it anticipates, represents and ensures that end and goal. True, Judaism lies outside history, but what seemed to constitute its weakness now appears as its unique strength. History itself moves into a relative position. It is not itself the realm of the Kingdom but only the intermediate realm (*Zwischenreich*), and whilst Rosenzweig the historian can do full justice to Christianity as the decisive power in the intermediate realm, Rosenzweig the Jew is more vitally interested in the final Kingdom of which Judaism is the representative and trustee. "For me God alone is reality; I am a member of the intermediate realm only by the compulsion of nature (i.e. history), not by free will. Jesus belongs to the intermediate realm. Whether he was the Messiah will become clear only when the Messiah comes. Today he is to me as problematic as the whole intermediate realm. I am sure only of God and His Kingdom, not of the *Zwischenreich*."[26]

Rosenzweig holds that it is the task of the Jew to sacrifice life in the world for the purpose of testifying to the messianic goal of

[24] Cf. *Briefe*, p. 405.

[25] See the present writer's article in *The Journal of Religion*, Vol. XXIV, 4 (Chicago, 1944), pp. 258–270, and Nahum N. Glatzer's in *Judaism*, Vol. I (New York, 1952), pp. 69–79.

[26] Cf. *Briefe*, pp. 302, 316–317, 331–332.

nach der Rückkehr aus dem Exil die Hoffnung auf das unmittelbare Eintreten der messianischen Zeit enttäuscht wurde und das Judentum sich in der gegenwärtigen Welt einzurichten hatte. Es musste sich mit ihr abfinden und fühlte sich doch letztlich nicht zu ihr gehörig. Es lebte gleichsam in einem dauernden Provisorium, musste sich den Ordnungen der gegebenen Welt einfügen, die es doch innerlich nicht bejahen konnte. Seine Aufgabe in dieser Übergangszeit bestand darin, in seinem Kreise das göttliche Gebot zu halten, nicht aber diese Welt als solche umzubilden."

history. Judaism, he repeatedly declares, lives and has its being in the *eschaton*: It "is alive only in so far as it is with God. Only when the world too will be with God, will Judaism be alive also in a worldly sense. That, however, will happen only beyond history."[27] The inevitable price Israel has to pay for being the people of the Kingdom is a loss of worldly creativity. "The sacredness which attaches to it as a nation of priests sterilizes its life." It prevents it "from surrendering its soul to the yet unconsecrated world of the nations".[28] War and revolution, the only realities which the state knows and which create the epochs of world history, do not affect the inner life of Israel.[29] The formula which Rosenzweig uses to denote the metahistorical existence of Judaism is: The Jew is at the goal of history, the Christian is eternally on his way.[30] This phrase expresses not only a theological belief but a historical truth as Rosenzweig sees it. It means, as the context of its discussion in the *Star of Redemption* clearly shows, that, in contrast to the Christian, the Jew has no inner conflict which history is expected to solve. The Christian soul is divided between nation and Church, between "Siegfried" and Christ, between myth and revelation. For the Jew no such inner discord exists. His sense of national destiny and his allegiance to God find themselves in complete harmony.[31] Whereas the history of Christianity is one of constant growth—represented by the succession of the

[27] Cf. *ibid.*, pp. 311–312.

[28] Cf. *Der Stern der Erlösung*, III, p. 91.

[29] *Loc. cit.*, III, pp. 93–94.

[30] *Loc. cit.*, III, pp. 86, 91, 104–105, 127. Rosenzweig's view of Judaism as standing at the goal of history may be regarded as a Jewish answer to Hegel's and Schelling's interpretations of Judaism. For Hegel the Jewish religion represents the stage of "negativity" against nature ("the angry God") which is inferior to both Hellas and Christianity. See H. J. Schoeps's article, "Die ausserchristlichen Religionen bei Hegel", *Zeitschrift für Religions- und Geistesgeschichte*, ed. E. Benz and H. J. Schoeps, Vol. VIII, 1, 1955, pp. 27–32. Schelling, who was much more sympathetic to Judaism. nevertheless, describes it similarly: "Das Judentum war eigentlich nie etwas Positives, es kann nur entweder als gehemmtes Heidentum, oder als potentielles, noch verborgenes Christentum bestimmt werden." Cf. *loc. cit.*, II, iv, p. 148. Whereas the idealist Jewish philosophers (S. Formstecher; S. Hirsch) tried to refute Hegel and Schelling by employing their dialectical method in reverse direction, Rosenzweig takes Judaism completely out of the historical process. In a sense, he may have been influenced by Schelling who, from a Christian point of view, regards Judaism as being outside history: "Indem sie den Übergang zum Christentum versahen und versäumten, schlossen sie sich von dem grossen Gang der Geschichte aus. Sie *mussten* aufhören ein Volk zu seyn, unter die Völker zerstreut und zerstiebt werden. Sie waren nur *etwas* als die Träger der Zukunft . . . es ist im eigentlichen Sinn *ausgeschlossen* von der Geschichte." (*Loc. cit.*, II, iv, p. 150.)

[31] Cf. *Der Stern der Erlösung*. III, pp. 87–88; *Briefe*, pp. 335–336.

three Churches—Judaism has no history after the first exile and, particularly, after the year 70. It has left behind the contradictions which lie at the back of the historical life. It has reached the goal.

Yet for all its intrinsic remoteness from the course of history Judaism fulfils a messianic purpose in the world. Living at the extreme point of history, symbolizing and anticipating it, Israel is the incarnation, we might say, of the Kingdom, the messenger of hope. Moreover, in this world of the dissolution of the hierarchical (Petrine) Church and of the (Pauline) Church of the Word there is no real substance left in the Christian life. In this epoch of "naked Christianity" the Jew is the only reality which binds Christianity to the Kingdom.[32] It prevents it from disintegrating into a myth or philosophy. It reminds the Christian that salvation comes from the Jews, not from the Greeks.[33] And it urges the Christian to realize that the world is not yet redeemed, that faith is not yet redemption. In Christianity the eschatological orientation is somewhat indistinct and easily merges with either creation or revelation. The Jew who hallows his flesh and blood under the yoke of the Law and continually lives in the reality of the Kingdom serves as a reminder to the Christian that redemption cannot be achieved by the mere inwardness of feeling.[34] He is the "eternal *enfant terrible*", the "mute admonisher",[35] whose function is always resented yet is indispensable.

Rosenzweig's view of the ahistorical character of Judaism accords, in a way, with certain traditional attempts at Jewish self-interpretation. The exclusion of the Jewish people from the realm of history was keenly felt in many epochs and led to the doctrine of God's exile (*Galut Shekhinah*), a theme with wide and profound ramifications in Jewish mystical thought. His concept of Christianity as a missionary of Judaism to the Gentile world, preparing it for the Kingdom, also stands on traditional ground. It is taken from the medieval Jewish philosophers and their modern disciples (S. Formstecher; S. Hirsch; Hermann Cohen). In support of his view Rosenzweig is able to preface and conclude his chapter on Christianity with quotations from Maimonides and Jehudah Hallevi, respectively. How far Judaism may be said to have "reached the goal" is another matter. Rosenzweig's idyllic notion

[32] Cf. *Briefe*, pp. 706–708.
[33] Cf. *Briefe*, pp. 74–75.
[34] Cf. *Der Stern der Erlösung*, III, pp. 197–198.
[35] Cf. *Briefe*, pp. 202, 75, 690.

of the freedom of the Jewish soul from inner conflict can hardly stand the test of closer scrutiny. The strong antinomian tendencies which reveal themselves in certain kabbalistic writings—notably in the *Sefer ha-Temunah* and in the literature which it engendered[36] —and in the Sabbatian movement clearly show the stresses and tensions within Judaism itself.

II

Rosenzweig's view of history is carried a stage further in the very conception of the Kingdom as outlined in the *Star of Redemption.* Revelation from which redemption flows as from its source is the dialogue between God and man. More particularly, it is the experience of the love of God. This experience has not necessarily a historical place but is a happening between God and man wherever and whenever they meet. Revelation is not an end in itself. The love of God challenges man to love his neighbour. This is the only commandment, and all the others are but its derivatives.[37] In German Idealism revelation tends to be regarded as the one and only concern of the soul.[38] Rosenzweig warns against all mystical enjoyment of revelation.[39] He insists that Schleiermacher's and Fichte's "Being immortal in every moment" is "a mere phrase"; that *all* the time must be fulfilled in order that the fruit of eternity may ripen.[40] What he means by the ripe fruit of eternity is the ensouling (*Beseelung*) of the world through love, something analogous to the ensoulment of an object of nature by the artist.[41] By loving what comes our way ("our neighbour";

[36] Cf. G. Scholem, *Ursprung und Anfänge der Kabbala*, pp. 417ff.

[37] Cf. *Der Stern der Erlösung*, II, pp. 114–115, 163–165.

[38] Cf. J. L. Fichte, *Die Anweisung zum seligen Leben*, Sämtliche Werke, II, 3 (Berlin, 1845), p. 481: "Dieses—bei Gott Seyn nun . . . wird ferner charakterisiert als Logos oder Wort. Wie konnte deutlicher ausgesprochen werden, dass es die sich selbst klare und verständliche Offenbarung und Manifestation, sein geistiger Ausdruck sey,—dass . . . das unmittelbare Daseyn Gottes notwendig Bewusstseyn, theils seiner selbst, theils Gottes sey . . ." Fichte rejects the concept of creation. Cf. *loc. cit.*, pp. 479–480, and tends to equate the *eschaton* with the *Reich der Vernunft* within us. See H. Ehrenberg's analysis and critique in his *Fichte*, pp. 144–146. Fichte's denial of creation was opposed by Schelling, *loc. cit.*, II, iv, pp. 101–103. On the young Hegel's metaphysics of love see Jakob Taubes, *Abendländische Eschatologie* (Bern, 1947), pp. 149ff. Schleiermacher's mysticism belongs to the same climate of thought.

[39] Cf. *Der Stern der Erlösung*, II, pp. 154–156; III, pp. 18–20.

[40] Cf. *Briefe*, p. 314.

[41] Cf. *Briefe*, p. 222. On the "Beseelung" and "Durchseelung" of the world through love see *Der Stern der Erlösung*, II, pp. 195–197.

der Nächste) we endow it with soul and life. Each individual waits for the loving response of his fellow men by which alone his individual character can be redeemed from the tragic futility of self-enclosure.[42] The notion of individuality lay at the root of German Idealism and Historicism, and engaged Rosenzweig's interest already in his student days when he meant to write a book on "the history of tragic individuality in Germany since Lessing".[43] The kingdom of the world, i.e. the natural path of world history has laws of its own expressed in terms of state and legal order. But they are merely the ground-work of creation from which the Kingdom of God has to emerge. Love is the force which brings about redemption. It creates the Kingdom.

The Kingdom, Rosenzweig emphasizes, is not the result of "progress" as the philosophers of *Aufklärung* suggested. As he remarks in one of his letters (dated 30th May, 1917), every progress in the direction of the good entails *pari passu* a corresponding growth of evil: Democracy means both responsibility and release of anarchic power; tolerance means conviction and indifference; Goethe is both Faust and Mephisto.[44] The problematical nature of progress could not have been seen more clearly.[45] Hegel's optimism he had discarded long ago. "Why should we be in need of God if history were God-like, if every deed, once it entered history, became *ipso facto* God-like and justifiable?" No, he says, every human deed is liable to become sinful precisely after it has entered history and has become part of it, since through the interrelation of acts in history no act is merely personal but is caught up in an impersonal nexus of cause and effect beyond the control and intention of the doer. For this reason God must redeem man not through history but—there is no alternative—through religion.[46] Rosenzweig rejects the ideology of progress for yet another reason. Revelation, he says in the *Star of Redemption*, is the ground and source of the Kingdom. In revelation eternity breaks into time, and it is this element of eternity which defies any attempt to account for the coming of the Kingdom in terms of a

[42] Cf. *Der Stern der Erlösung*, II, pp. 173–177, 196–199.

[43] Cf. *Briefe*, p. 60. On the significance of the concept of individuality in German thought see Friedrich Meinecke, *Schaffender Spiegel* (Stuttgart, 1948), pp. 221ff.

[44] Cf. *Briefe*, pp. 212–213. The paradox that "the world can become good only through the good" is quoted here and in *Der Stern der Erlösung*, II, p. 182.

[45] The ideology of progress is refuted, both in its "Islamic" and modern form, in *Der Stern der Erlösung*, II, pp. 177–181.

[46] Cf. *Briefe*, p. 55.

continuous, linear time-process. Eternity in the sense of the Kingdom is the fullness and totality of all the single moments in which revelation is experienced.[47] Eternity, he says in another place, is "not a very long time but a tomorrow which could equally be a today". It is the dimension of the Kingdom. "A being that has once entered into the Kingdom can never drop out of it; it has become eternal."[48] The rapturous words, "But we are eternal" which Hermann Cohen uttered at the end of his last lecture,[49] and which Rosenzweig quotes at the end of his chapter on Redemption[50] are understood by him in this sense. "Eternity" in Cohen's original meaning was "an ethical concept", the "eternity of the progress of moral endeavour", "the orientation (*Blickpunkt*) for the restless, infinite striving of the pure will": "eternity means the eternal task, the task of eternity".[51] Rosenzweig himself re-echoes this concept during the period prior to his writing the *Star* when he describes the ethical deed as determined by the infinite and unconditional, and as acted as if the fate of eternity depended on it.[52] But in the *Star of Redemption* eternity is more than the horizon of the ethical. It is the triumph of redemption over death, man's glorious release from his temporal existence,[53] the reality of the Kingdom.[54]

The eternity of the Kingdom implies a paradox: it is both presentness, the "eternalizing of the moment"[55] and future, being "eternally on its way".[56] Rosenzweig defines it as "a future which without ceasing to be future is nevertheless present".[57] It grows but the time required for its growth is not determined; more precisely, its growth has no relation at all to time.[58] For "eternity consists in this that no time is allowed between the present moment and the end, but the future is already seized today".[59] It is characteristic of the eschatological future that the end must be expected any moment. This constitutes its eternity. "That every

[47] Cf. *Der Stern der Erlösung*, II, p. 99. [48] Cf. *ibid.*, II, p. 176.

[49] Cf. Rosenzweig's Introduction to *Hermann Cohen's Jüdische Schriften*, edited by Bruno Strauss (Berlin, 1924), Vol. I, pp. lxi–ii.

[50] Cf. *Der Stern der Erlösung*, II, pp. 212–213.

[51] Cf. Hermann Cohen, *Ethik des reinen Willens*, 4. Aufl. (Berlin), pp. 412–416.

[52] Cf. *Briefe*, p. 157.

[53] Cf. Karl Löwith, "M. Heidegger and F. Rosenzweig or Temporality and Eternity", *Philosophy and Phenomenological Research*, Vol. III (1942–1943), pp. 53ff., where Rosenzweig's position is contrasted with Heidegger's "Sein zum Tode".

[54] Cf. *Der Stern der Erlösung*, II, pp. 212–213; III, p. 172.

[55] Cf. *ibid.*, II, p. 179. [56] Cf. *ibid.*, II, p. 176.

[57] Cf. *ibid.*, II, pp. 176–177. [58] *Ibid.* [59] Cf. *ibid.*, III, p. 87.

moment may be the last makes it eternal."[60] Nothing, Rosenzweig says, is more objectionable to the ideology of progress than this notion that the ideal goal may be reached at the next, nay at the present, moment instead of as the result of an infinite progress in time.[61] Yet this is the very essence of the Kingdom. It would be wrong to assume that Rosenzweig wishes to deny altogether the relevance of time for the growth of the Kingdom. No one is more emphatic than he that time is needed for the growth of the world into the Kingdom. It takes time until man experiences the love of God,[62] and it takes time for the world to come across the fructifying and ensouling love of man. God alone knows the hour. He has given the world the law of its autonomous growth. His revelation calls forth the response of love. Redemption issues from Him at the hour of grace.[63] In his essay, *Das neue Denken*, Rosenzweig left no doubt that there is in his view an irreversible order of time in every single happening and in reality as a whole.[64] Yet for all this there exists, strictly speaking, no history of the Kingdom, only a pre-history of it. Eternity has no history.[65]

In the light of eternity eschatology itself takes on a new meaning. It is no longer the end of history but the eternity beyond history. And this eternity is presentness and future at the same time. It is a dimension of existence rather than a fixed point to be reached. The "waiting for the Messiah" is not mere passive expectancy, but means entering into eternity, living in the Kingdom, and giving birth to the Kingdom. "Das Warten entbindet das Reich aus der Welt."[66] The future ceases to be an historical category. It no longer denotes a time to come but the Kingdom to come. Future, the Kingdom and eternity become synonymous terms in Rosenzweig's eschatological thinking. They are existential terms, not concepts denoting objective reality. They do not deny and invalidate history. On the contrary, they seek to give meaning to history. Rosenzweig realizes that the meaning of history cannot be spun out of its temporal substance. Historical time is incapable of yielding meaning unless it is related to the horizon of eternity. It is through revelation that eternity penetrates time, fulfilling and redeeming it. In a sense, the *eschaton* is in the present,

[60] Cf. *ibid.*, II, p. 179. [61] Cf. *ibid.*, II, p. 180. [62] Cf. *ibid.*, II, pp. 98–99.
[63] Cf. *ibid.*, II, pp. 198–199; III, pp. 16–17. [64] Cf. *Kleinere Schriften*, p. 385.
[65] Cf. *Der Stern der Erlösung*, III, pp. 16, 119. [66] Cf. *ibid.*, II, pp. 181–182.

and eschatology points to the future only in so far as it is realized in the present. In the concept of *Kairos* Paul Tillich expresses a similar eschatology.[67]

It might seem that Rosenzweig's interpretation of history as the *locus* of eternity obliterates the distinction between past, present and future, and altogether destroys the character of history as an order of time. Yet this is certainly not his meaning. On the contrary, he emphasizes that it is precisely revelation which "brings an absolute symbolical order into history".[68] "Revelation is orientation." It establishes not only "a real above and below" but also "a real and firm before and after in time". It means the *Verabsolutierung* of time and creates an "absolute history".[69] What Rosenzweig intends to convey by these metaphysical notions is this: Through the irruption of revelation history receives a clear and definite articulation. What lies before revelation is paganism and what flows from it is redemption. Moreover, revelation orientates our historical perspective by offering an absolute standard of what is truly meaningful in history. It "creates the stage and content of world history". Neither Plato nor Aristotle knew anything like this. The terms "the end of days" and "the whole earth" are missing from their vocabulary.[70] "Only for Jews and Christians exists that firm orientation of the world in space and time, exists the real world and the real history."[71]Rosenzweig repudiates Troeltsch's *Historismus* which equalizes all historical phenomena and speaks of the "nations of the Christian *Kulturkreis*", a term which obliterates the distinctiveness of revelation.[72] "Jews, Greeks and Romans will remain the eternal content of history." For they are the figures in which revelation and its counterfoil appear on the stage of history. In them history possesses its eternal, classical theme. "The Sumerians, the Accadians will not neutralize Moriah, Marathon, Brutus."[73] "Immortality in history belongs only to what positively or negatively belongs to revelation."[74] Revelation creates an absolute history.

[67] Paul Tillich, *The Kingdom of God and History* (London, 1938) (in The Church, Community, and State Series, Vol. 3).

[68] Cf. *Briefe*, p. 710.

[69] Cf. *Kleinere Schriften*, p. 358; *Briefe*, pp. 166, 221. In *Briefe*, p. 710, and *Kleinere Schriften*, p. 358, Rosenzweig credits Eugen Rosenstock with the authorship of this concept. Rosenzweig's letter outlining the idea is found in *Briefe*, pp. 676ff.

[70] Cf. *Briefe*, pp. 211, 429ff.

[71] Cf. *ibid.*, p. 717.

[72] Cf. *ibid.*, pp. 145, 710.

[73] Cf. *ibid.*, p. 710.

[74] Cf. *ibid.*, p. 227.

III

It is a long road which Rosenzweig travelled from his erstwhile preoccupation with German Imperial history to his theology of creation, revelation and redemption. What drew him away from purely secular history was not, as Meinecke suggested, a sense of despair arising out of the German collapse of 1918[75] but, already prior to the War, a deep yearning for eternity, an eschatological urge in which he discovered his Jewishness. From the very start he was troubled by such metaphysical questions as "the origin of evil, God and history".[76] He also moved away from Meinecke's German orientation and developed an interest in universal history. But, again, history tended to become mere "material for rambling", it was to him "neither Hegel's *Gang* nor Ranke's *Mär*",[77] neither the process of universal reason nor factual story. Clearly, he moved towards a viewpoint outside history itself, towards religion. His antipathy to Hegel grew stronger with the years. In 1918, after reading Fichte's *Die Grundzüge des gegenwärtigen Zeitalters*, he wrote: "The contrast to myself became so fully clear to me. Fichte, like Hegel, is perfectly transparent to me, free from contradictions in detail, but *en bloc* contrary and to be rejected."[78] In another letter from the same time: "I am an anti-Hegelian and anti-Fichtean."[79] Hegel's contemplative approach to history antagonized him.[80] He felt much more akin to Schelling[81] whose impact on Rosenzweig's view of history is pronounced. Schelling's description of myth and revelation as presenting a necessary process and free history respectively is reflected in Rosenzweig's concept of the relationship between the pagan world of myth and the truly historical world of revelation.[82] Rosenzweig was particularly impressed with Schelling's great Fragment of "The Ages of the World" (*Die Weltalter*) in which the philosophy of the future is announced as one in the form of narrative (*Die künftige Philosophie wird bloss erzählend sein*).[83] What is implied in this statement Rosenzweig elucidates in his essay, *Das neue Denken*. He feels that

[75] See n. 4. Meinecke himself reacted to the events of 1918 with a feeling of great despondency. In the words of Carlo Antoni (*loc. cit.*, p. 147), "Under the tremendous pressure his soul succumbed and abjured historical idealism." It seems that he projected his own despair on Rosenzweig.

[76] Cf. *Briefe*, p. 53.

[77] Cf. *ibid.*, p. 59.

[78] Cf. *ibid.*, p. 298.

[79] Cf. *ibid.*, p. 299.

[80] Cf. *Briefe*, pp. 55, 409, 476.

[81] Cf. *ibid.*, pp. 298–299.

[82] Cf. Schelling, *loc. cit.*, II, iv, pp. 3–4, 121.

[83] Cf. *Briefe*, pp. 208, 711, 718.

the method he himself adopted in the second book of the *Star of Redemption* conforms to Schelling's precept. By tracing creation, revelation and redemption not as pure concepts but as the stages of world history he had in fact fufilled Schelling's promise.[84]

In comparing Rosenzweig's concept of history with Hegel's and Schelling's one is struck by a strange anomaly. For all their idealist tendencies, Hegel and Schelling retain in outline the Biblical view of history as a field of Divine action and providence. Both echo Schiller's famous sentence in which this view is expressed: "*Die Weltgeschichte ist das Weltgericht*."[85] As Ernst Benz has shown in a recent study,[86] German Idealism reflects in many ways the theological doctrines concerning history which were current among the Swabian Pietists of the eighteenth century. Its eschatological orientation which was alien to the spirit of *Aufklärung* derives from here. Hegel's *List der Vernunft* which exploits the private egotism of man in the service of universal Reason is a secularized form of the Biblical idea that the rulers of the world are but the instruments of God's providence. In Rosenzweig this Biblical heritage is silent. History ceases to be the manifestation of Divine Providence, of Judgment, the dialectic of freedom and necessity. It becomes instead the realm of dialogue, of eternity, of the growing Kingdom. History does not move along with the urge which Providence alone could instil into it. It somehow hovers between time and eternity, and one fails to see how the final day can be reached with the Jew eternally at the goal and the Christian eternally on the way.

The reason which prevented Rosenzweig from introducing Providence into history is the same which enabled Hegel and Schelling to do so. In idealist philosophy history culminates in the complete self-realization of God, the absolute Spirit. In Schelling's words. "The last period is one of complete realization, i.e. the complete humanization (*Menschwerdung*) of God . . . Then

[84] Cf. *Kleinere Schriften*, p. 383.

[85] Cf. Schelling, *loc. cit.*, II, iv, p. 322: "Die Geschichte ist die unwiderstehlichste Auktorität. Ich möchte nicht eben das bekannte Schillersche Wort 'die Weltgeschichte ist das Weltgericht', mit dem sich jetzt manche viel wissen, besonders nicht in gleichem Sinne wiederholen, wohl aber: die Urteile der Geschichte sind Gottes Urteile." On Hegel's use of Schiller's sentence see Karl Löwith, *Meaning in History*, p. 58.

[86] Cf. Ernst Benz, *Schelling, Werden und Wirken seines Denkens* (Zürich, 1955), pp. 29–55.

God will be indeed *all in all*, and pantheism will be true."[87] History is a Divine process in the sense that in it God realizes himself. The New Testament phrase describing the final day as one in which God the Father will be "all in all" plays a prominent part in German Idealism.[88] It has a pantheistic ring—already in Swabian Pietism (F. C. Oetinger) it is interpreted to mean that in the end God will be "all in all *in us*"—and lent itself admirably to an expression of the final goal of the historical process. Providence was introduced into the idealist concept of history at the price of identifying it with the self-realization of God in and through history. Rosenzweig who was at home with this idealist conception and its antecedents in Christian theology refused to pay the price they paid. For him God remains wholly outside history. He need not "become", for He "is". He is not identical with the world but stands in relation to it. Providence, therefore, cannot mean the self-realization of God. It means the love of God as expressed in revelation. The eschatological goal within history is the Kingdom. Eschatology in its absolute sense falls outside history. Neither God nor the eternal have a history.[89] God who is the first will also be the last. He will be the *One above all*, not the *One in all*.[90] The final day beyond history belongs to God alone.

[87] Cf. Schelling, *loc. cit.*, VII, p. 484. See also Paul Tillich, *Mystik und Schuldbewusstsein in Schellings philosophischer Entwicklung* (Gütersloh, 1912), p. 121.

[88] Cf. I. Kant, *Die Religion innerhalb der Grenzen der blossen Vernunft*, in *Werke*, edited by Ernst Cassirer (Berlin, 1923), Vol. VI, p. 282; Schelling, *loc. cit.*, II, iv, p. 333; Benz, *loc. cit.*, pp. 41, 45, 47.

[89] Cf. *Der Stern der Erlösung*, III, pp. 16, 119.

[90] Cf. *ibid.*, III, pp. 159–160, 182–183, 195–196.

SOURCE REFERENCES

1 "The Delphic Maxim in Medieval Islam and Judaism": Philip W. Lown Institute of Advanced Judaic Studies, Brandeis University, Studies and Texts: Volume I, *Biblical and Other Studies*, edited by Alexander Altmann, Harvard University Press (Cambridge, Mass., 1963), pp. 196–232.

2 "The Ladder of Ascension": *Studies in Mysticism and Religion presented to G. G. Scholem on his 70th birthday* (Jerusalem, 1968), pp. 88–119.

3 "Ibn Bājja on Man's Ultimate Felicity": *Harry Austryn Wolfson Jubilee Volume*, English Section, Volume I, American Academy of Jewish Research (Jerusalem, 1965), pp. 47–87.

4 "Essence and Existence in Maimonides": *Bulletin of the John Rylands Library*, Volume 35, no. 2 (Manchester, 1953), pp. 294–315.

5 "A Note on the Rabbinic Doctrine of Creation": *The Journal of Jewish Studies*, Volume VII, nos. 3–4, 1956, pp. 195–206.

6 "Saadya's Theory of Revelation: Its Origin and Background": *Saadya Studies*, edited by Erwin I. J. Rosenthal, Manchester University Press (Manchester, 1943), pp. 4–25.

7 "Eleazar of Worms' Symbol of the Merkaba" (original title: "Eleazar of Worms' *Ḥokhmath Ha-Egoẓ*"): *The Journal of Jewish Studies*, Volume XI, nos. 3–4 (1960), pp. 101–112. The critical edition of Text 4 is not reproduced in this Volume.

8 "The Motif of the 'Shells' in ᶜAzriel of Gerona": *The Journal of Jewish Studies*, Volume IX, nos. 1–2 (1958), pp. 73–80.

9 "Moses Narboni's 'Epistle on *Shiᶜur Qomā*': Philip W. Lown Institute of Advanced Judaic Studies, Brandeis University, Studies and Texts: Volume IV, *Jewish Medieval and Renaissance Studies*, edited by Alexander Altmann, Harvard University Press (Cambridge, Mass., 1967), pp. 225–254. Full title: "Moses Narboni's 'Epistle on *Shiᶜur Qomā*'. A Critical Edition of the Hebrew Text with an Introduction and an Annotated English Translation", pp. 225–288. In this Volume only the Introduction is reproduced.

10 "William Wollaston: English Deist and Rabbinic Scholar": *The Transactions of the Jewish Historical Society of England*, Volume XVI (1948), pp. 185–211. The Appendix ("Wollaston's Hebrew References traced to their Sources") is here omitted.

11 "Moses Mendelssohn on Leibniz and Spinoza": *Studies in Rationalism, Judaism and Universalism in Memory of Leon Roth*, edited by Raphael Loewe, Routledge & Kegan Paul (London, 1966), pp. 13–45.

12 "Franz Rosenzweig on History": *Between East and West—Essays Dedicated to the Memory of Bela Horovitz*, edited by Alexander Altmann, East and West Library (London, 1958), pp. 194–214.

INDEX OF NAMES

Index of Names

INDEX OF SUBJECTS